A Persevering Witness

A Persevering Witness

The Poetry of Margaret Avison

ELIZABETH DAVEY

Foreword by David A. Kent

PICKWICK *Publications* · Eugene, Oregon

A PERSEVERING WITNESS
The Poetry of Margaret Avison

Pickwick Publications
An Imprint of Wipf and Stock Publishers
199 W. 8th Ave., Suite 3
Eugene, OR 97401

www.wipfandstock.com

PAPERBACK ISBN: 978-1-4982-2392-8
HARDCOVER ISBN: 978-1-4982-2394-2
EBOOK ISBN: 978-1-4982-2393-5

Cataloguing-in-Publication data:

Names: Davey, Elizabeth.

Title: A persevering witness : the poetry of Margaret Avison / Elizabeth Davey

Description: Eugene, OR: Pickwick Publications, 2016 | Includes bibliographical references and index.

Identifiers: ISBN 978-1-4982-2392-8 (paperback) | ISBN 978-1-4982-2394-2 (hardcover) | ISBN 978-1-4982-2393-5 (ebook)

Subjects: LCSH: | Avison, Margaret, 1918–2007. | Canadian poetry—20th century. | Religion and poetry. | Title.

Classification: PR9199.3 D19 2016 (paperback) | PR9199.3 (ebook)

Manufactured in the U.S.A.   05/13/16

Excerpted from *Momentary Dark* by Margaret Avison. Copyright © 2006 Margaret Avison. Reprinted by permission of McClelland & Stewart, a division of Penguin Random House Canada Limited.

Excerpted from *Listening* by Margaret Avison. Copyright © 2009 Margaret Avison. Reprinted by permission of McClelland & Stewart, a division of Penguin Random House Canada Limited.

Excerpted from *Always Now* (in three volumes) by Margaret Avison. Copyright © 2003, 2004, 2005 the Estate of Margaret Avison. Reprinted by permission of the Porcupine's Quill.

"The Butterfly" by Margaret Avison. Published by Oxford University Press, Don Mills, Ontario. Copyright © 1991 Margaret Avison. Used by permission.

"In time the author of being, with authority," "Nothing I do or know or speak or feel," and "He breathed on the dust in His hand." Published by John Deyell Ltd. © 1971 Margaret Avison. Used by permission.

Excerpts from letters and unpublished poems in the Margaret Avison Fonds, University of Manitoba Archives. Used by permission.

The Scripture quotations in this publication are from the New Revised Standard Version, © 1989 by the Division of Christian Education of the National Council of the Churches of Christ in the U.S.A., and used by permission.

Contents

Foreword

MARGARET AVISON (1918–2007) is one of Canada's most respected and admired poets. The youngest child of a Methodist, then United Church minister, she grew up as a brilliant child of the manse—a "preacher's kid"—inevitably marked by some of the complexes associated with that role. With her mother's encouraging of her creative gifts from an early age, Avison became a compulsive reader and writer, finding in literature her vocation as an artist. The time span between her first published poems in the children's section of a Toronto newspaper and her final collection exceeds a remarkable seventy-five years. However, her apprenticeship as a poet was protracted by her elevated aesthetic standards and a reluctance to step into the limelight. As a result, her publication history is highly asymmetrical. Her first collection of poetry appeared when she was forty-two, but most of her books appeared after she had reached the age of seventy. In her main archive at the University of Manitoba the number of poems left in manuscript (those she deemed "unpublishable") virtually equals the number of poems she published.

Avison's early life as a poet was marked by a singular dedication to her craft and an estrangement from her Christian upbringing. Unlike several of her friends who became social workers, teachers, or librarians (three of the limited number of jobs open to her generation of women), she rejected any idea of an orthodox career path, and so her work history is irregular. After graduating from Toronto's Victoria College in 1940, she often sought the life of a Bohemian artist, living in a rented room close to the University of Toronto, taking jobs as a free-lance editor when needed, and fleeing any long-term work commitments that she felt would compromise her integrity and reduce time for writing. She did work for three and a half years at the Canadian Institute for International Affairs (1941–45) during World War 2 and then for about seven years in the order department of the University of Toronto Library (1947–54), but she quit the latter as soon as a promotion was offered and a career commitment threatened. After several years as a research assistant to Coleridge scholar Kathleen Coburn, ghost writing a doctor's autobiography, and helping to translate Hungarian poetry, she returned to university for graduate study in English. She then taught at university for two years (1966–68), worked in an outreach mission for four years, spent four more at CBC Archives, and finished her working life with several years in the office of Mustard Seed Mission (ending in 1986).

Throughout her life, Avison was a resolutely independent spirit. Nevertheless, her gift for friendship also revealed a correspondingly dependent nature. Her personality and talents inspired friends, both male and female, to help ensure her exposure to the public by publishing her work, promoting her reputation, securing publishers for her books, and, latterly, organizing her papers. Among writers and academics, these friends and mentors included A. J. M. Smith, Northrop Frye, Kathleen Coburn, and Denise Levertov. In the latter part of her life, long-time friend Joan Eichner devoted her energies to helping Avison on many fronts, and in a number of projects requiring editorial work (such as her collected poetry and her autobiography), Stan Dragland joined her.

Avison's life is neatly bisected by her conversion experience in early 1963, just before her forty-fifth birthday. It was a life-changing experience that she felt obliged to describe and did so in interviews and in print on several occasions. When I spoke with her in 1984, she stated that whatever takes one's allegiance away from Christ is idolatry; that is essentially how she retrospectively regarded her life before her conversion.[1] From this point of view, Avison's testimony about her conversion was one way in which she fulfilled what Elizabeth Davey sees as a central impulse in her life and art: witnessing to the power of God and to her savior, Jesus Christ. But witnessing to the Christian faith could be challenging for someone who was temperamentally shy and who harbored "an intense longing for privacy."[2] For example, when I described her as "Canada's foremost religious poet" in the draft of my short monograph about her life and work, she retorted in an annotation, "meaningless stereotyping surely." I therefore altered the phrasing to the more muted "major religious poet."[3] Avison was also aware that too strident a statement of Christian commitment would diminish an already fragmented audience. She sensed that we no longer live in a "coherent" society. When more people know about karma than about Christ, she

1. Interview with Margaret Avison, May 23, 1984, Toronto.

2. She used this phrase in our telephone conversation of November 25, 1987.

3. The phrase occurs at the end of the section on biography in *Margaret Avison and Her Works* (Toronto: ECW Press, 1989). I had given her the entire essay to read before I submitted it to the publisher.

told me, there is a barrier to communication—"Some things are not heard." People "on the other side say, 'What gives?'" She also believed strongly in the importance of a Christian writer seeking publication in the mainstream media rather than remaining in the safer confines of the religious presses where fewer people will hear you.[4] When my anthology of Canadian Christian poetry was launched in 1989, Avison was in the audience but did not participate, though the selection from her work was the largest representation of any writer in the book. She sometimes did not want to be identified as a poet and on one occasion told me that she did not like being categorized as a Christian poet since she thought the label would deter potential readers.[5]

In her significant study of Avison's poetry, Elizabeth Davey demonstrates how complex the issue of witnessing is, how multifarious its manifestations are in Avison's work, and how the poet managed and balanced the competing imperatives of her vocation. It is important to note that Davey's study of Avison is the first book-length commentary on the poet to appear. There have been several shorter studies of Avison's work and many essays, but a substantial engagement of this kind is long overdue and is to be much welcomed. Davey carefully situates her approach by first stating what it is not—psychological, developmental, or historical. Her study instead takes as its major theme the varied ways in which Avison's artistic expression embodied the particular issues of Christian witness. Whether organizing her remarks (to take a few examples) around an Avison motif such as the pivot, the use of typology, favorite natural images (trees, birds, the sun), or the Advent poems of *sunblue,* Davey skillfully and systematically provides close readings of many Avison poems and shows acuity, good sense, and sensitivity in her readings. Given the large body of Avison's poems, her choice of representative poems is especially effective and the result is a comprehensive survey of the major themes and concerns.

As a literary scholar, Davey speaks with authority about Avison's achievement and grounds her commentary in a comfortable familiarity with existing literary criticism and important writers such as Hopkins, Milton, and C. S. Lewis. She is also alert to Avison's subtle use of language and poetic form. As a Christian, she places Avison's religious poetry within trends in modern theology (using concepts from Paul Ricoeur and Karl Barth, to name just two) and is sensitive to allusions only the biblically literate reader will recognize. For Davey, Avison's poetry exists at the nexus

4. *Christian Poetry in Canada* (Toronto: ECW Press, 1989; rpt. in 1993 and co-published with the Anglican Book Centre). Interview with Avison, October 29, 1987.

5. Telephone conversation of September 24, 1988 and conversation with Avison, August 19, 1989. *Christian Poetry in Canada* was launched at St. Aidan's Church, Toronto.

where the theological, the biblical, and the poetic meet. With knowledge of all three fields, Davey explores the diverse ways in which Avison witnesses to her faith. She begins defining witness by reference to its roots in the legal concepts of Greece and Israel: witness is knowledge that is reported and, ultimately, legal testimony. Davey's approach then offers a model featuring two scripturally based imperatives: "come and see" (John 1:39) and "go and tell" (John 20:17). The first addresses poems that bring the reader into contact with the particulars of both the book of nature and the book of human nature; the second addresses the book of the Scriptures and goes on to explore the missionary imperative in Avison's poetry. Davey also stresses that Avison's language of witness is invitational rather than defensive (with words as pointers, not weapons) and demonstrates how she draws the reader into her poetry to experience the complexity and even ambiguity of certain issues. Above all, Avison wants readers to venture beyond the habitual so that the "optic heart" will discover and empathize with human suffering, acknowledge personal failure, encounter the hidden depths of experience and meaning, and recognize the saving grace of Christian faith.

A highly sophisticated and self-conscious poet, Avison embraced Presbyterianism's stress on the centrality of Scripture, and she internalized the narratives by rigorously studying the Bible with more than usual concentration. In fact, she regularly participated in Bible study classes (using the Scripture Union Study method where the text is read through over a period of five years) and wrote many of her poems in response to the stories and personalities she found in Scripture. She kept all her copious notes, and they can now be consulted in her principal archive at the University of Manitoba. As Davey acknowledges, Knox Church in Toronto, where Avison was a member for about forty years, certainly affirmed the primacy of Scripture and the importance of witnessing in its evangelical practice. Davey's own knowledge of the Bible enables her to disclose Avison's theological premises as well as her methods and practice as a devotional poet—how she models the pattern of witness on Paul and depends on such forms as psalm, prophetic text, and the gospel for precedents in her poetic practice.

In each section of her discussion, Davey effectively uses illustrative texts from Avison's published work. For example, while exploring her use of New Testament accounts, she selects poems such as "A Story" (with its several layers of witnessing) from *The Dumbfounding* (1966) to show how elusive and challenging Avison's poems typically are. They are not saccharine or even, in the majority of cases, explicitly devotional. They are frequently ironic, ambiguous, and parabolic, laced with hidden meanings. They range in tone from the celebrative to the indignant, from the whimsical to the compassionate, and from the declarative to the meditative. The post conversion poems may be more open to their audience than the earliest of her poems but they are no less demanding. Above all, Avison seeks to engage both the reader's heart and his or her intellect. While the nature of her poetry may limit her audience among the faithful, Avison's achievement continues to appeal to those beyond the household of faith. It is that very reaching outward that confirms the central importance of witnessing that Davey examines in Avison's relationship with her audience. If Avison has acted as a spiritual mentor for Davey, as she states, then this work of scholarship embodies Davey's own act of witness in response.

David A. Kent
retired, Department of English,
Centennial College, Toronto,
author of *Margaret Avison and Her Works*

Acknowledgments

IN HER COLLECTED POEMS, Margaret Avison has a lyric "To Joan" which calls attention to the peculiar nature of acknowledgements:

> The pulpit led a prayer:
> "Thank God who brought us here."
> I prayed, "We couldn't come unless
> Joan came by car for us . . ."

The closing stanza of her tribute begins, "The act of God is found / lovely for being through my friend . . ." (AN 2.242). I echo Avison's sentiments as I think of the people who contributed to my life during the years of working on this book. Truly "the act of God is found / lovely for being through my friends."

I appreciate those connected with the T. Glendenning Hamilton Research Grant Program of The University of Manitoba who awarded a grant for archival research at The Elizabeth Dafoe Library. Joan Eichner, Margaret Avison's friend and executor of her estate, offered encouragement and generous assistance in accessing Avison's poems. My friend Brian Stiller, former president of Tyndale University College, encouraged me to write, matching his words with tangible assistance.

The Oxford Centre for Mission Studies, and in particular, Bernard Farr, created an invaluable research environment for me. David Kent, in his own work on Avison, was a model of careful scholarship. Finally, I treasure the wisdom, rigorous questioning, and gentle prodding Haddon Willmer brought to my thinking as I navigated the difficult terrain of Margaret Avison's lyrics. The journey was less arduous for his company!

My family—Natalie and Clifford, Rebecca and Simon—have been bright lights for me in their good humor, stimulating conversations, and shared love of learning. Finally, my husband Alan consistently offered his support and steady love. He himself models the very perseverance and passion of which Avison speaks. With the poet, I say, "[H]elp me tell truth in this [who brought me here] / while praying thus" (AN 2.242).

Introduction

My first exposure to the lyrics of the poet Margaret Avison occurred in the 1970s when I moved to Canada from the United States. One of my early teaching assignments at Tyndale University College was a course in Canadian literature, a field with a large body of texts about which I knew very little. I read a small selection of Avison's strange and difficult poems in *The Oxford Anthology of Canadian Verse* and admired her immediately for her sophisticated and intellectual verse, applauding her as a defender and promoter of the Christian faith in the highly secularized world of the Canadian academy.

There is another connection of which I was unaware. That first year in Toronto, my husband and I attended Knox Presbyterian Church, the large university church on Spadina Avenue. Unbeknownst to me, this was Avison's church as well, illustrative of her invisibility in that context as a prominent published poet. While she enjoyed the quiet recognition of select sensitive and thoughtful readers who recognized her worth as a writer, in the church community Avison seemed to be appreciated more as a vital force in her passion for evangelism and outreach.

Years later, I wanted to study her poetry from the angle of a woman's voice speaking from the margins of both society and church. Why, I wondered, was she invisible in the church with her intelligence, giftedness, and spiritual sensitivity? Why was she not given a platform to speak of her insights about Scripture—about God? Was it because she was a woman? What critique of society and of the church would she reveal from her place on the margins? What anger or disappointment, however veiled, might she express? As I wrestled with these questions while reading poem after poem, I gradually came to admit they were not her concerns. Her body of poetry is conspicuously silent on issues of gender inequality and lack of women's opportunity for expression and advancement. While her life may have been circumscribed by particular circumstances, her fertile mind was exploring larger theological and philosophical issues with a clearly articulated sense of identity. Fundamental was her deep sense of calling as a witness to Jesus Christ. Therefore, if I wanted to appreciate Margaret Avison's contribution to both the world of letters and the world of the church, I needed to explore how this passion is realized in her poetry.

My understanding was relatively circumscribed as I saw Christian witness as a process of introducing and defending Jesus Christ to those who have not embraced the good news. I anticipated cheering from the sidelines this modern and unusual champion of the faith who ably defends the claims of the gospel in my sphere of activity and interest. This understanding, in part, remains true. But in the slow process of unpacking the meaning of complex and dense lyrics, I learned and now know her witness to Christ and for Christ to be much larger. The poetry has been, in fact, a profound witness to me, a Christian reader, as well. Margaret Avison has become a spiritual mentor, calling me to a corresponding life of witness and service, much more mysterious and reflective than I have known before, the outlines of which emerge in the pages that follow.

In the posthumous collection *Listening*, the poem "Witnesses" (*L* 36–37) introduces the poet's complex method of accessing Christian witness, starting the process of re-directing assumptions about the most basic of attitudes and action.

Witnesses

How could the runners-after the
crowds running ahead, how could any of them
have known they'd find them-
selves there? I.e., at the
hangman's side? No,
on it? One by
one in the exhausted
afterwards, fidgeting, miserable, at
home, each had to find him-
self immured with the
undeservedly dead, for good.

What's "good"?
Springtime? The cat just
brought me a chewed
fledgling, his love-token.

            the afterward
    is a forever never knowing how
    the cords of who and what we are
    entwined and twisted so. I am

    implicit in a
    levigating of the incon-
    venient scree, grinding it down with
    the promise di-
    versely given all of us.

    Giver, I know now, anyone's
    survival is to be on
    Your side. If it is
    not too late, may the many
    be there, not to be eased, but to learn how
    losing is not
    negation. Oh it *is* that, but
    inside-out, under the
    merciful down-side-up of,
    for example, sky.

From the outset of the poem Avison establishes the focus of the witness on another—in this case, "the undeservedly dead," identified more clearly in the last stanza as "Giver." The event of Christ's crucifixion is suggested in the details of the opening stanza. At the same time, the witnesses are named as "crowds running ahead" and "runners-after the crowds"—people unclear in both motive and action. They think they are "at the hangman's side" but the preposition necessarily shifts to "on" [the hangman's side]. When they leave the scene they are no longer part of the crowd, but individuals, carrying their own consequences: "One by / one in the exhausted / afterwards, fidgeting, miserable"—unsurprising reactions to the profound experience. The surprise is in the closing lines, as each witness

    had to find him-
    self immured with the
    undeservedly dead, for good.

The connection with the event and the person is permanent, it seems.

The next stanza introduces familiar wordplay and double-meaning, requiring the reader to revisit the first stanza. "What's 'good'"? Furthermore,

in the puzzling images of the second and third stanzas there is a parallel
word with "immured"—"implicit." Avison suggests two pictures of inadver-
tent destruction—of the "undeservedly dead"—the dead bird killed by the
cat. The bird was "[the cat's] love-token"; the cat by his nature has been on
the side of the hangman. The next stanza suggests "I am / implicit" in the
grinding down to powder of the "inconvenient scree" of a mountainside.[6]
The reason is unclear but "the promise di- / versely given all of us" could
be the creation mandate to "subdue the earth and have dominion" over its
creatures (Gen 1:28). This dominion in reality has meant in many ways
"destruction," not unlike the cat's killing of the bird. People are on the hang-
man's side just by being who they are:

> the afterward
>
> is a forever never knowing how
> the cords of who and what we are
> entwined and twisted so.

The closing stanza transforms the witness who looks to the cross and
the crucified One with repentance and hope:

> Giver, I know now, anyone's
> survival is to be on
> Your side.

Being "immured with the / undeservedly dead" now seems "good"—in
its several meanings of mixed blessing. Furthermore, the witness wants
others to join in the seeing. "May the many"—"the crowds"—turn and look,
"not to be eased," but to learn the spiritual principle of not saving one's life
to lose it but losing one's life to save it (Mark 8:35). This is "the inside-out"
paradoxical way the gospel works. When Avison explores what it means to
be witnesses in her poetry, she invites the reader to read the "script of the
text" with her—to share in the experience of "the most intimate of poetic
forms."[7] The invitation cannot be taken lightly, because she deals with pain-
ful matters of the heart that take a lifetime of perseverance to work out.
"Losing is not / negation," she muses, and then backtracks,

---

6. "Levigate" means "to reduce to a fine powder; to rub down" (OED); a "scree" is
"material composing a slope" . . . the "mass of detritus forming a precipitous stony slope
upon a mountain side" (OED).

7. This is Helen Vendler's particular phrasing, providing a distinct perspective
on lyric poetry: "A lyric poem is a script for a performance by its reader. It is, then,
the most intimate of genres, constructing a twinship between writer and reader." See
Poems, Poets, Poetry, xl.

> . . . Oh it *is* that, but
> inside-out, under the
> merciful down-side-up of,
> for example, sky.

The music of the poetry combines with the puzzling language reversal "down-side-up," softening any sense of awkwardness in the enjambment of the closing lines and offering a startling picture of grace.

This book is an exploration of what the poet calls "a kind of perseverance"—her obedient and deliberate response to the biblical mandate of Christ's disciples to be his witnesses as particularly evidenced in the poems she has published.[8] My engagement with both her poetry and her avowed witness does not attempt to legitimize her corpus of poetry; earlier literary critics whom I cite in chapter 1 and elsewhere in the text have already established her contribution to modern Canadian letters in English. While I make frequent mention of such Christian poets as George Herbert, Gerard Manley Hopkins, and T. S. Eliot, whose influence on her seems obvious, my focus is not an extended comparison with any of them. Though I frequently refer to earlier and later poems in her collection and suggest shifts in her thinking, this exploration is not a study of her development as a poet. I take seriously her context in my discussion; at the same time, I am not taking either a psychological or developmental or historical approach to her poetry. I am not doing philosophy or theology in any formal systematic way though I refer to both in the construction of my argument. Rather, I am offering a close reading of her difficult lyrics to call attention to her singular accomplishment of providing a particular space where different kinds of thinking can take place—where the theological and biblical merge with the poetic, producing a compelling witness to the Christian faith.[9] In that process of reading, I inevitably draw on the reader's participation in completing the meaning of the text.

8. The title of her Pascal lectures on Christianity and the University published as *A Kind of Perseverance.*

9. As such, this exploration might finally be identified as an exercise both in critical poetics and hermeneutics, a distinction Jonathan Culler articulates in *Literary Theory: A Very Short Introduction.* "Poetics," Culler explains, "starts with attested meanings or effects and asks how they are achieved. . . . Hermeneutics, on the other hand, starts with texts and asks what they mean, seeking to discover new and better interpretations," 58. Importantly, he qualifies the method of critics in actual practice. In spite of fundamental differences in purpose of analysis, "works of literary criticism often combine poetics and hermeneutics, asking how a particular effect is achieved or why an ending seems right (both matters of poetics), but also asking what a particular line means and what a poem tells us about the human condition (hermeneutics)," 58.

My approach to Avison's work initially hearkens back to the formalist criticism of the American New Critics—literary analysis that specializes in the lyric poem. As a practitioner in a literature classroom, I echo Leland Ryken's assertion that "[n]o matter what else teachers of literature do, they interact with literary texts in terms of the categories bequeathed by formalist criticism."[10] A close reading of the text brings clarity of focus, helping one arrive at an initial interpretation of difficult poems. As the concrete language of images takes precedence over abstract concepts, practical criticism's emphasis on accessing meaning via the imagination provides direction for my argument. When Ryken speaks of "care lavish[ed] on written texts" with a concomitant response of humility, this interpretive strategy seems particularly apropos for the lyrics of a poet who demonstrates her own meticulous and humble preoccupation with her craft. Furthermore, as Ryken emphasizes, "This reverence before a literary text" is particularly congruent with a poet such as Avison

> who accept[s] the Bible as an authoritative repository of truth and are therefore committed to the principle that language can be trusted to convey understandable meaning. Christianity is a religion in which the word has a special sanctity. Openness to receive what the Bible has to say instead of imposing one's own meanings on it has been at least the theoretic aim of many segments of Christianity through the centuries.[11]

Her commitment to the scriptural text invites a similar perspective from a sympathetic reader and critic.

At the same time, an exclusive insistence on the autonomous text limits understanding of the poem. It becomes merely a piece of art, creating a disconnection with my central theme of witness. Witness by its nature involves more than aesthetics, and Avison's poems, I suggest, are texts involved in a very specific form of communication. Throughout this book the consideration of Avison's poetry as Christian witness directs the close reading and is more akin to a study in rhetoric and communication. As a result, the "literary transaction" of the reader-response theorists seems to naturally emerge when a poet suggests that one "come and see" and "go and tell," the proposed model present in Avison's writing.[12] Focusing on the process of the act of reading—the mental and emotional activity engaged in receiving the poetic text—can affirm Avison's declarations of witness. Trying to

10. Ryken, "Formalist and Archetypal Criticism," 1.

11. Ibid., 18.

12. See Vander Weele, "Reader Response Theories," 140. In contrast to the formalist's spatial view of a text, Stanley Fish emphasizes reading as a temporal process.

unlock her difficult poems matches the possible paradigm M. H. Abrams describes: "The experience of reading is an evolving process of anticipation, frustration, retrospection, reconstruction, and satisfaction."[13]

Further, an engagement with reader-response criticism and texts re-opens the gate to both the context of the work and the context of the reader. Assumptions can be freely acknowledged.[14] A false sense of detachment and unbiased and objective reading is named for what it is, allowing for more integrity in the proposed interpretations. The close reading of the text of individual poems is integrated throughout this study with a view toward the collection as a whole. I identify the assumptions implicit in the text and in the larger body of Avison's work and the context of her recorded life experiences shaping her view of the world. Then I explore the assumptions of her implied and real readers as I interact with secondary critical material throughout the project. As a result, I explore the question of Avison's poetry as witness of or witness to what and through what means—giving a rhetorical rather than aesthetic emphasis to this analysis, modifying the close readings.

In chapter 1, I introduce Margaret Avison as a recognized national poet in Canada with multiple volumes of lyrics to her credit and as a Christian who self-identifies another vocation as Christian witness. I begin near the end of her life with one of the poems read for the Griffin Poetry Prize which reveals both her poetic skill and her religious faith embedded in her lyrics. Following is an overview of the publication of her poetry and a selection of critics' commendations, including their recognition of her distinctive Christian voice. Her biographical data is framed in terms of her twin vocations as witness and poet, detailing her developing understanding of their intersection. This entangled nature of witness and poetry raises a double-pronged problem for the reader, challenging assumptions about both: On one hand, how can her difficult poetry be witness in the effort required to understand it? On the other, might its Christian witness diminish its appeal as poetry to modern readers?

The call to spiritual and theological attention implicit in Avison's poetry suggested in chapter 1 is anchored in her interpretation of the mandate

---

13. Abrams, *A Glossary of Literary Terms*, 257.

14. I appreciate Roger Lundin's particular emphasis when he refers to Paul Ricouer's work in his conclusion about hermeneutics: "The Cartesian claim of a radical new beginning is belied by the fact that all of our thinking is rooted in language which is saturated with the history of human shame and glory. When we pick up a word in order to use it to express our individual meaning, that word is already charged with a history of significance. . . . [Quoting Ricoeur] 'There is no philosophy without presuppositions.'" See Lundin, "Hermeneutics," 160.

in Scripture to be Christ's witnesses. She invokes the same biblical texts as traditional apologists do with their language of defense, but she gives less emphasis to the juridical metaphor framing the discussion. In her declaration of her dual vocations she offers an alternative model of Christian witness, albeit indirectly. Her poetry is invitational rather than defensive in its witness—i.e., "without weapons," a model I am exploring in this book.[15] In chapter 2 I look at connections that can be established between the two independent activities of witness and poetry, especially as the poet intertwines the two. Then I turn to the Scriptures to locate the witness in authoritative precedent—the witness in the activities of the Lukan narrative of his Gospel and Acts of the Apostles and the witness declared about and to Second Isaiah's exiles. Finally, I turn to two metaphors from the Gospel of John that provide the paradigm for understanding Avison's poetry as witness.

The poet's lyrics are simultaneously clarifying and concealing in their complexity, ambiguity, and riddling playfulness. They are fraught with challenge both for the reader inclined to Christian belief and to the one opposed. The method of witness in her poems is redolent of Jesus's words in the opening scenes of John's Gospel, "Come and see" (John 1:39), inviting her readers to look deeply and meticulously and from odd angles with her as she looks into the book of nature and human nature, my theme in chapters 3 and 4, and the book of the Scriptures, the subject of chapter 5. Avison seeks and finds the hidden God paradoxically revealed and concealed, particularly in the person of the risen Christ.

Her poetry, reflecting her own persevering faith experience, is an obedient response to the risen Christ's directive to Mary Magdalene at the empty tomb, "Go and tell."[16] In chapter 6, I speak of the accompaniment of seeing with an unabashed telling, no matter how veiled the language appears to be. In Avison's own words, "The poet writes as a mix of the resurrection life and marred everyday living."[17]

---

15. In his chapter "The Witness That Was Karl Barth," Hauerwas explains the influence of "the theological teacher of [Barth's] student years," Wilhelm Herrmann, on Karl Barth. Tucked in a footnote, Hauerwas draws on Barth's comments on "Hermann's view 'that apologetics is a subordinate and temporary activity destined to vanish.'" "'Knowledge of God is the expression of religious experience wholly without weapons'" is Hermann's observation that Barth incorporates into his own thinking (Barth, *Theology and Church* 248). See Hauerwas, *With the Grain of the Universe*, 150.

16. "Go to my brothers and say to them, 'I am ascending to my Father and your Father . . .'" (John 20:17).

17. Avison, Letter to Tim Bowling, October 5, 2001.

Abbreviations

AN   Avison, Margaret. *Collected Poems: Always Now*, 3 vols. Erin, ON: Porcupine's Quill, 2003–5.

L   Avison, Margaret, *Listening: Last Poems.* Toronto: McClelland & Stewart, 2009.

MD   Avison, Margaret. *Momentary Dark.* Toronto: McClelland & Stewart, 2006.

SP   Avison, Margaret. *Selected Poems.* Toronto: Oxford University Press, 1991.

Always Now, volume 1 contains the poems of earlier collections entitled *Winter Sun* and *The Dumbfounding*. Volume 2 contains the poems of *sunblue* and *No Time*. Volume 3 contains the poems of *Not Yet But Still* and *Concrete and Wild Carrot. Momentary Dark, Listening*, and *Selected Poems* remain independent editions. To reference poems and lines throughout the book abbreviations will appear directly in the text. Hence, the first poem referenced "Rising Dust" from *Concrete and Wild Carrot* (now published in *Always Now,* vol. 3, 163–64) will appear in the text as from *AN* 3.163–64.

NIDNTT   *The New International Dictionary of New Testament Theology.* 3 vols. Edited by Colin Brown. Grand Rapids: Zondervan, 1978.

NIDCC   *The New International Dictionary of the Christian Church.* Rev. ed. Edited by J. D. Douglas and Earle E. Cairns. Grand Rapids: Zondervan, 1978.

OED   *Oxford English Dictionary*, Online. Oxford: Oxford University Press, 2008.

TDNT   *Theological Dictionary of the New Testament.* 10 vols. Edited
by Gerhard Kittel. Translated by Geoffrey Bromiley. Grand
Rapids: Eerdmans, 1967.

To distinguish ellipses in Avison's poems, I bracket [ ] my own omissions from the text and leave Avison's ellipses unmarked. In all other prose references, including Avison's, the ellipses indicate my variations from the complete text unless indicated.

American spelling and punctuation are used throughout except in the actual poems and occasional quotations using British and Canadian spelling which differ from standard American English.

CHAPTER 1

With or Against the Grain?

Avison's Poetry as Christian Witness

> Unclasp my heart
> from my own cramped story
> to new, in-threading light, a start
> towards searching out your glory.
> ("The Freeing" *AN* 2.227)

IN THE SUMMER OF 2003, in Toronto, the Canadian poet Margaret Avison shared the stage with the Irish poet Paul Muldoon in winning the prestigious Griffin Poetry Prize, the richest poetry prize in the world for a single volume of poetry. The Canadian selection was a slender collection of poems *Concrete and Wild Carrot*, then her most recent volume. Since that event, the three volumes of her *Collected Poems: Always Now* (2003, 2004, 2005), *Momentary Dark* (2006), and an unanticipated posthumous collection *Listening* (2009) have been released. The title of *Concrete and Wild Carrot* suggests a kind of comfortable familiarity with the subject matter—a book about the city and its citizens, the weather, the seasons and nature's particulars as observed in the urban setting. The publisher's jacket cover exudes enthusiasm for poems "startlingly youthful" and "words leap[ing] with life."[1]

---

1. Avison, *Concrete and Wild Carrot*, jacket cover.

1

Sprinkled throughout the collection of a mere thirty-five poems are several overt, unabashed Christian poems ("surprising probes of the Bible")—natural expressions of one who had committed her adult life to regular Bible study, church attendance, and deliberate, reflective Christian living.[2] The poet speaks here in this volume of poetry as she has consistently written—as a "wise old woman," with unusual spiritual insight. In the words of David Jeffrey, "Despite the centrality of her religious vision, she seems less a mystic than a sage, and her poetry less lyric than gnomic."[3]

Accolades that accompanied her award include the judges' citation that "Avison's *Concrete and Wild Carrot* is an occasion of beauty." They go on to say:

> Avison's poetry is also alive in its sublimity and its humility: "wonder, readiness, simplicity"—the gifts of perception Avison attributes to her Christian faith—imbue every poem in this book with a rare spirit of disorderly love. Margaret Avison is a national treasure. For many decades she has forged a way to write, against the grain, some of the most humane, sweet and profound poetry of our time.[4]

These commendations are obviously deliberate and thoughtful, reflecting a commitment to craft and vision inherent in the making of a poem. Sharon Thesen, one of the judges and editor of *The Griffin Poetry Prize Anthology 2003*, explains some of the criteria for excellence in her introduction to the anthology, speaking of "the range and flexibility of poetic voice—diction that prefers, despite many temptations, the sovereignty of language to anything else, and which, at its best, evinces the uncanny ability to show reality to itself."[5] In her enthusiasm, Thesen is overstating any poet's achievements to "prefer . . . the sovereignty of language"; Avison more modestly suggests "the whole-hearted use of language."[6] However, what is clear, in selecting her as the recipient of the Griffin prize, the judges have noted her consummate facility with words and perceptive understanding of reality.

2. Ibid.

3. Jeffrey, "Light, Stillness and the Shaping Word," 59.

4. The comments are specifically explained in the context of Alfred North Whitehead's definition of beauty as "'a quality which finds its exemplification in actual occasions,'" and "more completely exemplified in 'imperfection and discord' than in the 'perfection of harmony'" (Judges' Citation, http://www.griffinpoetryprize.com/short-list_2003), perhaps revealing as much about the judges as the poems, and illustrating a facet of witness that calls for response.

5. Thesen, *The Griffin Poetry Prize Anthology 2003*.

6. Avison, "Muse of Danger," 35.

At the same time, Avison's "humane, sweet and profound poetry" accomplishes something more mysterious and hidden with that familiar metaphor "writing against the grain" employed by the judges of her verse. In a cultural and literary environment wary of religious sentiment and expression, she is a peculiar figure, garnering acknowledgement and respect— sometimes in spite of her profession of Christian faith, but more often in quiet and bemused recognition of the power of her distinctive words of witness.

The night before the award was presented Avison participated with the short-listed finalists in a poetry reading at Toronto's Harbourfront. There she read several poems from *Concrete and Wild Carrot* before a crowd of more than 500 people. Two of her selections were "Christian" in content. The more veiled of the two, "Rising Dust" (*AN* 3.163–64), was preserved on podcast, available for viewing and listening on the internet.[7]

> *Rising Dust*
> The physiologist says I am well over
> half water.
> I feel, look, solid; am
> though leaky firm.
> Yet I am composed
> largely of water.
> How the composer turned us out
> this way, even the learned few do not
> explain. That's life.
>
> And we're in need of
> more water, over and over, repeatedly
> thirsty, and unclean.
>
> The body of this earth
> has water under it and
> over, from
> where the long winds sough
> tirelessly over water, or shriek around
> curved distances of ice.
>
> Sky and earth invisibly
> breathe skyfuls of

7. http://www.griffinpoetryprize.com/shortlist_2003.

water, visible when it
finds its own level.

Even in me?
Kin to waterfalls
and glacial lakes and sloughs
and all that flows and surges,
yet I go steadily,
or without distillation climb at will
(until a dissolution
nobody anticipates).

I'm something else besides.
The biochemist does not
concern himself with this.
It too seems substance,
a vital bond threaded on an
as-if loom out there.
The strand within
thrums and shudders and twists.
It cleaves to this
colour or texture and
singles out to a rhythm
almost its own, again,
anticipating design.

But never any of us
physiologist or fisherman
or I
quite makes sense of it. We
find our own level

as prairie, auburn or
snow-streaming, sounds forever
the almost limitless.

The poem presents vintage Avison, providing a good starting point for understanding both the poet and the witness of her lyrics as she engages the reader/listener in an intellectual and spiritual quest. This journey on which she takes her audience is not at all easy. As one critic remarks, her lyrics are "famously tangled, knotted and textured—so much so that one experiences the thrill of revelation each time the code of a poem is cracked."[8] His insight is crucial to emphasize. The brooding and reflective exercise of thinking long and hard about words, of reading and re-reading, of circling back and forth around a poem with that resulting "thrill of revelation" holds a key to apprehending Avison's particularly engaging Christian witness.

To begin, the title and opening lines of the poem are shrouded in ambiguity and uncertainty with the obvious disconnect between the title "Rising Dust" and its apparent subject—water. The initial factual proposition, "The physiologist says I am well over / half water," is humorously challenged by some contradictory experience: "I feel, look, solid; am / though leaky firm." What the speaker sees is not all that she sees. Avison's poetic use of enjambment, with "am" left dangling at the end of a line, vaguely echoes Descartes' famous declaration *cogito, ergo sum*, "I think, therefore I am." The witness posture is announced in these opening lines, as well, since the poet's use of the personal pronoun "I" is not particularly personal. This is not a confessional poem; it is not self-reflexive. It is the observer "I" seeing and pointing. "I am composed / largely of water" soon points to a "composer [who] turned us out / this way," but the careful word choice disarms challenge of premature religious implication.[9] The word "compose" is richly ambiguous, allowing for broader interpretation in the creative process; further, "compose" invites connection with music and artistry in the making. Nevertheless, the poet ends the stanza with the assertion "even the learned few"—the physiologists?—cannot explain how this came to be; she is in a realm beyond physical science.

The next short stanza suggests two functions of water—satisfying thirst and repairing uncleanness, both basic physical needs with potential metaphorical significance. The following two stanzas enlarge the discussion by replacing the personal "body" as subject with "the body of this earth." Sometimes water and world mix in highly visible and dramatic form, the poet muses:

> from
> where the long winds sough
> tirelessly over water, or shriek around
> curved distances of ice.

8. "and the truth of the thing, like the meat of the proverbial tough nut, may finally be enjoyed," Heft, "In Griffin's Grip: The Canadian Shortlist," 41.

9. C. S. Lewis develops a similar argument in *Mere Christianity*: The idea of a moral law assumes a law-giver. See particularly the chapter "We Have Cause to Be Uneasy," 28–32.

Other times "[s]ky and earth invisibly / breathe skyfuls of water" similar to human bodies until "it [water] / finds its own level." At mid-point in the first line of the fifth stanza, Avison visually signals her method of reading text—whether verbal or visual—with a question mark: "Even in me?" She connects the idea of the persona's body and the body of sky and earth, but also the repeated phrase "finds its own level." Persons and their world are related. More and more threads are untangling in this stanza as the flowing and surging waters of the earth are compared to the speaker's observation of herself. She too, "well over / half water" is "[k]in to waterfalls / and glacial lakes and sloughs." "I go steadily," "climb[ing] at will," she recognizes. Those alliterative words "distillation" and "dissolution" start creating links between water and dust.[10] Further, "go steadily" and "climb" connect with the title's first word "rising." The parentheses around "a dissolution / nobody antici-pates" signal an important event that could have been overlooked.

The mood changes again in the sixth stanza, suggesting a shift in the argument.

> I'm something else besides.
> The biochemist does not
> concern himself with this,

the speaker muses. "It too seems substance." This "something else" is harder to explain because it cannot be named, but only be identified by analogy and metaphor: It *seems* substance—"a strand, a vital bond; threaded on / an *as-if* loom." Activities such as "thrumming," "shuddering," "twisting," "cleaving," and "singles out to a rhythm" ensure its reality. "The something else" is vaguely reminiscent of George Herbert's more familiar poem "The Pulley," where personal restlessness functions like a connective chain, an instrument of drawing the created upwards to the Creator.

The last two short stanzas circle back to the beginning of the poem pointing to some possible allusions. Initially the poet's sense of alliteration may have suggested the juxtaposition of "fisherman" with "physiologist," drawing attention to the common but distinct interest in water between observer and participant. But the phrase may be taken further as it evokes association with Jesus's first disciples, the early witnesses, called from their vocation of fishing and becoming "fishers of people" (Luke 5:10), pointing to the biblical text. In light of the Scriptures, other phrases take on new con-notations. "Rising dust" of the title could be referring to the second account

---

10. "the action of falling or flowing down drop by drop" (OED); "the action of dis-solving, disintegration, decomposition" (OED).

of creation recorded in Genesis: "Then the Lord God formed man from the dust of the ground."[11]

Echoes of water and dust continue to sound throughout the biblical text. The

> need of
>
> more water, over and over, repeatedly
>
> thirsty, and unclean

has resonances of Isaiah's invitation: "Ho, everyone who thirsts, come to the waters" (Isa 55:1), echoed by Jesus's declaration, "Let anyone who is thirsty come to me, and let the one who believes in me drink" (John 7:37).[12] The "something else" of that sixth stanza could be "that breath of life" that God breathed into Adam's nostrils, making him a living being (Gen 2:7)—the miracle unaccounted for by the explanations of natural science. It seems that Avison's "vital bond" and "strand" could be the invisible means of raising a person to new life out of dust.

While the extent to which allusions, as I hypothesize above, can be attached to specific references in the larger text of the Scriptures remains tentative, her suggestive pointing to the Bible's words is the essential issue. Avison is not demanding assent to Christian belief; she is inviting exploration and opening dialogue in her subtle and imaginative formulations. They are not rhetorical postures to persuade; they are poems to experience with her. In writing lyrics she is taking what she knows is a risk.

In her essay "Muse of Danger'" on the subject of Christian witness, she asserts, "The practice of poetry is as dangerous as this next hour of life, whoever you are. Yet its advantages are great."[13] Here in "Rising Dust" she declares the result of inevitable choices: "We / find our own level," as if she has the definitive statement on human decision; at the same time she dismantles her confident assertion with no end-stop punctuation. There is still another three-line stanza. The stanza break delays the completion of the idea with "as prairie [. . .] sounds forever / the almost limitless." Or putting

---

11. "and breathed into his nostrils the breath of life; and the man became a living being" (Gen 2:7). Preceding these words in the Bible is a relatively detailed account of God's interest in the matter of watering the earth: "For the Lord God had not caused it to rain upon the earth . . . but a stream would rise from the earth, and water the whole face of the ground" (Gen 2:5–6). There is also the corresponding sad sequence after the fall when God announces the judgment on Adam: ". . . until you return to the ground, for out of it you were taken; you are dust, and to dust you shall return" (Gen 3:19).

12. Again, the word "unclean" suggests David's plea for God's mercy in his psalm of penitence: "Wash me thoroughly from my iniquity . . . wash me, and I shall be whiter than snow" (Ps 51:2, 7).

13. Avison, "Muse of Danger," 35.

it another way, "How can we catch the illimitable in our little bottles?" she queries in her Pascal Lectures.[14] Here is one danger of the muse for both poet and audience with the inevitable surprise in revelation. God is both hidden and larger than the poet's explanation, and she knows this.

> There are inherent beauties –
> crystalline structures under microscopes –
> hidden in cliffs and canyons from our glance who
> pick our way along there,

she observes in one of her meditations on Christ's passion, "Thoughts on Maundy Thursday" (*AN* 2.213–14). The analogy deepens as she meditates further on Christ's actions:

> more intricate structures
> are hidden still till the magnification
> comes, in glory.

The composer of physical and spiritual life—both the world and the humans who inhabit it—outstrips the composer of poems, but her task is to keep pointing towards the One who inhabits her words.

The audience at the Harbourfront Reading chuckled lightly as the poet read the opening lines of the poem; then they grew quiet and thoughtful as they strained to absorb the subtle observation of "finding one's own level." Undoubtedly any allusive complexity and even the basic argument was probably not absorbed on first hearing, but the music of the phrases, the curious blend of sound and sense, the provocative mixture of idea and image of the poetry sustained the attention and certainly invited a later reading and reflection. Earlier readers of the poem (including the judges) had already found themselves gently judged by the text when they recognized her writing against the grain.

Who is this poet whose voice is so distinctive and compelling? What has she written that has made such an impression on critics and lovers of poetry alike? What in her life experience has shaped her singular insight with its peculiar mixture of soft humor and wry wisdom? How has she acquired the particular vision that is simultaneously difficult and disarming? Surveying her collections of poems and recounting her personal journey helps draw us into the larger story she lives and tells with eloquence and vigor.

Margaret Avison has been in and out of the literary public eye throughout the years of her writing career, earning her reputation as an outstanding

14. Avison, *A Kind of Perseverance*, 64–65.

poet with a relatively small body of published poems. Individual poems and clusters of poems have appeared in a variety of journals, beginning in the 1930s, including *The Canadian Forum, Poetry* [Chicago], and *Kenyon Review.*[15] Besides A. J. M. Smith's seminal *The Book of Canadian Poetry: A Critical and Historical Anthology* (1943), other major anthologies have published her poems, including *The Norton Anthology of Modern Poetry* (1973); *The New Oxford Book of Canadian Verse: In English* (1983); and *A New Anthology of Canadian Literature in English* (2002).[16]

Her first published volume of poems *Winter Sun* won the Canada General Governor's Award for poetry in 1960. Her second volume *The Dumbfounding* was published in 1966; *sunblue* in 1978; in 1982, *Winter Sun/ The Dumbfounding: Poems, 1940–66.* In 1989, she again won the Canada General Governor's Award for poetry for *No Time.* In 1991, *Selected Poems* was published; in 1997, *Not Yet But Still,* and in 2002, *Concrete and Wild Carrot* (again, for which she received *The Griffin Poetry Prize* in 2003). Her *Collected Poems: Always Now,* released in three volumes in 2003, 2004, and 2005, include the poems of the earlier volumes, a significant number of poems that appeared elsewhere in miscellaneous journals and anthologies and "Two Towards Tomorrow: New Poems" (*AN* 3.183–209). *Momentary Dark* in 2006, her final volume before her death, came as a bit of a surprise when it seemed she had concluded her writing with the *Collected Poems.* Yet again in 2009, *Listening,* a posthumous collection, prepared for publication by Stan Dragland and Joan Eichner, was released.[17] The publishing of these lyrics has been peculiarly spaced out—almost decades apart and calling attention to her advancing age. David Kent observed in 2008 that Avison had published four new collections of poetry, a book of lectures, a selected

15. Earlier her poetry appeared in Victoria College's (University of Toronto) student publication *Acta Victorian* and *Contemporary Verse.*

16. Other anthologies include *The Penguin Book of Canadian Verse* (1958); *Poetry of Mid-Century 1940–1960* (1964); *20th Century Poetry & Poetics* (1969); *The Oxford Anthology of Canadian Literature* (1973); and *The Harper Anthology of Poetry* (1981).

17. It is difficult to give an accurate count of her poems since there has been some shifting of poems between collections and eliminating of some that were previously published but now pulled from her *Collected Poems.* Nevertheless, one can establish some idea of her productivity: In the three volumes of *Always Now* and *Momentary Dark* and *Listening* there are 678 poems plus three translations of Hungarian poems. Furthermore, she has been a more prolific poet than her published work indicates. For one, individual occasional poems sent to admirers and friends continue to surface. Second, the Margaret Avison Fonds at the University of Manitoba contain many hundreds of unpublished poems—not of publishable quality according to her own exacting standards and with stringent publishing restrictions specified—nevertheless, still a record of significant achievement in the world of letters.

edition, and a three-volume collected edition of poems—all after the age of seventy.[18]

A. J. M. Smith, poet and critic, "one of the founders of the modernist literary movement in Canada" and an anthologist who helped shape the Canadian literary canon, beginning with his 1943 anthology *The Book of Canadian Poetry*, gave Margaret Avison a jump start in her career as a poet.[19] In his essay "The Confessions of a Compulsive Anthologist," reflecting on a "fruitful" visit to Toronto in 1942, he tells how he was introduced

> to a young woman named Margaret Avison who was working for Gage and living penuriously, chiefly on coffee. She showed me her poems in manuscript, and the fact that I was able to bring the anthology to a close with a selection of her poetry, almost the first to be published, I consider one of the real forward-looking achievements of the book.[20]

"For nearly thirty years, [Smith] was her critical champion in the Canadian academic community," David Kent notes in his brief monograph *Margaret Avison and Her Works*.[21] Beyond Smith, Avison has gained a small, but significant, following of admirers among poets and other writers and academics who have recognized her achievement. For example, *The National Post* obituary notice reads: "She was a 'titan' in modern Canadian poetry, as great as Irving Layton and Al Purdy, Toronto poet Dennis Lee said in a telephone interview."[22] In another obituary, the writer reports: "'Her contribution to Canadian literature was incalculable,' said Joseph Zezulka, an English professor at the University of Western Ontario who met Avison in the early 1970s while she was a writer-in-residence at the university."[23] After the announcement of the Griffin Prize, the poet and critic Ken Babstock is more specific in his review of *Concrete and Wild Carrot*:

> her work—its moral depth, humanity, transcendent intelligence and sheer power shrinks prize, applause and ego down to their deserving littleness. Magnanimity is unquantifiable. Reading Margaret Avison is like being in the presence of a heart and mind quite simply bigger and more open than our own.

---

18. Kent, "Margaret Avison, Poet," 16.

19. Bennett and Brown, *A New Anthology of Canadian Literature in English*, 366.

20. Smith, *On Poetry and Poets*, 110.

21. Kent, *Margaret Avison and Her Works*, 10.

22. Kubacki, obituary in *National Post*.

23. *Globe and Mail* on-line obituary.

He goes on to speak of her poems in "their unflagging verbal precision, notional complexity and exuberance."[24]

Embedded in the recognition Avison has received is the inevitable confrontation with her avowed Christian witness. Babstock demonstrates sensitivity to her passion as he acknowledges that "[*Concrete and Wild Carrot*] is informed by an earned Faith . . . indeed Avison's entire body of work, amounts to a beautiful argument for Ongoingness and open-heartedness." He goes on to point out: "The resurrection (to some a pivotal hinge in history, to others an allegory) is re-envisioned at the end of each lived moment, and again after the next, and the next . . . [Babstock's own ellipses]."[25] The Montreal poet and critic Carmine Starnino suggests that "Canadian poetry learned to argue its way around Avison's innovations, namely by misreading her interest in Christian ideas as anti-experimental." He then proceeds to show how the experimental and religious are intricately connected in her poems:

> most striking and more risky—and virtually unique in Canadian poetry—is that Avison's sense of the religious is wrapped up entirely in syntactic difficulties. . . . She has spiritualized syntax; reading her poems always leaves one's relationship with language somewhat re-angled.[26]

Another critical response to the religious and spiritual quality of her poetry comes from David Jeffrey:

> The critic of Margaret Avison ought probably to be drawn, in apprehension, through a slow measuring of words to quietness. Indeed, if it could remain articulate, this would be of all responses the most just, since it would faithfully mirror the transformation of her own perception, through language, towards the quiet understanding that is her strength. . . . Her work as a whole rests securely as testimony to a philosophical and spiritual progress: it is a *chef d'oeuvre* on our slim national shelf of true "wisdom literature."

He goes on to speak of "a perceptible and peculiar stillness" "descend[ing] almost immediately in the reading" of her work,[27] drawing on Avison's own awareness of beckoning silence in "The Effortless Point" (*AN* 2.69):

---

24. Babstock, Review of *Concrete and Wild Carrot.*

25. Ibid.

26. Starnino, "Are You There, God? It's Me, Margaret."

27. Jeffrey, "Light, Stillness, and the Shaping Word," 58–59.

> Moving into sky
> or stilled under it
> we are in the becoming
> moved: let wisdom learn
> unnoticing in this.

Each of these thoughtful observations points in the direction of her distinct contribution to Christian witness. Both the "stillness" that attracts Jeffrey and the "religious wrapped up in syntactic difficulties" that fascinates Starnino are rightly focused in Babstock's observation of the "re-envisioned" resurrection "at the end of each lived moment," specified and particularized in Avison's writing.

POET, CHRISTIAN, AND CHRISTIAN WITNESS

Avison was born in Galt, Ontario, on April 23, 1918, into the home of a Methodist minister. The family moved to Western Canada shortly after, and she lived her childhood years on the prairies of Saskatchewan and Alberta. Though the urban environment of Toronto where she spent most of her life dominates her poetry, her early recollections of the prairies have proven a significant wellspring of imaginative reflection as well. Her childhood also reveals the influences of both Christian upbringing and classical reading. An early undated and handwritten poem in the Manitoba archives, "The Trojan Princess's Defiance," reveals both a precocious grasp of the stories of Homer's Troy and a familiarity with varied verse stanzas. The closing lines give a glimpse of the emerging poet:

> Her velvet cheeks were burned with angry red
> 'Go back unto your cowards and your slaves
> Go back unto the lands which make your graves
> Go tell the craven fool who sent you here
> That not while I have head and thinking clear
> Shall ever any Greeks,' her words were bold,
> 'Bribe me with offers of their paltry gold
> No, not until – good Zeus suspend the day –
> The very earth beneath be swept away.'[28]

28. In the Margaret Avison Fonds, the University of Manitoba. There is also a published poem from *The Globe and Mail*, May 7, 1932, by the thirteen-year-old Avison about the mythic figure Charon, boatman in the underworld, again revealing her familiarity with the great ancient myths.

At the same time she grew up in a Methodist parsonage, with two biblically literate parents who "taught us to read the Bible, to pray, to love, to enjoy." In a pseudonymous, autobiographical essay, written for Scripture Union in 1968, she mentions that she was dutifully religious as a child—connected to the Christian faith by her participation in family life and by a strong will to exemplify behavior of "being good." "I wish I had known," she writes, "that I was not somehow peculiarly close to all good simply by virtue of having grown up a much-loved youngster in a relatively protected world." As she explains, "I was glad to 'see God everywhere' but with comparative and comforting indistinctness." She describes her gradual drifting away from this religious experience: "I wish I had known that there was a reason why the Bible became to me more and more opaque. . . . I was increasingly substituting an invented person of my own designing for Jesus, the Word made flesh, the life of the Word of God."[29]

The family returned to Toronto where Avison completed high school. She credits a grade-nine teacher who led the school poetry club with valuable and encouraging counsel in her poetic endeavours: "For the next ten years do not use the first person in any poem you write."[30] This advice received in her adolescent and formative period of intellectual and emotional development was essential insight, surely affecting more than her poetry. The focus on looking outward rather than inward in her writing of poetry carried over into her later understanding of Christian witness.

She attended Victoria College, University of Toronto, studying under such professors as E. J. Pratt and Northrop Frye. After she earned her BA in English in 1940, she began her working life as a file clerk at North American Life Insurance Company where she was employed for two years.[31] During that time she also spent a few months at Gage Publishing Company where she learned proofreading and editing. (It was during this time that A. J. M. Smith "discovered" her). Kent comments that "[h]er working life since has been characterized by frequent dislocations and reorientations, in marked

29. Avison, "I Couldn't Have My Cake and Eat It," 88–89.

30. Foreword, *Always Now*, Vol. 1, 14.

31. My sources include a basic chronology available in the Margaret Avison Fonds of the University of Manitoba archives; an interview with Harry der Nederlanden in *Calvinist Contact*, October 19, 1979; Avison's chapter "I Couldn't Have My Cake and Eat it" in *I Wish I Had Known . . .* [Angela Martin, pseudo.] (1968); an interview with Rose Simone in *The Second Mile* (1994); and a fuller account from David Kent who wrote *Margaret Avison and Her Works* in 1989 as part of the *Canadian Writers and their Works*, Poetry Series. Many of the details "were kindly supplied by Margaret Avison," 41, fn. In addition, the posthumous autobiography *I Am Here and Not Not-There* (2009) provides additional nuances to some of the named events, places, and people.

contrast to her continuing, though unostentatious, dedication to poetry."[32] She worked two years at the Canadian Institute of International Affairs followed by a year in the Registrar's Office at the University of Toronto. One of her longest periods of employment in one place was in the Order Department of the Library at the University of Toronto, where she worked for eight years. "On Saturday mornings she taught servicemen who had returned to university for a degree" and did freelance editing on the side.[33] In the Archival Chronology detailing her employment, 1957 is noted as the first of six years of freelance work.[34] Kent points out, in fact, that she did editing work and wrote book reviews all during the 1940s and 1950s.[35] She also wrote an elementary textbook, *History of Ontario*, published in 1951. When she left the University Library Order Department she worked as a "nursemaid and homehelp" for a year to a family with four children, taking her to France for part of that time.[36] She did not see these many varied experiences of employment as her vocation, but as a means of earning a living; from early on she saw herself primarily a poet.

Important events and experiences for her regarding her vocation in poetry include her significant acquaintance with Cid Corman, American poet and editor of *Origin*, in 1953, and subsequent correspondence with him. In the early summer of 1954 Avison took two summer courses at Indiana University, "one in linguistics and the other with John Crowe Ransom on Thomas Hardy's poetry," increasing her exposure to the American writing culture.[37] The prestigious *Kenyon Review* published several of her poems. When she won a Guggenheim fellowship in 1956–57, she spent eight months in Chicago. Her first published volume *Winter Sun* is a product of this time. As well, she established important literary friendships during these years, including Frederick Bock, associate editor of *Poetry*.[38] Among her many writing projects, she translated Hungarian poetry; she was ghostwriter for *A Doctor's Memoirs*, the autobiography of A. J. Willinsky; she wrote abstracts of dissertations in social work at the University of Toronto. She was invited to a writer's workshop at the University of British Columbia in 1964, the Canadian representative among such American poets as Charles Olson, Robert Creeley, and Denise Levertov. In spite of

32. Kent, *Margaret Avison and Her Works*, 2.
33. Ibid., 2.
34. Chronology, Margaret Avison Fonds.
35. Kent, *Margaret Avison and Her Works*, 2.
36. Chronology, Margaret Avison Fonds.
37. Kent, *Margaret Avison and Her Works*, 3.
38. His correspondence with Avison is in the Margaret Avison Fonds.

the importance of the event for her and her connection with these poets, Kent cautions against assuming any strong link between her and the Black Mountain poets (or any other poets) because of her "independent posture and self-imposed isolation."[39]

While she was making strides in her poetry, she was also making important decisions concerning her religious faith. In an often quoted letter to Cid Corman, published with her poems in *Origin* in 1962, she commented: "There is some corner I have to turn yet, some confronting I have to do," revealing an on-going crisis of spiritual reflection.[40] Her journey to faith came about as she was encouraged by the minister of Knox Presbyterian Church to read John's Gospel—"instead of Ezekiel, at the time!" she recounts in an interview.[41] She is precise in dating what she calls her conversion to Christianity: January 4, 1963, truly the pivotal experience in her life. She emphasizes the demarcation of her changed life in both her prose and poetry. She describes her conversion to Simone:

> She was reading John 14, which starts with "Do not let your hearts be troubled: you believe in God, believe also in me . . . ." Suddenly, she felt the overwhelming presence of Jesus Christ in the room. Avison said she felt she couldn't breathe—as if all the air had been sucked from the room. She felt "the Jesus of resurrection power" making Himself known to her. She threw the Bible that she was reading down on the floor.[42]

Avison goes on to tell of her fear of having to give up her poetry to prove her new faith commitment: "When I said, 'Ok, take the poetry,' then everything was different."[43] Instead of having to give up her writing, however, her poetic output flourished. Two months of compulsive writing followed, in which she wrote most of the poems that later appeared in *The Dumbfounding* (1966), published with the encouragement and assistance of the poet Denise Levertov.[44] "During her short period as poetry editor for Norton, not only did Levertov solicit this collection from Avison but she

39. Kent, *Margaret Avison and Her Works*, 9.

40. Letter to Cid Corman in *Origin*, 11.

41. Avison and Simone, "A Religious Experience," 5–6.

42. Ibid., 6.

43. Ibid. In her later autobiography *I Am Here and Not Not-There*, she elaborates how she perceived "this strange visitation" from God as a contest of wills: "An ancient poet describes the confrontation: 'Put me in remembrance; let us contend together. State your case' (Isaiah 43:26). It infuriated me to feel that my 'case' was weakened and about to crumble. Finally I hurled the Bible across the room and said, 'Okay, take the poetry too!'" 142.

44. Avison and Simone, "A Religious Experience," 6–7.

also played a crucial part in preparing it for publication," explains Kent in a later biographical essay.[45]

Several poems clustered in the middle of *The Dumbfounding* articulate the same experience, but with particular lyrical poignancy. She begins "The Word" (*AN* 1.195–96) in language of the marriage service, "'*Forsaking all*,'" revitalizing a lover's metaphor "head over heels" with more intense and extended language of primal fire's aftermath and potential renewal:

> '*Forsaking all*' – You mean
> head over heels, for good,
> for ever, call of the depths
> of the All.[46]

Embracing the "All" and forsaking "all" seem welcome when the exchange is offered to the one "far fallen in the / ashheaps" of a "false-making, burnt-out self":

>   and in the
> hosed-down rubble of what my furors
> gutted, or sooted all
> around me – you implore
> me to so fall in Love, and fall anew in
> ever-new depths of skywashed Love till every
> capillary of your universe
> throbs with your rivering fire?

Love's "rivering fire," with its revitalizing intensity is an invitation she cannot refuse. The punning wordplay of "falling" and "fallen" coupled with "All" and "all," interwoven with multiple alliterative combinations of "forsaking," "false-making," "furors," and "fire" along with the internal repetitions of "Love's All," "falling anew," and "every throbbing capillary" draw listener and speaker alike into the enchantment of transformation. Furthermore, the sobering cost for the One "unsealing day out of a / darkness none ever

---

45. Kent further elaborates: "What we may surmise is that Levertov's role in selecting and arranging the poems in *The Dumbfounding* was formative and that she seems to have been largely responsible for the book in the form and shape we have come to know." See David Kent, "Composing a Book: Levertov, " 40–52, for a detailed discussion of the two poets' connection.

46. This is the first of two poems with the same title. Here the word is emphasizing Jesus, the Word, while never named, as Love. The later miniature four-line poem (*AN* 2.220) leaves the correspondence unspecified, instead focusing on the intense experience of the receiver of the Word. See Appendix for the complete text of this longer poem.

knew / in full but you" of the next stanza both intensifies the value of the wooing of the Lover and diminishes the sacrifice of the submitting beloved. The last pun embedded in the picture of the Cross in the final stanza seals the contract:

> But to make it head over heels
> yielding, all the way,
> you had to die for us.
> The line we drew, you crossed
> and cross out [. . .].

Avison refuses sentimentality in speaking of "what / you know is love." She ends the poem with a reminder of the identity of the Word. "I AM" occupies and fills the space of the poem's last line, emphasizing her emerging awareness of the One to whom she witnesses.

"The Dumbfounding" (AN 1.197–98), the poem providing the title of the collection, changes the picture with a more ambiguous image, suggesting both silencing and astonishing. Avison anchors the story in the biblical narrative,

> When you walked here,
> took skin, muscle, hair,
> eyes, larynx, we withheld all honour [. . .],

connecting the twentieth-century convert with the early disciples:

> Now you have sought
> and seek, in all our ways, all thoughts,
> streets, musics – and we make of these a din
> trying to lock you out, or in,
> to be intent. And dying.

The same struggle with resistance calls for another kind of intervention. Again dream-like, the poet combines the past of Christ's life and death on earth with her current world. Mixing of the senses and using words with their double meanings such as "sound dark's uttermost" all under the title "The Dumbfounding" deepen the profundity of conversion.

> Lead through the garden to
> trash, rubble, hill,
> where, the outcast's outcast, you
> sound dark's uttermost, strangely light-brimming, until
> time be full.

At the same time, the speaker's prayer, "Lead [. . .] to trash, rubble, hill" is a brave gesture of submission.

The third poem in this cluster, "Searching and Sounding" (*AN* 1.199–202), picks up again on the uncertain and exploratory verb "sounding," anticipating the painful perseverance required of the new convert and witness.[47] Her connection to Christ means an active sharing in his suffering.

> I run from you to
> the blinding blue of the
> loveliness of this wasting
> morning, and know
> it is only with you
> I can find the fields of brilliance
> to burn out the sockets of the eyes that want no
> weeping.

A few stanzas later she refers to herself as a burnt out star, "Dwarf that I am, and spent," accepting a new role of both "mirroring" the light and submitting to one whose name she earlier recognized as Love:

> touch my wet face with
> the little light I can bear now, to mirror,
> and keep me
> close, into sleeping.

In retrospect, the poet's surrender of her poetry becomes her greatest gift of witness.

In 1963 Avison returned to graduate school, writing a master's thesis on Byron's *Don Juan* ("The Style of Byron's *Don Juan* in Relation to the Newspapers of His Day"). She then enrolled in the doctoral program, completing all but her dissertation. In *A Kind of Perseverance*, she discusses the struggle she had in living in the two worlds of her new found Christian life and what she saw as the "counter-Christian assumptions and standards of the [secular] university."[48] Her nomadic career path continued with two years as a lecturer at the University of Toronto's Scarborough Campus 1966–68. Then she worked as a social worker for the Presbyterian Church Mission at Evangel Hall in downtown Toronto for four years. She taught poetry to patients at Queen Street Mental Hospital for a time. During this period she continued publishing poems and did more translations from

---

47. See chapter 6 for further commentary on "Searching and Sounding."

48. North, "Introduction," *A Kind of Perseverance*, 11.

the Hungarian.[49] She was Writer-in-residence at the University of Western Ontario in 1972–73. She also worked for a time in the Radio Archives of the Canadian Broadcasting Company. A longer stint of employment was as an office worker at the Mustard Seed Mission's Canadian office from 1978 to 1986.

In her years of retirement she continued to publish poems, earning recognition for their significance, as already noted. As well, in 1985, Avison was made an Officer of the Order of Canada and awarded an honorary DLitt by York University, Toronto. While she died at age eighty-nine, in July 2007, her writing continued when Stan Dragland and Joan Eichner published her unfinished memoirs *I Am Here* and *Not Not-There: An Autobiography* in 2009.

Avison was already attending Knox Presbyterian Church in downtown Toronto, close to the University, when she embraced wholeheartedly the Christian faith, and most of the years since her Christian conversion she was a vigorous and active member there. Friends and acquaintances at the church recall and letters and notes in her personal papers point to her particular interest in projects of evangelism and outreach.[50] In her last years she attended the services at Evangel Hall, the outreach mission connected to Knox, and then at Fellowship Towers where she lived.

The religious thought world informing her poetry, I suggest, derives primarily from the theological premises shaping Knox's teaching and practice. In his 1971 book *Knox Church, Toronto: Avant garde, Evangelical, Advancing*, William Fitch, Avison's minister until 1972, articulates in detail the doctrinal position of the church.[51] He describes Knox as standing firm through stormy years of rising secularism and liberalism. "All across the wider church she has been known as an evangelical church. This has meant that oftentimes she has been treated as obscurantist and dogmatic," he explains. The primary issue for Fitch and his church is defending the central position of Scripture:

> The Presbyterian Church in Canada holds to the Westminster Confession of Faith as her subordinate standard, and the

49. Kent, *Margaret Avison and Her Works*, 4.

50. In a conversation with me in 2004, Daniel Scott, then academic dean at Toronto's Tyndale University College, recalls her fervency for outreach in a team visit when he was initially attending Knox Church. In a letter to her friend Anne Corkett (Dec. 17, 1981), she speaks of her involvement in the "3-by-3" pattern of visitation in her church which she muses may be "an instance of conformity or of obedience," but nevertheless, something in which she regularly participates (Margaret Avison Fonds, the University of Manitoba).

51. Dr. Fitch was Senior Minister from 1955 to 1972.

statement in the first chapter concerning the Scriptures is the best possible statement of Knox's Biblical position. "Sola scriptura"—that is the ultimate statement of our theological stance; and this is so because it is through Scripture alone that we know of Jesus Christ, the full and final revelation of God the Father.[52]

Consequently, Knox Church prides itself in giving priority to "expository preaching" and study of Scripture, as reflected in Fitch's declarations.

"It must be biblical," writes William Aide, Professor of Piano and Chamber Music at the University of Toronto, in his personal memoirs, reflecting on his friendship with Avison and his familiarity with Knox.

Knox Church had only one ritual (save Communion). Before the service began, the Bible was brought in, opened on a cushion, by the church-caretaker in black gown. It was placed on the lectern with some ceremony, as a signal. Knox was a Bible-centred church; its Sunday service was sermon-centred and its ministers felt called to search the scriptures and illuminate them through expository preaching. Knox was dignified, intelligent, strict.[53]

Aide's description of this Book-centered ritual invites comparison with Avison's favorite poet in the English tradition, the seventeenth-century divine George Herbert. There is much in common between the two religious poets to confirm a decided influence of Herbert's style and content on Avison's poetry—"his metaphysical love of wit and paradox, of wordplay and minor drama" appearing in Avison's twentieth-century verse.[54] I suggest there is also an element not attributable to distance of time and style that both separates them and calls attention to her unique contribution to the English literary tradition. While the rituals and symbols of the Anglican Church

52. Fitch, *Knox Church*, 102.

53. Aide, *Starting from Porcupine*, 58. Aide is basically critical of what he calls the Knox critique and how he sees its expectations shaping Avison's poetic output: "I believe 'The Bible to be Believed' to be the central poem in *sunblue*, Margaret's third book. In that book and *No Time* a new kind of poem appears—the biblical gloss. Precision in understanding the Bible presses poems from Avison. They are often intricately rimed, always linguistically felicitous. They do not move me . . . Margaret, like C. S. Lewis before her, is a defender of the faith. She will continue to write poems declarifying doctrine. Knox will edit them in her mind" (ibid., 58–59). His comments about declarifying doctrine with its opposing editing are suggesting two contradictory impulses in Avison. Furthermore, declarifying is not the same as defending, so is he meaning the "Knox edits" turn mystery into rhetorical persuasion? If so, he misses much of her delicate handling of text. See chapters 4 and 5 for further comment on her working with the shape of the biblical text.

54. Kent also notes this comparison. See *Margaret Avison and Her Works*, 7.

shape George Herbert's devotional poetry in his single volume *The Temple*, the plainer symbolic ritual re-enacted week after week in Knox Church directs Avison's imagination towards a religious experience grounded in text. As a result, "biblical glosses" and a preoccupation with scriptural texts are not surprising. Furthermore, the seeming limitation becomes a strength, a point I develop in chapter 5.

Avison's firm embrace of the Knox tradition can be seen in a peculiar collaboration with Fitch in his book about Knox Church. He outlines his seven cardinal points beginning with "The Divine Inspiration, Integrity and Authority of the Bible." "The Scriptures themselves," Fitch explains, "are not the result of some unusual cross-fertilization of gifted and creative minds. No! They are God's revelation and gift, a unique part of the divine creation."[55] He goes on to emphasize the Bible's integrity: "It is impossible to be led astray by the Bible"; "it can be utterly trusted." In his passionate prose there is the insertion of three short poems for support—whether fragments or complete, it is not clear—introduced anonymously, almost implying his own authorship. Their style gives them away. Reinforcing his explanation of integrity, one poem asserts:

> Nothing I do or know or speak or feel
> or ever shall
> but this One puts into my hands
> and fully comprehends.
>
> Entering wholly in
> heard to the end, and known,
> it brings me on to silence,
> and into listening presence.
>
> Words become the Word, the choice
> offered one, a Voice.

He goes on to celebrate the diversity and unity of "this divine library." Again, he quotes what he calls "four lines of exquisite poetry":

55. Fitch's rhetoric earlier in the explanation gives some indication of his persuasive enthusiasm: "'Holy men of God spoke as they were carried forward as on a wave of the sea by the Holy Spirit,' writes Peter. This means that they wrote with divine authority and candour. Absolute honesty shrouded them. Truth enveloped them. They were transported into a realm of consciousness in which they wrote what God meant them to write and yet not one of their faculties was in limbo. The Scriptures were no accident of history. This was the divine genius God showed when he chose the book method of transmitting His message to all men," *Knox Church*, 133.

He breathed on the dust in His hand,

He stooped and wrote in the sand,

He cleared blind eyes with His clay:

Who shall open that book, on that day.

To strengthen the discussion on authority he calls on the Muse again:

In time the author of being, with authority

lived out in all the dimensions of flesh and dailiness

the spoken word of God

even unto the silence.

And now – O, listen! – out of the stillness He

speaks, to us, our utter hurt and healing.[56]

The minister's Acknowledgements page confirms my suspicions.[57]

Even a cursory reading of the poetry suggests the poet exceeds the didactic intentions of the preacher chronicling the history and outlining the orthodox teaching and purposes of Knox Church. Integrity is too small a concept for what Avison is talking about when she speaks of being brought "on to silence / and into listening presence." Her multiple meanings of "the spoken word of God / even unto the silence" harkening back to "the author of being" intimates an authority far beyond the assurance of the reliable nature of the words of Scripture. This blending of two different discourses in the book provides a powerful metaphor for understanding her Christian witness. She has planted herself in a narrowly prescribed and described orthodoxy to which she vigorously adheres, as many of her prose statements confirm, but her poems transcend the simple faith declarations.[58]

In Avison's Christian poems there is more than the obvious. Perhaps it is just the inevitable outworking of poetry that emphasizes the metaphorical nature of language, immediately opening up multiple levels of complexity and highlighting ambivalence and paradox. She is clearly a self-conscious and deliberate poet and she naturally employs the poet's ways of making sense of the world in her religious context. When Aide says, "She will

56. Ibid., 133–37.

57. Ibid., Acknowledgements, *Knox Church*. "The author wishes to express sincere appreciation to the following colleagues, and acknowedges [sic] their contributions": "Miss Margaret Avison," followed by the first lines of the poems as titles as well as "Mr. J. Samuel Thompson" for another poem in the book. Curiously, Fitch uses other poems in his book but identifies the authors in the context of inserting their poems.

58. The preacher in the pulpit may do so as well, but he is not demonstrating that enlarged and mysterious sense of the gospel in his articulation of doctrine here in his book *Knox Church*.

continue to write poems declarifying doctrine. Knox will edit them in her mind," perhaps he has it backwards.[59] It is Avison who is editing Knox. She is constantly editing and reshaping what she has read, heard, and seen; then in turn, she paradoxically both "declarifies" and clarifies what she is taught from pulpit and lectern in an imaginative and reframed response. When writing about the Catholic novelist and short story writer Morley Callaghan, Avison commends him for his transparency and undistracted and honest perceptions:

> "Your beliefs will be the light by which you see, but they will not be a substitute for seeing," said Flannery O'Connor. Callaghan's struggle, in the telling, is to make convincing to others remote from his beliefs the light by which he sees; and he does not provide himself, or us, with any comfortable substitutes for seeing.[60]

What she says about Callaghan, she embodies in her own lyrics. Her friend Aide recognizes her complexity of thought, but perhaps misses the profound import of transformations emerging in her witness to the Truth.

Fitch continues in his book to identify the cardinal points of the "evangelical" position of the Christian faith. The second, "the Deity of our Lord Jesus Christ," follows from the reverence for Scripture. Quoting Griffith Thomas, he writes, "'Christianity is inextricably bound up with Christ. Our view of the person of Christ determines and involves our view of Christianity.'" He reiterates the point, "[The doctrine] is absolutely fundamental to all true Christian faith." Third is "The Need and Efficiency of the Sacrifice of the Lord Jesus Christ for the Redemption of the World." "Public enemy number one is Sin," he exclaims. "And it is this that Knox has been declaring through all its ministry. Preacher after preacher has pointed sinners away from themselves to Calvary." Fitch assures his readers that the fourth of the "seven guiding principles on which [Knox] has taken her stand," "The Presence and Power of the Holy Spirit in the Work of Redemption," means that "the ministry of the Holy Spirit is marked as fundamental and all-embracing." When Fitch explains the fifth commitment to "The Divine Institution and Mission of the Church," he points out the obligation so central to Avison's understanding of herself as will be elaborated further in this paper: "The Church has a 'mission to fulfil.' The Church is sent out 'into all the world.' . . This is why every Christian is intended to be a witness to Jesus Christ." Sixth, "The Broad and Binding Obligation Resting Upon the Church for the Evangelization of the World" follows from the fifth principle.

59. Aide, *Starting from Porcupine*, 59.
60. Avison, "Reading Morley Callaghan's *Such Is My Beloved*," 206.

Finally, there is "an unconquerable hope" in the second coming of Christ: "The Consummation of the Kingdom in the Appearing of the Great God and our Saviour Jesus Christ."[61]

I have intentionally articulated these evangelical views in Fitch's voice to reinforce the same language and tenor of theological persuasion the poet would have imbibed in her formative experience of her adult conversion. How these doctrines inform her view of God, humankind, and the created world around her is reflected, of course, in the poems she has written. It is to the fifth cardinal point, the expectation of Christian witness—surrounded by and organically connected to the other theological assertions—that I turn with particular interest.

AVISON'S POETRY AS A CALL TO SPIRITUAL AND THEOLOGICAL ATTENTION

Avison has noted in various interviews the inevitable question concerning the interface between her poetry and her Christian faith. In the article written for Christian college students in 1968, "Muse of Danger," she places a clear priority on the side of what she then calls "witness": "But in His strange and marvelous mercy, God nonetheless lets the believer take a necessary place as a living witness, in behaviour with family and classmate and stranger, in conversation, or in a poem."[62] She recognizes and embraces the multi-faceted nature of witness in actions and behavior and in words of conversation and direct discourse. It is that last phrase "in a poem" that gives some cause for pause. What are the implications of this assertion, as Fitch articulates and she echoes and refracts? How does this missional obligation shape her art? How does her poetry succeed as poetry with its religious agenda or ethos? What do her religious sympathies mean to critics and lovers of poetry alike?

On the other hand, how does her poetry determine the witness? What does Christian witness look like in poetic form? What can be accomplished in a poem? How effective is the poem as a vehicle of communication? Is a poem's witness authentic or contrived and forced? The readers' questions are hers as well, and they do not recede for the poet in succeeding years. The issues for a Christian poet can become muddled and complex, she admits in one interview a decade after "Muse of Danger." Harry der Nederlanden, writing for the Christian magazine *Calvinist Contact*, asks a pointed question about the Christian aim of all her poetry, whether or not it had explicit

---

61. These cardinal points are elaborated in Fitch's text between pages 139 and 169.

62. Avison, "Muse of Danger," 33.

Christian content: "All my poetry writing has an evangelical anxiety," she responds:

> Am I faithful? I would love to say that when I move outside ex-plicitly Christian subject matter I am still writing Christianly. In my person, however, an expression of the two person [the old and the new man] is present. Pride or self-hate, the vanity cycle, the competitive drive play a role in any art. And you can very easily rationalize what people will accept and praise. Or you can also very easily run to the other extreme and do what they vilify and say that you are being persecuted because you are a Christian. So it is very tricky.[63]

Here she is offering a kind of artist statement for the press, as she points to the inevitably haunted poet lurking in the shadows of her poems. The atten-tion is on the writer's struggle to be a faithful and true witness—one who composes poems with integrity and sincerity.

Sixteen years later, in a letter to Denise Levertov in 1995, Avison re-veals her ongoing "evangelical anxiety" as she reflects on the differences of their individual approach to their vocation as writer, but the emphasis has been refined and refocused on the poetry, perhaps partially because it is a shared confidence with a sister poet. She comments on what she calls the "opened world" for Levertov from her experience—[Levertov's pull from Europe, her Jewish past, the American cultural community]—"even as it took away rootedness." In contrast, Avison notes, "[I]n almost every respect it has been opposite for [me]," and concludes her letter:

> I love the inexplicit witness to your faith in the poems and in [Levertov's volume *Tesserae*], the ample evidence, those atti-tudes of the heart that confess their source without your design or maybe awareness. I who speak explicitly feel often an iden-tity with Mr. Sludge the Medium and it shows, as every-mortal thing must, thank God. God help us both.[64]

---

63. Nederlanden, "Margaret Avison: The Dumbfoundling [sic]," 4.

64. Letter to Denise Levertov, 1995. The allusion to Mr. Sludge, the Medium, in Robert Browning's *Dramatic Personae* confessing his dishonesty to his benefactor, in-vites the readers of her letter to Levertov into multiple levels of complexity. "I [who] speak explicitly," she confesses and feels Mr. Sludge's convoluted admissions. "'Preach-ers and teachers try another tack, / Come near the truth this time: they put aside / thunder and lightning,'" he proposes in lines 1128–29; several stanzas later he coyly suggests, "'[M]y fault is that I tell too plain a truth,'" in line 196. In fact, in reality, Mr. Sludge is merely a sham medium.

Avison's awareness of the tension in the Christian who is a poet and the poet who is a Christian spills over to readers of that poet's work. One can struggle to place her poems, even as Aide has earlier. Who is her audience? In what particular reading community does the reader position herself? Her books of poetry are not typically found on the shelves of Christian bookstores; instead, they are side by side with other poets' works in libraries and bookstores with a specialized section in Canadian literature. There is an expectation of muted and subtle exploration of religious themes—if mentioned at all. As a result, Avison, from the very outset, disturbs, disorients, and surprises, for she is sometimes muted and subtle, but sometimes uncomfortably direct.

In bold declarations she reveals an unapologetic interest in Scripture, her primary literary source, and she openly wrestles with faith issues—not in every poem—but often enough to anchor her oeuvre in her deep commitment to her life vocation of Christian witness. The overtly Christian lyrics in the three volumes of *Always Now* and *Momentary Dark* tempt her readers to see religious, and even Christian, overtones in other poems in their ambiguous phrases and syntax. She is obviously an intense and passionate poet. She is equally emphatic about the central focus of her Christian beliefs. These two vocations, entangled as they are in her work, create a curious tension in readers who approach and slowly learn to appreciate her poetry.

At the same time, immersing oneself in Avison's poems can bring an unexpected reward to the alert reader. As was suggested in the opening poem of this chapter, "Rising Dust," the poet's witness begins with a compelling call to attention in her quiet, but complex lyrics. In our highly verbal and wordy world with all its clutter, the modernist lyric in its particularly lean form calls attention to the white space on a page. While observing the words, the reader is vaguely aware of the context—the seemingly empty space around the words. It can be seen as "intimidating margins of silence,"[65] drawing the reader to think negatively about what is not said; but more positively, it can beckon to silence or set the stage for silence—a prelude for a particular kind of attention, noted in Scripture: "Be still and know that I am God" (Ps 46:10). In the silence one is stilled and drawn out of the self. This out of the ordinary discourse, language compressed and arranged to call attention to itself, can be a kind of burning bush which compels a reflective person to step aside.[66]

---

65. Culler, *Literary Theory*, 23.

66. "Then Moses said, 'I must turn aside and look at this great sight, and see why the bush is not burned up.' When the Lord saw that he had turned aside to see, God called to him out of the bush, 'Moses, Moses!'" (Exod 3:3–4).

Spiritual writers and theologians alike commend the discipline of "attention." Simone Weil insists: "Never in any case whatever is a genuine effort of the attention wasted. It always has its effect on the spiritual plane . . . for all spiritual light lightens the mind."[67] Austin Farrer observes in his essay "Poetic Truth":

> And the chief impediment to religion in this age, I often think, is that no-one ever looks at anything at all: not so as to contemplate it, to apprehend what it is to be that thing, and plumb, if he can, the deep fact of its individual existence.

Farrer goes on to suggest an antidote to this lack of attention:

> The mind rises from the knowledge of creatures to the knowledge of their creator, but this does not happen through the sort of knowledge which can analyze things into factors or manipulate them with technical skill or classify them into groups. It comes from the appreciation of things which we have when we love them and fill our minds and senses with them, and feel something of the silent force and great mystery of their existence.[68]

This appreciation of things to which he is referring calls to mind that unique function of the poetic voice that calls attention to and mediates that special "knowledge of creatures" for a receptive reader-listener. Take for instance, Avison's early sonnet "Snow" (AN 1.69), (composed before she became a professing Christian), and introducing her particular understanding of a call to attention.

> Nobody stuffs the world in at your eyes.
> The optic heart must venture: a jail-break
> And re-creation. Sedges and wild rice
> Chase rivery pewter. The astonished cinders quake
> With rhizomes. All ways through the electric air
> Trundle candy-bright discs; they are desolate
> Toys if the soul's gates seal, and cannot bear,
> Must shudder under, creation's freight.
> But soft, there is snow's legend: colour of mourning
> Along the yellow Yangtze where the wheel
> Spins an indifferent stasis that's death's warning.
> Asters of tumbled quietness reveal

---

67. Weil, *Waiting for God*, 106.
68. Ibid., 38.

Their petals. Suffering this starry blur
The rest may ring your change, sad listener.

In this enigmatic sonnet the poet recreates the experience of being out of doors when snow is falling, perhaps, as one writer suggests, with city lights in the background.[69] The physical experiencing of falling snow can unleash multiple puzzling images from someone with alert senses and an active imagination. One can be both disoriented and exhilarated in the changing moods and pictures generated, as Donald Hair points out:

What snow does to the landscape—and we all, as Canadians, ought to know this—is blot out everything that clutters the eye, revealing the essential pattern of things. So the tumble and the blur are revelatory and change-inducing.[70]

The opening lines—arguably Avison's most famous declaration—promise clarity, direction, and purpose:

Nobody stuffs the world in at your eyes.
The optic heart must venture: a jail-break
And re-creation.

Here is the basic formula of her poetics—not requiring a religious interpretation, but lending itself to one as her Christian experience unfolds.

In her essay "The Dissolving Jail-Break in Avison," Katherine Quinsey suggests that the poet is proposing a highly conscious and self-conscious activity for one embracing her particular vision: "The optic heart unites sense (eye) and inner being (heart) in a multi dimensional, imaginative vision that breaks through conventional structures of perception."[71] One is not casually observing sensory phenomena—in this case, falling snow. "Such seeing is a willed activity," Quinsey suggests, "done by the 'I' behind the eye, 'I/eye' being one of Avison's unlocking puns, identifying the optic heart with the self, the person who looks out from those eyes," implying she is pushing her readers outward, away from "a self-centred point of view" and involving a kind of death.[72] This movement is the jailbreak the poet advocates as she

69. Donald Hair team teaching a course on Canadian literature and culture in the 1970s remembers colleague James Reaney's comment on the difficult lines of "All ways through the electric air / Trundle candy-bright discs": "[H]e said that's what neon lights look like when you observe them through snow flakes or raindrops on your eyelashes. " See Hair, "Avison at Western," 55.

70. Ibid.

71. Quinsey, "The Dissolving Jail-Break in Avison," 22.

72. Ibid.

pushes towards the puzzling images she sees in the snow. Quinsey's pains-
taking analysis shows the poet's capacity to generate in her readers intense
metaphysical reflection emerging from the complex images juxtaposed in
the sonnet.[73] Furthermore, these musings are certainly moving in Weil's and
Farrer's direction of spiritual attention.

A later poem, "Old Woman at a Winter Window" (*AN* 3.15), is a sim-
pler, less convoluted picture of one who is still "venturing" with "the optic
heart," but much quieter and even more intense. No longer out in the whirl-
ing kaleidoscope of snow, the meditating woman is silent and still, as her age
and situation suggest, focused on fewer images:

> I stare into the glittering
> quartz of the air, marbled with
> tiny streamers from
> valiant chimneys down along the valley.
>
> It is as if we pit ourselves
> against a congealing It.

The woman broods on "the encroaching ice" but concludes that it signifies
something however mysterious and fearful, also wonderful:

> the ice that somehow
> signals another space, a fearful,
> glorious amplitude.

Here she is the psalmist's picture of one who has "calmed and quieted [her]
soul, like a weaned child with its mother" (Ps 130:2).

This call to attention and reflection achieves intensity, in the poet's
own words, with "the whole-hearted use of language" required in any effec-
tive poem.[74] "When he is writing poetry a person is at his most intense, his
most clear sighted," she insists. Poetry should reflect "that pressure point of

---

73. Quinsey and Hair are only two of many critics who have been attracted to
"Snow." In fact, no poem of Avison's has received more attention than this sonnet. To
name a few, some of the discussions include Michael Taylor, "Snow Blindness" in *Stud-
ies in Canadian Literature* 3, 288–90; Robert Lecker, "Exegetical Blizzard" in *Studies in
Canadian Literature* 4, 180–84; Zailig Pollock, "A Response to Michael Taylor's 'Snow
Blindness'" in *Studies in Canadian Literature* 4, 177–79; Francis Zichy, "A Response to
Robert Lecker's 'Exegetical Blizzard' and Michael Taylor's 'Snow Blindness'" in *Stud-
ies in Canadian Literature* 4, 147–54; David Jeffrey, "Margaret Avison: Sonnets and
Sunlight" in *Calvinist Contact* 19, 3–4.

74. Avison, "Muse of Danger," 35.

crystallization."[75] That pressure point emerges in both the deceptively simple images of her "selved" and "thinged" and "earthed" people of "People Who Endure" (*AN* 2.191) and the more complicated transformations of snow in the mind's "re-creation" in the elusive "Snow" sonnet.[76]

Avison is often a very short distance from religious considerations in her trio of "venture," "jail-break and re-creation." In fact, these themes emerge in explicit and undisguised form throughout the lyrics of her several volumes of poems. There is, for instance, the transformation of the initially unbelieving father of John the Baptist in *The Dumbfounding's* "Christmas: Anticipation" (*AN* 1.221–22):

> The old man with his censer, dazed down the
> centuries, rays his
> dry-socketed eyes, dimming
> still, till he could believe, towards,
> with, joy.

The evocation of

> Zacharias dumb with unbelieving,
> flame-touched, to front
> the new sky

is in the context of "the street-lot's unlit needles of wet trees / waiting for Christmas buyers" and "hoar stone / cliff of an unfamiliar church," with its "pigeons flap[ping] and chuckl[ing] invisibly" and "tire-slop and motor-hum" and "buyers wedge[d] in doorways / waiting for lights, lifts, taxis."[77] The poem's call to attention occurs in its opening lines: "For Christmas week the freezing rain / stings and whispers another presence." In all the activity of the city's pre-Christmas preparations, only the attuned and stilled listener—like the priest Zechariah forced into silence—catches the sound in nature that points to something larger and of ultimate importance.

Both sympathetic critics and editors anticipate that this call to spiritual awareness may and does draw resistance. The editors of the third volume of *Always Now: The Collected Poems* frame her poetry on the back cover in terms of Elizabeth Hay's musings:

---

75. Avison, Review of *Day and Night*, 67.

76. See chapter 2 for a fuller discussion of "People Who Endure."

77. or Zechariah. Avison is using the Authorized Version's variant spelling of the name.

> . . . how is an unbeliever to approach not just parts of the work
> but all of the work of a poet who believes, through and through,
> in a personal God? . . . I listen to her infinite sympathy for the
> natural world, her sensitivity to the physical weather of the soul,
> her razor-sharp vision which moves like a hawk's and a sighted
> mole's, her wry debates with herself, her ornery, unfashionable
> courage, her poetic genius for placing words in such a way that
> I feel as if I'm meeting them for the first time.[78]

To begin, Hay enthuses, her poetry is significant poetry, no matter what the topic and deserves a hearing. For the sake of the intriguing poetry—with its singularity of vision and voice—readers can approach the collected poems with some sense of anticipation. If Christian witness shines forth, so be it. Readers can focus on Avison's "infinite sympathy" and "razor-sharp vision" if they choose and sidestep the religious themes. The editors of a recent anthology suggest something similar when they point out that her poems "reflect the reverence and wonder of Christian beliefs" but her poetry "does not proselytize."[79]

Starnino, however, embraces the essential spirit of her concerns in his review of Volume 2 of *The Collected Poems*. He takes his interest in her work further as he appreciates her "profoundly unconservative" innovations flowing out of—not in spite of—the religious vision. "Many of Avison's poems are extreme acts," he avers. His review ends with a perceptive summation of her Christian witness:

> But God—the "light / shining from beyond farthestness" [Avison's words]—is the true creative direction in her work. Avison clearly takes her ideas on journeys many of us no longer travel, so that encountering these poems means encountering down to the micro level—a lost world of devotional thinking.[80]

It is possible that this creative direction—this "journey many of us no longer travel" and "lost world"—is worth re-exploring and re-interpreting. The poet thinks so and resolutely and openly announces in "Other Oceans" (*AN* 3.146–54),

> How different it would be, today, to
> "take up your cross and follow Me," to
> "take My yoke upon you, learn. . . ."

---

78. Hay, endorsement, back cover of Avison, *Always Now*, Vol. 3.
79. Moss and Sugars, *Canadian Literature in English,* 200–201.
80. Starnino, Are You There, God? It's Me, Margaret," D5.

Her innovations may extend far beyond syntax and diction as she imaginatively creates space for God. Speaking out of our culture's silence about the idea of a personal God involved in the world's creation and redemption, she addresses that silence.

The contemporary theologian Rachel Muers explains the concept of "the problem of benumbment."[81] Muers writes, "Benumbment is the condition of defensiveness produced by exposure to warring discourses. It is a refusal to listen or be listened to, as a means of defending one's own discursive space against the predatory invasion of other discourses."[82] Avison disarms, breaking the spell of modern enchantment and this particular "benumbment." She opens a window—or even a door—on the possibility of renewing dialogue between traditions of faith and unfaith. Across the years of her writing and across the separate volumes published sometimes decades apart are poems that explore an alternative vision to modernity's secularity. The poet returned to traditional Christian beliefs, having taken a lengthy hiatus in "the far country" (Luke 15:13), and with confidence offers a fresh and unique perspective on the faith she embraces. On topics sometimes directly religious, sometimes not, she offers a peculiar and strikingly honest vision that indicates a particular directional pull God-ward.

The poems in the chapters that follow are representative of her distinctive and singular Christian witness, articulating directly or obliquely that Christian vision. Memorable phrases excerpted from her lyrics are gentle invitations to see with her against the grain of our expectations but in harmony with the grain of the universe: "Part of the strangeness is / Knowing the landscape," she suggests ("From a Provincial," *AN* 2:85); "For everyone / The swimmer's moment at the whirlpool comes," she muses ("The Swimmer's Moment," *AN* 1:89). That vision may be "A calling from our calling?" ("Our Working Day May Be Menaced," *AN* 1:110–12) or "The kind of lighting up the terrain / That leaves aside the whole terrain, really" ("Voluptuaries and Others," *AN* 1:117). She calls attention to that perennial "seek[ing] out some pivot for significance" ("The Mirrored Man," *AN* 1:125–26) or "merely persever[ing] / along the borders of / the always unthinkable!" ("Other Oceans," *AN* 3:146–54), spurring her readers on to spiritual attention.

In *A Kind of Perseverance*, the poet speaks of what she calls an authentic act or utterance: "Rarely is an act or utterance so authentic that one is stilled by it—far past the ugly stage of 'understanding' that reacts to goodness with

---

81. Muers is drawing on the work of the linguistic philosopher Gemma Fiumara in *Keeping God's Silence*.

82. Ibid., 56.

guilt, i.e. with vanity."[83] In the context of her lecture she is speaking of a kind of receptiveness nurtured in the self that results in hope. The thread that joins the disparate poems in the chapters that follow, selected to reveal Avison's carefully articulated Christian vision, is the sense of wonder she evokes as she points to something—Someone—out of the self. I sense rare and authentic utterances.

83. Avison, *A Kind of Perseverance*, 60.

CHAPTER 2

Towards an Understanding of Christian Witness

> But when someone tells it, something,
>
> a Presence, may briefly shine
>
> showing heaven again,
>
> and open.
>
> ("When We Hear A Witness Give Evidence" *AN* 2.168)

To begin exploring this alternative model of Margaret Avison's particular Christian witness in poetry (and conversely, the effect of that witness on the poetry), the terms of reference "witness" and "poetry," familiar as they are, need clarification, leaving aside for a moment the critical and fundamental descriptor "Christian."

CONNECTING WITNESS WITH POETRY

An obvious way to think about witness is to consider its etymology—its root meanings, one of Avison's own favorite exploratory methods. At a basic level, the word has to do with knowledge—a kind of seeing and hearing before one reports. Its etymological root in Old English is *witan* ("to know") from the Indo-European root *smer* ("to bear in mind," "to remember," "to be careful"); hence, a witness is one who "knows" and who is "mindful of."[1] This connection with knowledge filters into many sundry experiences of life and

---

1. See Strathamn, "Witness," 475.

everyday parlance: "I witnessed the strangest thing today" or "God is my witness" or "Would any witness to the accident please identify yourself" or "Her interest in the subject is a witness (or bears witness) to its importance."

Depending on how the word is used, *The Oxford English Dictionary* explains, witness is "(a) knowledge, understanding or wisdom"; "(b) attestation of a fact, event or statement; testimony, evidence"; or "(c) a person who gives evidence concerning matters of fact under investigation." These descriptions of witness suggest an increasing participation and activity. The first sense of the word corroborates the etymological root of knowing and seeing, suggesting a two-part process. Here the focus is on intake, on reception. A witness may be intimately involved in an event or merely a disinterested and involuntary bystander. Perception may be clear or confused; understanding may be full or partial. The action of witness may be aborted if the one seeing chooses not to disclose what was seen and remains silent.

Witness in the second sense, as "attestation of a fact, event or statement," implies the expected complementary report of the event. This attestation can be automatic and involve no speech.

> Attend. Attend.
> In pool and sand and riffled waters, here is
> significant witness of an event,

Avison points out in "The Ecologist's Song" (*AN* 2.266). This attestation may also be verbal manifestation or revelation, drawing attention away from a reporting self to something outside the self.

> I love to see birds walk.
> Oh yes of course, their singing,
> their soaring, their
> flocking in autumn branches [. . .]

the poet exclaims in a whimsical mood in "Resting on a Dry Log, Park Bench, Boulder" (*AN* 3.97). Giving testimony or attesting to a fact involves interpretation both by a speaker and listener who may or may not understand each other, as Avison observes in "Cultures Far and Here" (*AN* 3.50–51):

> We cluster
> telling each other
> stories that build the vault of a
> shelter from the wholly
> unknown, comforted by what

> is recognizable in our overlapping
> awareness.
>
> But sky and weather
> have a way of disregarding our
> walls, sweeping us on to
> not being an 'us.'

In the process, the multivalence of language complicates, enriching or hindering the transaction between witness and hearer. The witness event, in all its parts, is not necessarily a clean and unambiguous exchange of facts. Again, Avison articulates the difficulty:

> Learning, I more and more
> long for that simplicity,
> clarity, that willingness
> to speak (from anonymity . . .)
> all those impenetrables, when words
> are more like bluebell petals under
> an absorbed heaven. ("Concert" *AN* 3.65)

The latter description in the OED, the third sense of the word, a person who gives evidence, is perhaps the default understanding of the word, and not without justification. Courtrooms, lawyers and judges come to mind when the subject of witnesses is raised. The popularity of courtroom dramas in the media reflects the culture's fascination with the expectations on witnesses and their narratives. Many famous novels and plays are constructed around trial scenes. For example, the dramatic testimony of the witnesses in the Russian novelist Dostoyevsky's *Brothers Karamazov* plays a central role in the story.[2]

Other more formal reasons come to mind. For one, its etymology encourages this emphasis. Biblical scholars interested in the topic of witness often point out that the knowing and seeing and telling of a witness has mostly to do with disputation and disagreement, covenants and legal proceedings in the Old Testament setting. Strathman again, in his seminal article on "witness" in Kittel's dictionary, begins his discussion by explaining:

---

2. This particular work is noted here because Avison herself singles out the novelist in a footnote about a friend and subject of a poem. See *Always Now* 3.125. Her comments that he was one of two writers central to her (along with Jacques Ellul) suggest her interest in witness could easily be colored by her reading of Dostoyevsky.

[t]he proper sphere of μαρτυς is the legal, where it denotes one who can and does speak from personal experience and actions in which he took part and which happened to him, or about persons and relations known to him. He may be a witness at a trial, or in legal transactions of different kinds, a solemn witness in the most varied connection.[3]

In other words, the word's "native habitat"[4] is in the legal sphere of ancient Greece and other ancient communities such as Israel.[5] Other scholars follow suit in their understanding.[6] Allison Trites, in his book *The New Testament Concept of Witness,* remains convinced of the importance of the legal context, and he expands the theme of anchoring witness in what he insists is an environment of controversy and disputation.[7] He develops his influential argument for witness as legal defense from Second Isaiah's metaphor of two controversies or lawsuits between Yahweh and the world, and Yahweh and Israel in Isaiah 40–55, particularly focused in chapter 43:

> Bring forth the people who are blind, yet have eyes,
>
> who are deaf, yet have ears!
>
> Let all the nations gather together and let the peoples assemble.
>
> Who among them declared this, and foretold to us the former things?
>
> Let them bring their witnesses to justify them,
>
> and let them hear and say, "It is true."
>
> You are my witnesses, says the Lord, and my servant whom I have chosen,
>
> so that you may know and believe me and understand that I am he.
>
> Before me no god was formed, nor shall there be any after me (Isa 43:8–10).[8]

---

3. Strathman, "Martyr," 476.

4. Lewis, *The Four Loves,* 2.

5. See Homer's *The Iliad* and *The Odyssey,* and the Book of Ruth in the Old Testament for examples of calling for witnesses in legal transactions.

6. Among these others are Boice, *Witness and Revelation in the Gospel of John*; Harvey, *Jesus on Trial*; Stott, *Some New Testament Word Studies*; Moss, Jr., Bavinck, and Casey as quoted in Trites; Trites, *The New Testament Concept of Witness*; Coenen, "Witness," 1038–51.

7. See Trites, *The New Testament Concept of Witness,* 20.

8. Other biblical scholars share his view. For instance, from the outset of his discussion, Watts, in his commentary *Isaiah 34–66,* insists, "the Book of Isaiah, especially chaps. 40–66, is clearly controversial in tone and purpose" and that "[t]he basic apologetic character of the Book of Isaiah is particularly clear in the so-called disputation speeches," xxiii.

For Trites the prophet's metaphor becomes a working model for the witness of the New Testament, particularly as John's Gospel, Luke's Acts of the Apostles, and the Apocalypse unfold. In his concluding argument, he speaks of communicating the gospel "to a sceptical, questioning age,"[9] and in Christian apologetic language, "the frequent use of the witness theme stresses the importance of the historical foundations of the Christian religion."[10] One must learn how to argue persuasively for the validity of the Christian faith.

Obviously, Trites is viewing biblical witness through a very particular lens which could be argued is compatible to a litigious and nervous culture. The language of courtroom can resonate with people as apologetic works with titles such as *Evidence Demands a Verdict* and *God in the Dock* demonstrate.[11] It cannot be denied that there is a juridical metaphor in the Isaiah passage, but it seems reductive to overwork the metaphor, closing rather than opening up the text. Security in a specific kind of certainty can bring its own blindness.[12] For one, the metaphor is situated in a poetic form, thus providing a natural linguistic resistance to the structure of the witness metaphor. Legal suits by their nature require specific control and limitations of meaning. Poetry, on the other hand, exerts its energy and power through nuance and multiple meanings, evocation and suggestion. Consequently, the metaphor in action, so to speak, outstrips its legal derivation. Second, witness, by definition is pointing outward—towards another. The driving force of Second Isaiah's poetic treatise is the "new thing" that Yahweh is performing in front of and for the witnesses (but which they cannot see, for it is hidden).

Another reason one might emphasize the legal connotations of witness comes from philosophical enquiry, as Paul Ricoeur details in his essay "The Hermeneutics of Testimony." The cognate of "witness," "testimony," seems to derive much of its attention and energy from a juridical context. He narrows the discussion by emphasizing the point that "testimony is not perception itself but the report, that is, the story, the narration of the event.

9. Trites, *The New Testament Concept of Witness*, 225.

10. Ibid., 224.

11. See Josh McDowell, *Evidence Demands a Verdict* and C. S. Lewis, *God in the Dock*.

12. Martin Walton takes a similar view. In his review of the conversation among biblical scholars, *Witness in Biblical Scholarship*, he posits, "The general legal connotation of the witness terminology is undisputed. Disputed is to what extent the legal element plays a role in the NT. Further, the question is also whether the content of the testimony is not of more concern for the NT writers than the witness setting," 25–26.

It consequently transfers things seen to the level of things said."[13] An important implication follows:

> The witness has seen, but the one who receives his testimony has not seen but hears. It is only by hearing the testimony that he can believe or not believe in the reality of the facts that the witness reports. Testimony as story is thus found in an intermediary position between a statement made by a person and a belief assumed by another on the faith of the testimony of the first.[14]

Therefore, Ricoeur implies, the character of the witness becomes important. Is the person reliable, sincere and with honest intentions? Is the witness willing to testify and prepared to speak truth about a situation or person? Does the person have the requisite skill to interpret and articulate what has been perceived? Is there competence for naming and identifying relevant information and constructing a coherent narrative from the garnered data? What natural biases and motives affect the reporting?[15] As a result, he observes, "[T]estimony is at the service of judgment," suggesting that the context of listening to testimony from a witness is a trial, whether literal or figurative—"all situations in which a judgment or a decision can be made only at the end of a debate or confrontation between adverse opinions and conflicting points of view."[16]

What Ricoeur has noted about witness is not a new idea, of course. Avison confronts the same concern in her lecture "Misunderstanding is Damaging," as she spells out the perils for both the one reporting and the one receiving the report of an event. Boethius's observation in the sixth century in his *Consolation of Philosophy*—"As we have shown, every object of knowledge is known not as a result of its own nature, but of the nature of those who comprehend it"—she remarks, sounds very much the same as the Heisenberg Principle from the twentieth century—"willing to doubt the veracity of the observed because the observer's presence is an inevitable part of the process and may screen or skew what is seen."[17] As a result, the role of the witness cannot be minimized; the reality embodied in the narration includes the narrator.

At the same time, there are related implications in the juridical situation. Drawing on the difference between descriptive and what is termed

13. Ricoeur, "The Hermeneutics of Testimony," 123.

14. Ibid., 123.

15. This latter question is what is behind Avison's "evangelical anxiety" over the integrity communicated in her poetry. See chapter 1.

16. Ricoeur, "The Hermeneutics of Testimony," 123, 125.

17. Avison, *A Kind of Perseverance*, 36.

"ascriptive" discourse, Ricoeur points out that juridical statements can be contested.[18] Ascriptive and defeasible discourse, the language of witness, can be tested and contested at various points of exchange, but the "truth" of the situation may remain elusive. Jacques Ellul explains it this way: "One person's word against another's is the only possible fragile pointer to truth, like a compass quivering in its case." But there is no other alternative, as he goes on to suggest: "In order to live, we need truth to be expressed by the most fragile agent, so that the listener remains free."[19] Straining to achieve certainty with deliberate rhetoric of persuasion may or may not achieve the goal.

What does this mean for the poet? Or better still, what can the poet bring to the juridical setting of witness? To begin, the poet recognizes, accepts, embraces and reveals human limitation. In the theological realm, for example, as Jasper observes,

> poetry disturbs theological certainty, making its signs danger-
> ous, indirect and provisional, reminding us that God is always
> greater than what is revealed to us, and that the *truth* of Chris-
> tian believing is more important than its definition as uniquely
> *Christian.*[20]

At the same time, the inherent limitation is also a source of rich artistic tension to be mined for the poet who declares a commitment to both witness and the "wholehearted use of words" noted in "Muse of Danger." Avison explains:

> a poet chooses to accept the full halo of values in the words he
> uses. He accepts the personal identity they reveal. He develops
> his sense of their echoes across developing centuries. . . . Conse-
> quently, his words have potential effect at every level—not only
> the intentional or logical levels.[21]

Meaning will be larger—will range farther—than the small context of the literal or figurative trial. Meaning is already fluid in poetic discourse. While

---

18. Ricoeur speaks of the character of legal judgment as "defeasible"—"susceptible of being invalidated, abrogated." This characteristic "is not secondary" but "the touchstone of legal reasoning and judgment itself," 126. Meaning and interpretation are assigned to juridical statements and these statements are capable of differing interpretations on the part of both witness and judge and jury. Further on in his discussion, Ricoeur observes that testimony is "caught in the network of proof and persuasion," placing a particular burden on both the speaking witness and the listening witness, 127.

19. Ellul, *The Humiliation of the Word*, 41.

20. Jasper, *The Study of Literature and Religion*, 33.

21. Avison, "Muse of Danger," 35.

the poet labors for clarity and precision, she embraces the radiating echoes of ambiguity and allusion and the multi-leveled movement of metaphor.

Avison has one poem where she uses the word "witness" in the juridical sense in its title, providing a vivid example of poetry's capacity to enlarge and transform experience—in this case, the enactment of witness itself. But though there is a suggestion of a metaphorical trial in its title, the situation in the poem belies the juridical emphasis. It is not a poem of apologetics with a controversy of warring discourses. Instead, the poem intimates a situation where God shows up and the heavens open in some miraculous unexplained way.

> *When We Hear a Witness Give Evidence*
> Who heard the angels' song?
> Those on the night-shift. Maybe
> the animals. Not mother and baby,
> not Joseph, innkeeper, wise men,
> not the soldiers or Herod. Not Elizabeth's John.
>
> The glory (that *once*) was clear
> of those in waiting on him who now
> was clothed with only our here.
> Heaven knew this was the hour.
> The Father gave Himself over.
> A few heard the angels shine, stricken with wonder.
>
> Joblessness now, or night-shift,
> nine-to-five or in Chronic
> Care waiting it out:
> we like to quibble, we hear
> and are faintly afraid, are sore.
> No, there's no angel-song
> tonight. But when someone tells it, something,
> a Presence, may briefly shine
> showing heaven again,
> and open. (*AN* 2.168)

Avison takes a familiar scene of the Christmas story as told by the historian and defamiliarizes it. She does not mention the shepherds, only implying them by their night-shift obligations. The central actors in the nativity do not hear the witness of the glorious choir, the list indicating it has nothing to do with merit: Mary and Joseph in their submission to the will of God, Jesus himself who has left the glory of heaven, the oblivious innkeeper who does not know whom he is turning away, the wise men who are so diligent and intent on worship, the soldiers and Herod who will cause such mourning with their massacre; not Elizabeth's John, either—the man, like the angels, sent from God to herald Christ's coming. Who gets to hear then?—and by extension, to see?

The second stanza slows the pace of reading with the difficult syntax and familiar diction, but strange in this context. What is meant by "glory," a very Johannine word? Two other familiar words feel strange: "once" and "clear." Is "once" referring to a specific time—a date, or only one time? Is "clear" suggesting understandable, the human veil removed temporarily, or removed from, or distanced from? The riddling language continues, describing "him who now / was clothed with only our here." The present human reality is all the clothing the human Christ will wear. "Heaven knew this was the hour," and hence, the song: "Glory to God in the highest heaven and on earth peace among those whom he favors" (Luke 2:14). The supreme moment of witness has occurred; in turn, the response to the verbal witness is again provocative: "A few heard the angels shine." Shine, of course, is a visual word. But then to those who heard the angels' song, stricken with wonder, perhaps hearing and seeing were all of one piece.

The last stanza connects to the present mundane and painful realities of current existence—even at its most hopeless and desolate: "in Chronic / Care waiting it out." "We like to quibble"—evade the truth. "We hear"—hear what? Instead of being "sore afraid"—stricken with wonder, we are merely "faintly afraid" and "sore"—in pain, irritated. There is no miraculous intervention tonight—no peace, no favor. "But when someone tells it"—what meaning fills that little pronoun? When a person hears a witness give evidence of God's redemptive presence in his or her confined and night-shift world, what might that witness look like? Would she or he recognize it as witness?

> something,
>
> a Presence, may briefly shine
>
> showing heaven again,
>
> and open.

Avison has taken the witness language of the courtroom and transcended the basic understanding of defeasible evidence. She has pointed to a numinous reality that is apprehended only occasionally in the darkness of humankind's existence. The playful ambiguities throughout the poem set the table for the climaxing mystery of the glory of "The Father['s] giv[ing] Himself over" to those now who "are faintly afraid, and sore."

Poetic discourse, as Avison has shown above, is both a form which calls attention to itself and a particular language which already suggests witness. The poet perceives; the poet apprehends; the poet knows. The poet names an experience, bearing witness to what has been seen or heard or felt or imagined. The poet may shape a particular work of art with distinctive lineation, syntax, rhythms, and diction that call attention to what has been seen or imagined. At the same time, the poem is not merely description (or only description). Rowan Williams speaks of a poetic text "offering a frame of linguistic reference other than the normal descriptive/referential function of language," echoing Ricoeur's assertion that "[p]oetic discourse suspends this descriptive function. It does not directly augment our knowledge of objects."[22] Earlier Ricoeur has suggested that witness is ascriptive discourse in contrast to descriptive discourse, implying the possibility of the familiar Wordsworthian combination "[o]f eye, and ear,—both what they half create, / And what perceive."[23] From both directions, then, witness has a distinctive character in poetic form.

The poets and critics themselves have their own ways of explaining their particular discourse. Avison herself reminds her listeners in "Understanding is Costly":

> "The poet's job," according to Megroz, is "to prove that we are wiser than we know. . . . Philosophy, science and morality are essentially empirical; poetry . . . and religion necessarily transcend and anticipate demonstrable experience and therefore cannot be *fully* expressed or understood rationally" (The italics are mine, Avison explains). Our wisdom waits, in the wings![24]

She intimates a freedom from the need to control, to fix meaning, as she suggests in her sonnet "Butterfly Bones: Sonnet against Sonnets" (*AN* 1.71):

> The cyanide jar seals life, as sonnets move
> towards final stiffness [. . .]
> Insect—or poem—waits for the fix, the frill
> precision can effect, brilliant with danger.

---

22. Williams, *On Christian Theology*, 133. That is, "at least if we identify [the referential function] with the capacity to describe familiar objects of perception or the objects which science alone determines by means of its standards of measurement." Ricoeur, *Essays on Biblical Interpretation*, 100–101.

23. See Wordsworth, "Tintern Abbey," 210.

24. Avison, *A Kind of Perseverance*, 52.

In the theories of an earlier century, the Romantic poet Wordsworth delineates the poet as "a man speaking to men: a man, it is true, endowed with more lively sensibility, more enthusiasm and tenderness . . . and a more comprehensive soul . . . ."[25] In his poetic manifesto, the poet goes on to identify poetry as the language of passion:

> Aristotle, I have been told, has said, that Poetry is the most philosophic of all writing: it is so: its object is truth, not individual and local, but general, and operative; not standing upon external testimony, but carried alive into the heart by passion; truth which is its own testimony, which gives competence and confidence to the tribunal to which it appeals, and receives them from the same tribunal.[26]

There is a curious emphasis on witness language—"not standing upon external testimony," "truth which is its own testimony," "tribunal to which it appeals"—as Wordsworth articulates Romantic poetics of the "truth of the human heart." Echoing her great predecessor in the opening lines of her early sonnet "Snow," Avison speaks of the venturing "optic heart" making "a jail-break / And re-creation." In his essay, "Stevens, Wordsworth, Jesus: Avison and the Romantic Imagination," Lawrence Mathews calls attention to her initial "indebted[ness] to the English Romantic tradition" when he draws the parallel between her optic heart and Coleridge's "famous definition of the secondary imagination, which 'dissolves, diffuses, dissipates, in order to re-create.'"[27]

At the same time, Avison early on shows herself wary of "[this] tendency begun by Wordsworth, to see poetry through the state of mind of the poet," and clearly reacts against her Romantic ancestry, as Mathews notes.[28]

---

25. See Wordsworth, "Preface, Lyrical Ballads," 324.

26. See Stephen Prickett for an extended discussion of the connection between the religious and the poetic in *Words and the Word*. In his historical account of the connection between religious language and what evolved into Romantic aesthetics, he discusses the work of John Dennis, who concluded in his essay *The Grounds of Criticism in Poetry* (1704) that "'Poetry is the natural Language of Religion' . . . 'Poetry . . . is an Art, by which a Poet excites Passion'" (quoted by Prickett, *Words and the Word*, 42. Prickett points out that "[f]or Dennis, the link between poetry and religion was that both relied on passion and supernatural persuasion to restore the inner harmony disrupted by the Fall," (ibid., 43). Avison, as will be pointed out, is more interested in perception than passion even while she evokes great feeling in particular lyrics. Wordsworth, "Preface, Lyrical Ballads," 325.

27. Mathews, "Stevens, Wordsworth, Jesus: Avison and the Romantic Imagination," 36.

28. Prickett, *Words and the Word*, 46. Mathews offers a comparative reading of Avison's post-conversion poem "Searching and Sounding" with Wordsworth's "Tintern

In an anecdote about her friendship with Avison, the poet Gail Fox comments that she

> has greatly curbed my tendency to write confessional poetry
> and poetry that is a cry from the heart. Characteristic of her
> response to such is an exchange I had with her recently which
> wasn't about poetry: "Well, I've given up smoking." "Yes, and the
> rain on the street is *violet*."[29]

Avison insists in her poem "Is Intense Sincere?" (*MD* 26), published in her last collection before she died,

> Neither passion nor
> prophecy is
> poetry. They come before, or are
> premonished.

She suggests instead,

> Prophecy and passion become
> poetry after,
> after long bearing-with.

Example follows assertion in a kind of reminiscence of "sea-wideness, the sure / promise of sungold towers":

> Yes, the sixteenth century
> poets were light on prophecy.
> Singing does that to poets – remembering
> that Shakespeare always is the
> exception. Desdemona's
> presence remains private to herself,
> Only to Miranda, calm
> and undemanding, came the
> sea-wideness, the sure
> promise of sungold towers
> with Ferdinand, exalting, at her side.
>
> That comes of exile.

Abbey," suggesting that her poetry is also "post-Romantic." See "Stevens, Wordsworth, Jesus," 36–50.

29. Fox, "Dancing in the Dark," 56.

In invoking Shakespeare's supreme example, Avison discreetly shifts the focus from the poet's inner awareness of "after long bearing-with" to the "exile" of the persona in the poet's play. *The Tempest's* Miranda and Ferdinand compel the audience's interest, not the playwright's emotional state.

Her poem "Is Intense Sincere?" also points to Avison's affinity with the modernism of Eliot and Stevens in its preoccupation with language as art. In her modern outlook and emphasis on her craft, she echoes W. H. Auden's suggestion that "[a] poet is, before anything else, a person who is passionately in love with language."[30] She resonates with Ezra Pound's formulation of "an intellectual and emotional complex" rather than "a cry from the heart," as she reviews the art of other poets.[31] Speaking of the poet Pablo Neruda, she comments: "his words are an incident in the mind, a low murmur on the nebulous shore of that sea all men know in common."[32] Of a particular work of Edith Sitwell, she exclaims that

> there is a fascination here, like watching in slow motion while the winged horse gathers his muscles for the triumphal leap; and because that ultimate moment comes, again and again, this is great poetry, in spite of the wracked times that have framed its creation.[33]

She celebrates in these colorful responses to the lyrics of other poets, poetry's capacity to "give words multiple meaning: literal, associative, mimetic, musical."[34]

Language as art shifts the discussion from speaking of the poet as witness to focusing on the text as testimony or witness. W. H. Auden asserts:

> Poetry can do a hundred and one things, delight, sadden, disturb, amuse, instruct—it may express every possible shade of emotion, and describe every conceivable kind of event, but there is only one thing that all poetry must do; it must praise all it can for being as for happening.[35]

This peculiar comment "it must praise all it can for being as for happening" points to several implications of this particular form of discourse. For one, in its naming of a reality poetry also alters it, and not unlike witness, interprets

30. Auden "from *The Dyer's Hand and Other Essays and Poetics*," 156.

31. Pound, "A Few Don'ts," 1042.

32. Avison, "Review of *Selected Poems*, by Kenneth Patchen; and "Residence on Earth and Other Poems," by Pablo Neruda," 21.

33. Avison, Review of *The Canticle of the Rose*, 263.

34. Avison, Review of *The Rocking Chair and Other Poems*, 191.

35. Geddes, *20th-Century Poetry and Poetics*, 157.

that reality. Owen Barfield speaks of *"fresh meaning"* when he describes the poetic: "It operates essentially *within* the individual term which it creates and recreates by the magic of new combinations."[36] As Michael Edwards suggests, drawing on insights of Mallarmé, "A line of verse—constituting a 'new world' alters the thing that it connotes, so that the reminiscence of the named object bathes in a new atmosphere."[37] In the same essay he refers to a phenomenon of sound affording Wordsworth's "visionary power," therefore "induced by another sense"—another poetic alteration.[38]

Avison playfully demonstrates a particular crossing over into another in moving one preposition "in" in "Poetry Is" (*MD* 27–8), a deceptively simple poem ostensibly explaining how poetry works.[39]

> *Poetry Is*
> Poetry is always in
> unfamiliar territory.
>
> At a ballgame when
> the hit most matters
> and the crowd is half-standing
> already hoarse, then poetry's
> eye is astray to a
> quiet area to find out
> who picks up the bat the runner
> flung out of his runway.
>
> Little stuff like that
> poetry tucks away in
> the little basket of other
> scraps [. . .]
>
> [. . .]
>
> Scraps. Who carries the basket?
> What will the scraps be used for?
> Poetry does not care
> what things are for but is

36. Barfield, *Poetic Diction*, 151.

37. Edwards, *Towards a Christian Poetics*, 152.

38. Ibid., 149–50.

39. See Appendix for the complete poem.

> willing to listen to
> any, if not everyone's
> questions.
>
> It can happen that poetry
> basket and all *is*
> the unfamiliar territory
> that poetry is in.

The poem is doing far more than playing with prepositions, however. It is both talking about and embodying what Williams calls "revelation" in his *On Christian Theology*: "Revelation . . . is essentially to do with what is *generative* in our experience—events or transactions in our language that break existing frames of reference and initiate new possibilities of life."[40] That generative experience may not be easily named with simple referential correspondence; rather, there is a kind of mystery about the way the poetic works. The idea of liminal intuition may help clarify. As Edwards points out,

> Verse is also described as a veil; and Wordsworth is surely right to imply that words veil rather than show, their role being not to describe a world merely given but, since it is a world excluded from Eden in expectation of Paradise, to conceal it in such a way as to change its appearance. "Transparent veil" is in fact formidably precise: almost an oxymoron, it suggests both our no-longer quite seeing the object when poetry has intervened, and our seeing yet not seeing the object as transformed in the poem. As we look, not "through a glass, darkly" but through a transparency, veiled, we catch, by flashes, a kind of other radiance.[41]

Hence, some poets and critics will argue that poetry "is the language of the body-self and of dreaming" or "the language of the unconscious and of dreaming."[42] Using religious language instead of psychological, David Jasper suggests something similar about poetic language (in its broadest sense):

---

40. Williams, *On Christian Theology*, 134.

41. Edwards, "Wordsworth and the 'Mystery of Words,'" 153.

42. Geddes is drawing on the work of the Australian poet and psychiatrist Craig Powell who goes on to suggest that poetry "has its roots in primary process experience and is closer to the primordial union with the mother than the secondary process language of prose. . . . Poetry, by the very regressive nature of its language, has the potential to evoke tears even when the manifest content of the poem has nothing to do with loss, *20th-Century Poetry and Poetics*, xix. Both writers are attempting to account for the deep emotion felt in the encounter with poetic language.

> [Good or great literature] works on us not only by what it *means*,
> but also because of what it *is*—its shape, its devices (irony, meta-
> phor, allusion). Its power to affect and persuade is, it seems to
> me, mysterious and ultimately beyond the grasp of author or
> reader fully to understand . . . the autonomous activity of the
> text [is like] the mysterious workings of divine grace.[43]

In the disorienting title of Avison's poem "Is" seems awkwardly placed
as an intransitive verb, but it signals a kind of ontological reality and hints
at yet another implication of the earlier observation of Auden. Poetry ex-
ists, the poem asserts; therefore one has to reckon with its presence. In
this sense, poetry witnesses—or is a witness. It is calling attention to the
thing itself. In less simple language Paul Ricoeur explains what he sees is
the process operating in a poetic text, not limiting himself to "something
opposed to prose" (i.e., verse), but certainly including it: "[It] restores to
us that participation-in or belonging-to an order of things which precedes
our capacity to oppose ourselves to things taken as objects opposed to a
subject."[44] Williams interprets Ricoeur as saying, "The truth with which
the poetic text is concerned is not verification, but manifestation (Ricoeur
102)." Williams continues:

> That is to say that the text displays or even embodies the reality
> with which it is concerned simply by witness or "testimony" (to
> use Ricoeur's favoured word). It displays a "possible world," a
> reality in which my human reality can also find itself: and in
> inviting me into its world, the text breaks open and extends my
> own possibilities. All this, Ricoeur suggests, points to poetry as
> exercising a *revelatory* function . . . it manifests an initiative that
> is not ours in inviting us to a world we did not make.[45]

Again, Avison is suggesting something similar in her poem about poetry.

---

43. Jasper, *The Study of Literature and Religion*, 63.

44. In *Essays on Biblical* Interpretation, Ricoeur goes to great lengths to explain his
understanding of poetic discourse: "This function is in no way to be identified with
poetry understood as something opposed to prose and defined by a certain affinity of
sense, rhythm, image, and sound . . . to speak like Aristotle in his *Poetics*, the *mythos*
is the way to true *mimesis*, . . . a transposition or metamorphosis—or, as I suggest, a
redescription. This conjunction of fiction and redescription, of *mythos* and *mimesis*,
constitutes the referential function by means of which I would define the poetic dimen-
sion of language," 101–2. I am following the lead of others like Rowan Williams who do
not seem to make this distinction, but instead, use Ricoeur's definition to interpret how
poetry *as* verse can function.

45. Williams, *On Christian Theology*, 133.

The first line of her poem promises some clarity, at least temporarily with its comforting addition of the preposition "in," returning "is" to its familiar capacity as linking verb: "Poetry is always in / unfamiliar territory." Unfamiliarity calls for close attention, as the poet describes the unusual details coming into her focus and gathered up into a "little basket of other scraps" of details she has collected. The central metaphor of the poem—the basket and the scraps—shifts place in the subtle re-arrangement of little words in the closing stanza:

> It can happen that poetry
> basket and all *is*
> the unfamiliar territory
> that poetry is in.

Now readers must attend to more than the original data, the scraps, to understand the unfamiliar territory. Somehow words have swapped places and now poetry—basket and all—*is* the unfamiliar territory. Now her audience must "see" the unfamiliar poetry—to clarify the original sightings. She shows what she means in any one of the three "scraps" she has selected from the "basket." For example:

> There's the
>
> cradling undergrowth in
> the scrub beside a
> wild raspberry bush where
> a bear lay feet up feeding
> but still three rubied berries
> glow in the green.
> He had had enough.

In the earlier stanza "poetry's / eye is astray" to see what others are not noting. Now "poetry's eye" is peering in "the / cradling undergrowth in / the scrub" to juxtapose two unequal images—"a bear lay feet up feeding" and "three rubied berries" the bear apparently missed. And then there is the poem's speaker's deduction, "He had had enough." The witness of the poem (that is, this part of the poem) is the whole generative event of the multi-level unfamiliar territory—literally, the cradling undergrowth with its bear in the vulnerable pose, the uneaten berries, and the commentator—but also metaphorically, the words selected and arranged by the poet both for sound and meaning, inviting the reader's participation in the experience.

For example, the delay and disruption—"There's the"—at the end of one stanza before the new stanza and the strange image. Or again, the naming of the raspberries as "rubied"—treasures the bear somehow left. Or there is the strange fact that one can even see the berries at all in the bear's presence. "Poetry Is," Avison insists. It is its own witness to the world that it is. "It must praise all it can for being as for happening," Auden agrees. David Jasper affirms, "Enactment is all."[46] In response, readers may accept poetry's invitation to "come and see."

In "People Who Endure" from the collection *No Time* (*AN* 2.191), readers are invited to "participate-in" or "belong-to" a very particular world of suffering, a reality all too close to twentieth- and twenty-first-century people saturated with images of multiple survivors of unspeakable disasters. The poet dares to name the reality and readers respond with some corresponding picture of some people who have "endure[d] terrible things."

> Some people who endure terrible things
> become terrible, are
> selved, yes
> then thinged, lumped together, then
> earthed.
> Earth goes slowly
> down (as Noah remembered but said water).
>
> Raining and levelling, clear
> eyes only, the unlidded only.[47]
>
> There is for Noah who
> trusted, a rainbow:
> who built, who dared the lonely deeps,
> who woke,
> a sun again, and sons.

At the outset the seeming simplicity of the language and the sparse use of descriptive words call attention to the theme. Enduring and suffering have that stripped down quality. There are only three adjectives in the poem

46. The context of Jasper's statement is a discussion of "proper theodical discourse and 'true perception'": "The poet is one who sees and contemplates most profoundly . . . creative in the perception of things in abandoned love even to the point of their created mystery. Enactment is all," *The Study of Literature and Religion*, 130–31.

47. The poem "Rising Dust" discussed at the beginning of chapter 1 has curiously re-visited this theme. The two poems are published decades apart so the duplication is striking.

and all of them are key: "terrible," "unlidded," and "lonely." The pace of the reading is abruptly halted on that awkward verbal "selved"—only to be followed by a neologism "thinged." The familiar phrase "lumped together'" and the less familiar "earthed"[48] complete the quartet of verbals describing what the people who endure terrible things become. The tragedy of the existence for some is accentuated by Avison's experimentation with unfamiliar forms of familiar words with their attendant metaphorical significance. The stanza ends with a new sentence connecting the one "earthed" to a strange fate: "Earth goes slowly / down," implying a vivid sense of burial. The sentence is interrupted by the parenthetical "(as Noah remembered but said water)." Naming a specific person in the poem has altered the emotional and intellectual response. The allusion is puzzling because in the story of Noah (Gen 6–9) the water did recede and the focus is customarily on his preservation. Avison seems to be beckoning to the context—the survivor's memory of the rising waters and the destruction of the earth around him.

The two-line middle stanza calls attention to itself with its images of raining and "levelling". There is awkwardness in the line with the comma after "levelling," but the awkwardness provides a radical turn in the poem: "The raining and levelling, clear." Clear what? With the break in the line, the focus is on "eyes only, the unlidded only." The poem opens up into something unexpectedly redemptive and healing. For the one who has eyes to see—as Noah, "who trusted" in the last stanza—there is a new aggregation of images paralleling the first stanza: the verbs "trusted," "built," "dared," and "woke" are now answered by "a rainbow," "lonely deeps," "sun," and "sons." While the complete Noah story moderates and complicates the hope—the sons of Noah are a mixed blessing—nevertheless, the isolation and darkness of the one who has been earthed in the first stanza ("having dared the lonely deeps") have been replaced with the revitalization and hope of the rainbow, sun, and sons.[49] In this initial exploration of witness Avison provides a "manifested" or "enacted" truth that disarms and invites readers to join her. At the same time, the poem opens up the possibility of a more pointed witness. Evoking Noah's story has awakened religious consciousness in the responsive reader, and leads naturally to Avison's specific witness to Jesus Christ in her poetry.

48. "plunged or hidden in the earth; covered with earth" (OED).
49. See Gen 9:20–27.

CHRISTIAN WITNESS SUGGESTED IN SCRIPTURE

As mentioned in the beginning of the chapter, Avison's poetic witness draws on the familiar biblical texts that speak of the same, but her practice in her lyrics suggests a minimizing of the juridical metaphor. Instead, she shifts attention to "the mystery, hesitation and hiddenness of religious experience"[50] inevitably connected to the transcendent and ineffable God of the Scriptures. In the Margaret Avison Fonds in the archives at the University of Manitoba there are several boxes filled with handwritten Bible study notes, reflecting a systematic and disciplined approach to familiarity of the text.[51] This capable scholar submits herself to a basic discipline as a lay reader of questions from the Scripture Union Study method of reading the Bible through in five years, an exercise obviously repeated more than once. She interprets her method in a 2005 interview for *Image:*

> Poetry has helped me to know that in reading the Word, scripture, it's important to read every word. I don't know Greek and Hebrew, but I've got lots of translations to help me. Similarly I think in poetry it's always true that every word matters. You revise by cutting out and boiling down. Words are a good training for realizing the unchangeableness of the Word.[52]

Typically, as in that last sentence, she extends the meaning beyond technique. Her notes are, for the most part, recorded observations of data, liberally sprinkled with question marks that sometimes make their way into the text of a poem. She explains in that same interview: "One reason I do it [i.e., slip a question mark onto a statement, or a single word] is in order to get under the text. I particularly like to ask these questions of something familiar in scripture, to try to read it in a new way."[53] A poem that emerges from that text of the Bible demonstrates that a transformation has taken place filtered through her particular sensitivity to the power of the multifaceted "Word."

This particular "seeing" she visualizes in the "weeping eyes" "stung" with the "spray" in the landscape of the "The Word" (*AN* 2.220), one of her shortest lyrics. The startling image of "huge waterfalls," normally anchored in the physical landscape, now pours from the heavens:

---

50. Jasper, *The Study of Literature and Religion*, 32.

51. They consist of single random sheets which are often obviously scrap paper and are written in a tiny and almost undecipherable hand.

52. Avison and Martin, "A Conversation with Margaret Avison," 66.

53. Ibid., 70.

> Huge waterfalls in ever-travelling skies
>
> sting us with their spray
>
> in weeping eyes
>
> even in our present shadow-form of day.

There is something in the book—the Word—that makes the speaker in the poem weep. Perhaps it is too much reality for "our present shadow-form of day."[54] The heartfelt emotion of the speaker creates uncertainty. Perhaps "The Word" is not the book Avison so delights in, but the Logos of John 1, and the weeping eyes are those of Mary Magdalene at the empty tomb (John 20:11–18). Or the indeterminate Word is perhaps a curious blending of both—the poet apprehending the Logos/Word/Christ in The Word/Scriptures. Here is Avison's method in miniature. The striking image attracts the reader first to the poem, and then to the text that inspired and generated the poem, and then in turn to the One both concealed and revealed in both texts. The direction is clear enough, but the ambiguities along the way linger and do not allow for clean closure. In this peculiar combination of clarity and lack of the same, her poems have become a mediating presence for the often puzzled but strangely yearning reader.

Helen Vendler speaks of processes going on for the poet and reader:

> To counter the common practice of separating the idea of lyric from the idea of responsible thinking, I want to illuminate, if possible, the way thinking goes on in the poet's mind during the process of creation, and how the evolution of that thinking can be deduced from the surface of the poem—that printed arrangement of language that John Ashbery has brilliantly called a poem's "visible core."[55]

Watching Avison think is one of the keys to understanding her poems as effective Christian witness. There is a power, perhaps hidden, in the aesthetic pleasure she affords in the perfect image of an idea combined with sounds that match the rhythms of the beats of the heart. The poet speaks of "writing with my ear in our good language" with "Adam's lexicon" ("Butterfly Bones: Sonnet against Sonnets," *AN* 1.71) and by now, the familiar venturing "optic heart" ("Snow" *AN* 1.69).[56] Her readers have the same tools

---

54. Connections with other twentieth-century witnesses can be inferred: C. S. Lewis in his fantasy story *The Great Divorce* contrasts the physical reality of heaven with the newly arrived "man-shaped stains" on the bright air who find the grass painful to walk on: "Reality is harsh to the feet of shadows," one of the Bright People explains to one of the Ghosts from Hell, 20, 39.

55. Vendler, *Poets Thinking*, 76.

56. Avison and Martin, "A Conversation with Margaret Avison," 76.

at their disposal. Further, the rigors involved in participating in her thought processes stimulate perceptions of the text of the Scriptures as well as the One to whom they point. In other words, her witness beckons the reader to join her in the witness.

Looking at two poems in *Not Yet But Still* on the same biblical text yields some significant understanding of both her method and perceptions. The title of the first of the two poems is unusually long, containing the entire text, which cleverly imitates its meaning. "'Tell them everything that I command you; do not omit a word' (Jer. 26:2b)" (*AN* 3.35) is an excerpt out of one of the prophet Jeremiah's warnings of impending doom to the king of Judah in a context of the people's skepticism and persecution of Jeremiah for his dire warnings.[57] A few chapters earlier in Jeremiah's writing, the prophet has lamented the false prophets of hope who have not called God's people to repentance for grievous sins: "They speak visions of their own minds, not from the mouth of the Lord. They keep saying to those who despise the word of the Lord, "It shall be well with you" (Jer 23:17).

The poem deals with the aftermath of those who reject the word of God. The lyric recreates the "eerie quiet" and the "crack and rustle of fear" with the impending "storm/doom" of a people who have been defeated by invading armies of another nation. The poem concludes,

> Yes, they had heard
> his long-range forecasts.
> But now, they knew, believing now
> had them closed in with seeing.

The few survivors knew now how to read the signs of their times and knew which prophet had spoken truth. The poem allows for an allegorical reading, extending the impending doom to one who does not respond to the words of Christ and the Word/Logos, but it still has profound import in its original context with its dominant image of people who have had their eyes opened to truth they have been denying.

Tucked in this prophecy of doom, however, are words that stretch beyond the situation and change the meaning of "long-range forecasts." In the third stanza the poet writes:

> with force and immediacy, heard
> by every child, woman and man,
> came the word, spoken
> through Jeremiah who
> moved past darkness.

57. See Appendix for complete text.

The "long-range forecasts" "mov[ing] past darkness" suggest the restoration promised for Israel and Judah and the return of the exiles. Further, Jeremiah sees in the future even greater hope: "The days are surely coming, says the Lord, when I will make a new covenant." The prophet clarifies, "I will put my law within them . . . I will forgive their iniquity" (Jer 31:31). Avison, in her poet's proclivity towards multiple meanings and figural thinking, is anticipating the "better covenant" mediated by Jesus Christ (Heb 8) announced to the disciples in the Last Supper.[58]

Strangely, she is not done with this short text. In a second poem, she revisits the excerpted phrase from "the word of the Lord to Jeremiah." Does she sense an incompletion of a thought or is the new theme just a variation of the theme? This time, the title is condensed to a single word "Proving." An ironic accompanying subtitle, ". . . do not omit a word," condenses the sentence and calls attention to the process with ellipses. Even more, she herself omits the first clause of the sentence, "Tell them everything that I command you," embodying the poet's process of crystallization of meaning. In this poem "Proving" (AN 3.79), she intertwines the abstract concepts of truth and word, placing Jeremiah's voice in the background in its opening words:

> Truth speaks
> all things into being.
> No word more, but
> not one left unspoken.[59]

In these two concise poetic statements she draws the reader to another writer in the Scriptures who opens a New Testament letter with "Long ago God spoke to our ancestors in many and various ways by the prophets" (Heb 1:1). These poets include Jeremiah, for one, who must not omit a word. The writer to the Hebrews continues,

> . . . but in these last days he has spoken to us by a Son, who he appointed heir of all things, through whom he also created the worlds. He is the reflection of God's glory and the exact imprint of God's very being, and he sustains all things by his powerful word (Heb 1:1–3).

In a fascinating move of concision, the creating and sustaining of "all things" "by his powerful word," including "the worlds" of the Scripture has been stripped down in Avison's language to "[n]o word more, but not one

---

58. Matt 26:28; Mark 14:24; Luke 22:20.

59. See Appendix for complete text.

left unspoken." She has clearly moved away—in fact, beyond—the original context of the command.

Launched in the book of Hebrews, she continues to blend the two senses of "word":

> Truth carves, incises,
>
> to the bone,
>
> and between bone and marrow,

echoing the biblical writer's assertion of the power of the words of Scripture and/or the Son: Indeed,

> the word of God is living and active, sharper than any two-edged sword; . . . it is able to judge the thoughts and intentions of the heart. . . . And before him no creature is hidden, but all are naked and laid bare to the eyes of the one to whom we must render an account (Heb 4:12–13).

"No wonder / we want none of him," the poet comments on the inevitable, contemporary and past responses of rejection of that word. One wonder generates another wonder, in poetic simplicity, as the words spill out:

> The wonder is
>
> truth loves;
>
> died of it, once.

In these epigrammatic sentences, one after the other, the reader sees the poet Avison thinking, to use Vendler's phrase, meditating on a phrase in the Old Testament, drawn to one in the New Testament, circling in large concepts to land in the middle of her poem at the central image of the gospel, the cross. In her process, she is also inviting the reader to enact that same circle. The last stanza of the poem distils further the complete work of Christ, as the poet returns to the words given to the prophet:

> Truth lives.
>
> Acting on what is spoken,
>
> not a syllable extra,
>
> nothing omitted,
>
> brings into being
>
> just what is prophesied.
>
> That is the test –
>
> not of what has been spoken
>
> but for the hearer,
>
> his act.

In her complex and compressed logic, she recalls the familiar test that a prophet's word is verified in the prophecy's fulfillment.[60] "Truth lives" (*AN* 3.79). The sentence cannot be reduced to fewer words, as the poet again enacts the words of the Old Testament prophet. Christ's resurrection, "his act," verifies his role as the greater prophet of Hebrews. His words of completion at the cross, "It is finished" (John 19:30), are fulfilled and the witnesses see the risen Christ. Words are spoken for hearers, but not words alone. Words and act have fused. Now the truth, the test of his prophetic effectiveness (for the one who has "incised to the bone" the hearts of the hearers), is in the redemptive act. The hearers of the prophet's complete word have the proof; now they can participate in the proving.

The effort involved in participating in Avison's thought processes of looking into Scripture apply to the books of nature and human nature, as well, and yield the same stirrings that may point to Christ. It is not a matter of persuasion, but of intense looking and reflection with receptivity to the witnessing lyric. The reader, in the completion of the poetic process, is invited to join in Williams's "revelation"—"the generative in our experience."

In the meantime, the question still lingers whether these difficult lyrics function as witness in the biblical sense. Their subject matter may be texts of or allusions to Scripture; they may speak to the heart of a persevering reader. But do they reflect the energy, passion, urgency, and action of the initial witnesses, articulated in the four Gospel accounts and The Acts of the Apostles? Words such as "profession," "confession," "proclamation," and "preaching" dominate this new mode of witness discourse as the four evangelists announce the gospel message—the good news of Jesus Christ. Are these words articulations of Avison's particular poetic language? All four Gospels center on the "testimony par excellence," the "confessional kernel" "that Jesus is the Christ."[61] All four Gospels emphasize the pivotal historical event of Christ's passion and resurrection. Is this testimony the poet's emphasis?

---

60. Moses speaks the Law of God to the Israelite people: "You may say to yourself, 'How can we recognize a word that the Lord has not spoken?' If a prophet speaks in the name of the Lord but the thing does not take place or prove true, it is a word that the Lord has not spoken" (Deut 18:21, 22). Even more connected to the text Avison is dealing with is Jeremiah's own struggle with prophets prophesying peace when he is prophesying doom to Judah: He speaks against Hananiah: "As for the prophet who prophesies peace, when the word of that prophet comes true, then it will be known that the Lord has truly sent the prophet" (Jer 28:9).

61. Ricoeur, *Essays on Biblical Interpretation*, 134. See Matt 16:13–16; Mark 8:27–29; Luke 9:18–20; John 1:41, 49; John 6:67–69.

WITNESS IN THE GOSPELS OF LUKE AND JOHN, ACTS OF THE APOSTLES, AND SECOND ISAIAH

Three particular places in Scripture articulate the manner and matter of biblical witness germane to Avison's own expression: The Gospels of Luke and John, Acts of the Apostles, and Second Isaiah. In the dedication to Theophilus prefacing Luke's Gospel, the writer presents himself as "a plain honest man, concerned with plain truth." Twice he uses the phrase "orderly account" and assures his intended audience that he has investigated everything carefully from the first, gleaning his information from "eyewitnesses and servants of the word" (Luke 1:2). In Willmer's words, "Luke-Acts is a text narrated as witness literature, appropriate for the law court, emphasizing what is clear and not clear."[62] The singularity of the Christian message—Christ crucified and risen—speaks through the voices of its many eyewitnesses. Sermons of the apostles include a variation of the familiar declaration, without subtlety and nuance: "This man . . . you crucified and killed . . . . This Jesus God raised up, and of that all of us are witnesses" (Acts 2:23).[63] In the Lukan record the proof is initially in the eyewitness account, making the question of the legitimacy of an eyewitness paramount.

From the outset of Luke's Gospel he presents witnesses who demonstrate an emerging faith and who need illumination.[64] From Zechariah at the beginning of the Gospel to the unnamed disciples on the Emmaus Road at the book's conclusion—all need clarity. When the great John the Baptist, languishing in prison, has his doubts about the One he has represented, Jesus sends John's disciples back to his key witness with the cryptic message:

> Go and tell John what you have seen and heard: the blind receive their sight, the lame walk, the lepers are cleansed, the deaf hear, the dead are raised, the poor have good news brought to them. And blessed is anyone who takes no offence at me (Luke 7:22–23).

Eyewitness accounts of emerging faith merge into emboldened preaching and empowered declarations of confident and enabled witnesses. The blunt language used in the sermons in Acts suggests Luke's passionate insistence that the evidence offered is clear; refusal to believe in and respond

---

62. Willmer, personal conversation, July 2005.

63. See also Acts 3:15; 5:30–32; 10:39–41; 13:28–31.

64. He is not unique among the Gospel writers in this emphasis. The importance of the parable of the Sower recounted in all three of the Synoptic Gospels (Matt 13, Mark 4, and Luke 8) suggests a common concern with spiritual apprehension. John, of course, has his own unique understanding of "seeing."

to the risen Christ reflects blindness based on resistance. Peter addresses the crowd on the day of Pentecost with language of indictment:

> You that are Israelites, listen to what I have to say: Jesus of Nazareth, a man attested to you by God with deeds of power, wonders, and signs that God did through him among you, as you yourselves know—this man, handed over to you according to the definite plan and foreknowledge of God, you crucified and killed. . . . But God raised him up (Acts 2:22–24).

Peter is unequivocal in his address to the people amazed at the lame man's healing: "But you rejected the Holy and Righteous One," he exclaims. "You killed the author of life, whom God raised from the dead. To this we are witnesses" (Acts 3:14–15).

The second of three direct statements that Jesus makes to his disciples about witness at the end of the Lukan Gospel emphasize their role first as observers.[65] Jesus concludes, "You are witnesses of these things" (Luke 24:48)—the whole complex of fulfilled Old Testament Scriptures, his completed ministry, his death, and now his resurrection. Karl Barth, in his extensive discussion on witness in his multi-volume *Church Dogmatics,* repeatedly insists, "[A]s he lives, Jesus Christ speaks for Himself, that He is His own authentic Witness, that of Himself He grounds and summons and creates knowledge of Himself and His life, making it actual and therefore possible." Jesus Christ makes Himself known: "He introduces Himself."[66] That introduction here at the end of Luke's Gospel is that of the now resurrected Christ. In turn, this resurrected Christ requires an active response. In Barth's words again, these witnesses are

> not idle spectators merely watching and considering; not for the enjoyment of spectacle granted to them; not for the vain increase of their knowledge of men, the world and history by this or that which they now come to know of God; not inquisitive reporters; but witnesses who can and must declare what they have seen and heard like witnesses in a law-suit.[67]

The historian's voicing of Luke lends authority to a clear missional agenda, and he writes his account as a document to persuade and affirm belief.

The third of the three witness declarations in the opening of Acts, recorded as Jesus's last words before he ascended into heaven—words co-opted by every serious follower of Jesus early on in her or his faith

---

65. The three statements are (1) Luke 21:5–11; (2) Luke 24:44–49; (3) Acts 1:8.

66. Barth, *CD*, IVa 69.2: 46.

67. Ibid., IVb71.4: 576.

journey—emphasizes the divine assistance and power the Holy Spirit provides: "But you will receive power when the Holy Spirit has come upon you; and you will be my witnesses in Jerusalem, in all Judea and Samaria, and to the ends of the earth" (Acts 1:8). The disciples are told to wait for the Spirit to descend on them, who will, when he comes, empower the fledgling witnesses on that special day of Pentecost with all its drama.[68] In the face of persecution and attack, Peter explains to his questioners the source of the apostles' courage and power: "And we are witnesses to these things, and so is the Holy Spirit whom God has given to those who obey him" (Acts 5:32).

There is a boldness in Avison that echoes Luke. Her passion, her sense of obligation, her awareness that she is a "sent one" is evident in some of her private correspondence. One set of letters passes between Avison and Stephen Scobie, a poet and critic, who requested her endorsement of his book *Gospel*, "a presentation, in the form of a documentary poem, of the life of Jesus."[69] Her guarded but uncompromising reading of his poem is revealing: "I am still struggling to get clear of me in order to read your poem with the 'literarily' requisite openness . . . ."[70] Her comments get more direct as she draws to a conclusion:

> Here is a poem about the one who is, alone and always, one in whose (to use a metaphor) imagination, vividly now always, we exist—an imagination whose least flicker would be my obliteration, yours, everything's and everybody's . . . a piece purportedly imagined, (this one purportedly speaking, for him making this one obliterable,) by one of us who are instantaneously, faithfully sustained! And the entangling rude unmanageable harsh parts of the apostolic are not here to trouble me, which troubles me who have to struggle.[71]

Scobie's subsequent response helps to clarify her concern and suggests he well understands her position: "I thought that your letter does indeed strike to the heart of the paradox implied by the choice of narrative position

---

68. See Acts 2.

69. This is the same Stephen Scobie who reviewed Avison's *sunblue* in *Queens Quarterly* in 1980, remarking on his disappointment with the collection: "There are the same intricate patterns of thought, the same packed, unusual language, and the same proclamation of an unequivocal Christian faith. Yet . . . the poems seem more diffuse, they lack the tension and the fine edge of complexity of Avison's best work. Some of the urgency seems to have gone out of her voice," 158. Scobie, Letter to Margaret Avison, November 10,1993.

70. These enigmatic ellipses throughout the exchange are Avison's own.

71. Avison, Letter to Stephen Scobie, December 30, 1993.

in that book: to 'create,' as it were, one's own creator."[72] He explains to her that he is not a believing Christian and that he wrote the entire draft without consulting the biblical account, an admission she would not admire. Any mistakes would be his "personal signature"![73]

In response, she concludes her correspondence with Scobie in another lengthy letter with a probing challenge, "Are you reading the Gospels again now that the book is out?" Then she tells him her own story of coming to Christian faith, concluding,

> God knows none of us know much, after Jesus, resurrected and ascended in Renaissance beauty, becomes Jesus living, inexorably, present at every moment, vulnerable stil [sic] to hurt, betrayal, but putting up with that and quickening possibilities all the time that one never knew existed. It is still so.[74]

On the back of an envelope attached to the letters is a scribbled sketch of a poem revealing her troubled musings. In part, she writes:

> It is the builders, those
> whose towers have filled
> the skies with their
> significant bulk – they cannot
> , so, have missed the
> cornerstone.

> We have that idiom
> 'beside yourself'
> and there you stood, and wrote? . . .
> (undated and untitled poem, Margaret Avison Collection)[75]

Another such exchange in correspondence is between the then *Toronto Star* Religion editor Michael Higgins and Avison. Higgins had sent Avison a copy of his book about Thomas Merton entitled *Heretic Blood*. A paragraph out of her lengthy reply is cryptic and pointed: "As I felt my way through the

---

72. Scobie, Letter to Margaret Avison, February 17, 1993[sic]. The sequence of the letters indicate an error in dating.

73. Ibid., November 10, 1993[sic.]

74. Avison, Letter to Stephen Scobie, March 15, 1994.

75. One of the conditions of access to her unfinished poems and correspondence in the Margaret Avison Fonds is limiting the quoting of unpublished (and not publishable by her standards) material to fragments. I respect her wishes in this partial reflection.

baffling new landscape of new ideas, I kept yearning to see on the page the stark lowly name that shrivels earth and sky like lightning: Jesus."[76]

These two excerpts from letters reveal the willingness and capacity of this difficult poet to speak plainly amidst her characteristic complexity. She embraces the divine calling to be a witness to and for Christ with utter commitment and earnestness. As she declares in her Pascal lectures,

> [W]e are in the miasma of this violent, headlong, desperate, fragmenting world. The salt that checks corruption has to be rubbed against the corruptible. And the salt is not ourselves, except as Jesus Christ presences himself, in mercy, even in us, even here and now. We may not know when this happens. It is certainly not in our power to make it happen. We are all, alike, in His hands, in or of the world though we be.[77]

At the same time, while Avison is forthright and occasionally direct in her faith declarations, the poet inserts her habitual questioning and multiple meanings, even in the plain speech of prose statements. For sure, she is not straightforward and direct in her poems. The confessional kernel of the gospel message is there but it is often like the parabolic treasure, buried in the complex field of her poetry (Matt 13:44). Even her various prose accounts of her own Damascus experience are transformed in her poems with hesitations and expressions of doubt and mystery.

The witness theme emphasized in Second Isaiah's vivid rhetoric of Isaiah 40–55 may be a model closer to Avison's indirect witness in her poetry than the narrative of Luke. Isaiah's words of comfort and admonition written in poetic form, suggest a parallel in complexity and multivalence, evocation, and suggestion rather than plain speech. It is true that the poet-prophet inserts in his poetic argument the genre of trial speech and employs the metaphor of witnesses, calling on them to "justify" other gods or Yahweh.[78] At one juncture Yahweh calls on his people, "Accuse me, let us go to trial" (Isa 43:26). However, disputation does not stand alone; rather

---

76. The paragraph bears completing: "In your March 13th letter you spoke of your keen interest in 'the interfacing of religious sensibility with the literary imagination.' Indeed I understand why you knew that I know the edginess, the sometimes grating against each other, of the imperious demands of poetry and the absolute demand of my Lord. Oddly, the oftener I deny the first, the more gently does He indulge me with unearned freedom to write. For me, it so often comes down to a choice between ego/vanity, and submission—that struggle which Merton records in many ways." Avison, Letter to Michael Higgins, April 4, 2000.

77. Avison, *A Kind of Perseverance*, 35.

78. See Isa 41:1–20; 43:8–13, 22–28; 44:7–8 for a sample of direct juridical references.

it is juxtaposed with another rhetorical strategy in the text—the salvation oracles. As Brueggemann observes:

> These twin modes of *speech of disputation* and *oracle of salvation* are quite distinct and move in opposite directions. But they need to be seen in relation to each other, for together they permit the exilic community to "see Yahweh" (40:9), who makes a decisive difference in its life.[79]

The two literary forms together are used effectively to call attention to Yahweh's larger message of comfort—that he is working on behalf of the exiles in Babylon. The prophet is countering hopelessness, skepticism and doubt with an exhortation to hope and belief. The juridical metaphor is a powerful rhetorical device but it neither subsumes the larger meaning of the text nor is it the only metaphor or organizing structure driving the argument.[80]

Furthermore, part of the rich complexity of the text is its multiplicity of suggested witnesses, not just the ones instructed to assume the role. There is the prophet speaking: "Comfort, O comfort my people, says your God" (Isa 40:1). The "Voice" of God—Yahweh himself as witness—asserts his presence (Isa 40:3, 6). The nations and their gods are called to be witnesses (Isa 41:1). The fearful and despairing exiled people are the nations' counterparts (Isa 43:10). The ambiguous and shifting "Servant" (42:1–4) assumes varied witness roles.[81] The text itself is witness as it blends and blurs seeing and telling.

What is not ambiguous in the text is its dominant theme and the focus of its witnesses, articulated repeatedly in the extended poem: "Say to the cities of Judah, 'Here is your God'" (Isa 40:9b). In the context of the developing dialogue between Yahweh and his witnesses, Yahweh poses key questions: "Who has measured the waters?" (Isa 40:12); "Who has directed the spirit of the Lord?" (Isa 40:13); "Who taught him the path of justice . . . of knowledge?" (Isa 40:14). The questions build towards implied accusations: "Have you not known? Have you not heard? Has it not been told you from the beginning? Have you not understood?" (Isa 40:21). There is irony in this announcement of good news for the initial hearers of the prophet's words. As Brueggemann points out, "the *announcement* of the gospel is a lyrical, poetic, imaginative one. . . . But the actual *substance of the news* . . . is an 'event' to which exiles have no access."[82] The testimony of the poem is

79. Brueggemann, *Isaiah 40–66*, 29.

80. See, for instance, the kinsman-redeemer motif in Isa 41:14.

81. There are multiple references in these chapters of Isaiah delineating the various witnesses.

82. Brueggemann, *Isaiah 40–66*, 12.

a story, a narration of Yahweh's creative power and intervention on Israel's behalf, which the exiles must believe based on the words they hear, not on what they have seen.

While Yahweh is working his as yet hidden salvation, the people, as his servant, have their witness role to play. He recognizes their fragility as witnesses in the context and registers impatience with their predicament:

> Listen, you that are deaf;
>
> and you that are blind, look up and see!
>
> Who is blind but my servant,
>
> or deaf like my messenger whom I send? (Isa 42:18–19)

Between two salvation oracles, "Do not fear, for I have redeemed you; I have called you by name, you are mine" (Isa 43:1) and "Do not remember the former things . . . I am about to do a new thing, now it springs forth, do you not perceive it" (Isa 43:18–19), Yahweh calls two sets of witnesses: "the nations" (Isa 43:9), and by implication, their false gods, and Israel, "my servant whom I have chosen" (Isa 43:10) in this climactic lawsuit.

The tension is obvious: How can the listeners witness or even be expected to witness when they are blind and deaf? As commentators and critics confront Yahweh's strange injunction, their resolution of the dilemma signals their own understanding of the nature of biblical witness. Strathmann, particularly focuses on the prophet's own witness, positing an "evangelistic confession" or a witness to beliefs about God as the dominant emphasis for witness here:

> For the prophets the deity of God is a fact . . . which is certain only to faith, which only the man who is not blind and deaf can see and attest, 43:8. The content of the witness is thus a religious truth of which the witness is convinced on the basis of his experience . . . grounded, then, on the prophetic experience of revelation which is original, and which by nature is not subject to rational control. This is certainty to the prophet.[83]

For Brueggemann, on the other hand, the essential point in the context involves the concrete existential implications for the called witnesses whose lives and futures are at stake. He explains:

> The trial is not only god versus god; it is also witness versus witness and truth versus truth. Israel is placed by the poet in a context of contested truth, where it is not known ahead of time which truth will be vindicated and accepted by the court. The

---

83. Walton, *Witness in Biblical Scholarship*, 21. Strathman, "Martyr," 484.

dispute about truth concerns theological claim about God, but it also concerns historical possibility.[84]

Ricoeur extends Brueggemann's suggestion by insisting, "It is not possible to testify *for* a meaning without testifying *that* something has happened which signifies this meaning." The fundamental example, he explains, is "[t]he conjunction of the prophetic moment, 'I am the Lord,' and the historical moment, 'It is I, the Lord your God, who has led you out of the land of Egypt and out of the house of bondage' (Exod 20:2) . . . ."[85] Willmer muses on these options to conclude:

> This modern distinction of fact and belief may not be true to Scripture or to life, where the more crucial distinction is between observable [and] manageable and what must be hoped and ventured, where we are thrown not onto beliefs, but on to faith, into the arms of God.[86]

In short, Willmer is pointing to the world of both poets—the writer of Second Isaiah and Avison. The biblical text presents a "hoped and ventured" witness in poems of exploration, which lead sometimes simultaneously to seeing and telling. In some mysterious way the process of witnessing itself is the healing of the blindness and the deafness, as Avison intimates in her poems which articulate the challenge of faith in what is not readily apparent.

Avison understands well the hidden character of God's activity. For instance, in her late collection *Not Yet But Still* and in one of her many poems about the central events of the Christian faith—the death and resurrection of Christ—she reflects on what cannot be seen:

That Friday – Good?

At least the twentieth century is ending.

Wretched insignificant
hurt-all-over all-through
is all there is.
Alone in the universe

and even then (feebly) the "Why?"

Someone, if present,

84. Brueggemann, *Isaiah 40–66*, 56.
85. Ricoeur, *Essays on Biblical Interpretation*, 133.
86. Willmer, in conversation, June 2007.

would make it go back to before
or at least make it better?

That's not true.

Abandoned.

What if the someone
were to be, every sinking moment,
were to have been,
present, all along?

You mean – that's true? (*AN* 3.84)

Not a word in the actual poem refers to Good Friday and the salvation achieved on the cross, but the shadow of its title affects every questioning line of the poem's summary of the twentieth century's record of human suffering. The anguish of the twentieth-century doubter parallels the exiles' dirge, "By the rivers of Babylon—there we sat down and there we wept when we remembered Zion" (Ps 137:1). The prophet's call and the poet's admission are similar—requiring some revelation to blind and deaf witnesses. On the adjacent page of *Not Yet But Still* is "Interim" (*AN* 3.85), a reflection on what follows from the "Easter trumpets, lilies, clamouring / in a blare of sun." She painfully observes,

Our troubled faces clear to see Him, being
radiantly here, somehow between
familiar days and what's beyond imagining.
We cannot take it in.

Our severed lives are blundering
about in what's been done,
appalled, exultant, sensing
freedom, we seem alone,

but doggedly set out, against a sting
of rain, moved by His plan,
through night and shale-blue dawn, remembering
at least to follow on.

Here in the companion poem the witness can "doggedly set out," "remembering / at least to follow on"; she also can write about it, making the witness even more plain.

Isaiah 40–55 contains a drama with high stakes where the truth of God's dealings with his covenant people and the nations prevails over his accusers' challenge and skepticism and the world's oblivious indifference. The text emphasizes Yahweh's triumph. Not the least is it articulated in another metaphor introduced at the end of the unit. This time it is in terms of the practical every-day miracle of harvest—an organic process that begins out of sight. As the rain waters the earth and helps the seed to sprout, which in turn, furnishes bread from its harvest, "[my word] shall accomplish that which I purpose, and succeed in the thing for which I sent it" (Isa 55:10–11). The poet-prophet has come full circle—back to the power of the divine witness now strangely hidden in the individual and collective witness of all involved in the seeing and telling.

Somewhere in the performance, one becomes subtly aware, in Avison's faith-filled and faithful words, that

> a Presence may briefly shine
> showing heaven again,
> and open.

The nuanced meanings, the evocations and suggestions, the repetition of images, the metaphors and symbols sprinkled throughout the dramatic poem work their own miracle wherever the text is recited. Second Isaiah gives passionate and eloquent demonstration of a poet-seer communicating his own testimony. While the prophet presents Yahweh pleading for the exiled people to claim their right and responsibility as His witnesses, the prophet himself is fulfilling that servant role. Like the psalmist mediating nature's witness, the prophet models the process for every subsequent person who picks up his text to read.[87] The Ethiopian eunuch puzzling over Isaiah's text and Philip carrying on the witness as "he proclaimed to him the good news about Jesus" (Acts 8:35) in Luke's story of Acts provide the

---

87. The psalmist explains creation's witness in extravagant metaphor:
The heavens are telling the glory of God;
And the firmament proclaims his handiwork,
Day to day pours forth speech,
And night to night declares knowledge
There is no speech, nor are there words;
Their voice is not heard;
Yet their voice goes out through all the earth
And their words to the end of the world (Ps 19:1–4).

Bible's own internal verification. If Avison's poetry is even a miniature echo of these great texts, her lyrics carry these same profound implications.

While Luke's account of the Christian message plainly identifies the mandate for witness, and the poetry of Second Isaiah evokes the hopeful impetus of a hidden God at work, it is perhaps in the Johannine Gospel that the poet's resonance with the story of Jesus is best seen. As has been noted earlier, Avison herself came to Christian faith by reading and responding to that Gospel's testimony, suggesting its importance in her own spiritual journey. Further, witness is a dominant theme in the Fourth Gospel; the word *martyria* (witness) and its cognates are found in John's text more often than any other section of the New Testament.[88] The language of controversy and trial in Jesus's discussion with skeptical and resistant religious leaders in chapters 5 and 8 are filled with juridical dialogue. But perhaps most relevant, John's Gospel is not like the Lukan "orderly account" of detail as evidence in this courtroom of contested belief. A new kind of witness takes the stand and offers a portrait of Jesus, but one more akin to lyric poetry with its aim of "utter centripetal coherence."[89] Hence, the Gospel writer offers Avison a model of perception and expression that can illumine and confirm her own understanding of spiritual truth.

The whole Gospel is a seeing and telling of Jesus as Messiah, the Son of God. As Bultmann suggests, "The Gospel of John fundamentally contains but a single theme: the Person of Jesus. The entire Gospel is concerned with the fact of his presence, the nature of his claim, whence he comes and whither he goes, and how men relate themselves to him."[90] Its witnesses arrive on the scene without any explanation of context. Its narration is spare in events and details, with only seven "signs" in contrast to the many anecdotes of Jesus's teaching and miracles in the Synoptic Gospels. The account is strangely clear and elusive at the same time, as the evangelist, like a poet, weaves incidents in and around each other with curious fluidity. Like a poem, its strange words and silences prevent closure. At an obvious level, any of the metaphors Jesus uses to reveal his identity—whether shepherd, bread, light or vine—illustrates both clarity and uncertainty. For sure, their meaning is multivalent.

---

88. For instance, Coenen explains that of the 76 instances of the verb *martyreo* in the New Testament, 43 are in John and the Johannine Epistles, 1042–43.

89. Vendler makes this cogent observation that "it is this centripetal force that most distinguishes lyric from the linear forms of writing that also have literary aims. Lyric tends to be like the systole and diastole of the heart: it has a center of concern around which it beats." Author's Notes, 3.

90. Bultmann, *The Gospel of John*, 5.

As a consequence, the witness to the mysterious hiddenness of God in Isaiah finds its counterpart in the mysterious witness of the revelation of God in Christ in John's Gospel. The paired phrases of Jesus's words to the first enquiring disciples in John's account, "Come and see" (John 1:39) and the risen Christ's directive to Mary Magdalene at the empty tomb, "Go and tell" (John 20:17) are freighted with eternal consequences. Avison's poem "When a Witness Gives Evidence" is essentially as much about Word becoming flesh, water turning to wine, a large crowd feeding on one small lunch, and a dead man walking out of a tomb, as it is about hearing the angels' Christmas song during the night watches. It is strangely all about the witness—the apprehension of the Son of God and the resulting declaration, but it is cloaked in wonder and paradoxical hiddenness. The Gospel begins with a word—The Word—and ends with the expressed satisfaction that a witness has given evidence: "A Presence has briefly shined."

The Gospel begins with a witness, John the Baptist, sent from God, who suddenly appears, "testifying to the light" (John 1:7). John is the archetypal witness with his pointing hand and preparing "voice crying in the wilderness" (John 1:23). Jesus takes over the witness role after John's presentation of "the Lamb of God who takes away the sin of the world" (John 1.29). Jesus is the one who beckons his first disciples to "come and see," invoking the formula for starting the process of faith. When Jesus shows his disciples "his glory" in turning the water to wine at the wedding in Cana (John 2:11), he sets in motion a very specific set of signs according to the Gospel writer, affirming their decision to follow and "see."

John presents seeing and believing Jesus as a mysterious process. Why do some "see" and others do not? The same data is presented to two audiences; some respond with loving faith, others with deep hostility. Throughout the Gospel there is an ongoing struggle to make connection between the world "above" and the world "below," as Jesus declares (John 8:23). "Seeing" is crossing that great divide. The Son, "close to the Father's heart" (John 1:18), reveals himself to the Beloved Disciple who is close to Jesus's heart (John 13:25); that disciple, in turn, has written his testimony "so that you may come to believe" (John 20:31). To read the Gospel of John with perception and understanding means to receive John's witness as from the Father, true and full of light and life. Faith begets faith in his telling. Seeing produces more seeing. It is no accident that one of the major signs is the healing of the man blind from birth recorded in chapter 9. While the miracle naturally generates awe and amazement, it is also symbolic, as John demonstrates, using poetry's language of metaphor. Can people spiritually blind from birth also be healed?

The meaning of Jesus's great declaration, "I am the light of the World" (John 8:12), expands beyond the narrative. The announcement is framed by the continuing and growing controversy between the unbelieving religious leaders who are spiritually and perversely blind. The truth of Jesus's identity remains opaque for the blind who ironically insist they can see (John 9:41). In chapters 5 through 12, leading up to the end of Jesus's public ministry, Jesus initiates important dialogue with these religious leaders. He provokes attention with his works and his dramatic declarations. These events and word-events are signs to promote belief, or if not belief, in Barth's words again, "direct confrontation with and at the very heart of [their] own reality."[91] They are grace-events if his audience choose to "come and see." Unfortunately, they respond with hostility to his claims to divine authority, and hence, contribute to a confrontational atmosphere.[92] Jesus describes their resistance in his flat assertion: "There is no place in you for my word" (John 8:37). In Avison's words, "A Presence" has briefly shone, "showing heaven again, / and open," but they are "afraid, and sore" (AN 2.168). The poet understands their rebel spirit, and several of her key poems in *Winter Sun* play out their ancient unbelief, particularly "The Fallen, Fallen World" with its "learned" rebels who "stubborn, on the frozen mountain cling / Dreaming of some alternative to spring" (AN 1.75–76).[93] The religious leaders and their modern counterparts refuse to "see"; instead they provoke controversy. But they are doing worse as they align themselves on "the hangman's side," which Avison notes will mean later

> each had to find him-
> self immured with the
> undeservedly dead, for good. (L 36–37)

In contrast, the blind man, the focal point of the second discussion, receives his physical sight. He also gradually receives his spiritual sight when Jesus shows him he is not yet seeing what he sees! "Do you believe in the Son of Man?" Jesus asks him. "And who is he, sir? Tell me, so that I may believe in him." Jesus says to him, "You have seen him, and the one speaking

---

91. Barth, *CD*, IVa70.1: 416.

92. In the setting typical of early Christian discourse they argue, putting each other on trial. With the frequent use of the terms "witness" and "testimony" and "judgment, a number of interpreters of the text have identified these scenes specifically as the "controversy" or "trial" scenes referred to earlier in the chapter, each deriving significance of the forensic motif as a major theme throughout John's Gospel. Again, see Trites, *The New Testament Concept of Witness*; Harvey, *Jesus on Trial*; R. Brown, *The Gospel According to John*; Stibbe, *John's Gospel*; Edwards, *Discovering John*.

93. See chapter 4 for a fuller discussion of this poem.

with you is he" (John 9:35–37). Here, in literary terms, is one of a series of the Gospel's *anagnorises*, or "recognition scenes," a motif used throughout John's Gospel narrative to demonstrate the progress of Jesus's revelation of himself.[94]

It is not a matter of clever intellectual capacity to understand signs. The prologue to the Gospel in its measured and poetic phrases has already established the polarization between light and dark that Jesus elicits in his encounters with people: "The light shines in the darkness and the darkness did not overcome it" (John 1:5). In her lyric "Meditation on the Opening of the Fourth Gospel" (*AN* 2.148), Avison's voice calls out:

> Even in this baffling darkness
> Light has kept shining
> (where? where? then are we blind?)
> But Truth is radiantly here.[95]

When Truth arrives, a person is forced to face his or her own reality, just as the frail Samaritan woman acknowledges her multiple marriages (John 4:17). There is clearly a personal dimension intended in the evangelist's portrayal of the Roman ruler Pilate's much less happy ending (John 18:28–19:38). His witness—assigning the title "The King of the Jews" to Jesus's cross—does not exonerate him of responsibility for his own personal unbelief. Barth, like Avison, speaking of that final confrontation of the crucified Jesus, makes the Gospel encounters vivid and real for his readers:

> But let us imagine . . . we are ready to receive instruction—this instruction—from Him and therefore from God Himself concerning God. . . . It means that we must be ready to be told by Him that we shall find Him precisely where we do not think we should look for Him, namely, in direct confrontation with and at the very heart of our own reality, which whether we like it or not, reduces itself with the crumbling and tottering of all our previous genuine or illusory possibilities and achievements to the one painful point where each of us is stripped and naked,

---

94. This literary device, explained in Aristotle's *Poetics*, is frequently found in both Hebrew literature and Greek drama such as Sophocles's *Oedipus the King*. Luke has his recognition scenes as well, as seen earlier with the disciples on the Emmaus Road (Luke 8:31). See Culpepper's discussion of this thread running through John's Gospel in *The Gospel and Letters of John*, 71–86.

95. See chapter 5 for a detailed discussion of "Meditation on the Opening of the Fourth Gospel."

where each is suffering and perishing, where each is engaged in futile complaint and accusation, where each is alone.[96]

The prologue puts it simply, powerfully and quietly: "He came to what was his own, and his own people did not accept him" (John 1:11). The Gospel is about "seeing"—about recognition. "But to all who received him, who believed in his name, he gave power to become children of God" (John 1:12). Fortunately, while Jesus sees the truth about everyone and "needs no one to testify about anyone" (John 1:25), his "glory" is also "full of grace and truth" (John 1:14). His witness in words and signs is also his offering of grace, whether to the Samaritan woman, Pilate, the paralytic, or the man blind from birth. In sum, Jesus's presence becomes a two-pronged witness—to those who "see" and in turn become witnesses, and to those who resist the words and works of Jesus and eventually push him to the cross where they ironically accelerate and bring to a climax his own witness and triumph.

John's Gospel is unique in its portrayal of the crucifixion—the final "lifting up of the Son of Man" (John 8:28). The horror and agony of Jesus's death is not emphasized in John's account. Instead Jesus's accomplishment, "his glorification (his ascent to heaven by way of the cross)" and triumphant return to the Father, is foregrounded.[97] "It is finished" (John 19:30) are the words from the cross that echo in the Beloved Disciple's heart. When he sees the soldier pierce Jesus's side and blood and water come out, he sees the fulfillment of the Scriptures: "They will look on the one whom they have pierced" (John 19:37).

Soon after Jesus's public ministry is concluded, a new witness is introduced in the text. In those intimate last words with "his own," the disciples, Jesus explains how the witness will continue after He has returned to the Father: "When the Paraclete comes, whom I will send to you from the Father, the Spirit of truth who comes from the Father, he will testify on my behalf" (John 15:26a).[98] Here in the person of the Holy Spirit is the first part of the equation of witness. The second involves the disciples themselves, the eyewitnesses of Jesus's works and words: "You also are to testify because you have been with me from the beginning" (John 15:26b). The witness of the Spirit is an invisible witness—one who will only be recognized by Avison's "optic heart." The readers of John's Gospel are those who must receive the Spirit's witness and John's witness that Jesus is truly the Son of God and be drawn into the light and life that such faith entails. Part of the mystery is

96. Barth, *CD*, IVa 70.1: 416.

97. R. Brown, *The Gospel and Epistles of John*, 47.

98. How *paraclete* translates into English—whether Advocate, Comforter, Helper, Intercessor, or Mediator—shapes the modern reader's apprehension of him.

the form that witness takes—what it looks like in the shape of each person's individual story.

The resurrection events described in John's Gospel are the beginning of the rest of the disciples' lives as "sent ones": "Go to my brothers and say to them, 'I am ascending to my Father and your Father, to my God and your God,'" Jesus says to Mary Magdalene beside the empty tomb (John 20:17). He later commissions the disciples, "As the Father has sent me, so I send you" (John 20:21). There is the same hiddenness and mystery involved in the telling as in the seeing. Sometimes "the night shift," "the nine-to-five," "the joblessness," and "waiting it out in Chronic Care" seem all there is— "until a witness gives evidence" (*AN* 2. 168).

In the closing stanzas of another of Avison's poems "Branches' (*AN* 1.185–86), she talks of the motif of "come and see" and "go and tell" in an organic image of newly splitting seeds from dying and diseased elms. Her picture of the cross is strangely Johannine in its delicate presentation of Christ's triumph.

> But he died once only
> and lives bright, holy, now,
> hanging the cherried heart of love
> on this world's charring bough.

There is life on the "charring" (burned out) branch of both one's personal world and the larger world in a sweet red fruit interpreting Christ's heart of love. The poet continues:

> Wondering, one by one:
> 'Gather. Be glad.'
> We scatter to tell what the root
> and where life is made.

"Come and see" in John's Gospel is the story of "wondering, one by one," gathering and gladness as Jesus's disciples have listened and learned. "I have made your name known to those whom you gave me from the world," Jesus prays for his disciples on the eve of his glorification and death (John 17:6). And then comes the scattering of the seed: "As you have sent me into the world, so I have sent them into the world. . . . I made your name known to them, and I will make it known, so that the love with which you have loved me may be in them, and I in them" (John 17:18, 26). Ironically, of course, as Jesus well knows and warns them, they will first scatter in fear: "The hour is coming, indeed it has come, when you will be scattered, each one to his home" (John 16:32). But the re-gathering after the resurrection and the receiving of the Holy Spirit ensures the new life in the seeds of their fledgling faith will be scattered. Avison explains in "Branches" that it continues to be, each generation telling "what the root / and where life is made."

So what do these scriptural models of witness mean for her? She recognizes the inevitable controversy inherent in the polarization of belief and unbelief. Hence, she says emphatically in "Witnesses" (*L* 36–37),

> Giver, I know now, anyone's
> survival is to be on
> Your side.

"Seeing" the Unseen is urgent—is essential. This seeing is in the context of the "momentary dark" of one's existence which may make the signs more difficult to recognize. Equally imperative is the compulsion to share what she sees and to help others to see for themselves:

> If it is
> not too late, may the many
> be there [on the Giver's side].

Jesus's invitation to "come and see" contains its inevitable counterpart of obedience to "go and tell." This kind of witness Avison pursues with relentless perseverance.

CHAPTER 3

"Come and See"

"All Lookings Forth at the Implicit Touch"

> Sparrows in the curbs
> and ditch-litter at the
> service-station crossroads
> alike instruct, distract.
> ("Prelude" *AN* 1.62)

> Attend. Attend.
> In pool and sand and riffled waters, here is
> significant witness of an event.
> ("The Ecologist's Song" *AN* 2.266)

> To contemplate is an
> indulgence, distancing
> a self, an object.
> ("Neighbours" *AN* 2.80)

LEARNING TO SEE

Jesus's words "Come and see" (John 1:39) to those early disciples in John's Gospel can be an invitation to accompany a skilled traveller on her own journey to see the living Christ. The logic of the writer's question, "How can you love God whom you have not seen if you do not love those whom you do see?" suggests a parallel challenge concerning perception and understanding[1]: How can a man "see" Jesus (whom he has not seen), if his perception of the world around is dull? How can a woman recognize spiritual reality if she is unaware of the physical world? Again, in Avison's words, "Nobody stuffs the world in at your eyes" ("Snow" *AN* 1:69). There must be some seed of desire to see—some motivation to move in the direction of awareness. That motivation may need to be awakened.

Avison writes in her poem "The Promise of Particulars" (*AN* 2.210) that "all, everywhere / burns with minutiae and risk and wonder." Whether it is the "shore of remote foaming sea" for the foreign traveler or the "doorway at home" for "the first-stepping child" there is this promise:

> For the spirit released,
> too, all is
> vivid, nothing
> routine or lost to awareness,
> and yet in that one-eyed
> heart-whole wonder
> tiny particulars will be
> known within wholeness.

The gift of seeing—of risking, of stepping out to see—is a kind of miracle. It is a matter of spirit released, the jail-break of the poem "Snow" explained in metaphysical or religious language. It is like foreign travel; it is like the first-stepping child in her or his early experiences of seeing. But it is more. The objects of perception are all vivid, nothing routine or lost to awareness. When she speaks of "that one-eyed / heart-whole wonder," the poet is referring to a particular kind of acuity. She has transformed the senses' "everyday eyework," as she calls it later in "The Fixed in a Flux" (*AN* 3.185), to the eye of the heart. Emotions, feelings, imagination are all employed now. What accompanies the miracle is more seeing, in vivid specificity, and then the "tiny particulars will be known within wholeness," which the poet interprets in the last lines of "The Promise of Particulars":

> The moment winks, is gone.
> But everything is shaped in prospect of the
> glory.

The Johannine word "glory" does not go unnoticed.

---

1. a loose paraphrase of 1 John 4:20.

Avison is distilling in few words what Annie Dillard, the Pulitzer Prize winning essayist, in *Pilgrim at Tinker Creek*, details is the reward of the attuned observer of the natural world:

> Unfortunately, nature is very much a now-you-see-it, now you-don't affair. A fish flashes, then dissolves in the water before my eyes like so much salt. Deer apparently ascend bodily into heaven; the brightest oriole fades into leaves. These disappearances stun me into stillness and concentration; they say of nature that it conceals with a grand nonchalance, and they say of vision that it is a deliberate gift, the revelation of a dancer who for my eyes only flings away her seven veils. For nature does reveal as well as conceal: now you don't see it, now you do.[2]

Nature's playful elusiveness described in Dillard's ebullient prose refracts the strangely hidden and revealed nature of the spiritual world. The poet's "prospect of glory" has its own hidden mystery about it, cloaked in religious language that hints at access to the mystery of seeing the one whom no one has seen, mediated through "the Word become flesh . . .the glory as of a father's only son, full of grace and truth" (John 1:14).

Avison has led the way with a lifetime preoccupation with perception and apprehension—particular and peculiar, off-angled seeing. "Poetry is always in / unfamiliar territory," she writes near the end of her life ("Poetry Is" *MD* 27),[3] and what she achieves in her varied verse over and over is "a particular instance of / The kind of lighting up of the terrain" ("Voluptuaries and Others" *AN* 1.117). Donald Hair notes the demand placed on the reader of an Avison poem to respond to its particularities: "The struggle with the text startles the reader out of the torpor of ordinary perception and effects a revolution in our ways of seeing."[4] He recalls hearing her lecture at the University of Western Ontario, pointing out the "opaque world, a world up against your eyeballs." Her advice to aspiring writers, "Write at the limits of vision—when you've got it, you can see farther," is the measure of the gift she offers the readers of her difficult poetry.[5]

The world is a little less opaque with awareness of some of nature's oddities: Avison's "winter pigeons walk the cement ledges / Urbane, discriminating" ("To Professor X, Year Y" *AN* 1.87); her trees have "tremulous-aching fingers / shaping the quiet airflow" ("April" *AN* 2.157); her "Milky

---

2. Annie Dillard, *Pilgrim at Tinker Creek*, 16.
3. This poem is discussed in detail in chapter 2.
4. Hair, "Avison at Western," 53.
5. Ibid.

Way / end over end like a football / lobs" ("The Hid, Here" *AN* 2.139). In "Natural/Unnatural" (*AN* 1.217),

> Evening tilt makes a
> Pencil box of our
> Street.
> The lake, in largeness, grapy blueness,
> Casts back the biscuit-coloured pencil-box, boxes, toys, the
> Steeple-people, all of it, in one of those
> Little mirrory shrugs.[6]

The striking strangeness in the examples above comes, of course, from the poet's transformations of her ordinary sightings in nature. Dillard, equally preoccupied with nature's revelations, suggests,

> Seeing is of course very much a matter of verbalization. Unless I call my attention to what passes before my eyes, I simply won't see it. It is, as Ruskin says, "not merely unnoticed, but in the full, clear sense of the word, unseen."

At the same time, while the poet puts expression to what is experienced, and hence, shapes what is seen, Dillard posits

> another kind of seeing that involves a letting go. When I see this way I sway transfixed and emptied . . . the difference between walking with and without a camera. . . . When I walk without a camera, my own shutter opens, and the moment's light prints on my own silver gut.[7]

She is echoing Avison's assurance that "for the spirit released, / too, all is vivid" (*AN* 2.210). Both essayist and poet are sensitively tuned to what passes before their eyes, and the gift that emerges in the text extends the "lighting up of the terrain" (*AN* 1.117).

Further, noting particular phenomena is often only the beginning of Avison's seeing: "Move your tongue along a slat / Of a raspberry box from last year's crate," she writes in "Thaw" (*AN* 1.92); "Smell a saucepantilt of water / On the coal-ash in your grate." The poet juxtaposes that peculiar sensory data with an even further reach of the imagination as the poem moves on:

6. "Steeple-people" condenses a childhood limerick: The adult demonstrates to the child with entwined fingers closed: "Here is the church"; index fingers raised, "Here is the steeple"; opening the hands and twisting them outward, "open the doors and see all the people."

7. Dillard, *Pilgrim at Tinker Creek,* 30–31.

> Think how the Black Death made men dance,
> And from the silt of centuries
> The proof is now scraped bare that once
> Troy fell and Pompey scorched and froze.

The reader is expected to make connections between these extreme, disparate particulars. Yet again, in "From a Provincial" (*AN* 1.85):

> On evening tables
> Midges survey their planes of brief discovery
> At a half-run. In Milton's candle's light
> They so employed themselves.
> Some die before the light is out.

The poem abruptly shifts its subject:

> In Caesar's camp was order,
> The locus of their lives for some centurions
> Encircled by forests of somber France.

Midges and centurions have little in common—except the central metaphor of the poem: "Part of the strangeness is / Knowing the landscape."

One literal and metaphorical landscape that Avison knows well is a Toronto street in winter's constraints. In "Dark Afternoon" (*AN* 2.141), an unassuming (and enigmatic) lyric, she precisely visualizes the details of a common scene. She defamiliarizes it with off-angled syntax and strange diction such as the neologisms "snowblear" and "unfurnitured" and noun-become-verb "parlours" and the compound epithet "one-day day":

> The sun is white,
> snowblear all stained, and
> radiostore music
> parlours this grimy salt-besplattered
> sidewalk.

The "radiostore music" is the only part of the scene that makes it habitable—that "parlours" the space. She continues,

> The time is furtive, seeming late,
> unfurnitured, fit for hunched
> non-householders, and for ghosts of a
> pre-city, one-day day.

Robert Merrett offers one helpful window into the poet's distinctive formulations of what and how she sees—her interpretation of the world. He suggests that "syntax . . . reveal[s] how our minds work and how we react to the world." Therefore, to see with her lenses, the reader needs to embrace her "unpredictability" and work with her imaginative and often jarring rearrangement of sentence structure. Merrett explains:

> her world is not limited to the phenomenal. She realizes speech can point to things that do not factually exist: she trusts that language refers to the ineffable and to elements of reality not normally envisaged. Using syntax oddly, Avison offers us a challenge; breaking conventional relations between concept and referent, she invites us to mend these fractures. We respond only if we reconceive the relation of language to creation imaginatively.[8]

In the poem above, she is beckoning readers to "come and see"—see deeper into the visible reality of the "salt-besplattered" sidewalk paired with the invisible "furtive" and "unfurnitured" time "fit for hunched / non-householders." Place and time are merging in the imagination and calling up another ephemeral scene—a strange transformation of "ghosts of a / pre-city, one-day day." The suggestion is indeterminate, but it hints at the other-worldly. In offering his particular interpretive key to Avison's poetry, Merrett is also intimating a possible connection between seeing the natural world mediated and aided by the poet, and seeing in the religious sense.[9]

The poet explains the guiding principle of her poetry in the foreword to her *Collected Poems: Always Now*, drawing on a hitherto unpublished poem "City of April" (*AN* 1.14–16), "written shortly before the ten years [of following her high school teacher's advice to avoid using the first person in any poem] had elapsed."[10] Calling it a poetic manifesto (*AN* 1.14), she is playful in the poem's candor and vulnerability in the opening stanza:

> This is about me, and you must listen
> You who sit naked on the bed, folding your hands about your
> > toes
> Knowing how foolish it is to do so
> but alone, so safe and free to be foolish.

8. Merrett, "Faithful Unpredictability," 83.

9. There are hints of Ricoeur's thinking here: "[W]e too often and too quickly think of a will that submits and not enough of an imagination that opens itself[;] . . . the imagination is that part of ourselves that responds to the text as a Poem," *Essays on Biblical Interpretation*, 117.

10. This idea is introduced in chapter 1.

The speaker leads her readers down a Prufrock-like street of ambiguity, where even the "you and me" are blurred and indeterminate. The articulated manifesto of the mature poet emerges in later lines:

> This is about me, and you must listen
> Because tonight *I have been staring*
> *At the shadow of chairlegs on this attic floor*
> *Seeing them as they are.* [italics mine]

She proceeds to expand that particular shadow of chairlegs to other particular images of place and people, each with their accompanying vistas of feeling and thought. She blends the seeing with her other senses: "the spring night breathes through my window"; "I feel nights on the foothills desolate dark"; "And hylas loud in the sloughs"; "the train-whistle far and far." The young poet draws from Eliot and Wordsworth in their understanding of poetic memory:

> And I know that there are no hylas now
> And the footprints down in the area pavement
> Are indistinguishable from a million others
>
> This being city, and long years passed.
> At the same time knowing it is a train [. . .][11]

The narrator proceeds to draw a picture of that train and its imagined occupants, including an

> old woman, bunchy skirted
> alert and placid and chatting endlessly
> to the young stranger who submits.

Carrying on in literary tradition, Avison imitates Coleridge's "Rime of the Ancient Mariner," drawing first the stranger listening to the old woman and then the "you" of the poem into the position of wedding guest.

The poem is a paradigm for interpreting Avison's poetics. Her focus is not on the emerging woman but on the emerging woman who sees. The seeing involves all the senses, heart, and soul of a sensitive, intelligent, and intuitive artist. The narrator repeats for a third time in the poem, "This is about me, and you must listen / For I make no claim on you else." Avison

---

11. Her lines here sound similar to Eliot's lines of "Burnt Norton." Intimations of Wordsworth's familiar opening words of "Tintern Abbey" are suggested as well. It makes sense that a developing poet, as Avison was in this very early poem, would have the masters she has absorbed ringing in her ears.

explains through the voice of the speaker what she expects and desires in an empathetic reader:

> So bear with me and look
> At that shadow of chairlegs on the floor
> Till your throat is swollen with tears and exultation.

The response she wants from her reader sounds very much like Barfield's "felt change of consciousness."[12]

Avison's passionate admonition to "come and see" in this late-released, but early poem is important to note for several reasons. For one, it highlights her paradoxical stance expressed in the monologue: "This is about me / this is not about me . . . This is about what I see." Ken Babstock, speaking as both a poet and critic, in his review of Avison's later volume *Concrete and Wild Carrot*, comments on the "many labourings and movements of spirit that occurred—must have occurred—prior to each poem's creation."[13] While this observation rings true in the depth of feeling released in the varied lyrics, these efforts and movements of the spirit are not the focal point of her art. "City of April" is suggesting that it has been "a kind of perseverance," a deliberate fastidiousness in habit of pointing to something other than the self. Avison's poetry beckons her readers on this journey of perception—to come and see what she sees. In the process of absorbing the poems the poet emerges, but only as a witness, not the key player in the drama. Furthermore, and most important, it is finally the witness of the poems, not the poet, that compels attention.

Avison's posture is one of watching from a window or sitting on a park bench—a looking out and observing—in a number of her poems. "Grammarian on a Lakefront Park Bench" (*AN* 1.77), "Rich Boy's Birthday Through a Window" (*AN* 1.109), "Old Woman at a Window" (*AN* 3.15), "Beyond Weather, or From a Train Window" (*AN* 3.15), and "Resting On a Dry Log, Park Bench, Boulder" (*AN* 3.97) are titles of some poems that emphasize the poet as a meditative, but alert observer with a pointing hand. Her vision is in sympathy with C. S. Lewis, another great twentieth-century Christian witness who explains in his own manifesto written near the end of his career and life, *An Experiment in Criticism*, his view of the receiving process of sightings and seeings of a writer:

> The primary impulse of each is to maintain and aggrandize himself. The secondary impulse is to go out of the self, to correct its

---

12. In explaining his phrase "aesthetic imagination," Barfield goes on to say, "By 'felt' I mean to signify that the change itself is noticed, or attended to." *Poetic Diction*, 48.

13. Babstock, Review of *Concrete and Wild Carrot*, D13.

provincialism and heal its loneliness. In love, in virtue, in the pursuit of knowledge, and in the reception of the arts we are doing this.

The role of the critic and reader of literature for Lewis is a participation in this specific seeing:

> it is *connaitre* not *savoir*; it is *erleben*; we become these other selves. Not only nor chiefly in order to see what they are like but in order to see what they see, to occupy, for a while, their seat in the great theatre, to use their spectacles and be made free of whatever insights, joys, terrors, wonders or merriment those spectacles reveal.[14]

If readers follows Lewis's suggestion with Avison's poetry—pausing with her at her window or park bench, putting on her spectacles, to see what and how she sees—they accept the risk and demand of attention, but also the promise of nothing "lost to awareness," "in that one-eyed heart-whole wonder," "known within wholeness" ("Promise of Particulars" *AN* 2.210).

When the young woman of "City of April" exclaims, "[L]ook / at that shadow of chairlegs on the floor / Till your throat is swollen with tears and exultation," she obviously suggests something beyond a mere clinical recording of visible data. Looking at the shadow is different than focusing on the chairlegs. There is an element of seeing the unseen that elicits the strong emotion of "tears and exultation." D. G. Jones corroborates the thinking of several contemporary poets when he suggests, "If there is a world [for the poet] to make articulate, it is a world that has been suppressed by the hegemony of the eye."[15] The implication is the overemphasis on images, particularly as the media has drawn one's attention to the visual.[16] Jones goes on to suggest,

> For the writer it is not simply a question of naming what he sees; to name what people cannot see, what is not already in the language, he must go into the dark and somehow see what is there in the dark . . . whatever world remains mute, invisible, requires a new language.[17]

---

14. Lewis, *An Experiment in Criticism*, 138–39.

15. D. G. Jones, "Cold Eye and Optic Heart," 173.

16. Jacques Ellul, so influential to Avison's thinking, has similar sentiments in his concern for the modern addiction to images but places different emphasis in his critique: "Anyone wishing to save humanity today must first of all save the word." *The Humiliation of the Word*, vii.

17. Jones, "Cold Eye and Optic Heart," 174.

Obviously, this naming what people cannot see is intangible, often elusive, and often what makes Avison's poetry so frequently puzzling and difficult to access. Nevertheless, the implication of "City of April" is that the youthful poet has started on a journey toward the ineffable and spiritual and invites her readers to join her.

In "To Someone in That Boardroom" (AN 2.188) the poet speaks to a person she imagines working late in a high rise office building:

> so late?
>
> Tired to your wool sox, sir?
>
> Eyes gritty with paper encounters?
>
> Listen, then:

Here is one of Avison's many calls to attend to nature through the imaginative faculties.

> There is a throb, outside,
>
> a hyacinth-core, impacted, under
>
> the rolling wind and night.

Her call is not unambiguous, of course, because the referents are multi-faceted; a tentative meaning can only be intuited. Nevertheless, the "inflooding, dark swirls over / tinkertoy town" of "the rolling wind and night" and the "throb, outside, / a hyacinth-core" compel attention. The environment around and outside the confinement of the building is pulsing with some kind of living energy. What is this "hyacinth-core, impacted"?[18] While precise signification is elusive, something similar to "the vital bond" of "Rising Dust" (AN 3.164), is suggested again.[19] In "Rising Dust" the connection is inward: "The strand within / thrums and shudders and twists." Here in "To Someone in That Boardroom" it is "a throb, outside," external, but functioning to point to something—to someone, out of the self, and in the dark.

In "A Nameless One" (AN 1.225), she watches an insect live out its day and die in the "lodgers' bathroom."[20] The attention to the time suggests

18. She could be referring to a precious stone, the hyacinth gem of the ancients or the flower with its spikes of bell-shaped and fragrant flowers or the bulb of the flower. Or she could have in mind the mythological story behind the flower, "said to have sprung up from the blood of the slain youth Hyacinthus and the ancients thought they could decipher on the petals the letters AI, or AIAI, exclamation of grief" (OED). (See Ovid, Metamorphosis 10.211 for one version of the myth.)

19. See chapter 1.

20. This poem from The Dumbfounding is one of several that has been frequently anthologized and has received considerable critical comment from earlier reviewers and critics: D. G. Jones, "Cold Eye and Optic Heart," 55–56, Redekop, Margaret Avison,

a repeated and intentional seeing. The details she records sound like a scientist clinically gathering data, but the interpretation of the data reveals a particular point of connection more intimate. She watches and notes and in some inexplicable way, cares about its fate—its "insect-day." Dillard suggests, "The lover can see and the knowledgeable," and the detail Avison has recorded implies she herself is both.[21] She moves to reflection:

> now that it is
> over, I
> look with new eyes
> upon this room
> adequate for one to
> be, in.

The bathroom has strangely become a sacred space, hallowed by a living, nameless creature. She views creation, not as a disinterested viewer, but as one connected, and participating. Something healing has occurred in the observer as she has shared the brief reality of the

> narrow winged
> long-elbowed-thread-legged
> living insect,

mirroring her own, and transforming the experience of both:

> Its insect-day
> has threaded a needle
> for me for my eyes dimming
> over rips and tears and
> thin places.

Learning to see—to really see—takes courage and determination, as a person confronts both light and darkness in events, ideas, and things. In *Winter Sun*'s "A Conversation" (*AN* 1.123), it is a curious matter of dealing with the death of a fish. The man in the restaurant telling the story of his encounter to "no particular listener / For few can listen, on Saturday afternoon" remarks on "the queer pocket of quiet" "before the debacle":

> 'Fish have a way of wavering through water.
> They don't beat with their fins. What is their death

16–18; Neufeld, "Some Pivot for Significance in the Poetry of Margaret Avison," 39. See Appendix for the complete poem.

21. Dillard, *Pilgrim at Tinker Creek*, 18.

> To me? I can't confront
> A tree to really know it, and feel odd
> To exchange glances with a squirrel,
> And wish to keep my springs of life
> Private from the Big Eye.
> Well then. The fish had died. I'll not intrude there.'

Yet in the poem, ironically, he is unable to release himself from the memory of the event, as he continues brooding on the details of the death of the fish. The poet herself is not like her fictional characters. Her poems are all about "confront[ing] / a tree to really know it" and "exchang[ing] glances with a squirrel," even if it means extreme psychic pain.

One of her earlier published poems "The Butterfly" (*AN* 1.23) records the brief event of a trapped butterfly in a violent storm: "It clung between the ribs of the storm, wavering, / and flung against the battering bone-wind." Its brief delicate life ended, "glued to the grit of that rain-strewn beach." The storm has been

> An uproar,
> a spruce-green sky, bound in iron,
> the murky sea running a sulphur scum,

originating, it seems, in Milton's hell. The rain-strewn beach is anthropomorphized as it "glowered" in helpless sympathy with the butterfly it "swallowed" in its "unstrung dark," again laden with human characteristics.

In memory, the event is even more sinister. Some looming malevolent force, wild and enveloping, in one violent gesture of entrapment deliberately destroyed the vulnerable and delicate life of one of its creatures:

> That wild, sour air, those miles of crouching forest, that moth
> when all enveloping space
> is a thin glass globe, swirling with storm
> tempt us to stare, and seize analogies.

The analogy is harsh and accusing and full of unanswered questions: What is the new "fierce and subhuman peace?" Why is the "east sky, blanched like Eternity?" The final stanza intones repetitively, "The meaning of the moth, even the smashed moth, / the meaning of the moth," as the poet continues to mourn. Furthermore, the meaning extends to the human situation. As David Jeffrey notes, speaking of Avison's other butterfly poem, "'Butterfly Bones': Sonnet against Sonnets" (*AN* 1.71), "The butterfly is a fragile messenger: age-old symbol for the spirit (*psyche*) and for transformation (*metamorphoses*)."[22] Here its message is dark and foreboding:

> can't we stab that one angle into the curve of space
>
>   that sweeps so unrelenting, far above,
>
>   towards the subhuman swamp of under-dark?

Again there is this word "subhuman,'" now coupled with "swamp." It is a strange juxtaposition—this "far above" with "under-dark."

The 1943 poem was revised in 1989, at which time Avison commented, "This is a revision, because I have learned that 'moth' and 'butterfly' are not interchangeable terms (as I had written them in ignorance in the earlier version), and because the 'angle' seems indicated in Rom. 8:21 and Eph. 1:10."[23] In this second version she simplifies the second stanza: Rather than "tempts us to stare, and seize analogies" (*AN* 1.23), the line merely reads, "tempts one to the abyss" (*SP* 1). This rendering, of course, alters the meaning of the temptation, but also implies the speaker is coming from a different place. The biblical story of "The Voice that stilled the sea of Galilee" (*AN* 1.23) has disappeared, and the closing stanza has taken on a much quieter and resigned acceptance of the suffering of the created order in light of the Christian hope of future restoration of creation:

> The butterfly's meaning, even though smashed.
>
> Imprisoned in endless cycle? No. The meaning!
>
> Can't we stab that one angle
>
> into the curve of space that sweeps beyond
>
> our farthest knowing, out into light's
>
> place of invisibility? (*SP* 1).

In the revised version the meaning of the moth/butterfly and its suffering is still unresolved, but there is no sense of alienation.[24] "Light's / place of invisibility" (*SP* 1) has replaced "the subhuman swamp of under-dark" (*AN* 1.23). That which cannot be seen is light rather than darkness—much more in keeping with Avison's own faith journey into light. Nevertheless, in

22. Jeffrey, "Margaret Avison: Sonnets and Sunlight," 4.

23. See Avison, *Selected Poems* (*SP* 1). St. Paul writes to the Romans, "The creature itself also shall be delivered from the bondage of corruption into the glorious liberty of the children of God" (Rom 8:21); Again, he writes to the Ephesians, "In the dispensation of the fullness of times he might gather together in one all things in Christ, both which are in heaven, and which are on earth" (Eph 1:10).

24. Jon Kertzer suggests one of the ways we might interpret Avison's early poetry is that "of alienation relieved by imaginative insight." See "Margaret Avison and the Place of Meaning," 7.

the recent publication of her *Collected Poems: Always Now*, she has reverted to the original poem for this final consideration and reconsideration of the poems she wishes to preserve, implying several possibilities: the original version is the better poetry; it is the more authentic confrontation with the darkness—the cry of the cross, "My God, My God, why have you forsaken me?" (Mark 15:34); it better maintains the mystery of the "smashed moth" as the speaker/poet experiences it.[25]

Finally, learning to see the created world and its inhabitants means learning to read signs. Implicit in seeing carefully, looking closely, seeing the hidden, and seeing with courage is the understanding of reality's mystery and ambiguity. In the poem above, the poet's litany "the meaning of the moth" already speaks of that reality, even in her despairing and questioning stance. When that reality and mystery connect and point to the ineffable and invisible God, the task becomes more urgent. Reading signs means first assuming the presence of Jesus Christ in the world, and then responding to that reality and mystery embodied in the incarnation.

However, even on a basic level people are not naturally attuned to signs, a fact she laments.

> Earth-dwellers tend to
> amble about in spite of
> being alerted,

the poet notes in "Reconnaissance" (*MD* 24–25). The signs should be obvious, but people miss them or do not recognize what they see.

> Signs and symptoms
> speak out, but when
> embossed on persons are
> rarely discerned in
> preventive time.

Nature's pointers are also not recognized:

> Signs and runes
> gleam out in the last
> tapestried evening sky.
> Symptoms, all spent, open on
> silence.

---

25. Avison, *Always Now*, Vol. 1, "A Note on the Text," 17.

One reason they may be missed is that they are not necessarily obvious. John Tinsley, in *Tell It Slant*, observes that indirection is fundamental to signs. "Signs, to be signs, are necessarily ambiguous, mistakable, indirect," he asserts, suggesting the imaginative energy required of the sensitive witness. Furthermore, "revelation is provisional. He who reveals is greater than what he reveals."[26] Therefore, humility, a sense of wonder, and expectation seem necessary accompaniments to sign-watching. To "see" nature—creation and its creatures—is both performance and rehearsal for the greater seeing. The observer gradually becomes aware of the "Knower" who sees and "waits / our turn" ("Exposure," *MD* 16–17).

NATURE'S DISPLAY

Avison's overt Christian witness in her devotional poems or glosses on biblical passages invites expectation of similar emphases in the lyrics that call attention to nature's revelations. For instance, how is one to interpret "News Item" (*AN* 3.99) from *Not Yet But Still*?

> Today, May 9th,
> the chestnut trees
> pagoda'd in full
> seven-fold leaf
> out of a blue sky

or "The Cloud" (*AN* 2.234) from *No Time*?

> The August storm
> is tall as a wall.
> How eerily the cosmos
> unflutters like a feather
> in this waiting stillness?

Does their context in collections with devotional lyrics influence a "Christian" reading or are these lyrics about natural seasonal events in and of themselves poems of Christian witness? These questions mirror in an odd sort of way the same kinds of questions asked about the possibility of knowing God through nature and creation. The familiar biblical texts of Psalm 19, Romans 1:19–21, Acts 14:15–17 and Acts 17:24–29 imply some sort of "general revelation," but theologians through the centuries have not been

---

26. Tinsley, *Tell It Slant*, 14, 17.

in agreement about the extent, nature, or effectiveness of these inferences. Avison's poetic witness inadvertently becomes tied into this larger question.

How she perceives and speaks of nature's gifting in her beckoning to "come and see," I propose, is a strong indicator of her unique creativity and independence of spirit. While she is anchored in one tradition, she seems willing to move in a larger stream of Christian thought, ultimately resulting in an extra measure of vitality in her Christian witness. Her theological formation is through Reformed Christianity with its tradition of deep skepticism regarding natural theology, part of which claims "that God actually has made himself known in nature[;] . . . truth about God is actually present within the creation."[27] To use the language of this book, "nature witnesses to God, reveal[ing] God in some way, which is intelligible to all persons as human beings with reason and good will."[28] Her minister William Fitch is conspicuously silent about any witness of creation in his description of the beliefs of Knox Church; rather he affirms the commitment to *sola scriptura* of the Westminster Confession of Faith, emphasizing "it is through Scripture alone that we know of Jesus Christ, the full and final revelation of God the Father."[29] As discussed earlier in chapter one, Avison embraces this commitment to regular and rigorous Bible study. Consequently, it is not surprising that her poetry includes a significant number of poems based on specific passages of Scripture.

On the other hand, it is curious that her conversion to Christianity signals a deeper shift in her poetry than just the obvious introduction of devotional poems. The inward transformation she chronicles in such poems as "The Word" (*AN* 1.195–96), "Searching and Sounding" (*AN* 1.199–202), and "A Prayer Answered by Prayer" (*AN* 1.203), is accompanied by an increase in attention to creation. Details of the natural world woven throughout the poet's earlier verse, often more context than subject, take center stage in many post-conversion lyrics. *The Dumbfounding* begins with several striking images of nature's varied display. "Old . . . Young . . ." (*AN* 1.147) speaks of

> The antlers of the ancient
> members of the orchard lie
> bleaching where the young grass
> shines, breathing light.[30]

27. Erickson's skepticism is implicit in his use of the word "actually." *Christian Theology*, 181.

28. Willmer, private conversation, July 2009.

29. Fitch, *Knox* Church, 102. See chapter 1 for a fuller discussion.

30. Avison's ellipses.

The poem's last stanza suggests a reason to take notice with its initial itali-cized conjunction, perhaps a veiled and metaphorical allusion to her own changed spiritual condition:

> *because* cobwebs are forked away
> and the wind rises
> and from the new pastures long after longstemmed sunset,
> even this springtime, the last
> > light is mahogany-rich,
> > > a 'furnishing.'

The next poem to follow in the revised collection, "Two Mayday Selves" (*AN* 1.148–49), continues the celebration of spring, this time in the heart of the city:

> The grackle shining in long grass
> this first day of green casts
> an orchid-mile of shadow
> into the sun-meld, that marvel, those
> meadows of peace (between the bird
> and the curved curb
> of the city-centre clover-leaf).[31]

Spring's arrival has its multiple observers, including the essential transcen-dent and immanent "other beholder" in

> [t]he aloof
> tiers of offices, apartments, hotels,
> schools, park branches, opal
> heaven-hidden stars, the other
> beholder – out there, here.

The poet concludes in her invitation: "Old ghoul, leather-tough diaphragm, / listen! – I am holding *my* breath." With spread out and enjambed lines she beckons her other self,

> Come out. Crawl   out of it.   Feel
> it.   You,
> too.

---

31. In the original edition there is another conversational lyric, "The Two Selves," facing and paralleling "Two Mayday Selves." Avison removed it from *The Collected Poems*.

Both early poems are invitations to joy anchored in a baptized perception of the natural world, beginning a pattern that increases in subsequent verse.

Jonathan Edwards, the eighteenth-century Puritan divine, writes in his "Personal Narrative" of a parallel conversion experience of religious import: "I began to have a new kind of apprehensions and ideas of Christ, and the work of redemption, and the glorious way of salvation . . . ." One of the outcomes was a vivid perception of God in nature:

> The appearance of everything was altered: there seemed to be, as it were, a calm, sweet cast, or appearance of divine glory, in almost everything. God's excellency, his wisdom, his purity and love, seemed to appear in everything; in the sun, moon and stars; in the clouds, and blue sky; in the grass, flowers, trees; in the water, and all nature; which used greatly to fix my mind . . . in viewing the clouds and sky, to behold the sweet glory of God in these things.[32]

This excerpt from Edwards' narrative is a possible accounting for the invitational impulse to "come and see" creation in Avison's poems. Both writers—preacher and poet—are expressing a witness to and of creation in their playful joy. They may also be enacting Calvin's accommodation of special revelation to general revelation with his analogy of spectacles:

> Just as old or bleary-eyed men and those with weak vision, if you thrust before them a most beautiful volume . . . yet can scarcely construe two words, but with the aid of spectacles will begin to read distinctly; so Scripture, gathering up the otherwise confused knowledge of God in our minds, having dispersed our dullness, clearly shows us the true God.[33]

The implication is a kind of "limited natural theology available from creation."[34] If a person has these "spectacles of faith" of which Calvin speaks to interpret correctly the created world, she or he may recognize God in his creation.[35] Robert Newman clarifies in his brief summary of the various positions one view that has been compatible to "conservative theologians":

> a limited natural theology stemming from natural revelation, sufficient to reveal God but insufficient to redeem man, hence

32. Edwards, "Personal Narrative," 181.

33. Calvin, *Institutes of the Christian Religion*, I.6.1, 70.

34. Newman, "Natural Theology," 695.

35. Erickson extrapolates the phrase "spectacles of faith" from Calvin's explanation. *Christian Theology*, 195.

the need for special revelation—especially as depraved man has perverted this natural knowledge (cf. Rom. 1).[36]

If Avison were to articulate her theological understanding of creation she may well endorse this position.[37] What is obvious in her poetic output is that her conversion, her spiritual awakening, has sparked an interest in the creation, and now she is particularly receptive to the psalmist's announcement: "The heavens are telling the glory of God; and the firmament proclaims his handiwork. Day to day pours forth speech, and night to night declares knowledge" (Ps 19:1–2).

There is another influence on her nature poetry that needs to be factored in. Her long acquaintance with and participation in the English literary tradition has provided a natural link with the nineteenth-century Catholic poet Gerard Manley Hopkins in his religious perspective on the created world. His influence on Avison is seen in a number of ways. It is seen in matters of style, syntax, and diction.[38] Kent observes, "Both poets dare to stretch and twist language, to fashion compound epithets and fracture

---

36. Newman, "Natural Theology," 695.

37. Mazoff suggests Avison takes this perspective of a limited natural theology, using lines from "Oughtiness Ousted" as verification:

God (being good) has let me know
no good apart from Him.
He, knowing me, yet promised too
all good in His good time.

This light, shone in, wakened a hope
that lives in here-and-now. (s 64)

Waiting for the Son, 16–17. Since the poem's subject is not nature, this connection does not seem obvious, but his assessment makes sense given her general theological commitments.

38. Curiously, Avison semi-parodies Hopkins through the voice of her cranky "Local" in her early poem, "The Local and the Lakefront" (*AN* 1.38), in which the irritated lobbyist sees the "barges and brazen freighters" with their imported goods damaging the landscape of the lakefront of Lake Ontario. He brings his grievance to the "Committeeman":

At Sunnyside
Toronto lakefront west,
          with a bricked sooted railwaystation and
                    a blueglass busstation)
the sunset
blurges through rain and all
man tinfoil, man sheetlead
shines, angled all awry,
a hoaxing hallelujah.

One cannot miss the echoes quoted above of Hopkins from the poems "God's Grandeur," "Pied Beauty," and "Hurrahing in Harvest."

syntax, and to experiment with rhythms in order to recreate . . . vitality."[39] But it is in Hopkins's reflections on nature that he could particularly impact her expression of witness in the created world. Hopkins himself has drawn on the Romantic poets' understanding of the significance of the natural world both in its particularity and in its emphasis on the poet's role in interpreting and re-interpreting nature through the imagination. He, in turn, draws the focus to what he sees as the incarnational witness of creation. He is explicit in his theological assertions in his famous celebratory poems: "The world is charged with the grandeur of God," he declares in the opening line of "God's Grandeur." "He fathers-forth whose beauty is past change: / Praise him," is the benediction ending "Pied Beauty." Even more specific in "Hurrahing in Harvest," he exclaims, "I lift up heart, eyes, / Down all that glory in the heavens to glean our Saviour." His creative formulations of "inscape" in "As Kingfishers Catch Fire" ("Each mortal thing . . . / Acts in God's eye what in God's eye he is— / Christ—for Christ plays in ten thousand places") —and "instress" in "The Wreck of the Deutschland" ("His mystery must be instressed, stressed")—direct one to the nature of witness.[40]

Admittedly, Hopkins's understanding of sacrament and mode of witness are not Avison's. While both poets would acknowledge the general Augustinian definition of sacrament as "a holy sign (image, symbol, expression) through which we both perceive and receive an invisible grace," Hopkins takes the concept further, seeking "Christ's sacramental Real Presence" "in nature as much as in the Church."[41] At the same time, Loomis describes the difficulty in applying the term "sacramental" even to Hopkins. I quote him at length because his comments are applicable to interpreting Avison as well.

> Yet the term *sacramental* has surely not meant the same to each Hopkins scholar who has used it. . . . It is also true because Hopkins—a far more multifaceted contemplative person than he often receives credit for being—saw the sacramental experience at various stages of his life (and sometimes simultaneously) from variant perspectives. For him, authentic contemplative openness superseded dogma.[42]

39. Kent, *Margaret Avison and Her Works*, 7.

40. "Inscape" has to do with the nature of being. Just by existing each living thing represents Christ in the process. "As Kingfishers Catch Fire" is Hopkins' most direct discussion of inscape. "Instress" involves apprehension and appreciation of what one has accomplished in that process.

41. Loomis, *Dayspring in Darkness*, 17, 19.

42. Ibid., 24.

An example of this diversity of perspective is the understanding Hardy and Ford assign to the word "sacrament" in their work *Jubilate: Theology and Praise*. They quote "Pied Beauty" and "God's Grandeur" to illustrate the sacramental in a "wide sense"—"taking up any aspect of the material universe into being a sign or symbol of its Creator" (in contrast to the traditional "narrower" sense of the rites of the church).[43] They observe, "The sacramental concern is to enter into God's way of using and enjoying his world. . . . In the sacramental, the media are both appreciated in themselves and also as pointers to God."[44]

Avison herself does not use the word sacrament to speak about nature. She also does not announce discoveries of Christ in the creation. In fact, she explains in a letter to David Mazoff, "[A]sk me about my idea of Nature and I boggle. Ask me about this particular weed at this hour of this unique afternoon mix of light and weather and I know what you want and can answer."[45] Nevertheless, critics sometimes employ the word to speak of her nature lyrics, probably intuiting the meaning from their own religious persuasion. Her letter of response to Mazoff about his book *Waiting for the Son* includes several specific "quibbles" about his interpretations, but she passes over his analysis of her "sacramental view of nature," leaving at least a suggestion by inference that it is not a misreading to connect her poems to a sacramentalist outlook—at least in Hardy and Ford's wider sense of pointers to God.[46] Furthermore, it is obvious in her lyrics that she is sensitive to the particulars of creation in unusual ways; it is also evident that she carries a deep concern for the care of the environment, not always an emphasis accompanying the impulse of Christian witness.[47]

In the relative vacuum of silence regarding nature's witness in her own theological tradition—at least at Knox Church—it is not surprising if she sometimes draws on Hopkins for her meditations on the created world. His vision with his "authentic contemplative openness" harmonizes with her sense of wonder for the created world.[48] Her poems about nature are equal to Hopkins' in intensity and direction upwards. Her record of nature's peculiarities—both in its splendor and sometimes wonder, and even terror—is one of expectancy and faith in the mystery of Christ's presence in and power over (and, noting Hopkins's enigmatic phrasing,) *under* the phenomena of

---

43. Hardy and Ford, *Jubilate*, 17–18.

44. Ibid., 17.

45. Avison, Letter to David Mazoff, January 4, 1990.

46. Mazoff, *Waiting for the Son*, 13.

47. See chapter 6 for a fuller discussion of her particular interest in the environment.

48. Loomis, *Dayspring in Darkness*," 24.

what God has created. She too is sacramental in startling phrase after phrase and varied lyrical expression, but the witness is implicit and even hidden.

While both church and literary predecessor may influence Avison's perspective regarding a witness of creation, she is too sophisticated and original to be controlled by either. Her nature poems do suggest an implicit Christian witness, but often only available to the reader who makes connections with the vision of her more explicit lyrics. She writes about the changing seasons with their contrasting weather and landscape (and accompanying weather and landscape of the human heart in response); the shifting hours of the day and night (and the corresponding moods to light and dark); the activity of the creatures of the earth, particularly the little ones—insects and birds; the trees and flowers, the stars and the sun. In most of these lyrics there are no overt signals of theological or biblical import in the language of the poem, but echoing St. Paul in his letter to the Romans who points out a particular witness in creation, Avison, with her "spectacles of faith" discerns the witness, and in turn, points in a Godward direction.[49] How she accomplishes this varies in subtlety and intensity.

I suggest several avenues of exploration, uneven in complexity and detail, but each highlighting a different aspect of the poet's creative and challenging witness in her creation lyrics. To begin, Avison's conversion to Christianity means she sees God's world with a new sense of playfulness that is itself a witness. Second, nature provides a vehicle to communicate spiritual longing. Third, specific parts of creation attract her attention. In her interest in birds and trees, the poet sends strong signals of religious significance. Fourth, the dominance of the image of the sun in Avison's poetry has been a marker of spiritual awareness throughout her years of writing. Finally, on occasion the poet explicitly announces connections between the natural world and the biblical text making the witness obvious.

NATURE'S CREATIVE PLAYGROUND

As mentioned earlier, Avison has grappled openly with the meaning of the "smashed moth"/butterfly "glued to the grit of that rain-strewn beach" in "The Butterfly" (AN 1.23). Somehow, the observer in the early poem has a fearful recognition of "somebody" as creator, far removed from personal

---

49. "For what can be known about God is plain [to those who have suppressed the truth], because God has shown it to them. Ever since the creation of the world *his eternal power and divine nature, invisible though they are, have been understood and seen through the things he has made. So they are without excuse.*" (Rom 1:19–20) [italics mine].

relationship. Her attitude here is similar to C. S. Lewis's observation at the beginning of his argument in *Mere Christianity*,

> . . . I think we should have to conclude that He was a great artist (for the universe is a very beautiful place), but also that He is quite merciless and no friend to man (for the universe is a very dangerous and terrifying place).[50]

In contrast, "Scarfover" (*MD* 3), in her later collection *Momentary Dark*, presents a more comfortable and familiar stance between creator and observer of nature. Long acquaintance has mellowed the perspective. The spontaneous outburst of implicit praise in the opening phrase "Glorious, rigorous, sun-flooded, / snow-iced morning," sets the tone even while what follows suggests the challenge and difficulty latent in the extreme cold. The "snow-iced morning" is also "scoured by the north wind, marble-hard to today's / human designs." The weather's gift has inadvertently set in motion a small contest of wills:

> we do not dare defy you but
> still our defiance is
> summoned up. We are
> human creatures,
> resolute. We'll go
> our this day's way,
> plunge into, become party to
> the frieze of this iron and
> brilliant, uncompromising
> artwork,
> its foil.

Putting a scarf over the face (and hence, the poem's title) is one determined way of submitting—of "becom[ing] party to / the frieze" (a pun, of course, on the freezing temperature), of the "uncompromising / artwork" of the winter scene; the person is now humbly nature's "foil," not the lead role in this little drama of nature's making. The poet has transformed an old feeling,

> The sickness has passed from me
> of thinking that the flinching leaves
> are frozen of all motion because my eye
> falls on them ("Extra-Political: The Thorned Speaks (While Day Horses Afar)," *AN* 1.96),

50. Lewis, *Mere Christianity*, 24.

into one of active and participatory celebration, ironically when it physically takes more effort.

Avison's spiritual transformation has enabled her to approach nature with a curious sense of playfulness. This playfulness is rooted in what Lewis Smedes suggests is a cluster of characteristics: "freedom, adventure, unproductivity, pleasure, and a sense of 'trans-seriousness'—a dialectic between seriousness and non-seriousness." The key for the theologian is an awareness of grace. He explains:

> [S]ince the resurrection, the cross invites us to a trans-serious attitude about life. We are serious players; but, since Calvary, we know the game we play no longer has ultimately serious consequences. We can be "dialecticians of play" because of God's one undialectical act.[51]

It is this sense of playfulness of which Smedes has spoken that is released in the poet, particularly evident in her observations of the creation—notations that often seem like doxologies. A new light-heartedness and sense of whimsy assert themselves in her focus on nature.

Avison's poems call attention to creation in many ways, often focusing on phenomena so familiar, people no longer see them. In "Grass Roots" (*AN* 2.25) she does double work: she defamiliarizes a commonplace metaphor and revitalizes the language while calling attention to the creative and active world underneath one's feet:

> There is a grass-roots level:
> small ears and weed-stems;
> necklacing ant-feet; robins' toe-pronging and beak-thrust;
> raindrops spotting in, or
> cratered, sluicing, and wrenching
> grass flat, gouging
> earth, to enrich.
>
> Summer is so.
>
> Winters, that level
> is ore, deep under snow.

In each of the details she is deepening the significance of the activity with her magnifying glass. She uses strong words—"cratered," "sluicing, and wrenching grass flat," gouging"—in reference to miniature activity, but with

---

51. Smedes, "Theology and the Playful Life," 50, 61.

intentionally good results—"to enrich." Summer's rain produces "ore" in winter, "deep under snow."

A telescopic focus, in the other direction—though "I with the naked eye still standing see"—turns to the sky, where she notes the infrequent appearance of a newly sighted comet, particularly visible in the winter of 1973–74, in a poem taking on its name, "Kahoutek" (*AN* 2.96).

> The comet
> among us sun and planets
> I saw with naked eye, i.e.
> nothing between my ice-
>> keening
>> tear-washed
>> seeing
>> from earth-mound (here) to
> ocean-deep navy-blue out-there (there).

Her movement from the familiar "grass roots level" of "Grass Roots"—here simplified to "earth mound" in "Kahoutek"—to "ocean-deep navy-blue out-there" is accompanied by deep unexplained emotion of "tear-washed / seeing." She conveys understanding of its actuality in her comparison to earth:

> In the traffic-flow
>> a frozen lump
>> from a jolting fender
>> spins meteor-black
>> towards the midwinter bus stop where I stand
>> under the tall curved night.

Its deep significance for the poet is in its strangeness, its location "veering weird-brightness / from somewhere else":

> we solar-system people flinch
>> as at a doom-sign,
> and find you cryptic
>> from far unlanguaged precincts
>> soundlessly hollowing past us.

She does not take this unusual sighting casually.

In "Silent Night in Canada 1848" (*AN* 2.153–54) the poet sees a natural event but only imaginatively, creating a picture of what observers might have experienced. What has piqued her interest is an unusual occurrence in

March 1848 when the flow of water over Niagara Falls stopped—the only time this has been known to occur. The details in her poem fit the various reports of the two-day phenomenon.[52] Accounts of the event emphasize the stunning silence which Avison captures in her opening lines:

> The night, a winter moon's was distinctively
> still.
> The farmers near the gorge
> heard it emerge
> large and unreal, and lit their lamps to pull
> on boots and sheepskins and go look.
> They saw Niagara-no-Falls moony rock
> with here and there a slack
> curbed puddle in the moonshine,
> table-paving and threshold of cataract
> as actual, still, stone.

The unusual silence of the falls in this relatively isolated section of the world in 1848 is contrasted with the human turmoil and bustle of political activity around the world. England's unshakable solidity—in "tallow snowlight fingers / warmed branches on the hedge"—is far away. There are wars on the other side of the world, "Europe [is] in turmoil" and "in Chile the intellectuals too / [are] infected with revolt." Seen historically, these events bear more weight on human affairs. At the time, as well,

> [Lake] Erie is wide and shallow and windswung
> in a black-bushed stump-rough nowhere.
> News is hard come by here
> and who's to care on the escarpment in March weather?

The same moon "floats around" and "over" Africa where the isolated explorer-missionary David Livingstone is making his discoveries, and "over / the cradle of – eyes buttoned shut in / sleep – one Paul Gauguin," the famous post-impressionist painter. An ice jam stopping the water flow over Niagara Falls is merely one piece of news in a world filled with happenings.

Nevertheless, there is still the event and the silent night in Canada. While the world does not bear witness, those who hear reckon with its silence and interpret it in the light of the moon. The opening line suggests the night is "distinctively" "a winter moon's" night. When the farmers go to look at the silence they see "moony rock" where usually there were torrents

52. Facts about Niagara Falls.

of water. Twice in the poem as this event of silence is juxtaposed with other events around the world, the phrase "[t]he moon floats round . . ." and "[t]he moon floats over . . ." is used. Before a kind of order has been restored, "[t]he farmers stare at the rock, rock at the moon." They sense they are in the midst of an event charged with religious significance, and they are participating in primitive urges to turn to the heavens for explanation and comfort. The ending three lines, in contrast, suggest miracle enough for modern viewers of the falls:

> Now while it snows we linger
> stunned by the roar of the Falls
> and the river unrolls, unrolls.

"Unspeakable" (*AN* 1.226), the closing poem of *The Dumbfounding*, in contrast, includes nothing remarkable. Rather, the worth of each detail is in the noticing. The lyric is a single exuberant sentence, a witness to what the poet calls "excellent indolence," calling attention to creation's capacity to just be, and again, one of the characteristics of play. Associative thinking generates the connections between birds and roof and leaves and cat:

> The beauty of the unused
> > (the wheatear among birds, or
> > > stonechat)
> the unused in houses (as a
> portion of low roof swept by the
> buttery leaves of a pear tree
> where a Manx cat is
> discovered – just now – blinking his
> sunned Arctic sea-eyes in the
> sun-play).

The associations expand to the human with its curious phrase "excellent indolence":

> the beauty of the
> > unused in one I know, of
> > excellent indolence
> > > from season into
> > > > skyward wintering
> should be
> confidently, as it is

copious and new into the morning,
celebrated.

Robert Merrett points out that "[t]his poem climaxes Avison's attempt to sing of the world in a religious way [at the end of *The Dumbfounding*]; it expresses the poet's sense that being is to be trusted."[53] The appropriate response for poet and reader is to simply rejoice.

At the same time, a sense of lighthearted playfulness contains its own dialectic between seriousness and non-seriousness, As a result, all is not light and joy; celebration is muted. The title of one of the sketches in *sunblue*, "End of a Day *or* I as a Blurry" (*AN* 2.23), emphasizes its provisional and evocative form and initially communicates a kind of intimacy and identification with the multi-layered detail of an autumn scene. "I as a blurry groundhog bundling home / find autumn storeyed," the poet announces, seeing the outdoors with busy movement of eyes as well as feet, from sidewalk to clouds above her head:

underfoot is leafstain and gleam of wet;
at the curb, crisp weed
thistled and russeted;
then there's the streetlight level;
then window loftlights, yellower;
above these, barely, tiers
of gloaming branches,
a sheet of paraffin-pale wind,
then torn cloud-thatch and
the disappearing clear.

However, the particular sightings of this hasty twilight walk match the "blurry groundhog's" compulsion to get indoors. The distinctive naming of "leafstain, "weed thistle," "gloaming branches," "torn cloud-thatch" and "cold layered beauty" do not invite the traveler to linger and suggest a particular distancing and separation from her surroundings. Only the yellow streetlights and "window loftlights" signal the lights of home for the groundhog-person.

---

53. In his detailed discussion of the poem the critic admires "the comfortable subversiveness which Margaret Avison is able to exert in order to share her confidence in the sacramental nature of reality . . . putting off . . . the usual formalities of utilitarian and anthropocentric ways of thinking." Merrett, "The Ominous Centre," 14, 16. His reference to the "sacramental nature of reality" is an example of a generic and non-Catholic use of the term.

> Indoors promises
> such creatureliness as disinhabits
> a cold layered beauty
> flowing out there.

At the same time, there is a potency about nature's disfigurements—remnants of life and gestures toward death—that both repel and attract simultaneously.

Frequently, Avison's lyrics intimate an intentional hiddenness about natural phenomena and about one's apprehension of its mystery. All the words in her sketch "CNR London to Toronto (II)" (*AN* 2.20) point to the last italicized one "*invisibility*." The rider in the train assigns an adjective to badger, sun, and frost (emphasized in the unfamiliar syntax), but she knows she is imagining because she cannot see them from her vantage point.

> In the Christmas tree and
> icing sugar country
> they listen under banks
> badger foreheads sleek
> the sun uncaring, frost
> squeaky, bright with
> berries: *invisibility*.

Her senses are obviously not passive, but are "half-creating," like Wordsworth's, "see[ing] into the life of things" and "instressing," to again borrow from Hopkins, the distinct design of each miracle of creation.[54] At the same time, she seems to be emphasizing the hiddenness and the invisible that she has been able to penetrate.

In "The Hid, Here" (*AN* 2.139), she plays with perspective from another window:

> Big birds fly past the window
> trailing string or vines
> out in the big blue.

From this vantage point—up close—birds seem big. In fact, the next lines make no particular distinction in size:

54
While with an eye made quiet by the power
Of harmony, and the deep power of joy,
We see into the life of things [. . .]
("Tintern Abbey," ll. 46–48,).

Big trees become designs
of delicate floral tracery
in golden green.

Size and distance merge in her next sighting:

The Milky Way
end over end like a football
lobs, towards that still
unreachable elsewhere
that is hid within bud and nest-stuff and bright air
where the big birds flew
past the now waiting window.

The point of interest for the watcher is "that still unreachable elsewhere" beyond the Milky Way "hid[den] within bud and nest-stuff and bright air" but close—within reach of her "waiting window."

Avison's occasional poems about snow, both earlier and later, have to do with a person's capacity to see and engage in observation of what often is hidden.[55] The earlier snow sonnet of *Winter Sun* (*AN* 1.69) emphasizes an active imagination interacting with the snowflakes. A later snow poem "Not Quite Silently" (*AN* 3.21), from *Not Yet But Still*, implies a quieter passivity:

Though light is overshadowed, yet the far
Comes close, the unknowable
Near; the random usual 'here'
Is sifted down
Feathering eyelid, lashes, blank
Eyeball, as if with holy
Fear.

The snowflake is a miniature incarnation—of "the far / comes close, the un-knowable / near." Again, "Beyond Weather, or From a Train Window" (*AN* 3.15) is a meditation on all the "[s]nowflakes in starlight, obliterated into / weft and stippling" and what happens to them as they lie in layers—"buried under / combed sweep and depth." The "mineral beauty" of these "round little pools / bright with the lift of the sky they left last autumn" suggests an upward pull—the connection of earth and sky; but the poet acknowledges, "Most such is still / long, for long, hidden." There is mystery that she cannot

---

55. See also "Christmas Approaches, Highway 401" (*AN* 2.97); "Not Quite Si-lently" (*AN* 3.21); "Making" (*MD* 29–31); "3 A.M. By Snowlight" (*MD* 36–37).

penetrate, even in the snowflake. Here, the imagination is inadequate to dislodge the secret. Sometimes seeing involves both the tranquil acceptance of creation's silence; at the same time, there is at least an intimation of something beyond the physical, however subtle.

In her lament "Hid Life" (*AN* 2.28),

> Red apples hang frozen
> in a stick-dry, snow-dusty
> network of branches,

the narrator mourns.

> Heavily in my heart
> the frost-bruised fruit, the somber tree,
> this unvisited room off winter's endless corridors
> weigh down.

She strains to see what she cannot see. Worrying about the seeds that are not in the ground, she struggles with a sense of hope. "Botanist," she asks,

> does the seed
> so long up held
> still somehow inform
> petal and apple-spring-perfume
> for sure, from so far?

And then the insight comes in the play on words in the ending query: "Is the weight only / a waiting?" The weight on her heart of the seemingly abandoned fruit, exposed to the elements in "this unvisited room off winter's endless corridors," so reminiscent of the "smashed moth/butterfly" of the earlier poem, carries a new sense of expectation. This desolate scene is really another one of those "ten thousand places" in which "Christ plays" in Avison's assertion of Christian hope.

STIRRINGS OF LONGING

Some of Avison's nature poems, while still indirect, allusively offer an orientation towards the religious, and ultimately towards the God of Scripture. Sometimes the placement of poems in the collections establishes connections. As well, repeated motifs and recurrent images suggest her deep faith commitment. Then there are internal cues, subtle allusions within the poems—at least for those initiated in a literary tradition—to direct the spiritual eye Godward. For those with basic acquaintance with Old and New Testament Scriptures, these allusions and images coalesce even more obviously. The poems "Thirst" (*AN* 2.35) and "Sounds Carry" (*AN* 2.34) in *sunblue*, just after "Water and Worship: an Open-air Service on the Gatineau River" (*AN* 2.33) and just a few pages from a block of poems directly on biblical texts, carry these allusive qualities. Both poems simultaneously register sensitivity to natural detail and spiritual longing.

Like an impressionistic painting, there is a surreal quality to the undefined and vague setting of "Thirst" (*AN* 2.35):

> In the steeped evening
> deer stand, not yet
> drinking
> beyond the rim of here;
>
> and crystal blur
> clears to the jet
> stream, pure, onflowing:
> a not yet known –
>
> beyond the grasses where the deer
>
> stand, deep in evening
> still.

Visually the poem is striking with its repeated phrases "beyond the rim" and "beyond the grasses" and its phrase "deer stand" twice noted. "Steeped evening" and "deep in evening / still" direct the focus to the middle stanza's "a not yet known." The psalmist's longing is called to mind: "As a deer longs for flowing streams, so my soul longs for you, O God" (Ps 42:1). The deer in Avison's poem seem to be waiting for something in the "beyond the grasses." "Beyond the rim" hints at a pool or pond, but there is no clear mention of water.[56] The standing still (whether it means "quiet" or "always" or "yet") is

56 It is also reminiscent of her "rim" from "The Swimmer's Moment" (*AN* 1.89) and "Pace" (*AN* 1.150):
And so their bland-blank faces turn and turn
Pale and forever on the rim of suction
They will not recognize ("The Swimmer's Moment" *AN* 1.89).
and
Pedestrians linger
striped stippled sunfloating
at the rim of the
thin-wearing groves ("Pace" *AN* 1.150).

in contrast to the jet stream—the high-altitude winds moving east at high speed—"pure, onflowing" like the psalmist's "flowing streams." Here the stream is only "onflowing" upwards. The allusion to the deer of the psalm gives her poem about thirst new intensity. At the same time, her interpretation of longing as skyward takes the sense of personal thirst out of the self: "My soul thirsts for God, for the living God. When shall I come and behold the face of God?" (Ps 42:2).

"Sounds Carry" (*AN* 2.34) might be another expression of spiritual longing, suggesting both the mystery of God's presence and the intense desire to experience that mystery. As the title suggests, the longing for presence may be indicated in sound: "Nimbus of summer"—the dark gray, rain-bearing cloud—is creating a sound chamber that amplifies even breathing:

> undefines place and
> time imitates an immemorial dawn
> > – dogs at the white gates . . . .
> Breathing is palpable, and
> breathes response to amplitude
> and hidden tendril,
> yearning for large and little.

Any sound bears significance. The poet goes on to note "flies / and bird cheepings" as muted sounds present in a sultry summer day under the "nimbus of summer," but also part of "a clarity beyond the mist." The poem is a delicate mood piece calling attention to the experience of "misty summer," satisfying in a straightforward reading; but the potential is there to understand the lyric as suggesting more. In mythology nimbus also means a bright cloud surrounding gods or goddesses appearing on the earth or a halo or bright disk surrounding the head of a divinity or a saint. When these nuances are added to the word, the last four lines above with their "breathing," "amplitude," and "yearning" take on deeper significance. It is not just a matter of the effort of breathing in humid pre-storm weather. Now it is deep spiritual longing. Under the dark rain cloud cover/halo, the summer sounds of a present divinity have been carried to the sensitive listener/participant.

In the sketch "Overcast Monday" (*AN* 2.18) there is a reversal of expectations:

> In this earth-soakt air
> we engage with
> undeathful technicalities,
> hurt that they click.

An oil of gladness, in
the seafloor Light
quickens, secretly.

The "earth-soakt air" (rather than air-soaked earth) imitates the strange
action of the title "Overcast Monday"—cloudy, but also thrown over. The
gloomy sky encourages the focus on "undeathful technicalities, / hurt that
they click"—not a sickness unto death, so to speak. Avison reveals the secret
of the reversal in an image reminiscent of Hopkins's "ooze of oil" in "God's
Grandeur": "An oil of gladness" "quickens, secretly," she suggests. The allu-
sion is even closer to a direct reference to biblical lyrics of joy.[57] The poet
looks at the overcast sky of Monday and sees where oil is needed to stop the
clicking; she also sees the oil in the "seafloor Light" (*AN* 2.18).

Avison works with the familiar theme of life within a seed in her epi-
grammatic poem "Potentiality" (*AN* 3.37). "Humble is the intensity of /
a seed" is the cryptic opening as she juxtaposes two attributes not immedi-
ately apparent—humble and intense. The poem's form matches the theme
as the contrast is made in its simple two-line stanzas. The size of the seed
compared to the one who made it is explained in terms of light and shadow:
"It lies there / too small to cast a shadow." In contrast, "the invisible is too
large, compassing / light and shadow both." The seed's humble properties
are obvious then, but where is the intensity? The closing couplet, "yet there
is / a bond that makes them one," is the witness's announcement of the hu-
man yearning for the invisible, drawing humankind homeward, and similar
to Herbert's "The Pulley." Further, the allusive connection of the seed's "po-
tentiality" to familiar comments of Jesus in the Gospels adds poignancy.[58]

57. The ode for a royal wedding of Psalm 45 has the psalmist exclaiming, "Your
God has anointed you with the oil of gladness beyond your companions" (Ps 45:7). The
theme is picked up again in the poet-prophet Second Isaiah's good news of deliverance,
where he uses the same phrase to suggest that those who are sad in Zion will be given
"the oil of gladness instead of mourning" (Isa 61:3). Jesus declares himself the fulfill-
ment of these great Isaiah passages of "good news to the poor, release to the captives,
recovery of the blind" in Luke's Gospel (Luke 4:18–19).

58. One time he compares the kingdom of God to a mustard seed, but when it is
sown in a field (put in the ground—in essence, dies), it grows "into the greatest of shrubs
and becomes a tree" (Matt 13:31–32). Another time, referring to his own impending
death (and resurrection), Jesus again employs the seed as an essential analogy—"if it
dies, it bears much fruit" (John 12:24).

Trees in their rooted connection to the earth and their skyward direction are also powerful symbols of Avison's persevering hope and beckoning gestures.[59] Sometimes it is an "urban tree"—

> An orphan tree
> forks for air
> among the knees of
> clanking panoplied buildings ("Urban Tree," *AN* 1.226).

Sometimes it is a wintering tree without its show of leaves—

> A tree its twigs up-ending
> November had bared:
> drenched in height, brisk with
> constellar seed-springs, thrusting
> its ancient ranginess towards
> the cold, the burning, spared
> of leaf, sealed in, unbending ("And Around," *AN* 1.223).

"Trees wait their lifetimes / fragrantly forthright," the poet describes admiringly in "Enduring" (*AN* 2.219), as she endows them with personality.

> Tangle
> risks itself in space
> for contour's mysteries,
> self-disclosure,

she goes on to explain, as the trees make themselves vulnerable to mystery. When spring comes, a different sense of the tree's organic connection skyward emerges. "April" (*AN* 2.157) alerts the reader to a spring evening's sights and sounds—the clocks striking the night hour, "a robin's song, silence unraveling," and the emotion attached to "the trees with tremulous-aching fingers / shaping the quiet airflow." All this beauty must mean something. The trees are the directors, pointing towards the poem's penultimate conclusion, "[s]ick-faint dark / limp in the arms of the infinite." Further, in "Knowing the New" (*AN* 3.28), when "the detritus of winter" is "washed clean away," spring's announcement is most visible in the trees as they create their own cathedral: "Suddenly utterance is everywhere."

---

59. See also "In Time" (*AN* 1.156); "A Sad Song" (*AN* 1.209); "City Park in July" (*AN* 2.78); "Patience" (*AN* 2.140); "In the Hour" (*AN* 2.180); "The Fix" (*AN* 2.202); "Pacing the Turn of the Year" (*AN* 3.119–21); "Towards the Next Change" (*AN* 3.124); "Ramsden" (*AN* 3.129); "Responses" (*AN* 3.137); "No Dread" (*MD* 66–67).

And the magnolia has
haloed high around itself a dome
of space,
an eloquent soundlessness
the birds can understand and
revoice for the wide world.

A similar theme emerges in "News Item" with its "chestnut trees / pagoda'd in full / seven-fold leaf" (*AN* 3.99). Demonstrated in "Knowing the New," trees and birds go together in Avison's poems as signs of spiritual longing which may eventually direct the seeking heart to the living Christ. Before they are signs, however, they have to be seen.

BIRD SIGNS

Like the astute bird watchers in the ancient tales, Avison knows how to read bird signs.[60] To begin, she shows in her earlier volumes *Winter Sun* and *The Dumbfounding* her keen awareness of and attraction to birds as part of daily life. There are multiple references to sparrows, robins, pigeons, seagulls, crows, geese, and grackles, mostly with positive and whimsical designations, suggesting the pleasure they afford. Her robin "trills" with "flame tulip sound" ("Open Window," *AN* 1.22); her pigeons "flap and chuckle" ("Christmas Anticipation," *AN* 1.221–22); the "junco flits" ("The Fallen, Fallen World," *AN* 1.75–76); the "grackle shin[e] in the grass" ("Two Mayday Selves," *AN* 1.148–49); the park pigeons are "heavy with knowing / tame food" ("The Earth that Falls Away," *AN* 1.175–84); a "gill" "sloughs and slumps / in a spent sea" ("Grammarian on a Lakefront Park Bench," *AN* 1.77). The unidentified clicking in "Pace" (*AN* 1.150)

is perhaps the conversational side-effect
among the pigeons; behold
the path-dust is nutmeg powdered and
bird-foot embroidered.

---

60. Early in Homer's story, for example, "Zeus of the wide brows / sent forth two eagles" (*Odyssey* 1.146) for the sake of Telemachos, the son of Odysseus struggling to regain control of his family house. The men of the town watched in fear, the bard sings, "astounded at the birds" (1.155), needing someone to interpret the sign. Halitherses "was far beyond the men of his generation / in understanding the meaning of birds" (1.158–59).

She signals early that they mean something or point to something, reminiscent of another poet fond of birds, her more famous nineteenth-century predecessor, Emily Dickinson.[61] While Dickinson has alerted the reader to the meditative gaze in her minimalist still life portraits of birds, Avison, on the other hand, sees her birds in the busy atmosphere of the city. Their meaning is less enigmatic, more directed, and accessible in their varied movements:

> The sparrows
> in suet season, and through
> carbon monoxide summer till
> autumn's enlarged outdoors,
> quick in their public middle age
> keep hidden delicate and final things ("Sparrows," *AN* 2.158).

At the same time, "sparrows in the curbs" can "instruct, distract" ("Prelude," *AN* 1.62). Her emotionally and spiritually stunted character Agnes Cleves does not know how to read bird signs and turns away from their messages. "In March you can see the geese from the highroad / They are very white," she notes, and there is hope that she is going to intuit their significance. But her monologue dwindles into reasons for retreat into her own narrow focus:

> The rim of the pond is muddy
> And the keen blue of the sky and these voyaging clouds
> Show from the round water
> And a beat like echoes makes your eyelids flutter.
> A red and white collie fusses around the geese
> And it would be clumsy walking (after climbing
> The new wire fence) to go down there
> And why should courage be hailing you to go
> Because it is muddy and March and there are a few
> Sinewy snowy geese
> > Stretching their necks?
> ("The Agnes Cleves Papers," *AN* 1.132–43).

---

61. A sampling of Dickinson's many bird references and poems suggests the striking contrast to Avison—less particularized, more enigmatic: "I dreaded that first robin so, / But he is mastered now";

> A bird came down the walk:
> He did not know I saw;
> He bit an angle-worm in halves
> And ate the fellow raw.

Her lack of spiritual and mental curiosity is both enervating and disturbing. "Sinewy snowy geese / Stretching their necks" are pointing to something that matters more than she knows.

In "Controversy" ("and if some sparrows / dropt by [. . .] your god keeps accounts of" *AN* 1.163), Avison gives an early clue to her connection to the biblical text in its many reference to birds, inviting readers to make similar links.[62] There is Jesus's admonition in his Sermon on the Mount: "Look at the birds of the air; they neither sow nor reap nor gather into barns, and yet your heavenly Father feeds them. Are you not of more value than they" (Matt 6:26)?[63] These instructions are preceded in Scripture by other significant references to birds.[64] Spiritual longing is connected to birds in Psalm 84:

> My soul longs, indeed it faints for the courts of the Lord . . . .
> Even the sparrow finds a home, and the swallow a nest for herself
> where she may lay her young . . . . (Ps 84:1–3).

As a result, when the poet moves beyond the early mention of birds to entire poems in *sunblue, No Time,* and *Not Yet But Still* devoted to birds, she implies an instruction, a signal, a sign of some religious import.[65] For example,

62. See chapter 5 for a fuller discussion of this poem.

63. Jesus encourages his listeners, "Are not two sparrows sold for a penny? Yet not one of them will fall to the ground apart from your Father. . . . So do not be afraid; you are of more value than many sparrows" (Matt 10:29, 31; Luke 12:6–7).

64. In the initial Genesis account of creation, birds are singled out as they share their own creation day with the fish (Gen 1:20–23). "Birds of the air and beasts of the earth" is a repeated phrase in Scripture (Gen 1:26–30; Gen 2:19–20). The dove is Noah's harbinger of hope when he returns to the ark with a freshly plucked olive leaf (Gen 8:11). The psalmist refers to God's special awareness of birds: "I know all the birds of the air," Yahweh proclaims (Ps 50:11). God's care of his people is expressed in similes referring to eagles (Deut 32:11; 19:4), and Jesus speaks of his care as "a hen gathering her brood" (Matt 23:37; Luke 13:34).

65. "Sparrows" (*AN* 2.158)
    Only whiskered cats and the
    hidden lover see their stillness, and
    the devotees of cats
and "Seeing So Little" (*AN* 2.159)
    why have I never seen you walk?
    Toes yes, legs yes,
    but knees'?
on facing pages; and "City Birds" ("Pigeons are pedestrians / chiefly, therefore becoming threatened," *AN* 2.169) in *No Time*—all reveal affectionate concern and soft humor.

Seven birds toss
skyward and glide
and ruffle down:

birds on the TV wires
eye-mirroring the light of the
wild west,

in the sketch "The Seven Birds (College Street at Bathurst)" (*AN* 2.22), are known and watched and cared for by the Creator.[66] When they are called "stormy sunlit evening children" "under / the very shadow of / heaven," they are naturally connected to those who are worth more. Their gliding movement upwards suggests the same motion as the one in "Thirst" (*AN* 2.35). In the later volume *No Time* there are more direct bird signs to interpret. For one, the language in the opening stanza of "Seeing So Little" (*AN* 2.159) echoes biblical language:

In the tents of day,
under night's canopy so
long – why
do I still not know you,
sparrow?[67]

Second, birds and their activities become powerful metaphors for human life events. In "Resting on a Dry Log, Park Bench, Boulder" (*AN* 3.97–98), she calls attention to birds out of their element: "I love to see birds walk. / Oh yes of course, their singing, their soaring." Associative reflection moves her into theological musing:

But that a bird
comes simply among us,
steps as we must (though some,
sandpipers, robins, etc.,
like children bob or run)
touches us.

She returns to her description of the birds' activity,

---

66. Seven carries symbolic meaning of completion or perfection in the Bible. One obvious example is the creation account with the seventh day devoted to rest. It is possible (but certainly not necessary), then, to extrapolate some special significance in Avison's very specific use of seven here.

67. See 2 Sam 22:12; Ps 18:11; Ps 104:23; Isa 40:22.

com[ing] for seeds,
or crumbs perhaps, a comfortable
touching down we can well understand.

Again, the theological inserts itself:

although for us to
'consider the birds of the air' in this regard
can be uncomfortable.

Without further comment she returns to her whimsical observation, "I like to think birds walk / for fun." She has only hinted at the incarnation, but nevertheless, the idea is incipient in the playful lyric.

Both "Migrant Impulses" in *No Time* (*AN* 2.186–87) and "Making a Living" in *Not Yet But Still* (*AN* 3.31) have similar themes of the anticipation of death. To leave the earth, she suggests is to

[s]wim the updraught of air   dotty
as birds, mysteriously
instructed migrants

Like the birds,

We twitter and flip
but not in the thinning branches
who have left forms known as trees
　　　　forever. We are
　　　　　　　　left to the aloning power
　　　　who gathers us   now
(tossed, tossing)
　　　　　　I sit in this tree.
　　　　We twitter and flip.
The gloaming draws near.

There is fear in the unknown as "[t]he sky-valve lets in a / pallor and chill," but "[t]he flocking, the high homing / in Jetstream" points "to a new power, radiant, / fearsome, for flight, far coursing." Migrant impulses lead to one's rightful destination. "Making a Living" is more hopeful in its subtlety. The poem sets up contrasting scenes of sandpipers—"the industrious young"—and herons—"the old stand hunched":

motionless, like a morning
heron on mist-smoking water standing,

>   the way a lightning-crippled oak
>   mimicking lightning in its
>   old blasted branches
>   seems forever bereft of leafing.
>   Earth under water; sky over all,
>   waiting; though
>   there will be, abruptly, a
>   brief tussle: life, from death.
>   Another fast is broken.

The last five lines completely upend one's understanding of the diminishment of old age and point to the Christian hope of a new life—after an "abrupt" and "brief tussle"—an ambiguous phrase that could point to a person's death. The emphasis is reversed from the expectation of loss. Instead the "fast" of the "old" ("like a morning heron" and "a lightning-crippled oak") will be rewarded in an upcoming new day.

Finally, Avison connect birds with herself as a poet in her lament for the Canadian writer Margaret Laurence, "Just Left or The Night Margaret Laurence Died'" (*AN* 2.149). She mourns in the opening stanza:

>   Bare branches studded once with jeweled birds
>   Someone inexorably plunders
>   One by one till an
>   Impoverished wintry sky from hill to
>   Darkening hill reveals
>   Untreasured tree-spikes, almost only
>   (One bunched bird left
>   His eye aglimmer there).

In the suggested aloneness of being the one remaining bird,

>   The perched, askew,
>   Will ruffle still as the day-ocean
>   Lips in and foams towards flood of
>   All emptiness exposed,

the poet will still carry on in double awareness. In many of the bird poems she has called to mind the one who "sees the sparrow fall" (Matt 10:29–31). At the same time, she shares the role of "the songsparrows" "improvising their immemorial singing" (*AN* 3.36) and the "robins' trilling" (*AN* 1.22). She "revoices for the wide world" "the eloquent soundlessness" that the "magnolia has / haloed high around itself" (*AN* 3.28). In other words, Avison knows how to read her bird signs; and like the birds, she is a witness in her poetry.

AVISON'S SIGNATURE SUN METAPHOR

In his introductory article on Avison for *Profiles in Canadian Literature,* Jon Kertzer notes what critics have long observed: "The image that has dominated her work for forty years is the sun."[68] That dominance has continued for almost another three decades right up to the closing pages of *Momentary Dark,* where in a seniors' residence,

> A spinney of old women, thin-
> branched valley of old men – all
> find the sunlight dim ("Shelters" *MD* 80–88).[69]

Her poems yield images such as these: "The men of Mytilene waited restive / Until the yellow melt of sun" ("Birth Day" *AN* 1. 127–28). Or again, in "The Engineer and the Asparagus" (*AN* 2.79),

> Asparagus, once established, bustles
>
> it grows so vehemently,
> cone by cone nosing out towards
> those (unseen) garbled acres and the sun's
> tusks of flaming.

The picture shifts:

> through the early murk
> the sun, a tangerine ball,
> bulged briefly ("When the Bough Breaks" *AN* 3.27).

68. Kertzer, "Margaret Avison," 34.

69. The posthumously published collection *Listening* (2009) has very few poems alluding to the sun. It is hard to suggest whether this lack of emphasis is merely coincidental. Avison keeps good company in her preoccupation with the sun, and there is ample precedence in the long poetic tradition: Spenser's "Phoebus fiery carre" (*The Faerie Queene*); Shakespeare's "eye of heaven" with "gold complexion dimmed" ("Sonnet 18"); Donne's "Busy old fool, unruly sun" ("The Sun Rising"); Herrick's "the glorious lamp of heaven" ("To the Virgins, to Make Much of Time"); Blake's call to "The little Black Boy" to "look on the rising sun"; Wordsworth's "sky rejoices in the morning's birth" ("Resolution and Independence"); Byron's "Child Harold bask'd him in the noontide sun ("Child Harold's Pilgrimage"); Yeat's reference to "a gaze blank and pitiless as the sun" ("The Second Coming")—all suggest the sun's prominence.

Image merges naturally into metaphor in the many references to the sun with the implicit directive to come and see by its light—to understand what it reveals, particularly as it illuminates divine presence and power in the universe.

Initially, Avison's sun is not identified with the Creator, as Kertzer suggests in his overview of the poet's early works:

> In her poetry, the sun represents the power of human apprehension at its most acute: the spark of genius, the "golden contemplation" of the brilliant thinker, the "sunbright gaze" of the visionary, the "inrushing floodlight" of imagination of the poet. The sun permits vision and sustains life. It invigorates the earth in the spring. It dispels the shadows of ignorance, doubt and fear.[70]

He interprets what he sees as her developing aesthetic in his later essay, "Margaret Avison and the Place of Meaning," which involves a refinement of the sun-metaphor's meaning. Without naming it as such, this explanation is one of witness—with a gesture outside the poet's self:

> The sun shines (or is obscured) in all her poetry, and like Kahoutek, its brilliance comes "from somewhere else," from the depth of the cosmos, infinity, God, or the Son. Light illuminates and makes vision possible, but is not itself visible. Rather, it is the condition of seeing.[71]

Within the broad range of references to the sun in her verse, there are some key poems, published both before and after her conversion, where the sun is central and the poet invites significant religious connection. This link evolves in the transition between early and later lyrics, but she employs biblical and Christian language even before she embraces the Christian faith. Her earlier poetry of "searching" and reflecting a "post-Christian or lost Christian," darkened landscape in *Winter Sun*, in reality, points to the light and warmth of the sun.[72] The metaphor emerges in succeeding poems.

In the wistful "Prelude" in *Winter Sun* (*AN* 1.61–63), with its haunting head note,

---

70 Then he demarcates a division, one I am not making: "In her religious poems, the sun is Jesus Christ: the son of God and the 'Sun of righteousness' (Malachi 4:2)." Ibid.

71 Kertzer, "Margaret Avison and the Place of Meaning," 23.

72. Doerksen, "Search and Discovery," 7–20. M. Anderson, "'Conversation with the Star Messenger,'" 89.

> The passive comes to flower, perhaps
> a first annunciation for the spirit
> launched on its seasons,

there are scenes of contrasting youthful pastoral memories and city weari-
ness. Bridging the two scenes is "the honeycombing sun" which strangely
seems to have both

> opened and sealed us in
> chambers and courts and crooked butteries,
> cities of sense.

The government building's "stone lip of a flower" "stares through a different
sun." She sees a person close by with hair "fixed like a corpse's" and who
seems "closed like a bank's vault." Yet, when the sun touches the woman—as
it touches the stone flower and the speaker in the poem—"she knows day,
abruptly." This prelude is a signal of an awakening in the landscape, in the
woman the speaker observes, in the speaker, and perhaps in the poet herself:

> Light, the discovering light, is a beginning
> Where many stillnesses
> yearn, those we had long thought long dead
> or our mere selves.
>
> In the moment of held breath
> the light takes shape.

The witness is slowly coming to flower and acknowledge light's power, but
the metaphor is still veiled.

It is surprising that in this early group of pre-conversion poems of
Winter Sun the poet goes on to establish both the importance of the sun as
metaphor and specifies its meaning in a Christian sense in the poem "The
Fallen, Fallen World" (*AN* 1.75–76). Here Avison pictures not passivity, but
open resistance to the sun. "Since Lucifer," the poem reports, fallen crea-
tures—whether revolutionaries, idealists or the learned—have apprehended
their "slow sure estrangement from the sun," and they are bearing the results
of their rebellion.[73] For rebels, "the sun comes still / Remote and chilly."
Similarly, in the sad and puzzling "Not the Sweet Cicely of Gerardes Herb-
all" (*AN* 1.64–65), another poem with heavy scriptural suggestions, the sun

---

73. I speak further to this poem in chapter 4; I mention it here because of its clear
announcement of the metaphorical application of sun representing the Son for Avison.

is "purifying, harsh, like sea-salt" to the "gardenless gardens" of the "house abandoned." For Agnes Cleves,

> much alone, as well as old,
> And fearful sometimes of the tedious fondness
> Peculiar to my kind,

in the closing dramatic monologue of Avison's first volume of poems (*AN* 1.132–43), it is not so much a matter of resistance, as fear: "Telling it in plain words / Makes me see how I feared the wrong thing." Agnes's dwindling thoughts eclipse the sun:

> this iris bed
> Is scarfed in dreadful mist
> and no sun comes
> Beyond the yellow stoneway. . . .

It is in the early part of her narration—

> Have you remarked
> How few persist in penetrating farther
> And all the rumour that subsides after them
> Is of some outdoor chill –

that the mention of the winter sun signals the title of these pre-conversion poems.

> And pomegranate seed spilled in the
> Cleft where sand and winter sun
> Drift to make small regular shadows?

The image is apt in its application to Agnes Cleves in her meandering memories of regret, nostalgia, and inertia.

The language of these poems shows Avison's familiarity with the tradition of the Christian faith, all the while offering a vague accounting for her own turning aside from its reality. The title of her first collection *Winter Sun* seems like code for a person struggling to live in the presence of a reality she cannot deny, must acknowledge, but does not want to embrace. Mia Anderson responds to the predicament the poet has outlined in naming her sun:

> Winter sun is a weak implication of summer but it's all we have,
> in this post-Christian or lost-Christian world where Dec. 25 and
> Jan. 6 mean a pale yellow sun over the winter solstice, and the
> new year waiting for spring, to a people who can only read one

level, the blessed natural one, who have no parabolic depth in their scanning of the universe—and to a poet who knows what's been lost but also knows why and is blocked, for now, from re-course to it, self-condemned to figure out salvation the natural route, as best a one she can.[74]

If *Winter Sun* were the end of the poet's expressed vision it would indeed be a melancholy conclusion.

In *Winter Sun*'s version of "Easter" (*AN* 1.95), the poet writes in full awareness of the significance of the apex of the Christian story, but only al-lows a glimmer of its hope to shine through. The imagery veils the Christian Easter story in nature's own resurrection of spring:

> the eve of April brings
> A delicacy of light at the day's end
> The bulge of earth seems again comic [. . .]

In the second stanza,

> the milky air
> Lulls, and listens, and there
> Is the sorrow of all fullness,

available for hidden meaning of awareness of what preceded the resurrec-tion. "But on the hillside the frail tremolo / Of a new dayspring, eggshell and lilac" signals the arrival of the Easter event—the culmination of the Magnificat's dayspring—but it is not spelled out. Instead, "an everywhere of sunwardness" is the strong hint that generates hope.

> A bird sings, forceful, glorious as a pipe-organ,
> And the huge bustling girth of the whole world
> Turns in an everywhere of sunwardness
> Among the cloudcarved sundering of its oceans.

The poem's climax is the earth's response "sunward"—a rehearsal of crea-turely gratitude.

There is a decided shift in mood and perspective towards the sun in the second volume of Avison's poetry, *The Dumbfounding*. As mentioned earlier, the collection opens with the poem "Old . . . Young . . ." (*AN* 1.147) as "the young grass / shines, breathing light" and "the last / light is mahogany-rich, / a 'furnishing.'" "Two Mayday Selves" (*AN* 1.148) speaks of "sun-meld" and

---

74. M. Anderson, "'Conversation with the Star Messenger,'" 89.

> the rice-
> perfuming light sifting
> between that pointing distance
> and this?

and "[t]he power of the blue and gold breadth / of day" "poured out, flooding, all / over all." There is the

> too much none of us knows
> is weight, sudden sunlight, falling
> on your hands and arms, in your lap,
> all, all, in time

in "July Man" (*AN* 1.160). Again,

> a Manx cat is
> discovered – just now – blinking his
> sunned Arctic sea-eyes in the
> sun-play

in "Unspeakable" (*AN* 1.227). There can still be a winter sun in these poems,

> this winter sun glisters on
> washed cottons, amid a branch-tangle
> and morning quiet,

but the speaker in "Until Silenced: To I. A." (*AN* 1.157) sees it differently.

In this brighter atmosphere there are, again, some poems emphasizing the metaphor of the sun with more than a passing reference. One, in particular, in *The Dumbfounding* is illuminating. In the poem "Once" (*AN* 1.210) the sun is at the center in an account of the natural events of earth's rotation and movements away from and toward the sun. In spite of the straightforward narrative, there is a sense of a living presence both in the sun and on the earth in its response or lack of response. When earth "turns its shoulder / on the ungrudging sun," it is "pole-tilted"—its natural appropriate gesture. In this position, with its "fronting / the eyes of utter dark," the poet creates a sense of waiting in the pause between stanzas: "snow forms and falls," as a living presence—

> breathing
> even by night of, as if,
> eyelid pallor.

The "melting, coursing sun" is in charge, however, and it counters the earth's movement away with its own moves—"(hurting and lilting, / dimming and flashing)." Avison recalls the medieval universe alive with its cosmic dance in the relationship between sun and earth:

> Earth is all pools and all the
> waters speak, in the new
> sky's language.

In the melting of the snow there is a kind of end to an ice age, as "the myths of earth-ferment" are recalled. Here is a miniature creation account, culminating in "spiking up swords of / green, bright under blueness." There is a merriment and joy in the sun's accomplishment and the concluding stanza should be a gesture of praise. Instead, the poet suggests,

> the myths [. . .]

> make shy our brutish,
> averted, black-drinking, still-
> ice-splintered
> eyes.

Transformation—a "seed-nub in dissolution / spiking up swords of / green"—is surely needed to enable people to turn sunward. The poet again calls to mind Jesus's observation about himself: "Unless a grain of wheat falls into the earth and dies, it remains just a single grain; but if it dies, it bears much fruit" (John 12:24).

The momentum of *The Dumbfounding* is maintained in *sunblue* with its season of spring dominating the early poems. Phrases like "swepth of suncoursing sky" ("Thaws," *AN* 2.17); "oils of sun" ("Cement Worker on a Hot Day," *AN* 2.19); "sun's butter fat" ("A Childhood Place," *AN* 2.19); "strong sun" ("Water and Worship: An Open-air Service on the Gatineau River," *AN* 2.33); "sweet with the sun" ("Sounds Carry," *AN* 2.34); "sunflooding sunfire" ("From a Public Library Window," *AN* 2.68); and "look to the sunblue" ("Light" II, *AN* 2.66)—all call to mind the warmth and life-giving energy of the sun. In "Released Flow" (*AN* 2.29), the poet speaks about the source of the flowing sap from the sugarbush:

> In the sunward sugarbush
> runnels shine and down-rush
> through burning snow and thicket-slope.

Several lines down the poet observes that "the motions of the light / close the flow as watertight." Creatures of the woods respond: "Squirrels flip and play / through sunsplash." "The extraordinary beyond the hill / breathes and is imperturbable."

> Across snowbush and sunstriped maples
> Honeyed woodsmoke curls and scrolls.
> Sunblue and bud and shoot wait to unlatch
> All lookings-forth, at the implicit touch.

The hints are bolder now of the interchangeable word play of Son/sun that characterize this third volume of poetry, and the sun metaphor seems to suggest more obviously the sacramental for Avison.[75]

The two poems side by side, "March Morning" and "March," convey the joy of nature's response to the sun.

> Peaking wafering snowbanks are
> sun-buttery, stroked by the
> rosy fingertips of young
> tree shadows
> as if for music;
> and all the eyes of God glow, listening,

exclaims the poet in "March Morning" (*AN* 2.30).[76] In "March" (*AN* 2.31), the spring thaw takes on sacred significance with eucharistic intimations of "earth-loaf, sky-wine":

> Though all seems melt and rush,
> earth-loaf, sky-wine,
>
> swept to bright new horizons
> with hill-runnel, and gash,
> All soaked in sunwash.

Avison maintains the sacramental hints of the sun in the subsequent volumes of her poetry, though not as frequently until *Momentary Dark*. In "The Promise of Particulars" in *No Time*, for instance, she speaks of "[t]he late sun, spoking under storm / against prune-coloured stormclouds to the west" (*AN* 2.210), bringing its gift of life as it "haloes and breathes" to the

---

75. From different perspectives both Redekop and Mazoff emphasize this distinctive wordplay. See Redekop, "sun/Son light/Light" and Mazoff, *Waiting for the Son.*

76. She is unmistakeably echoing Homer's distinctive "rosy fingers of the dawn."

receiving creation just by being what it is. In "The Ecologist's Song" (*AN* 2.266), she speaks of the interplay between water and sun:

> Absorbing, glittering, the beach at noon
>
> welters with silence. There a separate pool
>
> has formed, plum-coloured, richer than water, cool,
>
> shadowed by stillness in the naked sun.

Later in the poem she emphasizes the connection again: "Everywhere's ocean of sun, late-flowing, knows / the dark tides too." Her beckoning conclusion of the earth's connection of sun and sea—and humanity's responsibility for upsetting the delicate balance between the two—is a call for sharers in her poem to "come and see."

In Avison's last volume of poetry *Momentary Dark* there is a surge of references to the sun. "Glorious, rigorous, sun-flooded / snow-iced morning" opens the poem "Scarfover" (*MD* 3). "High Overhead" (*MD* 18–19) speaks of

> misty mid-
>
> morning sun
>
> flatten[ing] mere earth with the
>
> girth of its far but
>
> fatherly presence up there.

"Making" ends its cosmic reflections with "Just now a glint of / sunlight on glass alerts me" (*MD* 29–31). "Palette" (*MD* 68), with its closing lines,

> The little new-drenched leaves
>
> glow in the momentary dark,
>
> dancing,

implies the glorious opposite shining through. In "Window Conversation: 'Brightness falls from the air'" (*MD* 57), the poet notes the shared good fortune with a tree, concluding, "We are sun-gilded":

> The clouds, the morning
>
> sun are such that
>
> one lettuce-bright tree-tip
>
> over the roofs, like me,
>
> is singled out. We are
>
> sun-gilded.
>
> You smile away

out there.

You are I am
inexpert about timing.
How this instant was
hit upon is
beyond us. We in
passing can
only receive
this befalling, a
blissed one.

These sun pictures gently nudge toward any number of corresponding wit-
ness statements about the sun/Son in Scripture and are a short distance
from the less frequent witness in creation that Avison makes explicit.[77]

EXPLICIT CONNECTIONS BETWEEN THE NATURAL WORLD AND THE BIBLICAL TEXT

Probably the most direct connection between nature and the person of
Christ is seen in those poems that juxtapose and interweave two seemingly
distinct topics, but in play on words they come together. By its title "Psalm
19" (*AN* 1.162) appears to be one of her glosses on a piece of Scripture, in
this case, a psalm from the Hebrew psalter. But in fact, she is working with
only one half of one verse (verse 9) of the psalm, part of a series of charac-
teristic parallel statements having to do with "the law of the Lord":

The law of the Lord is perfect, converting the soul:
The testimony of the Lord is sure, making wise the simple.
The statutes of the Lord are right, rejoicing the heart:
The commandment of the Lord is pure, enlightening the eyes.
The fear of the Lord is clean, enduring forever.
The judgments of the Lord are true and righteous altogether (Ps 19:7–9
KJV).[78]

77. "For the Lord God is a sun" (Ps 84:11); "But for you who revere my name the
sun of righteousness shall rise, with healing in its wings" (Mal 4:2); "The people who
walked in darkness have seen a great light" (Isa 9:2); "By the tender mercy of our God,
the dawn from on high will break upon us" (Luke 1:78); "And the city has no need of
sun or moon to shine on it, for the glory of God is its light, and its lamp is the Lamb"
(Rev 21:22).

78. The first line of the poem using the word "clean" identifies The Authorized

The obvious theme in her poem is not "the law of the Lord" (though silently present in the background), but the "enduring sun" and its many variations mentioned throughout the lines of the lyric.

> *Clean* is the word with *fear.*
> Fear is to love high
> and know longing for clear
> sunlight, to the last ribcorner
> and capillary – and wonder
> if, so known, a sighing-
> over-the-marshlands me
> might all evaporate, wisp away.
> Yet to love high
> is with this very fear
> to shrink, *and* seek to be made plain,
> openly to own
> both the mists smoking from pure
> stone-cold lake-still sun-sweetened places
> and the dank mist that rises
> from the long-unsunned, sour
> pools, hid even from the storm's sluices.
>
> *Enduring* is the word with *clean.*
> The fear once won
> of sunward love, it proves – not boulderstone,
> baldness, slowly in fire consuming – but green
> with life, moss, cup-rock-water, cliff riven
> for a springing pine;
> and thus, trusted to fire, drawn
> towards an enduring sun.

Avison designs her own parallel structure. Stanza 1 of her short poem opens with the stark sentence, "*Clean* is the word with *fear*," echoing the style of the Hebrew psalm; stanza 2 opens with a parallel sentence, "*Enduring* is the word with *clean*. The spokes of thought radiating out from both phrases have to do with the speaker's relationship to the sun.

Version of the Bible (KJV) as the text Avison is using for her source.

> Fear is to love high
> and know longing for clear
> sunlight, to the last ribcorner
> and capillary [. . . .]

It is in this image of sunlight that the connection with the entire Psalm 19 becomes evident. Furthermore, as Daniel Doerksen observes the movement in the poet's thinking from *Winter Sun* to the transformed vision of *The Dumbfounding*, this interpretation of the sun defines the poet's emerging vision. He writes:

> The whole poem hinges on the sun-metaphor for God, an image which does not change, but is radically re-interpreted as the seeker becomes a finder, as the "fire," being "trusted," is revealed to be the life-giving "enduring sun."[79]

Preceding those accumulating assertions of God's presence in words in the psalm is the poetry of declaration of God's glory in the skies: "The heavens declare the glory of God; And the firmament sheweth his handy-work" (Ps 19:1). The sun occupies the dominant position and place of honor and function in the psalmist's heavens:

> In them hath he set a tabernacle for the sun,
> Which is as a bridegroom coming out of his chamber,
> And rejoiceth as a strong man to run a race.
> His going forth is from the end of the heaven,
> And his circuit unto the ends of it:
> And there is nothing hid from the heat thereof (Ps 19:4–6).

The poet has taken the ominous sense of "the fear of the Lord" and transposed it into "longing for clear sunlight"—longing so intense that it courses through a person's inner being the same way the psalmist's glory of God courses through the sky. She goes on to suggest ambiguously "and wonder, if, so known." Is it longing known? Or is it the sun known? Or the sun that knows the one with the longing?

> a sighing-
> over-the-marshlands, me
> might all evaporate, wisp away.

This anthropomorphized sun is sighing over what it sees "to the last ribcorner and capillary," and might as well vaporize these marshlands of the

79. Doerksen, "Search and Discovery," 16–17.

soul with the sun's heat. Yet to fear—"to love high," she suggests, is to both "shrink, *and* seek / to be made plain." Now the word *clean* makes a connection: A person shrinks in fear at what the sun will reveal:

> the dank mist that rises
>
> from the long-unsunned, sour pools,
>
> hid even from the storm's sluices

—obviously unclean places. At the same time there is a longing to own "the mists smoking from pure / stone-cold lake-still sun-sweetened places." These are two mists—one pure, the other not. The cleanness comes from the sun which achieves full disclosure—the total abandonment of "secret faults" and the "presumptuous sins" (Ps 19:12–13) the psalmist deplores. Further, there is a sense of sweet abandonment to the "bridegroom coming out of his chamber" (Ps 19:5). The phrase "loving high" does not suggest some amorphous undefined looking to the skies, but implies a clearly defined object of desire in this context.

"The fear once won / of sunward love" in the second (and final) stanza does not spell barren rock of "boulderstone, / baldness, slowly in fire consuming." This sunward love ensures fecundity and greenness:

> but green
>
> with life, moss, cup-rock-water, cliff riven
>
> for a springing pine.

The God who provides water that is needed for the growth for the "springing pine" also provides the essential light and heat. The final image of Avison's poem, "trusted to fire, drawn / towards an enduring sun," evokes an awareness that God has not been mentioned in this entire poem, and yet the universal "longing for clear / sunlight" has drawn reader and poet alike into his sphere.

The title of a second poem connecting the natural world and the biblical text, "What John Saw (Revelation 4)" (*AN* 3.74–75), this time indicates a biblical theme, but the poem proper suggests something else.[80] It begins with an imagined scene much closer in proximity than the vision of Revelation 4. Avison speaks of "the black holes out there, of pure (physical force)" in outer space, based on what scientific discovery has revealed.[81] As

80. See Appendix for the text of the complete poem. In the original publication "Revelation 4" is placed as a note, Avison's interpretive clue for identifying the person John and the object of his seeing. In the *Collected Poems* the note has moved to the title giving the signal more weight.

81. In astronomy, a black hole is "a region within which the gravitational field is so strong that no form of matter or radiation can escape from it except by

she muses on the mystery of the phenomena "out there," the text seems to suggest these black holes are "what John saw":

> those in-and-out plosions, focused,
>
> remote, in a rhythm of
>
> incomprehensible infrequency
>
> but nonetheless in time,
>
> speak the extremes absolute of a rhythm
>
> we mortals know.

Her fascination with the black holes elicits the awareness of the shared rhythm "contained in / creation's 'Let it be so'" which she anchors in a "bronzing beech tree" in stanza 3. The second stanza implies trauma and instability—"the uprooting / tremor of one event"—whether a person's or a celestial body's crisis, and calls her back to earth. She turns to the familiar and stable—

> this bronzing beech tree, the
>
> blackening myrtle at its foot
>
> (event in all my seasons,
>
> seasoned for this long before I was
>
> born) [. . .]

The day in and day out event of its being there for her seems to be hurtling away as well. As she recreates the disorienting experience of the visionary seeing compressed time and space moving towards she knows not what, she sees that the tree

> exists in a mere
>
> twitch, is rushing towards the node
>
> millennia away [. . . .]
>
> Time curls on itself.

In stanza 4, the poet's and the apocalyptic writer's visions converge, and she clarifies that, in fact, John has seen much farther than the black holes of space.

> Least moments given, though,
>
> can open onto
>
> John's comprehender.

---

quantum-mechanical tunnelling, and thought to result from the collapse of a massive star" (OED).

Here, at mid-point of the poem she introduces her biblical text. It contains a dramatic vision of a particular scene outside earth's time and space. "After this I looked," writes the Revelation's speaker, "and there in heaven a door stood open" (Rev 4:1). He continues,

> And the first voice, which I had heard speaking to me like a trumpet, said, "Come up here, and I will show you what must take place after this." At once I was in the spirit, and there in heaven stood a throne, with one seated on the throne (Rev 4:1–2).

The description of this other-worldly scene is conveyed in a series of similes of surreal grandeur and beauty.[82] The activity culminates in a worship service with creatures and twenty-four elders singing antiphonally a chorus of praise to the one on the throne. What/who John saw on the heavenly throne is the One who sees—who comprehends—both John and the poet—and the uprooting tremors of events. This one, the poet asserts is

> here,
> there, then, always
> now, because unchanging.

She echoes the words of the antiphonal heavenly refrain in her own idiom,

> who
> made light and ponderous rhythms, time, and all
> pulsing particulars.

How does she know?

> John saw him rainbowed in glory –
> compact of all our music, hearing the farthest
> compositions, and the most intricately
> present.

Packed in metaphor, it is not a clear and distinct picture, but one composed in shapes of jasper, carnelian, emerald, and crystal, blending sight with sound. In her own burst of understanding the poet also imitates the vision:

82. "And the one seated there looks like jasper and carnelian . . . and around the throne is a rainbow that looks like an emerald . . . and in front of the throne there is something like a sea of glass, like crystal." Later, "the living creatures around the throne' are described as "like a lion" or "like an ox" or "like a human face" or "like a flying eagle." The concrete images seem to be the throne and "the flashes of lightning and rumblings and peals of thunder" and "seven flaming torches" in front of the throne . . . (excerpts from Revelation 4).

> Magnet. Intensifier. Agonizingly
> rediscovering, in shards, the shapes
> design is satisfied to see.

The black holes are replaced by wordplay of satisfactory shards—one-word explanations: "One. White. Whole."

The poem ends back at the foot of the tree to the natural scene that is visible:

> Secret within
> all that John saw
> is the bronzing beech tree
> of this October twilight.

She remains firm in viewing nature's gifts in terms of secret messages from heaven. She is also quick to acknowledge human limitation—

> though I do not yet see,
> even in mind, being
> not yet out of time.

But she intimates a pointing gesture of faith. What John saw she is waiting expectantly to see, and the poem beckons the reader to join her.

These are two examples of explicit witness—combining biblical text and nature's text. The latter poem points directly to the living Christ. While she has named "the One," she does not release pictures indiscriminately. To see what she sees one has to look, and look deeply, "with a heart hungry / for meaning." These reflections lead to the crown of God's creation, human-kind, applying to both male and female what Milton's Adam ascribed to Eve,

> fairest of Creation, last and best
> of all God's Works, Creature in whom excell'd
> Whatever can to sight or thought be form'd. (*Paradise Lost* 9.896–98)

In light of the Genesis announcement that humankind reflects the divine image, there is anticipation of a clearer picture of Christ in Avison's poems focusing on people and their activities and actions.

CHAPTER 4

"Come and See"
Creatureliness and Imaging God

> Being human
> what can we do
> but bow, and believe
> now, or when glory
> leaves all he made
> transformed, or stricken.
> ("Nothing Else For It" *AN* 2.257)

In Hopkins's understanding of "selving," he alludes to "more"—a larger role for people than the rest of creation—as he speaks of humanity's capacity to reflect God's image:

> I say more: the just man justices;
> Keeps grace: that keeps all his goings graces;
> Acts in God's eye what in God's eye he is –
> Christ – for Christ plays in ten thousand places.[1]

This ability to "ac[t] in God's eye what in God's eye he [or she] is" is Avison's concern, as well, in her implicit witness, but she expresses her understanding of personhood and creatureliness in a different manner. I suggest three avenues of exploration loosely organized around a repeated motif of pivots

---

1. See Hopkins, "As Kingfishers Catch Fire": "Each mortal thing does one thing and the same: / Deals out that being indoors each one dwells;/ Selves."

in certain lyrics: the pivot of "Old Adam" in "Neverness" (*AN* 1.24–26), the pivot of the old man in "July Man" (*AN* 1.160) and the pivot of the Creator-Redeemer in "On a Maundy Thursday Walk" (*AN* 3.174–75). First, she recognizes the witness of *imago dei* is bound up in creatureliness with its inherent human limits. God's image in people is unfortunately linked with fallenness. Second, an implicit witness is seen in humankind's relational capacities. Shared humanity both as gift and need points to the Creator. Third, the most effective witness to Christ ironically is occasioned by collective and personal failure. God's provision of new creation becomes the visible gift.

THE MIXED REALITY OF *IMAGO DEI* AND FALLENNESS

As the poet draws on the tradition of Western literature and the words of Scripture, she demonstrates an orthodox Christian understanding of the human person as a created being. In the middle of *Concrete and Wild Carrot* is its longest poem, the mythic "Other Oceans" (*AN* 3.146–54), a symphonic performance in seven parts, each a meditation on a given preposition or adverb—on, within, under, when, where, out, after.[2] The account of creation in this first section "ON" (*AN* 3.146) is spare in its anthropomorphized detail:

> When the convulsive earth
> arched under the sea
> its craggy ribs were
> blurted out where reefs had been
> into the golden warmth for a
> fraction of a second of the one
> day that's a thousand years.

There are readily recognizable allusions to both Milton and the Bible, but this accounting for existence is different. The seven days of the biblical account are condensed to "a fraction of a second" and "in the same breath." There is no mention of God in this creation myth—an oddity for a Christian poet. Instead, her economy of allusion evokes additional connection with the Creator—a response from the creature. The "day that's a thousand years" could suggest one psalmist's observation, "For a thousand years in your sight are like yesterday when it is past, or like a watch in the night" (Ps

2. Section 7 "AFTER" of "Other Oceans" was briefly discussed in chapter 2. See Appendix for the complete text of "ON."

90:4), or another's, "a day in thy courts is better than a thousand elsewhere" (Ps 84:10). The miracle of "what had emerged to be / grasses of the field" connects to the frequent reminders in Scripture of a person's flourishing and fading mortality like grass (Ps 90:5–6; Ps 103:15). On the other hand, "grasses of the field" also speaks of Jesus's instruction in his famous Sermon on the Mount, not to worry, because "God clothes the grass of the field" (Matt 6:30), and by extension, will care for his human creation.

In the closing lines of this stanza, Avison uses the word "face" three different ways. "On the face of the earth" is yet again a phrase rooted in the Genesis account of humankind's beginnings—both of good and evil (Gen 6:1; Gen 7:4). She creates a puzzle with "trees and tiny Arctic flowers / alike fac[ing] upwards"— while

> animals
> with velvet paws, or hoofs,
> all seem to look away towards the
> falling-away edge of the earth.[3]

The mystery of the one "who sits above the circle of the earth" (Isa 40:22) is recognizably observing upright creatures from any point. Yet the animals are "look[ing] away towards the / falling-away edge of the earth." The poet may be hearkening back to Beddoes' *Death's Jest-Book* and including the fall and its consequent death sentence in this newly created earth.[4] As a result, the opening lines of the stanza are seen in a new ominous light: earth's "craggy ribs were blurted out" "into the golden warmth" for (only) "a fraction of a second of the one / day that's a thousand years."[5] Avison's third reference to face—

> My face, among these others,
> ours, are not as though
> among these others.

3. "Facing upwards" is reminiscent of Milton's Adam looking up towards the sky with his sudden awareness of his existence (*Paradise Lost* 8.257–58).

4. "Can a man die? Ay, as the sun doth set: / It is the earth that falls away from light" from Beddoes, *Death's Jest-Book* (II.2.39–40) which is the epigraph opening Avison's "The Earth That Falls Away" (*AN* 1.175–84). This longer poem on blindness and sight in her volume *The Dumbfounding* is her first exploration of the theme.

5. It is interesting that C. S. Lewis does a similar thing with his creation story in *The Magician's Nephew* of the Chronicles of Narnia. Before Narnia is an hour old evil has been brought in, the velvet-pawed Aslan tells the children observing, and he insists they must play a part in Narnia's protection and redemption.

—is strangely elusive. Perhaps she is merely acknowledging difference—voluntary and involuntary response to the Creator. On the other hand, there could be judgment inherent in the humans not looking face-upwards in creaturely acknowledgement and not alert to impending doom if they do not. To be "on the face of the earth" is a serious matter.

Even in her earliest "detour into darkness" with its pessimism and resistance to her Christian upbringing, Avison reveals assumptions of creatureliness in her poetic world. In cryptic fashion, the poet announces in "Civility a Bogey or Two Centuries of Canadian Cities" (*AN* 1.66–67):

> To walk the earth
> Is to be immersed,
> Slung by the feet
> In the universe,

and implies someone placed people on the earth, however unceremoniously. Her world is a created world as she evokes Adam's name—whether intentionally historical or mythical (or both)—in her early poem "Neverness Or, The One Ship Beached On One Far Distant Shore" (*AN* 1.24–26):

> Old Adam, with his fistful of plump earth,
> His sunbright gaze on his eternal hill
> Is not historical:
> His tale is never done.

Whether echoing the Genesis account of creation or Milton's *Paradise Lost*, she intimates the glory and privilege of *imago dei*.[6] The nuances of theology, however, contained in her understanding of what it means to be made in the image of God—whether substantive, relational, or functional—are not obvious.[7]

---

6. "Then God said, 'Let us make humankind in our image, according to our likeness; and let them have dominion over the fish of the sea, and over the birds of the air'" (Gen 1:26).
"where the Fiend
Saw undelighted all delight, all kind
Of living Creatures new to sight and strange:
Two of far nobler shape erect and tall,
Godlike erect, with native Honor clad
In naked Majesty seem'd Lord of all,
And worthy seem'd, for in thir looks Divine
The image of thir glorious maker shone,
Truth, Wisdom, Sanctitude severe and pure,
Severe, but in true filial freedom plac't" (*Paradise Lost*, 4.285–94).

7. These are the categories Millard Erickson uses to delineate distinctions between

In "One Rule of Modesty and Soberness"(*AN* 3.86–89), she contrasts the memories of humans to angels, drawing on "Calvin, on angels, *Institutes* I, xiv, 4":

> Our mortal memory structures
> in us what matters – to
> bury it, or
> re-celebrate so as to
> falsify it; we are
> made less than the angels, said the ancient
> poet, who knew.

In "Relating" (*AN* 3.135), she addresses an ant, one of the smallest of creatures, playfully suggesting their common predicament:

> The radii of power
> are focused down and in
> on you and me over our
> warped little shadows; they
> adjust, this midday instant, to
> us, moving.

In "Rising Dust" (*AN* 3.163–64), while discussing a person's physical make-up of largely water, she alludes to "something else besides"—"a vital bond threaded on an / as-if loom out there."[8] In "Leading Questions" (*AN* 3.166), she comments,

> Walking naked in Eden, they
> lived always in the light
> of the holy.

In "WITHIN" (*AN* 3.146–47), the second section of "Other Oceans," the poet intimates humans' efforts to interpret and act on their place in the world:

> Studies by night. By day
> blinks at the intricate
> script of the world [. . .]

---

positions of the theologians from Irenaeus to Aquinas to Luther and Calvin, and then to Brunner and Barth. See Erickson, *Christian Theology*, 510–36. In *The Image of God in Man,* David Cairns elaborates more fully on each theological position.

8. See the opening of chapter 1 for an extensive discussion of this poem.

> Intrudes
> the throb of self selecting self
> out of what was suggestive of a
> singing part. Unravels
> some syllables of the music, in
> withdrawing again.
> Waits [. . . .]

The most detailed and overt of Avison's poems articulating her understanding of creatureliness is the first part of her three-part poem, "Light" (*AN* 2.65–67). The three parts together comprise one of several poems whose altered perspective brings particular insight. In this case, the speaker is looking down from the wing-window of a plane, observing and interpreting both what she sees and how—"the source of light is high / above the plane." The light—both the sun and its source—is the central theme of the poem. "The light has looked on Light," she writes near the end of the first part; as a result, the Light has provided hope and blessing.

> [T]he Pure can bless
> on earth *and* from on high
> ineradicably

is the poem's ending declaration. In this context, looking down from the plane's window she observes people who look like "stick-men" and "plasticine-people" "strewn" like children's playthings:

> The stuff of flesh and bone
> is given, *datum.* Down
> the stick-men, plasticine-
> people, clay-lump children, are strewn,
> each casting shadow in the eye of day.

Then her imagination takes over as she re-creates an experience of receiving the wonder of life in "the breath of delighting." The "clay-lump children" become active and productive and "delighted":

> Then – listen! – I see
> breath of delighting rise from
> those stones the sun touches
> and hear a snarl of breath
> as a mouth sucks air. And with
> shivery sighings – see: they stir

and turn and move, and power

to build, to undermine, is theirs,

is ours.

The poet seems to echo the psalmist's fundamental question, "What are human beings that you are mindful of them, mortals that you care for them" (Ps 8:4) as she ponders these newly living creatures—"[t]he stuff, the breath, the power to move even thumbs / and with them, things: *data*." What do humans do with what has been given?

What is

the harpsweep on the heart for?

What does the constructed power

of speculation reach for?

Each of us casts a shadow in the bewildering day,

an own-shaped shadow only.

The implication from the three parts of the complete poem is a grateful turning to the Light, "look[ing] to the sunblue."

In each of these excerpts Avison is in keeping with Calvin's understanding of the divine image "that the image of God in man consists in the acknowledgement of God's goodness and greatness." David Cairns goes on to explain:

> There is thus a close resemblance between the image of God in the world of nature, and the image in man. In both cases there is a reflection of God's glory back to himself through praise, but inanimate creatures and creatures without reason do this unconsciously, while men do it in gratitude and humility when they acknowledge their complete dependence on God and give him their obedience. . . . As Torrance has pointed out, the picture of a mirror is the governing one in Calvin's mind.[9]

Avison uses the language of light and shadow to emphasize this "reflection of God's glory back to himself." In "Relating" (*AN* 3.135), she speaks of "our / warped little shadows" shared with the ants; in "Leading Questions" (*AN* 3.166) she notes Adam and Eve "lived always in the light"; and in "Light" (*AN* 2.65–67), she observes "clay-lump children," "each casting shadow in the eye of day." In "WITHIN" (*AN* 3.146–47) of "Oceans," she speaks of humankind's complete dependence on God in terms of "blink[ing] at the intricate / script of the world"—again, reflecting back what has been given.

---

9. Cairns, *The Image of God in Man*, 136, 137.

In her understanding of creatureliness, Avison is only too aware of the fall and its effect. In the lyrics above she has readily acknowledged the reality of sin, even while she is talking about the image of God. In "One Rule of Modesty and Soberness" (*AN* 3.86–89), the mortal memory is "re-celebrat[ing] so as to falsify" "what matters." The poem "Leading Questions" (*AN* 3.166) quickly moves to failure:

> Drawn to disobey
> they awoke to shame – and God –
>
> like comprehension of pain,
> of broken as well as good.

In "Light," after the "stick-men" come alive, "suck air," "see," and "turn and move," with their "power to build" they also use their power "to undermine." Like Christian thinkers who have gone before her, she wrestles openly with what it means to be made in God's image, and yet, a sinner. She both understands and articulates the theme of St. Augustine's opening words to his *Confessions*:

> "You are great, Lord, and highly to be praised" (Ps. 47.2): "great is your power and your wisdom is immeasurable" (Ps. 146.5). Man, a little piece of your creation, desires to praise you, a human being "bearing his mortality with him" (2 Cor. 4.10), carrying with him the witness of his sin and the witness that you "resist the proud" (1 Pet. 5.5). Nevertheless, to praise you is the desire of man, a little piece of your creation. You stir man to take pleasure in praising you, because you have made us for yourself, and our heart is restless until it rests in you.[10]

Initially, therefore, Avison's witness is not an unspoiled celebration of imaging God. Her witness to people's sin and God's resistance to pride and the accompanying restlessness of which St. Augustine speaks is what permeates the early collection, even as "Neverness" (*AN* 1.24–26) suggests in its image of the pivot: "We millions hold old Adam in our thoughts / A pivot for the future-past."[11] Adam plays the significant and singular role of pointing

10. St. Augustine, *Confessions*, 3.

11. See Appendix for the complete text of "Neverness." Northrop Frye recognized the importance of this poem early in Avison's publishing career, when in 1957 he suggested that "[e]very good lyrical poet has a certain structure of imagery as typical of him as his handwriting, held together by certain recurring metaphors, and sooner or later he will produce one or more poems that seem to be at the centre of that structure. These poems are in the formal sense his mythical poems, and they are for the critic the imaginative keys to his work." He went on to suggest that "Neverness" is one such

humanity to both glory and failure—both innocence and experience.[12] Adam's image is a reminder of short-lived pleasure and purpose in Eden, followed by expulsion and loss. Avison speaks of this pivot in somber realism as

> a core
>
> Of the one dream that never goads to action
>
> But stains our entrails with nostalgia
>
> And wrings the sweat of death in ancient eyes.

His fall is everyone's fall; "[h]is tale is never done," as people continue to repeat Adam's rebellious pattern. The accompanying nightmare-dream contains only regret and fear. Finally, in this dark and early poem, Avison speaks of a dream of a winding down of history into unending night where this image of Adam must be denied. When this happens, all will fall apart,

---

poem. Preface to an "Uncollected Anthology," 35.

12. Avison is peculiarly single-focused in this portrayal of Adam, departing from Milton's emphasis on Adam's and Eve's relationship shaping the pleasure of the Garden and their fall and subsequent expulsion. When her friend and colleague Al Purdy in his commemorative poem "On first looking into Avison's Neverness," pays tribute to Avison, he notes with his dry humor a peculiar absence in the poem: "lonesome Adam and no Eve." ("On First Looking into Avison's 'Neverness,'" 30). His observation, albeit playful, calls attention to a pattern in Avison's poetry. Most of the time her portraits of humans are truly "man"—i.e. men. Men and boys figure large in the people she notes. Key exceptions are the long poems "The Agnes Cleves Papers" and "The Jo Poems." One can only speculate. In a telephone interview, I queried her about her lack of interest in gender issues and she brushed the question aside. Her attitude toward the recognition of women in language or women's opportunities and corresponding limitations in the marketplace partly reflects her times and its traditional stance of church and home. More important to her as a woman is the prime position of onlooker/observer, without pressures of career opportunities derailing her focus on writing poetry (Telephone interview, April 6, 2004). She begins "A Women's Poem: Now" (AN 3.55) with

Women are breadwinners perforce
when their pay is their sole resource.
Or when couples aspire to arrive
at a house – not a cell in a hive.

These are not comments about women's aspirations of achievement or a challenge about roles of women. When it comes to her understanding of witness, gender is irrelevant.

However, with her keenly observant eye, it is still discomforting that men dominate the landscape of her thinking. For instance, in the children's textbook *History of Ontario* she wrote for Gage Publishers in 1951, there is virtually no mention of women in Ontario's formation. Perhaps it is the instinctive "other" that attracts her in her delineation of character. The reversed "other" (the woman looking through a window at the man) helps her draw the sharp focus and enables her to better understand the self by exploring that "other." Or perhaps it is a necessary distancing perspective, keeping the autobiographical at bay.

imitating Yeats's circling gyres in "The Second Coming." In her later poem in *Winter Sun*, "'The Mirrored Man" (*AN* 1.125–26), she revisits the theme of the pivoting Adam and Eden lost when she writes that

> So now we flee the Garden
> Of Eden, steadfastly.
> And still in our flight are ardent
> for lost eternity.

Like planets who have lost their orbit,

> All of us, flung in one
> Murky parabola,
> Seek out some pivot for significance.

"The Mirrored Man" enacts the restless heart that has not turned to Christ.

In the meantime, "Neverness" contains more than darkness in its pivot Adam. In the same poem she hurtles through the millennia to connect "Old Adam" with "Old Leeuwenhoek," sharing the same excitement of discovery. Adam may be content to hold a "fistful of plump earth," but his progeny want to see and understand what particles make up that dirt. Anton van Leeuwenhoek (1632–1723), pioneer in microbiology, was the first to observe single-celled organisms and "opened up an entire world of microscopic life to the awareness of scientists."[13] In describing the discoverer's excitement Avison imitates the process as she creates the word "ribby" to frame the elation of discovery:

> Old Leeuwenhoek must have had ribby thoughts
> To hoop the hollow pounding of his heart
> Those nights of spring in 1600-odd.

In later poems she continues this theme of discovery and advancement as she introduces other pioneers in science and thought, this time replacing microscope with telescope. Tycho Brahe (1546–1601) and Johannes Kepler (1571–1630), key contributors to the Copernican revolution in science— Brahe for revolutionizing astronomical instrumentation and Kepler for formulating his laws of planetary motion—and Buckminster Fuller (1895–1983), designer of the Dymaxion map of the world and the geodesic dome, are all key figures in Avison's poem "Dispersed Titles" (*AN* 1.55–59).[14] In

13. Waggoner, "Antony van Leeuwenhoek (1632–1723)."

14. Al Van Helden notes in *The Galileo Project* that Tycho Brahe "revolutionized astronomical instrumentation" and "observational practice profoundly." His "observations of the new star of 1572 and comet of 1577 . . . were instrumental in establishing

"The Iconoclasts" (*AN* 1.30), she acknowledges various and peculiar kinds of "explorers"—"[t]he cave-men, Lampman, Lief, the dancing dervish" who

> knew their doom to propagate, create,
> Their wild salvation wrapt within that white
> Burst of pure art whose only promise was
> ferocity in them.[15]

Here poet, explorer, and religious figure join scientists in their human urges—their fierce need to propagate and create.

In one of the last poems of *sunblue* "Creative Hour" (*AN* 2.104), published almost twenty years after "Dispersed Titles" and "The Iconoclasts," the mood is brighter but the irony is deeper as she relativizes these accomplishments of creativity and discovery with the image of a child at play:

> The universe our colouring-book:
>> 'Child, fill it in'? –
> or a waxy page to scribbling shade in, and make
> streaky pictures come plain?

She speaks of the failed, or at least imperfect art of the child/person as

> outlines vanish
> the tentative image fails.
> Chalks smear, all the paint spills,
> creation crumples and curls.

As a result, the person gives up:

the fact that these bodies were above the Moon and that therefore the heavens were not immutable as Aristotle had argued." Kepler, endorsing and supporting Galileo's discoveries, discovered that planets move in elliptical orbits around the sun. Among his accomplishments, he also introduced concepts into our language: "space ship earth" and "synergy" (from "Synergetics"—the "geometry of thinking") (World Transformation "R. Buckminster Fuller").

15. "Dervish" is "a Muslim friar, who has taken vows of poverty and austere life. Of these there are various orders, some of whom are known from their fantastic practices as dancing or whirling" (OED). "Lief Ericson is the Viking/Icelandic explorer credited with landing on North American soil (ca. 1001) before Christopher Columbus and creating a colony, Vinland, now Canada's Newfoundland (Ryne, "Lief Ericson"). Archibald Lampman (1861–99) is one of Canada's earliest poets, one of the "Poets of Confederation," known for his nature poetry.

> What is learned, I unlearn:
>
> and hunt out an art school
>
> that may require a model;
>
> or contribute a membership as an art patron.

By the end of the poem she is stating baldly the misunderstanding of the creaturely role:

> The evasive 'maker'-metaphor,
>
> thank God, under the power of our real common lot
>
> leads stumbling back to what it promised to evade.

The idea that the child has power over his or her elements by the ability to "make" can be an evasion of the greater Creator. Her discovery leads to yet another admission of limitation—but also gift.

> There is no one reviewed, no viewer,
>
> no one of us not creature;
>
> we're apparently at work.   But nothing is made
>
> except by the only unpretentious, Jesus Christ, the Lord.

In the context of *sunblue* this discovery is good news. People are free to energetically embrace the role as "subcreators," with the paradoxical freedom that comes with acknowledgement of creaturely limits.[16]

But in *Winter Sun*, Avison is not yet ready for this admission; rather, she is preoccupied with critique. In "Meeting Together of Poles and Latitudes (in Prospect)" (*AN* 1.73–74), she piles strong verb on verb, echoing John Donne's energy and capturing the intensity of ambition to achieve, to accomplish and to discover.[17] The picture is strangely harsh:

> Those who fling off, toss head,
>
> Taste the bitter morning, and have at it –
>
> Thresh, knead, dam, weld,
>
> Wave baton, force
>
> Marches through squirming bogs,
>
> Not from contempt, but
>
> From thrust, unslakeably thirsty,

16. See J. R. R. Tolkien, "On Fairy-Stories," 66, and C. S. Lewis, "On Three Ways of Writing for Children," 27.

17. Batter my heart, three-personed God; for you
As yet but knock, breathe, shine, and seek to mend;
That I may rise and stand, o'erthrow me, and bend
Your force to break, blow, burn, and make me new.

> Amorous of every tower and twig, and
> Yet like railroad engines with
> Longings for their landscapes (pistons pounding)
> Rock fulminating through
> Wrecked love, unslakeably loving – .

Unsatisfied human desire for achievement keeps people endlessly striving, she concedes; but there are cautionary notes in the dominant metaphor of the railroad engines with "pistons pounding" and "rock fulminating." The unfamiliar and coined constructions, "unslakeably thirsty" and "unslakeably loving," suggest the poet's deep ambivalence towards the price of accomplishment. As a result, the poet presents a jaded picture of modern humanity coping with its own creations.

> *People,* every one with a different world, from
> Supernovae to amoeba in his soul,
> Craving act, and harmony (shebang!).
> Bewildered / Each broods in his own world,

she laments in "Apocalyptics" (*AN* 1.107). "Old Leeuwenhoek's 'ribby thoughts'" (*AN* 1.24–26) could suggest more than excitement. He is discoverer, not creator. The iconoclasts (*AN* 1.30)—"cave-men, Lampman, Lief, the dancing dervish"—"knew their *doom* [emphasis mine] to propagate, create,"

> whose only promise was
> Ferocity in them, thudding its dense
> Distracting rhythms down their haunted years.

In "Dispersed Titles" (*AN* 1.56–57),

> The oak that cracked a quilted tumulus
> and rustled, all through childhood's
> lacy candle-drip of winter

still "wounded with whispers" the great Buckminster. In "Apocalyptics" (*AN* 1.105–08), "[t]he city is a jungle gym." In "Intra-Political" (*AN* 1.97–100), people are reduced to "comestibles"—"boxed, bottled, barreled in rows."

> Games are too earnest.
> these packaged *us*-es
> are to the gamboling of real nourishment
> as mudcake to transmuted sun.[18]

18. This poem sounds very much like the early lines of C. S. Lewis's well-known

These early poems all reveal the poet's deep uneasiness about accomplishments normally applauded.

The poet creates a more disturbing and pointed picture of modern thinking in "The Fallen, Fallen World" (*AN* 1.75–76). In its allusive language, beginning with its title, the lyric becomes a dramatic enactment of the biblical account of the origin of evil. The poet writes as if she were preaching, like Jonathan Edwards, a sermon to herself, or reading Dante's *Inferno* as she pictures open resistance to the sun. "Since Lucifer," the poem reports, fallen creatures—whether revolutionaries, idealists or the learned—have apprehended their "slow sure estrangement from the sun."

> When, breathing murk and apprehension of
> Slow sure estrangement from the sun,
> Night and the withering Arctic wind explore
> The vacant corridors that are allowed
> Us for our enforced passage,
> We are, in snow and sleep's despite,
> Straitly sustained.

For the revolutionaries, she speaks of a poor exchange between "the sun in happier days burnished" and present time "ungalaxied, to centre / Fuel and fume" and "self-consuming, burn." The idealists "in moan and misery / Stray desolate along the steely river." One such rebel

> repent[s]
> That under starlight, dissolute and lovely,
> He to the angel's urgency gave way
> And won a sunless summer for his soul.

The learned—those who share the poet's inclinations—are the most disturbing of all:

> And, some, alas, who from the summit see
> The season's sure resolve, and having sounded
> Dayspring in the Magnificat, and sensed
> The three-day darkness on the eternal's doorstep
> Not once, but more than once [. . . .]

---

sermon "Weight of Glory" where he speaks of people selling themselves short in their aspirations, "like an ignorant child who wants to go on making mud pies in a slum because he cannot imagine what is meant by the offer of a holiday at the sea," 26.

These intellectuals are particularly culpable with their knowledge of the truth of the sun and its favor. Here the metaphor is identified, connected with the Son in his incarnation in the "Magnificat" (Luke 1:46–55) and death and resurrection in "the three-day darkness." The alliterative trio of "see," "sound," and "sense" emphasizes the study, experience, and insight afforded these privileged people. Mary's Song, "The Magnificat," speaks of the mercy available for those who fear God. The hungry are filled with good things; the lowly are lifted up. Conversely, "he has scattered the proud in the thoughts of their hearts. He has brought down the powerful from their thrones" and he has "sent the rich away empty" (Luke 1:50–53). The learned have "sounded / Dayspring," have probed the depths, and have seen all of the consequences connected with turning towards the sun/Son or away from Him. They have "sensed" or intuited the meaning of "the three-day darkness on the eternal's doorstep." They have some idea what the cross meant to the Son and what its requirements are for them. But now the learned reveal their foolishness in their fallenness: "[N]ow are but weary / Because the hope is certain." "They, stubborn, on the frozen mountain cling / Dreaming of some alternative to spring"!

> Yet where the junco flits the sun comes still
> Remote and chilly, but as gold,
> And all the mutinous in their dungeons stir,
> And sense the tropics, and unwitting wait.
> Since Lucifer, waiting is all
> A rebel can. And slow the south returns.

The connection with Lucifer is sobering in his lowest icy circle of Dante's hell, but the closing lines also carry with them the glimmers of hope and rescue with the poet's sense of a slow return of the south and a sense of the tropics.

In delineating human limits, articulating rebellion, and voicing her own sense of dissatisfaction with no clear "pivot for significance" (AN 1.125–26), Avison achieves an emerging witness in pointing to the need for intervention and salvation. Even here, in Winter Sun's shadows, in the closing stanza of "Intra-Political" (AN 1.97–100), the poet gives readers a glimpse of the vision that will be full blown in later poetry:

> If with dainty stepping, we unbox ourselves
> while still Explosion slumbers,
> putting aside mudcakes,
> the buying, selling, trucking, packaging

> of mudcakes,
>
> sun-stormed, daring to gambol,
>
> might there not be an immense answering
>
> of human skies?

She evokes George Herbert's "transfiguring board / *Did sit and eat*" from his "Love (III)," hinting at the ultimate expression of creatureliness.[19] The poet implies recognition of the requirement of humility in acknowledging sin and submission in accepting the Creator-Redeemer's act of hospitality—the simultaneous Eucharist and cross.

THE WITNESS IN PEOPLE'S RELATIONAL CAPACITIES

Avison returns to the image of the coloring book of *sunblue's* "Creative Hour" (*AN* 2.104) years later in "Present from Ted" (*AN* 3.122–23). This time, however, there has been a shift in its meaning.

> The pictures that emerged
>
> were outlines? I remember
>
> only the paper, and the wonder of it [. . . .]
>
> There were no colours, were there?

the poet muses. But her memory and imagination have transformed the "no colours" to "glorious colours," "deepening colours, / patterns that keep emerging." In fact,

> Locked in the picture is
>
> missing the quality of the analogy of
>
> morning light
>
> and the delighted holder of the paintbrush.

The morning light and her delight suggest humanity's shared position with the rest of creation. She is not finished remembering, however. "Locked in the picture" and its analogy is also the poem's last line, which seems like an afterthought, but is actually its center: "and who gave him the book, and where he found it." The relationship is what matters, as the title of the poem suggests.

In another poem in the same volume, "Cycle of Community" (*AN* 3.156–57), Avison emphasizes the sense of shared community in

19. Love bade me welcome: yet my soul drew back [. . . .]
You must sit down, sayes Love, and taste my meat:
So I did sit and eat (Herbert, "Love (III)").

the hum

of a world going on,

untroubled by the silent witness, sky.

The poet explains the experience of walking on a city street in "[m]id-morning paraffin film over the / dayshine," and becoming aware of city sounds—the "little clanks and whirrs / out there." Her response to what she hears is one of tender identification with her fellow citizens and an acknowledgement that collectively they have a voice "to / open a bud of tremulous hearing":

We here are silent. Yet being

drawn into, with, each

creature, each machine-work

thump, each step, faraway bark,

buzz, whine, rustle, etc.

goes to give our city

a voice, dampered by distance;

serves, through outer

windless openness of skywash, to

open a bud of tremulous hearing.

This connection with another person that Avison conveys is a more subtle and implicit witness. The poet both senses and embodies in her verse humankind's relational capacities to image the triune God, an understanding that some modern theologians assert (in their own ways)—among them Brunner and Barth.[20] C. S. Lewis assumes this dynamic image in his distinction between what he calls gift- and need-love in his work *The Four Loves*. Lewis uses the language of contrasting "nearness by likeness" and "nearness by approach" to explain one's participation in divine love:

Hence, as a better writer has said, our imitation of God in this life—that is, our willed imitation as distinct from any of the likenesses which He has impressed upon our natures or

20. Erickson interprets Barth's later thinking on the image of God as "consisting not only in the vertical relationship between human and God, but also in the horizontal relationship between humans. The image is not something a human is or does. Rather, the image is related to the fact that God willed into existence a being that, like himself, can be a partner" (Erickson, *Christian Theology*, 525). Cairns speaks of Brunner's "Human I-Thou relation": "In his own being, the triune God is love; he is creator in his relation to the world. And man's true being, when it corresponds to God's own being, as God's image on earth, is a being bound to his fellow men in love" (Cairns, *The Image of God in* Man, 156).

states—must be an imitation of God incarnate: our model is the Jesus, not only of Calvary, but of the workshop, the roads, the crowds, the clamorous demands and surly oppositions, the lack of all peace and privacy, the interruptions. For this, so strangely unlike anything we can attribute to the Divine life in itself, is apparently not only like, but is, the divine life operating under human conditions.[21]

Avison reinforces the "Jesus . . . of the workshop, the roads, the crowds" in her empathetic sketches of ordinary people in their commonplace interactions. In one poem, "[a] boy alone out in the court / Whacks with his hockey-stick" ("Thaw" *AN* 1.92). In another,

After the surprising *coup* at a late luncheon meeting

the young man shifting for green concludes

the future makes his bitten thumb the fake ("September Street" *AN* 1.131).

In yet another poem a jarring picture disturbs: "[s]carred – beyond what plastic surgery / could do,"

he prows his life through

the street's flow and wash

of others' looks ("Scar-face" *AN* 2.78).

Blunt critique inserts some soft humor:

The fellow in the library who said

he was 'researching a

poem': you just

feel he is likely no great shakes ("Edging Up on the Writing" *AN* 2.205).

Here the observer reflects on common human feelings.

The divine image is more vivid as people express their desire for connection with one another. In the humorous observation, "Walking Behind, en Route, in Morning, in December" (*AN* 1.215), the poet notes, "This man is not entirely / ,by himself, satisfactory," calling attention to a seemingly out of place comma at the beginning of a line, nudging awkwardly the first word of the new line. She goes on to describe the limitations of clothes, shoes, and hair. Somehow at the sight of "his topcoat spli[t] at the / unbuttoned slit and / in the wind," she concludes,

---

21. Lewis, *The Four Loves*, 11.

> I admit that this man, since he is
> *not* by himself, is a
> one, is satisfactory.

In her wordplay she is noting her connection with him. The man is satisfactory—is a "one" in his particularity, but also not alone because she is walking behind, noticing his inherent inadequacies. She speaks in "The World Still Needs" of that "communal cramp of understanding" (*AN* 1.79–80). In "The Agnes Cleves Papers" (*AN* 1.132–43), the narrator struggles to articulate the experience of love—or almost love:

> One evening, just a year or two ago,
> The simple penetrating force of love
> Redeemed me, for the last perhaps. I've seldom dared, since
> to approach that.

"How for joy Mr. Jollyben cried" in "Diminuendo" (*AN* 1.36–37) is the story of loss and diminishment denied by the man obviously in pain, but compensation comes in the notation "(He said it was for joy.)" by the sensitive listener. Then there is the poignant picture of the widow who sees her husband's coat on an indigent man: "Still, he had his coat, / and she, the echoing years" ("Balancing Out" *AN* 3.130).

In "To Counter Malthus" (*AN* 3.72), Avison reacts to disturbing implications of the ideas of the theorist Thomas Malthus (1766–1834) in his "Essay on Population" (1798).[22] In her wordplay she constructs either a reply to the theoretical statistician, the "counter Malthus," or a challenge, countering Malthus's argument to anyone hearing it:

> None of us in this so
> burdened earth has known
> how to live, let alone
> who is too many.

This counting of persons and food supply is not a legitimate exercise, she protests. In the zeal to analyze and solve the practical questions of existence, Avison herself counters that human boundaries can be surpassed. In that

---

22 As Malthus seeks to establish the "perfectibility of society," he theorizes that unchecked population growth always exceeds the means to feed that population. He suggests that the world's disasters of disease and starvation are positive checks to overpopulation. There can also be more intentional "preventive" checks of population control. The sophisticated nuances of his argument are not emphases Avison appreciates. She is responding to the fundamental de-personalizing of humanity in the concept.

over-reaching, the very Person who gives sustenance and meaning to each person's unique life is missed:

> Presence, each day
> afresh, you give a
> purifying signal to
> sting us alive.

In the face of that reality—"Presence" implying the personhood of the Creator-Sustainer of persons—the proper life questions are not being asked. Her compassion moderates and alters Malthus's calculations of the masses of humanity:

> Vast territories and seashores
> still bear these thronging
> strangers,

but she exclaims, "May none die / without somebody caring." Like a post-script, she acknowledges, "To know even one other is / costly. And being known." Again, the delayed thought in the new line introduces a surprise. "Being known" throws the observation on the potentially self-serving theorist who has seemingly overlooked the fact that he is one of the "too many" and someone needs to care for him too. Ironically and graciously, "Someone" does, Avison gently asserts. While illustrating her earlier wry observation that "[t]he city is a jungle gym," in "Apocalyptics" (*AN* 1.105–8), she playfully describes the people climbing its bars, including those who penetrate the mysteries of earth's workings:

> Physicists have broken through; some are dismayed to find
> The new air they inhabit
> They share with poets.

If physicist and poet co-inhabit the same space, interrupting and disturbing one another with their reflections, the poets provide that essential reminder of humanity. She has played that role in countering Malthus.

In her appreciation of the human person Avison can recall Adam not only in his grandeur and strength, but in his potential frailty and latent fragility—in short, his creatureliness. The poet of the city experiences all the variety of the city's people, not the least, the visibly indigent, and one of their representatives speaks for all. In *The Dumbfounding's* "July Man" (*AN* 1.160), she creates the memorable picture of

Old, rain-wrinkled, time-soiled, city-wise, morning man
whose weeping is for the dust of the elm-flowers
and the hurting motes of time.[23]

Here he is—"in this grass-patch, this city-gardener's place"—a limited, ex-
posed and exposing garden, resembling Eden not at all. "In the sound of the
fountain / you rest, at the cinder-rim, on your bench." As she notes both the
person and his place of rest, Avison introduces the motif of pivots again:

The rushing river of cars
makes you a stillness, a pivot, a heart-stopping
blurt, in the sorrow
of the last rubbydub swig.

The man is a picture of humanity in all its creatureliness, a visible reminder of
the outcome of one's many addictions that threaten to overcome any and all.
    The old July man, like Adam initially, is alone. He is the "heart-stop-
ping" picture not only of addictions and failure, but isolation and loneliness:
"the searing, and / stone-jar solitude lost." From the distance of the "rushing
river of cars" he is a "stillness" and sorrow to the observer, but up close
(literally, or in the imagination), he is also "wonder (for good now) and /
trembling." There is a gentle and barely perceptible and surprising turn in
the poem, however.

The too much none of us knows
is weight, sudden sunlight, falling
on your hands and arms, in your lap,
all, all, in time,

Avison sighs. The lines are predictably ambiguous. The one in the rushing
traffic seeing "the July man" as a pivot acknowledges there is "too much
none of us knows." There is an invisible curtain of privacy concealing from
the viewer the man's own personal history of human struggle that has
brought him to this lonely place. The delay of the completion of the thought
"is weight" transferred to the next line is equally uncertain. In fact, the next
line connects that weight with "sudden sunlight, falling" logically making
no sense since light has no weight. However, there is witness to some hope,
however faint, reminiscent of many of Avison's other poems evoking the
sun. In the specificity of sunlight falling on hands and arms and lap, the
"pivot, a heart-stopping / blurt" has been particularized, and hence, cared

23. See Appendix for a complete and uninterrupted version of the poem.

for by both the One who sees and draws people into relationship, and the observant poet with parallel compassion.

THE WITNESS FROM HUMAN NEED

In their frailty and fallenness, Avison's pivots of "Old Adam" and her "'July Man" seem to be sorry representative witnesses to God's presence in the world. It is difficult to reconcile theological descriptions of God's image in persons with the blatant disregard for that reality in human conduct and practice. As part of his explanation of God's image in creation, Jürgen Moltmann suggests in his monograph *God in Creation*, "God is present in human beings. 'He appears wherever the human being appears.'[24] The human being is God's indirect manifestation on earth. To be an image of something always means letting that something appear, and revealing it."[25] Avison notes, in seeming contrast, humanity's weakness, limitation, and capacities to destroy.

In her poem "Known" (*AN* 2.179), her contribution to the *festschrift* in honor of the American poet Denise Levertov, she presents two observers scanning passenger lists after an airplane crash:

> eyes dart
> along, down, till at last we can
> relax: this horror was not to the heart.

The second observer has a different response:

> Oh, but His eyes are on
> the passenger list too;
> every mourning child tonight's well known;
> their dead He, nearest, knew.

She ends the stanza with its miniature theodicy, in subdued quietness: "for Him this horror is real, and to the heart." To be human means "[o]ur horizons stop at those we know / so we can bear it." In contrast, the divine observer has unbounded capacity to absorb everyone's pain:

> His [limits] not at what we know,
> compassing our sheer-edge-of-nothing panic
> and more; He though in peace and power, knows pain
> for time and space, Whom these cannot contain.

24. Moltmann is quoting W. H. Schmidt, *Die Schöpfugsgeschichte der Priester-schrift*, 2nd ed. See *God in Creation*, 28.

25. Ibid.

At the fundamental level of human sympathy, then, people fail to image God in his capacity to love and care for all.

There is more than passive failure, Avison avers. "We are despoilers" (*AN* 3.36); We leave "detritus" (*AN* 3.23; *AN* 3.28) and "ditch litter" (*AN* 1.62) everywhere. "My kind out there sullies / it all" (*AN* 3.36). She names the obvious damage of pollution from our technological capabilities in "The Ecologist's Song" (*AN* 2.266):

> Sometimes, where once the sky bent brown
> above a creased doeskin of new earth
> pillars plunge upwards, and through the thinning air
> the pelting hail sweeps down.

Human beings "muddle, mangle, despoil, degrade" (*MD* 29–31). The urban landscape is particularly affected:

> Sufferer of cities, hear me for
> green pastures are
> everywhere despoiled (*MD* 77–78).

Human relationships at both micro and macro levels reveal strain, tension, and a tendency towards destruction. The conflicts start over minor dilemmas such as the predicament outlined in the ironic title "Peace and War" (*AN* 2.253):

> A sharp-chinned boy
> in the automat
> tried the ice-cream bars
> but none came back
> though his coin went in.
> He asked at the counter.
> Said the counter-man, No,
> I've got bars in the freezer
> but I'll not hand one over
> till you pay me too.
>
> Should the boy go away?
> Who should say should?
> What makes the counterman so mad?

The child's conflict with an adult moves to larger adult tensions. "Tut-tuttery today / fits politics" ("In Our 'Little Nests'" *AN* 3.176), the poet observes. Raising the ante, she comments,

> Our own skills and
> achievements are imprisoned by
> managed relationships
> no one can manage quite
> ("Alternative to Riots But All Citizens Must Play," *AN* 3.179–82).

Even songs celebrate humanity's disharmony and lack of mercy and kindliness. "Inclemency," she calls it:

> Why is the source of song when we
> gather in the gloaming, or indoors
> when winter snarls and hurls
> rattling grains of snow against the shutters,
> why is a peaceable company nourished on the
> songs of railroad strikers, of
> shipwrecks, disastrous cyclones, fires
> engulfing whole communities
>
> as the strumming storyteller
> renders these? ("Songs" *MD* 32–33).

Nowhere is this attitude of pitilessness more obvious than in postures of war. In "*horror humani*" (*MD* 73–74), whether in today's Sudan or yesterday's "quiet places across the / Channel" from Flanders' fields

> the
> private reader relishing his
> book somewhere in
> his window chair is
> this very moment – O why? –
> *kaputt*. The air-raid
> 'achieved its purpose.'

In another poem in *Momentary Dark*, "Not Words. Alone" (*MD* 5), she changes perspective on human conflict and war, diminishing in Lilliputian style the consequences of human suffering. In "the dark of / outerness," the poet posits, our world's angry exchanges may be merely "squeakings and dots." With irony she laments,

<pre>
                                              may
     all the myriad noises of our
     everyday doings never,
     may they never give us away
     out there, tell to a
     universe who we are.
</pre>

There is perhaps no more vivid understatement in Avison's entire collection of poems then her dry conclusion to "Not Words. Alone":

> Or at least
> let's tune these up together
> a little, first.

While war and peace, framed as a child's conflict over an ice-cream bar, have been reduced here in the "dark of / outerness" to mere disharmonious sounds, the grave consequences, nevertheless, have not been negated.

Collective failure is painfully mirrored in the personal in *sunblue's* "Absolute" (*AN* 2.92). The poem images Lewis's observation "that our whole being by its very nature is one vast need; incomplete, preparatory, empty yet cluttered, crying out for Him who can untie things that are now knotted together and tie up things that are still dangling loose."[26] Avison puts a face on the possibility of the "worst there is / at the core of it" for any person to acknowledge:

> Right here on earth
> I've known One Person who would
> see me in the worst there is
>
> at the core of it – *see* me
>   e.g. the mocker making a frail rabbi
>   hop on the Warsaw pavement   yes   at the worst
>   would see me
>   lazing and lording it over him or e.g. nobody
>   making me do it
>   willing to hop on the pavement
>   fearful nobody really
>   making me
>   or e.g. would see me

26. Lewis, *The Four Loves*, 9.

> turning away from both in
> order
> to be beautifully alone –.

All parties in the confrontation are individually guilty and individually seen
by the "One Person" who the poet understands

> would
> nevertheless care
> enough to be past
> tears [. . .]

That same Person is one

> who means risking
> tireless loss
> in a real world   e.g.

> along the lake road with evening pale already
> and nowhere to turn off:
> right here on earth.

In this terrifying poem is a witness emerging from human sin. Failed crea-
turely response to other creatures and failed reflection of the Creator elicits
the remedy in the Redeemer-creature relationship—a motif that is repeated
numerous times in Avison's lyrics. On the one hand, "My kind out there
sullies / it all"; on the other, "[y]et we, providing an unlikely / context for
miracle" (AN 3.36), point to humanity's rescue and the person who achieves
it. As Cairns interprets Calvin's well-known antitheses from the Institutes:

> It at once becomes clear how closely in his thought our knowl-
> edge of God is interwoven with our knowledge of ourselves . . .
> the blessings which we owe to God, including the chief blessing
> of our very existence, should drive us in gratitude to think of
> him, while our very feeling of ignorance and depravity should
> remind us of our need of him.[27]

People provide more than context for Christ's intervention. Awareness of
failure becomes a peculiar but often effective form of witness, reminding a
person to act on that knowledge.

This Redeemer-creature relationship is announced in another
Creator-creature story in "On a Maundy Thursday Walk" in Concrete and

27. Cairns, The Image of God in Man, 134.

Wild Carrot (*AN* 3.174–75), published decades apart from "Neverness" and "Mirrored Man." The poem contains the third reference to a pivot, this time connected to the new Adam.[28] The title suggests its connection with the Christ-story of the Gospels in its reference to Maundy Thursday, the familiar observance of the Christian church during Holy Week, involving preparatory rituals in anticipation of Good Friday. The connection between Creator and Redeemer is immediately established between the title of the poem and its opening statement:

> The Creator was
> walking by the sea, the
> Holy Book says.

The witness of Scripture is asserted, and still in the same line, the initial witness of Christ (without being named as such) is established.

> Who can imagine it, sullied
> as our senses are? Faulty as are even our
> most excellent makings?

the poet asks. Sullied imagination is contrasted with imagination that can and did create

> At a word –
> the hot smell of sunned rock, of
> the sea, the sea, the sound of lapping, bird calls,
> the sifting sponginess of sand
> under the sandals, delicate
> April light – all, at a word
> had become this almost-
> overwhelming loveliness.

It is at this point in the poem that Avison provides a vivid emotional connection between "the walker-by-the sea," the Creator and Artist himself, and the sharers of the poem:

> Surely the exultation –
> The Artist

---

28. "For since death came through a human being, the resurrection of the dead has also come through a human being; for as all die in Adam, so all will be made alive in Christ. . . . Thus it is written, 'The first man, Adam, became a living being'; the last Adam became a life-giving spirit; . . . the first man was from the earth, a man of dust; the second man is from heaven" (1 Cor 15: 21–22, 45, 47).

> Himself immersed in
> His work, finding it flawless –
> intensified the so soon
> leaving (lifted out of
> mortal life for good
> forever).

They experience the same particulars of the natural environment of sun and sea. More poignant, He must die; so will the readers and the writer of the poem. Theological challenge has been set aside for reflection on mortality.

> That too eludes
> us who disbelieve that we
> also shall say goodbye to
> trees and cherished friends and
> sunsets and crunching snow
> to travel off
> into a solo death.

The common death fears

> that mak[e] me sweat with vertigo
> On this peculiar shelf /
> Of being ("November 23" *AN* 1.86)

add to the understanding of the intensity of the experience for the Creator to subject "the perfection of / created Being" to "go under / its Maker, and us all" (*AN* 3.174–75). It is at this point Avison reintroduces the pivot-image—this time, her picture of Good Friday's cross:

> How much more, that
> (suffering this
> creation to go under
> its Maker, and us all)
> He, the Father of love, should stake it all
> On a sufficient
> Indeed on an essential pivot.

The connection of Creator and creature is taken to the extreme in the story of the cross. It is not just the connection between the old and new Adam that brings awe to the reader, but the insertion of the cross in all its brutal physicality—"should stake it all"—as the necessary link for a rescue and restoration of the "millions" immured in the "nostalgia" and "sweat of death" in the picture of "Neverness" (*AN* 1.24–26). In its context of reflections on the goodness and loveliness of creation, the pleasure of the Artist and the wistful sadness of leaving, the pivot stands larger in its profound significance. As a result, the image is jarring as it transcends the surface of the poem. In a strange way, this irony heightens the demand for the reader to turn—as a pivot suggests—from the creation to its Redeemer.

A NECESSARY CODA FOR CREATURES

Mortality, of course, is the ultimate in limitation and creatureliness and the ultimate consequence of sin. Avison does not evade its reality; in fact, the theme of death runs through the pages of the poet's lyrics. Early on in *Winter Sun* she introduces the inevitable in the picture of the "little clay house" in "Death" (*AN* 1.81). The tight construction of the single-sentence lyric implies the swiftness of its arrival; at the same time, the multiple images of wet and wind, trains, bells, foghorn imply the busy environment that forestalls the event:

> I ask you how can it be thought
> That a little clay house
> Could stop its door
> And stuff its windows forevermore
> With the wet and the wind and the wonderful grey
> Blowing distracted in
> Almost night
> And trains leaving town
> And nine o'clock bells
> And the foghorn blowing far away
> And the ghastly spring wind blowing
> Through thin branches and
> Thin houses and
> Thin ribs
> In a quick sift of
> Precious terrible coldness?

"Death has us glassed in," she notes in a later poem "A Lament" (*AN* 2.38). Again,

> When you crawled over the ice to the crest
> and there was the deer the
> wolves had torn
> you had forbearance in the blast
> and blank of fear,

she tropes in "To a Fact-facer" (*AN* 2.231).

The intellectual and emotional acknowledgement takes on the clothing of acute personal mourning in *No Time* as she copes with the deaths of people close to her and of fellow poets and writers. These include the elegiac "Jo Poems" (*AN* 2.114–38); "Just Left *or* The Night Margaret Laurence Died" (*AN* 2.149); "For Milton Acorn" (*AN* 2.163); "My Mother's Death" (*AN* 2.170–78); "It Bothers Me to Date Things 'June the 9th'" (*AN* 2.225); "For bpn (circa 1965)" (*AN* 2.240). In *Momentary Dark's* "Never Alone" (*MD* 79), she speaks of memories of Thanksgiving and Christmas "festivals" "recollected through a haze of grave- / side standing." Later, she writes, "the flourishing trees / deep-bosomed" are

> like comforting cousins at a
> mourner's wake, that other
> family festival.

The closing poem, "Shelters" (*MD* 80–88), of this last collection echoes the same theme:

> When it is dark although
> the cemetery is in
> our blindly self-obliterating
> city, the trees
> gather, encircle
> benches and grassy places.

It is in the context of this particular kind of darkness—this "momentary darkness"—that the poet inserts a gentle and suggestive witness. In her oblique fashion she points away from humankind's limitation and need to the promise of fulfillment and newness:

> In here, looking up, the starry
> night is barely
> visible; yet its scent of *far*
> breathes gently.

In "Bereavement and Postlude (Remembering Angela Bowering)" (*MD* 21), she frames the hope in terms of sight instead of scent: "On the far shore, see? away over, *there*: / some little village twinkles down to bedtime."

Vision in Avison's poems undergoes many permutations, as her reflections on mortality suggest, but the end result points in the same direction—away from the self and towards the light. For example, in the collection *Not Yet But Still*, published just before Avison turned 80, an altered perspective seems to be suggested. The epigraph from a poem of the Canadian poet Eli Mandel, "*The sun a cataract in a blinding sky . . .*" signals, on the one hand, the familiar theme of the sun's dominance in Avison's poetry, but on the other, it suggests a subtle shift.[29] The cataract could have several meanings for the poet: a downpour or a large waterfall; or an affliction of old age—opacity of the lens of the eye; or both. What does a person see when the seeing is difficult? What does she hear when hearing dwindles? What is present in the mind's eye? In the diminution, there is also clarity—a second seeing, a looking again that brings new energy and hope.

In the opening poem of *Not Yet But* Still, "Old Woman at a Winter Window" (*AN* 3.15), the speaker of the poem adopts the posture of one most vulnerable.[30] Here is an aged woman confined indoors by icy winter weather to staring out through a mere "frosted pane." From her limited and potentially distorted window she reports what she sees, reflecting not limitation, but expansiveness. She, in her small space, looks out at the "immensity." The image of "the glittering quartz of the air" suggests both something to be attracted to and something to fear: "a congealing It," she imagines, "encroaching ice." Only the "'tiny streamers from valiant chimneys down along the valley" offer her temporary hope in her shared participation with others who do battle with nature:

> We claim these square ceilings and walls
> and floor from the immensity
> as all that have, for us,
> meaning, against the encroaching ice.

It is a bleak vision from that winter window. But the closing stanza transforms the vision and releases the speaker from her sense of vulnerability to an attitude of hope: "The encroaching ice"

---

29. The epigraph is not included in the final Collected Poems, *Always Now*, Vol. III.

30. "Old Woman at a Winter Window" was introduced in chapter 1.

somehow
signals another space, a fearful,
glorious amplitude.

The particulars of experience and vision are not the only and final reality. This "fearful, glorious amplitude"—this capaciousness, completeness, plenitude, richness—is another space awaiting the watcher at the window. The religious dimension is subtly introduced, reversing the limited acceptance of the woman's mortality and hinting instead at her anticipated immortality.[31] The closing two-word line "glorious amplitude" functions as a delightful surprise. The event seems intimate, imminent, and intuitive of a release from the confinement of inactivity and mere watching. It also signals an end to reading signs in the created world—both nature and human nature. The beckoning to "come and see" has been finally realized.

31. St. Paul's comment on the resurrection body of the Christian believer is hovering in the background of this poem: "Listen, I will tell you a mystery! We will not all die, but we will all be changed. . . . For this perishable body must put on imperishability, and this mortal body must put on immortality. When this perishable body puts on imperishability, and this mortal body puts on immortality, then the saying that is written will be fulfilled: "Death has been swallowed up in victory"" (1 Cor 15:51–54).

CHAPTER 5

"Come and See"
"Truth Radiantly Here"

> Today the blueness burns
> Inbetween new greens and space's
> Soundless blackness.
> Yet we even now
> Discern more, cry:
> No, lovely as May is
> We would hear more
> ("In Season and out of Season" *AN* 3.69–71).

Near the end of Milton's *Paradise Lost* when the archangel Michael is sent to expel Adam and Eve from the Garden of Eden, he first takes Adam up to a high hill where he "sets before him in vision what shall happ'n till the Flood" (11.Argument). Then he pauses "[A]etwixt the world destroy'd and world restor'd" and explains to Adam a shift in manner and method of his prophetic witness to the redemption of the now fallen creation:

> Much thou hast yet to see, but I perceive
> Thy mortal sight to fail; objects divine
> Must needs impair and weary human sense:
> Henceforth what is to come I will relate,
> Thou therefore give due audience, and attend (12.3, 8–12).

165

Whatever dramatic, philosophical, and theological reasons may be suggested in this narrative transition, for sure, an alternative form of witness is announced. "Thou therefore give due audience, and attend" echoes Jesus's concern for active listening emphasized in all four Gospels. In the Parable of the Sower, recorded in the Synoptic Gospels, the two senses, hearing and sight, merge as Jesus explains why he speaks in parables: "'seeing they do not perceive, and hearing they do not listen, nor do they understand'" (Matt 13:13).[1] On the other hand, Jesus commends the disciples for the two senses working in tandem: "But blessed are your eyes, for they see, and your ears, for they hear" (Matt 13:16). John's Gospel, too, refers to hearing as much as seeing. When the resurrected Jesus reveals himself to the doubting Thomas in one of the closing scenes of the book, he implies the priority of the word in his words, "Have you believed because you have seen me? Blessed are those who have not seen and yet have come to believe" (John 20:29).

This emphasis on hearing and word corroborates Ricoeur's observation cited earlier that "testimony is . . . found in an intermediary position between a statement made by a person and a belief assumed by another on the faith of the testimony of the first."[2] Margaret Avison can be said to "see" and beckon her readers to "come and see" with her in her poetry; but she has also received the testimony of other witnesses, particularly the witnesses in and of Scripture and has believed, and hence, speaks of what she has heard—what she has interpreted based on the testimony of the text. She suggests this blurring of terms in "When We Hear a Witness Give Evidence" (*AN* 2.168). "Who heard the angels' song?" she queries, calling attention to verbal content in the evidence of the poem's title. But the aural and visual come together a few lines later: "A few heard the angels shine."

Paradoxically, this witness dependent on language and text is more direct and specific about the One to whom it points than the witness of creation and human nature. On the one hand, as Ellul emphasizes, the word is "the most fragile agent" with its "blessed uncertainty" and "thick haze of discourse."[3] On the other, he insists, "Only the word can convey the Word of God, the sole means God used to reveal himself to us." Ellul offers his

1. Mark 4:1–20; Matt 13:3–23; Luke 8:4–18.

2. Ricoeur, *Essays on Biblical Interpretation*, 123. See chapter 2.

3. *The Humiliation of the Word*, 41, 18, 19. Ellul uses a vivid image from nature to explain the ambiguity and uncertainty inherent in language: "[Language] takes its place in the center of an infinitely delicate spider's web, whose central structure is fine, rigorous, and dense. As you move away from the center, the web becomes larger and distended, until it reaches incoherence, at its edge, where it sends off threads in every direction. Some of these threads go a great distance, until they arrive at the invisible spots where the web is anchored. This complex web is a marvel which is never the same, not for me at different points in time nor for another person," 18.

explanation, conceptualizing the central metaphor *Logos*, the "Word made flesh," informing key poems in Avison's collection when he writes:

> When I say that language normally deals with Truth rather than Reality, I only mean that there are two orders of knowledge, two kinds of references we use as human beings. There are references to the concrete, experienced reality around us, and others that come from the spoken universe. . . . We derive meaning and understanding from language, and it permits us to go beyond the reality of our lives to enter another universe.[4]

The hinting and hovering suggested in the poet's perceptions and interpretations of reality are given over to the signs pointing to God's presence and activity announced in the biblical text's fundamental declaration—God speaks.

It makes sense, therefore, to take seriously Avison's interest in the text of the Bible. The boxes full of the poet's Bible study notes preserved in her archives suggest not only a consistent and frequent habit of systematic reading, but a decision to maintain a private record of that reading not ultimately shielded from the public. At the same time, the poems that emerge from that base of reading are not study notes, but organic meditations that take on a life of their own. Poems formed around biblical texts reveal an eclectic collection ranging from the beginning to the end of the Scriptures. While this diverse choice of texts from the larger text of Scripture seems random, the narrative core of the Bible's account of creation, fall, redemption, and new creation emerges in often startling fashion, and hence, points to a dimension of Avison's unique contribution to Christian witness. While the poems demonstrate the poet's ease in ranging across the Scriptures, blurring distinctions between individual stories and their parts and inserting questions and allusions remotely suggested in individual texts, there is, nevertheless, a discernible logic in Avison's method of reading the Bible. With a paradigm of witness in the divisions I propose, the poet demonstrates "a reading of Scripture that takes place in faith"[5]: (1) She begins by announcing the witness of the Word, modeled after the Prologue to John's Gospel. (2) She connects Old and New Testaments with surprising typological links particularly focused on the Eucharist. (3) She reports the Christ story in varying literary forms of parable, vignette, Pauline analysis and fusion of literary traditions. (4) Her witness, like the New Testament witness, ultimately leads to Christ's resurrection.

---

4. Ibid., 107, 22–23.
5. Williams *On Christian Theology*, 56.

JOHANNINE WITNESS OF THE WORD

I concur with Ernest Redekop that "Avison's reading of the Bible really begins with the Gospel of John."[6] Her poetry often probes the mystery of the multiple meanings of Word/words as has already been noted in her miniature poem "The Word" (*AN* 2.220).[7] The cryptic and hidden referent of the poem's compact sentence is less oblique in three other lyrics in the same volume referring to the Johannine motif of the incarnate Word: "Meditation on the Opening of the Fourth Gospel" (*AN* 2.148), "The Bible to Be Believed" (*AN* 2.62–63) and "Listening" (*AN* 2.64).

"Meditation on the Opening of the Fourth Gospel" from *No Time* is a reading of the rich and complex Prologue to John's Gospel (John 1:1–18), where the Evangelist sets forth the mystery of the incarnation in majestic sweep.[8] His words echo the words of Genesis, but they prefigure creation: "In the beginning was the Word, and the Word was with God, and the Word was God. He was in the beginning with God" (John 1:1–2). *Logos* or Word is the name, the concept, by which John's readers are to understand "the only Son, who is close to the Father's heart, who has made him known" (John 1:18). The Gospel writer "wants a term that carries thought nearer to the heart of all reality," William Temple suggests. "He finds it in this word 'Logos,' which alike for Jew and Gentile represents the ruling fact of the universe, and represents that fact as the self-expression of God."[9] "Untense-able Being," Avison exclaims, calling attention to the Word as act, as she begins her poem, "spoken / for our understanding."

The Gospel writer continues, "What has come into being in him was life, and the life was the light of all people. The light shines in the darkness, and the darkness did not overcome it" (John 1:3–5). Further down in the text of the Prologue, the writer announces in several ways this joining of heaven and earth with the arrival of "the true light"—"the Word." "And the Word became flesh and lived among us," he declares in verse 14. Avison responds confidently, pointing back to the text of the Evangelist,

> speaking forth the 'natural world' –
>
> 'that,' we (who are part of it)
>
> say, 'we can know.'[10]

6. Redekop, "The Word/word in Avison's Poetry," 125.

7. See chapter 2.

8. See Appendix for complete text.

9. Temple, *Readings in St. John's Gospel*, 4.

10. Avison is simply stating here what Calvin explains: "It is as if he were saying that the life given to men was not life in general but life united with the light of reason

At this point of her poem, there is a shift in her commentary. The questions start flooding in.[11]

> Even in this baffling darkness
> Light has kept shining?
> (where? where? then are we blind?)

Even in her line spacing of "where? where?" the poet depicts this strained searching—or refusal to search?—for light/Light with all its many-layered implications. In these questions Avison has alluded to the major conflict in John's Gospel, brought to a climax in the conversations surrounding the healing of the man born blind, of ones who could "see" Jesus and those who refused to see. Jesus's interpretation of the Pharisees' response to the "sign" with his disciples in private is similar to his interpretation of the parable of the Sower in the other Gospels:

> "I came into this world for judgment so that those who do not see may see, and those who do see may become blind." Some of the Pharisees near him heard this and said to him, "Surely we are not blind, are we?" Jesus said to them, "If you were blind, you would not have sin. But now that you say, 'We see,' your sin remains" (John 9:39–41).

He is characteristically oblique and ambiguous in his response to these teachers of the law.

Avison responds, in kind, with an ambiguous phrase "this baffling darkness" and parenthetical and strained questions. She may be suggesting an anxious identification with those who cannot see, or an amazed incredulity at the patience of One who "has kept shining.""But Truth is radiantly here," she insists again, but only for those with spiritual perception, a reality echoed throughout the Gospels and embodied in a number of her poems. In "To Emmaus" (AN 2.59) she refers to the disciples of the Lukan account who fail to recognize Jesus in his resurrection appearance as "beclouded":

. . . since God effectually illuminates their minds with His light, it follows that they were created to the end they might know that He is the author of such a unique blessing. And since this light streamed forth to us from the Word its source, it should be as a mirror in which we may see clearly the divine power of the Word." *The Gospel according to St. John 1–10*, 11.

11. Again, her technique of the question mark in her own study of the Bible inserts itself in the poem.

> Their beclouding had not cleared
> and did not lift even from
> His word.[12]

In "Third Hand, First Hand" (*AN* 3.141), she presents the familiar story of doubting Thomas in his need for proof after the event, with his defensive assessment of his own motivations and that of the other disciples:

> They saw because they wanted to?
> They all half-doubted when
> He asked for fish and honeycomb,
>
> took it, and ate it too.

Thomas's skepticism in John's narrative (John 20:24–29) rises out of a second-hand report—the witness of the disciples who told him the Lord appeared to them and ate in front of them for proof of his substantial body—as recorded in the Lukan account (Luke 24:36–43). Now he is having his own first-hand experience with Jesus telling him, "Reach out your hand and put it in my side" (John 20:27). This reference to "third hand" in Avison's poem could be Thomas's own hand. Or it could be the peculiar verification of the original disciples' recitation to the physician Luke, the one so careful to establish the authenticity of the witnesses in his own story of Jesus: "It was the doctor later who / said it had been so." Or it could be both at once. The poem retains the poignancy of both original stories even while the doctor certifies the live body (instead of a dead one), giving credence to the original eyewitnesses and to both post-resurrection accounts. These hesitant witnesses to the Light stand in stark contrast to Avison's earlier rebels in "The Fallen, Fallen World" (*AN* 1.76) in the learned Pharisee fashion, "stubborn, on the frozen mountain cling / Dreaming of some alternative to spring."

The poet links the radiant Truth, Eternal Being, Word, and Creator of John's Prologue with the familiar gospel invitation, "[T]o all who received him, who believed in his name, he gave power to become children ['sons'] of God" (John 1:12). Her response is one of awe: "Being, giving us to Become: / a new unfathomable genesis" ("Meditation on the Opening of the Fourth Gospel" *AN* 2.148), leading to another cluster of questions:

> Come? in flesh and blood?
> Seen? as another part
> of the 'natural world' his word
> flung open, for the maybe imperiller,

---

12. See Luke 24:13–35.

in what to us was the

Beginning?

This stanza is dense with theological import and human pathos. "The Word became flesh and lived among us, and we have seen his glory, the glory as of a father's only son, full of grace and truth," writes the Evangelist (John 1:14). The *Logos*, the Light, the Son joins the splendid but fragile world he has made, becoming one of the parts of his creation. Avison calls attention to the "natural world," with its multiple meanings of creation, physical reality, ordinary life, but also fallen world. "[H]is word / [is] flung open," vulnerable and exposed to "the maybe imperiller," and suggestive of the darkness that has not overcome the light (John 1:5). In the Gospel account Jesus names this imperiller in one of several challenges to the religious leaders opposing him: "You are from your father the devil" (John 8:44). In the naming of the archenemy of truth, John's particular perspective of the cross is anticipated—Christ's ultimate glory. Here in the triumphant words of the Prologue, the means of becoming children of God is shadowed with Christ's suffering. Avison captures the sacrifice in the one puzzling word "imperiller."

The closing stanza of her meditation highlights the poet's veiled and indirect disclosures characteristic of her style, but also of the style of the writer of John's Gospel. There are three cryptic sentences, each progressively shorter, beginning with the *Logos* and ending with the witness. Jesus remains unnamed—consistent with many of her poems about Christ. In "A Story" (*AN* 1.164–67), he is identified only as "the one out on the water" and "Gardener/Seed-Sower" and "Storyteller." In "The Dumbfounding" (*AN* 1.98), he is directly addressed, titled as "the all-lovely, all-men's way / to that far country" and "outcast's outcast." "The Word" is the only identifier in "The Bible to Be Believed" (*AN* 2.62–63); no name is used in "Third Hand, First Hand" (*AN* 3.141). The hiddenness here in "Meditation on the Opening of the Fourth Gospel" (*AN* 2.148) is not surprising then.

The unknown, the unrecognized, the

invisibly glorious

hid in our reality

till the truly real

lays all bare.

This first sentence sums up both the book of John and its Prologue, but it has the witness's beckoning "come and see" encrypted in its lines.

The last two sentences introduce a surprise:

The unresisting
then, most, speaks
love. We fear
that most.

In this highly abstract poem with its limited images and story line it is a reasonable expectation for the emphasis to be on intellectual recognition, assent, and believing. Instead, the meditation draws to a close with a picture of what "seeing"—unresisting—will look like. Why does one "fear / that most"? Again, the answer is ambiguous, but at least one possibility lies in the Johannine story itself. The Prologue of the Fourth Gospel points to its end where Jesus asks Peter three times, if he loves him. Jesus's response to Peter's affirmations is to outline the great cost of that love, ending with a sobering implication of seeing: "Follow me."[13]

There are a variety of things going on in the second poem, "The Bible to Be Believed" from *sunblue* (*AN* 2.62–63).[14] For one, the text explains and defends the link between two understandings of "Word"—the living Word and the Scripture as Word. In this connection the poem demonstrates how Avison, the poet, reads the biblical text diachronically and figurally. She validates her own reading by using the "Word's" reading as a model. The Word in the poem reads himself into the text of Old Testament Scriptures, inviting the reader to do the same. In turn, then, the Word as Scripture is validated—"the Bible to be believed"—because of the Word's "reading."

The poem begins with the same Johannine metaphor *Logos,* the Word, the "'Un-tense-able' Being" of "Meditation on the Opening of the Fourth Gospel" and proceeds to announce a thesis in the shape of a riddle: "The word read by the living Word / sculptured its shaper's form" (*AN* 2.62–63).[15] The paradox is focused on the living Word who existed prior to any written word, but now, as incarnate Word, reads the words of the Hebrew Scriptures. In turn, he is affected, that is, "sculptured"— a word filled with connotations

---

13. "'Very truly, I tell you, when you were younger, you used to fasten your own belt and to go wherever you wished. But when you grow old, you will stretch out your hands, and someone else will fasten a belt around you and take you where you do not wish to go.' (He said this to indicate the kind of death by which he would glorify God.) After this he said to him, 'Follow me'" (John 21:18–19).

14. See Appendix for complete text.

15. The same mystery informs John Donne's "Annunciation" in Gabriel's word to Mary:
Ere by the spheares time was created, thou
Wast in His minde, who is thy Sonne and Brother;
Whom thou conceivst, conceived; yea thou art now
Thy Makers maker, and thy Fathers mother.

of both beauty and pain—by his reading. The link between living Word and scriptural Word is immediately established. The second declaration in the poem, an implied implication, is more obscure: "What happens, means. The meanings are not blurred / by Flood—or fiery atom." Redekop, in his reading of these lines, suggests "a sacramental unified field, as it were":

> Avison . . . interprets John 1:1 as both act and word: the life, death, and resurrection of Jesus and the relation of Old and New Testaments come under one heading . . . in which Creation and Redemption are one act of will existing outside time–or, more exactly, at the intersection of time and eternity. Thus the Word, embedded in history and reading history, is independent of history, speaking with equal clarity through ancient or contemporary apocalypses.[16]

The poem then proceeds to show how Avison reads Scripture diachronically and figurally as she reveals the Word "embedded in history and reading history."[17] Rowan Williams explains a diachronic reading as a "'primary' or authoritative level of reading that is bound to history,"

> read[ing] a text in a more or less "dramatic" way, by following it through in a single time-continuum, reading it as a sequence of changes, a pattern of transformations . . . a reading where the unity of what is read is worked out in time [rather than a reading worked out in something more like space].[18]

Here in Avison's poem there is an emerging picture of the God/man submitting to human limitations of a gradual unfolding of his self-understanding of purpose. It is a picture of the incarnate Word, never named in the poem as the Jewish boy Jesus, studying the Hebrew scriptures, learning about other young boys who grew into their God-appointed missions: Moses, "a Jewish-Egyptian / firstborn, not three years old"; Isaiah, "a coal-seared poet-statesman"; and Samuel, "an anointed twelve-year-old." The Word is learning indirectly about himself as the narrative of the Bible is unfolded.

The paradox of the Word reading the word is repeated in the poem, but the word "sculpturing" is more ominous: "The Word dwells on this word / honing His heart's sword." A new layer of intensity not accessible to the Word's personal reading of the text, but suggesting Avison's own diachronic reading, is added with Simeon's solemn prophecy to Jesus's mother Mary: "This child is destined for the falling and the rising of many in Israel . . .

16. Redekop, "The Word/word in Avison's Poetry," 126.

17. Ibid., 126.

18. Williams, *On Theology*, 45.

and a sword will pierce your own soul too" (Luke 2:34–35). The writer to the Hebrews is close at hand as well: "Indeed, the word of God is living and active, sharper than any two-edged sword, piercing until it divides soul from spirit, joints from marrow" (Heb 4:12). The Word's heart's sword is metaphorical but will also be literal before he is done with his life's work. In the meantime, Avison is using later New Testament material to interpret the Word's reading himself into the text of "an anointed twelve-year old."

Avison emphasizes a figural reading as well, which Christopher Seitz explains as the "letter of scripture . . . taken with utmost seriousness . . . God is figured and accessible to the eyes of faith."[19] In his work *Figured Out: Typology and Providence in Christian Scripture*, he elaborates:

> Figuration entails the trustworthy and truthful witness of the scriptures of Israel to the One Lord (YHWH, the "I am who I am in my disclosure of myself with Israel") toward which the New Testament's proclamation of Jesus as Lord is "in accordance" (1 Cor 15:3).[20]

Avison enacts her sense of this unity of witness in Scripture as the Word's Bible lessons continue: "Ancient names, eon-brittled eyes, / within the word, open on mysteries" (*AN* 2.62–63). Cain, "the estranged murderer, exiled, hears at last / his kinsman's voice": "Listen, your brother's blood is crying out to me from the ground!" the Lord tells Cain (Gen 4:10).[21] Isaac,

> the child, confidingly questioning, so close
>
> to the awful ritual knife,
>
> is stilled by another

in the famous account of Abraham's submission to God to offer his son as a sacrifice and God providing a ram as substitution.[22] "The Word alive" learns about doves (from Noah's ark, perhaps) and lambs (sacrifices and the exodus) and a whale (Jonah's rescuer). "Grapes, bread, and fragrant oil: / all that means"—again, familiar symbols of exodus history—he needs to understand, because he will also embody and experience and act out those same symbols in his divine mission.

All this knowledge comes to a climax for Jesus in his temptations in the wilderness at the beginning of his ministry:

19. Seitz, *Figured Out*, 3.

20. Ibid.

21. Redekop interestingly refers to "For the Murderous: The Beginning of Time" (*AN* 2.54) to explicate the mystery of this line—a good example of intertextuality within a poet's works. See "The Word/word in Avison's Poetry," 129.

22. See Gen 22.

Yes, he was tempted to wash out

in covenanting song

the brand on the dry bone;

he heard the tempter quote

the texts he meant and went embodying.

The stories and the symbols embedded in the history of God's people all point to Jesus's own story, particularly the cross and the empty tomb. He is "Jewish-Egyptian firstborn" and "coal-seared poet-statesman" and "anointed twelve-year-old." He is both the ritual sacrifice and the one preserved.

His final silencing endured has sealed the living word:

now therefore He is voiceful, to be heard,

free, and of all opening-out the Lord.

In these specific interpretive gestures Avison is echoing her close friend, theologian Victor Shepherd, when he explains Calvin's views on the doctrine of Scripture to theology classes:

The Church acknowledges that Scripture, whose authority is as self-authenticating as are the colours and shapes and tastes of objects. To say the same thing at greater length and more nearly in the spirit of Calvin's fullest theological logic: Scripture authenticates itself as through it people are brought to faith in the Lord of whom it speaks and *he* authenticates *himself*. I.e., as Jesus Christ authenticates himself in the power of the Holy Spirit, the book by which we heard of Jesus Christ is authenticated too.[23]

In the poem Avison is providing intellectual ballast for trust in the source of knowledge about Jesus Christ. If the *Logos*, who "in the beginning was" and "was with God and is God" (John 1:1), turned to "the word"—the Old Testament Scriptures with its ancient stories of Abraham, Isaac and Jacob, of Moses and the Prophets—where "[t]he meanings are not blurred / by Flood—or fiery atom," then a seeking person can trust the source.

Where these older stories of the Scriptures are types of Jesus Christ in his ministry and mission, the recorded stories of Jesus's life and death in the New Testament verify in their details what the earlier accounts prefigured. "His final silencing endured"—the cross and the tomb—the poet proposes, "has sealed the living word." The source is now trustworthy, first, by the suffering Jesus endured. Then,

---

23. Shepherd, "A Summary of Calvin's Doctrine of Scripture."

the Word was moved
too vitally to be entombed in time.
He has hewn out of it one crevice-gate,

pointing to the lesson of triumph he learned and then fulfilled in his resurrection. The one who was "sculptured," "honing His heart's sword," now "has hewn out" of the tomb his own exit. Readers of the poem can trust the living Word because He trusted the word of the Scriptures. Readers can trust the word of the Scriptures because of what the living Word accomplished in his life, death, and resurrection—the account given in the word of the Scriptures. The poem suggests no anxiety with the circularity of the argument.

The third poem in this Johannine sequence reads like a companion poem to "The Bible to Be Believed." The latter ends with the declaration that "He is voiceful, to be heard, / free, and of all opening-out the Lord." On the next page of *sunblue*, the lyric "Listening" (*AN* 2.64) begins with a personal acknowledgement. As the Word reads himself into the Old Testament stories of the earlier poem, now the speaker in the poem, as a modern witness, reads herself into the sacred text, applying its most poignant injunctions and promises to her own experience:

Because I know
the voice of the Word
is to be heard
I know I do not know
even my own cast burden,
or oh, the costly load
of knowing undisturbed.
There is a sword
enters with hearing. Lord,
who chose being born to die
and died to bring alive
and live to judge
though all in mercy, hear
the word You utter
in me, because I know
the voice.

The poem divides into two units, with the first focused outward to an unspecified audience; the second is a prayer. In the first section the speaker identifies herself as both a follower of Christ and a reliable witness. She is

like the sheep following the Good Shepherd who "knows his voice" in Je-
sus's metaphor (John 10:4), and she "belongs to the Truth" (John 18:37). The
witness word "know" is repeated five times in this short poem, emphasiz-
ing both "knowing the voice" but also suggesting implications of cost. She
knows two things she does not know: "my own cast burden" of the psalm-
ist's prayer, "Cast your burden on the Lord. . . . He will hear my voice" (Ps
55:16, 22), and the "costly load of knowing undisturbed."[24] Here the same
"sword" reappears from the last poem:

> The Word dwells on this word
> honing His heart's sword,
> ready at knife-edge to declare
> holiness, and come clear (*AN* 2.62–63).

The cross shadows both poems in this image—for both The Word and his at-
tentive follower. The second section of the poem suggests that other sword,
"the word of God living and active . . . able to judge the thoughts and inten-
tions of the heart" (Heb 4:12). There is relief from one's burden in knowing
the voice, but there is an accompanying purifying process that may bring its
own pain. The witness turns upward in a prayer of contrition: "Lord,"

> hear
> the word You utter
> in me, because I know
> the voice.

In this compact lyric the poet has addressed hard questions of the Christian
faith. What does it mean to believe, to hear, to obey, to "know the voice,"
to declare that one knows? There is a seal of authenticity about the kind of
witness that reflects such a depth of feeling and personal involvement.

CONNECTING OLD AND NEW TESTAMENTS

The whole of Scripture is the scope of Avison's Bible reading. Her poems
probe the well-known stories of biblical history revealing the God of Abra-
ham, Isaac and Jacob; she is also interested in the obscure and unusual
stories. She follows the movement of the Scripture figurally, pointing to the
story of Christ crucified and risen and assuming one overarching narrative
guiding a typological interpretation that often shows itself in images of the
Eucharist. Several very different Old Testament episodes point to Avison's

---

24. See also Matt 11:28.

distinctive understanding of the unity of Scripture, but two poems in par-
ticular from *sunblue* and one from *Not Yet But Still* focus on these close
textual readings and provide illustration of her method. The stories stand
on their own, carrying their own individual significance, but the poet takes
each of them beyond their own environs and points to an anticipated work
of Christ.

In "For the Murderous: The Beginning of Time" (*AN* 2.54), she recon-
structs the limited details of the familiar story of Cain and Abel and their
two sacrifices to God, one pleasing and the other not, as recounted but not
explained in Genesis 4.[25] "Cain brought grain on his forearm / and a branch
with grapes" begins the poem, more specific than the Genesis text of "an
offering of the fruit of the ground" (Gen 4:3). A single adverb "vaguely" is
Avison's only interpretive comment of Cain's failure to specifically follow
God's instructions (unidentified for the reader of the biblical account):

> vaguely he offered
> to the far-borne light
> what the slow days had sweetened.

The second stanza predictably tells of Abel's more acceptable sacrifice:
"[F]rom his flock / On the fire he made sacrifice," "and blood / darkened the
stone place." The poem here echoes the Bible's early introduction of its cen-
tral theme—the ritual of the slain animal representing the necessary atoning
for sins. The third stanza briefly describes the murder, in turn, in sacrificial
terms, with the word "kindled" triggering the connection: "That this was
'better' than that / kindled in Cain a murderer's heart." Now there is a slain
man instead of a slain animal. The concluding line of the stanza articulates
God's way of calling Cain to accountability, the emphasis in Avison's line
interestingly focusing on God's care: "[H]e was watched over, after; but he
kept apart." The line is also anticipating the typology expected in reflection
on blood sacrifices, which the poet notes in the last stanza in her reference
to "the paschal lamb."

The closing lines, however, contain a surprise:

> In time the paschal lamb
> before the slaying did
> what has made new the wine
> and broken bread.

The reference to Christ's blessing the wine and bread as symbols of a "new
covenant," his blood and body at the Last Passover supper (Matt 26:26–29),

25. See Appendix for complete text.

now strangely validates not just Abel's sacrifice, but Cain's as well.[26] There is the obvious and beautiful irony Avison is bringing out in her poem of God's care for Cain. St. Paul reminds the Christian believers in Corinth, "For as often as you eat this bread and drink the cup, you proclaim the Lord's death until he comes" (1 Cor 11:26). Christ is the "paschal lamb" who offers himself "for the murderous"—both Abel who sacrifices a slain animal and Cain and all his progeny (those sharing in the Passover and Eucharist). The symbols to remind readers of his sacrifice, however, will be the grain and grapes, "what the slow days had sweetened," the failed sacrifice introduced in "the beginning of time."

Two poems about King David reveal a similar process of reflection—of puzzling over New and Old Testament connections. There are no verbal puzzles in "Aftermath of Rebellion" (AN 3.57–58), the account of King David's response to learning his son Absalom's rebellion had been quashed and Absalom was dead (2 Sam 18). David's anguish is stark and unadorned, spoken in his own voice: "Would God that *I* had died for *him*."[27] The voice of the poet reflects on this famous picture of grief:

> The father's lament
> has lingered on the ancient air of grief
> at least till now.

The meaning of the lines seems filled with all the other suffering parents of the world who know the pain of a child who has

> flung off
> – forever now –
> in his young man's euphoria,
> his father's hand.

The poem seems complete in its simple portrayal of both parties in their tragedy; the one is dead, and the other wishes he were.

> For such a delinquent
> even, a sovereign, sick at heart,
> learned what it is when
> a father loves.

Avison's last lines transcend David's personal grief, and point to the deep love of the Sovereign God who loves delinquent children with unfathomably

26. See also Mark 14:22–25; Luke 22:14–20; 1 Cor 11:23–26.
27. See Appendix for complete text.

greater intensity—and the love of the Son is lingering in the shadows (John 3:16). For the love of one son, another will be sacrificed. Simply expressed poems such as this give poignant and powerful pause in the sweep of Avison's more often complex lyrics.

The import of Avison's complex thought processes is more disguised in "All Out *or* Oblation (as defined in 2 Sam. 23:13–17 and 1 Chron. 11:17–19)" (*AN* 2.55–56).[28] She again refers to the life of King David, but uses a more obscure pericope—a little event buried in the details of the records of the fighting men loyal to David in his various struggles to gain and maintain his power over Israel. In the vignette Israel's familiar enemies, the Philistines, have control of David's city, Bethlehem, and David and his men are in the stronghold at the cave of Adullam. While no motive is suggested in the biblical accounts, David gets "most likely, a sentimental longing for a drink of cool water" from a well of Bethlehem by the gate, "[his] own native place," one commentator notes.[29] Three of his mighty warriors demonstrate their profound loyalty to him, risking their lives to break through the Philistine lines to fulfill his wish and bring him water from the well of Bethlehem. The text in the account of 2 Samuel records David's appreciative response. "But he would not drink of it; he poured it out to the Lord, for he said, 'The Lord forbid that I should do this. Can I drink the blood of the men who went at the risk of their lives?'" (2 Sam 23:16–17). There is no further comment in either account to suggest the significance of the event. But out of Avison's musings on the story, an intense and strange poem emerges.

There are a number of features in the poem that call attention to the nature of witness. In the retelling of the ancient story Avison has invited readers to interpret the event anagogically and even Christologically. Significance begins with the title's key word "oblation."[30] "All out" directs the reader to the central action in the poem—pouring water out on the ground. "Oblation" interprets the action, signaling the reader to look for double meanings in her text.

The poet interprets (and re-interprets) the biblical account with her imaginative choice of details, emphasizing the setting as a desert "[w]here sandstorms blow / and sun blackens and withers" and implies another metaphorical desert in the closing stanza. Avison uses the theme of the desert in an earlier poem, "Searching and Sounding" (*AN* 1.199–202), where she speaks of the painful journey of both looking for and running from Christ:

28. See Appendix for complete text.

29. A. Anderson, *Second Samuel*, 276.

30. "The action of offering or presenting the elements of bread and wine to God in the Eucharist . . . the Eucharist understood as offering or sacrifice" (OED).

> [Y]ou have brought me to
> sandstone, baldness, the place
> of jackals, the sparrow's skull.

In both poems she introduces the biblical motif of desert spirituality. Further, Avison significantly alters a crucial detail of the story here in "All Out *or* Oblation." Instead of David pouring the water out, as the original accounts record, the emphasis is on the "little group of men":

> They are crazy. They are
> pouring it
> out.

The sacrifice becomes a shared allusion with the Johannine account of Mary anointing Jesus's feet with costly perfume—a parallel pouring out (John 12:1–8). Again, the repetitions of the central image of water throughout the poem give the sacrifice multi-layered significance, particularly in the singular phrase "living water":

> Clean   cold   water
> throat-laving
> living
> water.[31]

Contrasted with the "clean, cold water" poured out is the "saltwater" "etched [on] their cheeks, their mouthcorners," with no mention of David's strong reaction.

The peculiar lineation and layout of the poem direct the eye to other particular emphases in the story. In the middle of the poem's narration of the sacrifice and its accompanying emotion, repeated lines with the single referent "God" take ascendant position as the poem's center.

> Look! – a little group of men:
> sun flashes
> on the water poured from leather pouch
> into a bowl, shining,
> now uplifted.
> God.
> God.

31. It is tempting to see Jesus's declarations of "living water" to the Samaritan woman (John 4:14) and to the crowd on the last day of the festival (John 7:37–38) embedded in this very specific detail.

Saltwater has etched

their cheeks, their mouthcorners.

Then a new voice—a witness—is introduced in the upper case exclamation: "WHAT ARE THEY DOING?"

They are crazy. They are

pouring it

out.

The poem's longest line, highlighting the action of David's men, depicts in vivid terms what the water and the sand look like as one absorbs the other. The following lines merge two Old and New Testament gestures— that of the action of David's loyal men and an intimation of the gesture of Christ's death on the cross:

Sand coats the precious drops and darkens with the life-stain.

Earth's

slow and unspasmodic swallowing is slowly, slowly

accomplished.

The closing lines admit the mystery of the event(s) that the witness cannot access: "No. I do not understand." Nevertheless, there is compelling determination to

still gaze at them

to learn to expect to

pour it out

into desert – to find out what it is.

The ambiguity of the "it" in the closing lines does not prevent the sense of expectation that when desert and water and God converge, the witness will herself be ready to pour it out.

VARIATIONS ON THE CHRIST STORY IN THE NEW TESTAMENT

Poems drawing on New Testament accounts of the Christ story promise easier access with an obvious referent to the "Word made flesh" of the Gospel. These poems, while varied in style and form, point in the same direction to the person of Jesus: "A Story" (*AN* 1.164–67), a parable framing the Parable of The Sower, recorded in the three Synoptic Gospels; "The Circuit"

(*AN* 2.61), an emblematic interpretation of an early church hymn in Philippians; "Hope" (*AN* 2.71), a dialogue between heaven and earth; and "Music Was in the Winds" (*AN* 3.42–43), a blending of Greek myth and Christian story.[32]

These poems, both in spite of and because of their complexity, introduce the theological premises underlying much of Avison's poetic work. While appearing to be overt Christian witness—that is, pointing to Jesus Christ in their topical subject matter and familiar text sources—they embody a familiar Avisonian ambiguity that complicates the picture. Perhaps the opposite also is true: they clarify the mystery of God in Jesus Christ and the good news that follows. Embedded in her invitation to "come and see" are Jesus's familiar provisos, "if you have eyes to see and ears to hear"— seemingly a mysterious spiritual perception, available only to a select audience who have hearts open to apprehending his words and meaning. Hence, they are simultaneously both indirect and direct witness to Christ.

"A Story" (*AN* 1.164–67) is the first in her collected poems that directly—and indirectly—introduces the figure of Jesus.[33] The title is, once again, typically ambiguous, for the poet is telling a story to her readers of a young woman telling a story to her mother of Jesus telling a story to a crowd of a gardener sowing seeds (which in the biblical parable is also a story of telling and listening). In the four-layered story all levels of listeners are struggling with perception and understanding, making Avison's story-poem a new parable about what it might mean to see Jesus.

The main story is a dialogue between the mother and her young adult daughter who has unexpectedly returned home early from being with friends at the beach. She has witnessed a moving event and now wants to be alone, but the parent presses for details. What happened? What did she see and hear that disturbed her so? As the young woman tries to report what she experienced, her mother repeatedly interrupts with commentary

---

32. This is not an exhaustive list of her surprisingly short group of poems that could be said to present the Jesus of the Gospels. One might also include from *The Dumbfounding*, "Person" (*AN* 1.191) and "The Christian's Year in Miniature" (*AN* 2.206–07); from *sunblue*, "He Couldn't Be Safe (Isaiah 53:5)" (*AN* 2.58), "To Emmaus" (*AN* 2.59), "The Bible to Be Believed" (*AN* 2.62–63) and "Contest" (*AN* 2.72); from *No Time*, "Meditation on the Opening of the Fourth Gospel" (*AN* 2.148), "The Unshackling" (*AN* 2.208), and "From Christmas through This Today" (*AN* 2.248); from *Not Yet But Still*, "If No Ram Appear" (*AN* 3.73) and "Third Hand, First Hand" (*AN* 3.141); and from *Concrete and Wild Carrot*, "The Whole Story" (*AN* 3.155) and "On a Maundy Thursday Walk" (*AN* 3.174–75). Other poems, as well, include references to Jesus, but again, I am looking here at core unifying images.

33. See Appendix for complete text.

suggesting her limited and predictable understanding of her daughter, but
hindering the articulation of the story.

> You're not sick? Did you
> get too much sun? a crowd,
> I never have liked it, safety in numbers
> indeed!
>> He was alone.
> Who was alone?
>> The one
>> out on the water, telling
>> something.

The mother's comments provide the contemporary setting,

>> You all
> standing there, getting up
> out of the beach-towels and gathering
> out of the cars.

The daughter explains the event and her reflective mood, originating in the
attitude of the crowd intent on listening,

>> Because the ones
>> who started to crowd around were
>> so still. You couldn't
>> help wondering.

What was the man in the boat talking about?

>> It is a story. But
>> only one man comes.
>> Tall, sunburnt, coming
>> not hurried, but as though
>> there was so much power in reserve
>> that walking all day and night
>> would be lovelier than sleeping if
>> sleeping meant missing it, easy
>> and alive, and out there.

Then the daughter—the listener to the man telling the story—tries to explain how she heard Jesus's parable of the Sower of the Seeds (Mark 4:1–20).[34] The above stanza already reveals a different perspective on the parable than a customary reading assigns. Tinsley comments on this parable with attention to obvious but overlooked details that Avison particularly emphasizes. Jesus's interpretation of the parable to his disciples is, in reality,

> no explanation at all, but the parable over again, presenting the allegorical character of the original all the more starkly by identifying some of the subsidiary details, but not significantly the main figure—the sower. But if the seed is the Word of God, and so on, who then is the sower?[35]

The daughter is preoccupied with the singular "gardener," as she titles him ("but there was nothing / like garden, mother"). What the daughter sees in the seed-sower is "so much power in reserve" that the only way she can describe it is to suggest what she would do—give up sleep and willingly walk all day and night rather than miss "it." Does she mean the power of the man, or the story of the man or the man himself sowing the seed? The indeterminacy of the "it" intensifies her response.

> Only the queer
> dark way he went
> and the star-shine of
> the seed he spent,

she continues. The mother is puzzled. "(Seed you could see that way —)." The daughter hardly hears her mother:

> In showers. His fingers
> shed, like the gold
> of blowing autumnal
> woods in the wild.

The young woman falls into metaphor and enthusiastic description as she completes the story of the receptiveness of roadway, stone, waste and loam receiving the seed, "and the one who had walked,"

---

34. See also Matt 13:1–23, Luke 8:4–15. Tinsley notes "[t]he probability that this parable was a master-parable which provided the key to all the others and bears the distinctive marks of Jesus' allegorical manner of alluding to himself on his mission." *Tell It Slant*, 91.

35. Ibid.

> searching thirsty ones
> for his garden
> in all that place.

The girl ends her reverie with a peculiar observation:

> But they flowered, and shed
> their strange heart's force
> in that wondering wilderness –.

It is not clear whether the daughter heard this conclusion—"they [the seeds] flowered"—as part of the original tale, or whether she is reflecting metaphorically on her own heart as a "wondering wilderness." The mother's question of clarification which misses the significance of the story, jars attention back to the framing story: "Where is he now?"

>   The gardener?
> No, The storyteller
> out on the water?
>   He is alone.

There is a wistful sadness in the last lines of the young witness. What she has seen and heard she cannot capture adequately in words; it is a mystery she has only intuited. The storyteller in the boat out on the water has merged with that "giant" of a gardener and somehow the discovery is crucial to the young woman's existence, but she is not there.

> Perhaps a few
> who beached the boat and
> stayed, would know.

The daughter inadvertently recognizes what the Gospel writers note: "When he was alone, those who were around him along with the twelve asked him about the parables. And he said to them, 'To you has been given the secret of the kingdom of God'" (Mark 4:10–11). Here the young woman is home, wanting to be left alone, but wishing she were still under the spell of the storyteller.

This poem is Avison's witness at the height of indirection, telling a story of Jesus without giving his name, using his own parabolic and ironic method of introducing himself, by pointing back to the listener/see-er, looking for a receptive heart. The fearful part of the story is the mother who remains on the surface of its details and fails to perceive anything—even the profound effect of the story and its teller on her own child. She is a parable herself, illustrating Jesus's private reminder to his disciples: "The reason I speak to them in parables is that 'seeing they do not perceive, and hearing they do not listen, nor do they understand'" (Matt 13:13).

Avison understands the dilemma of wanting literally to "see" and speaks of her own struggle to come to the truth of Jesus. But she is uncompromising in her presentation of the truth of the gospel in all its mysterious and seeming elusiveness. She begins her witness to Christ in her poems much the same way she learns of Jesus in the Gospels—in parables and enigmatic signs. Again, Tinsley reminds his readers, "The Incarnation is not only a historical event but it is also a divine manner of speaking, the disclosure of God's style in communication." He goes on to explain the difficulty:

> The Incarnational and parabolic method of God is disturbing, puzzling, questioning and human beings have a natural momentum towards preferring a revelatory method which is reassuring, direct and "simple." The ambiguous "sign" has therefore to give way to the indubitable "miracle," the parable to the slogan. Christianity has constantly been threatened by moves to replace the personal, reticent, self-forgetting style of revelation by an assertive, over-powering, indisputable authoritarianism.

He goes on to suggest that the Bible is a story of teaching people "an ability to discern God in the 'sign' which, because it is always ambiguous, is inevitably a 'stumbling-block.'"[36]

In Avison's sophisticated, albeit simply told story, the gaze of the reader is constantly shifting first to the mother and daughter in dialogue, then the daughter watching the Teller of the story of the Sower of seeds, then the Teller of the story, then the Sower in the story, and back to the daughter and mother. It is through the response of stillness and yearning in the girl that Jesus becomes strangely visible. Again, Tinsley notes, "It is significant that, whenever Jesus asked a question about himself or his mission, he never answered directly or explicitly. His usual manner is to return the question to the speaker."[37] Avison's poem does the same. As a result, several layers of witness mediate the introduction to Jesus.

Avison also considers the apostle Paul's interpretation and analysis of the incarnation, this time in the manner of the seventeenth-century Metaphysical poets, with an elaborate conceit. In her poem "The Circuit" (*AN* 2.61), she recreates the hymn of the early church that Paul uses in his argument for divine humility in his letter to the church at Philippi. While faithful

36. Ibid., i–ii.

37. Ibid., 44.

to the text's theme, she nevertheless defamiliarizes it and points back to the text with new intensity in her metaphor.

The Circuit (Phil. 2:5–11)

The circuit of the Son
in glory falling
not short
and without any clutching after
His Being-in-Light,
but stripping, putting on
the altar-animal form
and livery of Man
    to serve men under orders
    to, into, death,
    trusting the silent Glory
    (though at that instant out of touch) –
        flesh marred, heart
        deliberately benighted
        till the spilt Blood on the criminals' hill
        split earth and Temple veil
        (then all was silent,
        cloth-cased and closed in a stone hole) –
    to prise, till touching with unflickering Breath
He prises even us free:

this circuit celebrates the Father of Lights
who glorifies this Son and all that He
in glory sows
of Light.

To begin, she depicts the completed electrical circuit in the twenty-four-line poem as one long unbroken sentence, drawing the eye toward the period in the short concluding stanza, set apart in a blaze of light. The poem announces the conceit in the opening line, "[t]he circuit of the Son" and then shows the downward pull:

in glory falling
not short
and without any clutching after
His being-in-Light.

The familiar phrasing brings to mind others' fall in St. Paul's writings: "[A]ll have sinned and fall short of the glory of God" (Rom 3:23), highlighting the unique quality of this falling. However, here in the conceit the meaning of "falling [not] short" takes on another meaning. The Son's falling is successful circuitry—not short-circuited and far enough to "prise even us free." This falling short is voluntary and intentional, and similar in mystery to John's Prologue with the curious mixture of Word, light, and flesh. "[W]ithout any clutching after / His Being-in Light," the Light of the World (John 8:12) can trust the circuitry to be effective.

The image temporarily shifts, following St. Paul's line of thought: The Son "emptied himself, taking the form of a slave, being born in human likeness and being found in human form" (Phil 2:7). Avison pictures the self-emptying as "stripping, putting on the altar-animal form / and livery of Man." "Livery" is the distinctive dress worn by servants heightened here by "altar-animal" form. The downward journey is not just taking the form of a human, but of an animal prepared for sacrifice on an altar, John the Baptist's "Lamb of God who takes away the sin of the world" (John 1:29). The Son's service to and for humankind is given intensity as the circuit metaphor is resumed, emphasized with new and increased indentation in the verse:

> to serve men under orders
>
> to, into, death,
>
> trusting the silent Glory
>
> (though at that instant out of touch) –
>
> > flesh marred, heart
> >
> > deliberately benighted.

In his death the connection with the Father is broken and his heart is "'benighted"'—in darkness. There is the double meaning of both flowing currents and flowing blood as the poem continues:

> till the spilt Blood on the criminal's hill
>
> split earth and Temple veil
>
> (then all was silent,
>
> cloth-cased and closed in a stone hole) –

Here the lights have gone out and silence accompanies the darkness. But his service to humankind is not over, and in his death and resurrection the circuit is not broken. Visually, in the indented lines, while the servant is "putting on the altar-animal form / and livery of Man," the ones he has served are "prised free"—extracted with difficulty—from their death sentence, and with the ease of "touching with unflickering Breath," are drawn mysteriously into the circuit.

The hymn in the Philippian text emphasizes the exaltation of the Son by the Father who "gave him the name that is above every name, so that at the name of Jesus every knee should bend" (Phil 2:9–10). His exaltation after his humiliation is the primary point. In her circuit metaphor, Avison too "glorifies this Son" in the closing stanza, reinforcing the purpose of the "falling," "stripping," and "serving," but this time guiding the eye emblematically in the shortening lines:

> this circuit celebrates the Father of Lights
> who glorifies this Son and all that He
> in glory sows
> of Light.

The poem ends in the singular announcement of Light, pointing directly to the circuit's purpose and the person who is Light. At the same time, the poet extends the witness and calls attention to "all that He / in glory sows," anticipating Paul's encouragement for the Christian believers to "shine like stars in the world" in the subsequent verse (Phil 2:14).

In "Hope" (*AN* 2.71) the same theme is enunciated, less heavily freighted with theological allusions, and with different emphases. The familiar human lament over loss of innocence opens the poem as the speaker notes the "clear bright world / from a shining source" has been "spoiled, / gross-warted by the cheap and coarse." The human solution is to obliterate, destroy, throw away what has been ruined:

> I'd thunderbolt it down
> to shred in withering smoke
> if that way everything could drown
>   in all I've found of dark –.

In the third stanza a new voice enters the poem: "The shining one looked, and said 'we,' / owning one source with us." The response is emotion-laden:

> That chokes the heart unbearably;
> here, where we grope and fuss,
> dully we hear, and dully wonder why
> we did Him in for this.

The shining one corrects the mistaken theology. He was not done in. It was divine intention and initiative:

> 'I chose to come
> and knew the way was through

> your flesh and blood and doom
> of death.   I, judge and lover, knew.'

The speaker is given fresh hope with this new understanding: "Somehow a clear bright world / wakens at the voice."

In "Music Was in the Wind" (*AN* 3.42–43), Avison follows in the tradition of the earlier poets Dante and Milton in their fusion of two stories, the Greek myth and the Christian story. Even more specific and particular, she may be drawing on the Middle English lai *Sir Orfeo* of the late thirteenth century.[38] "It was Orpheus all along!" are the striking opening words, inviting one into that imaginative "music of the spheres" that so entranced the medieval mind and Avison's as well. Mia Anderson, in her reading of Avison's earlier poems, comments on the indication of something good happening in Avison's poems with the mention of music. "Singing and music . . . are always touchstones of salvation in Avison," she suggests.[39] The names of Orpheus and Eurydice recall Ovid's haunting myth of the singer who loses his lover/wife to death and fails in the attempt to bring her back from the land of the dead. But the poem's opening details signal that the story is being altered.

> He carried Eurydice down, down
> into the earth
> in his arms, going himself with her
> since this was the only way
> out of her mortal maze now.

Avison recasts the myth in similar fashion to *Sir Orfeo*. Jeffrey explains the earlier story:

> an astonishing, unanticipated escape from death's dark dominion occurs. It happens in only two lines: Eurydice is freed from Pluto's power . . . the reader recognizes that a stunning reversal has come about, so to speak, in the twinkling of an eye. Because of Christ, a powerful old story has been retold precisely so that it might be transformed: death is overcome, the bride is restored and the world rejoices in an epithalamium that every worthy harper now can sound.[40]

---

38. See Jeffrey, *Christianity and Literature*, 160–61 or *Houses of the Interpreter*, 155–72.

39. M. Anderson, "Conversation with the Star Messenger," 117–18.

40. Jeffrey, *Christianity and Literature*, 160.

In this case, Avison is the new "worthy harper": The love story has been transposed into another love theme—still tender and awakening deep feelings akin to the love of lovers, but not the same. This new Orpheus risks all

> except a love strong and steady enough
> never to share her
> relief in this fine-sifted silence, nor
> her torn
> loyalties to this private place
> and to the devastated but remembered
> home where she was known.

The cost to procure this Eurydice's life does not mean relief for him; nor can he himself have divided loyalties to be successful.

> First it had to be down.
> He was no
> stoic, no ascetic, moved to
> goodness without experience
> of all our billion moments.

Two stories begin to merge in this second stanza as the identity of this new Orpheus is identified. The intensity of love so moving in the Greek myth of Orpheus's sacrifice for Eurydice is overlaid with the one who has "experience / of all our billion moments." The conceit of Christ's sacrifice in the earlier lyric "The Circuit" is repeated in the same downward movement but here in terms of the Singer's imagined experience of the music he hears about himself: "Did he / hear what the shepherds overheard? / sweet singing in the choir?" (*AN* 3.42–43). Perhaps the "sweet singing" sustains him in his downward journey. The tenderness of the love is haunting as "[h]e carried her he loved / the whole way down"; but even better,

> The strange travail home
> up into light
> emptied his arms.

Unlike the defeated Orpheus who mistakenly looked back on Eurydice just at the point of arriving back in the land of the living, this new Orpheus, "took [this Eurydice] by the hand, and she was walking." The words in the closing lines hint at the alternate source of the tale. This could be the account from Mark's Gospel of Jairus's young daughter whom Jesus brought back from the dead, taking her by the hand, and saying to her, "'*Talitha cum*,' which means, 'Little girl, get up'" (Mark 5:40–42). The last stanza blends the experience of both this new Orpheus and Eurydice, implying their intimate long-term relationship of love, complicated by the merging of the immortal with the mortal:

> And on the way they would be
> sometimes sensitive to a loss as she
> lived it out in a familiar
> and yet altered world,
> remembering a morning, in a song.

ALL STORIES LEAD TOWARD RESURRECTION

As the closing of "Music Was in the Wind" suggests, Avison's poems based on Scripture reveal a witness who has internalized, experienced, and appropriated the story she is telling over and over. She engages in what Rowan Williams has called "dramatic" modes of reading:

> We are invited to identify ourselves in the story being contemplated, to re-appropriate who we are now, and who we shall or can be, in terms of the story. *Its* movements, transactions, transformations become *ours* . . . our appropriation of the story . . . [is] an active working through of the story's movement in our own time.[41]

She has made the Christ story her own, melding the biblical story with her own life experience, providing a window for "an unbeliever to approach not just parts of the work but all of the work of a poet who believes, through and through, in a personal God."[42] Hers is an orthodox theology, pointing to and emphasizing the resurrection with its promise of future glory, as has already been observed in a number of the poems: for example, "That Friday—Good?" (*AN* 3.84), "Interim" (*AN* 3.85), "The Dumbfounding" (*AN* 1.197–98), "The Circuit" (*AN* 2.61), and "Music Was in the Wind" (*AN* 3.42–43). Williams articulates the common thread in Christianity when he writes: "The scriptural *history* has to be told, has to be followed diachronically or literally, *as it leads to* Christ and the cross of Christ."[43] To speak of the cross includes the climax of the resurrection: "the one focus of Christ

---

41. Williams, *On Christian Theology*, 50.
42. Hay, quoted earlier in chapter 1, *Always Now*, vol. 3, back cover.
43. Williams, *On Christian Theology*, 56.

crucified and risen that is the movement of Scripture."[44] As Avison tells and retells the biblical story of the incarnation, death, and resurrection of Jesus, there is deep and varied emotion expressed in the frequent tellings, always carefully controlled and disciplined. Her difficult lyrics engage the reflecting intellect, discouraging sentimentality. Sometimes she is explicit; more often, however, she "tells it slant," revealing as much as a receptive reader can receive in one telling.

To start at the beginning, the poet's Advent poems are mostly clustered in *sunblue* where she works and reworks from various angles the experience of the incarnation.[45] As a result, the poems seem as much, or more, about the city and contemporary practice of remembering the Christmas event rather than meditations on the biblical text. Though she draws on the outlines of Luke's and Matthew's narratives, she emphasizes how the modern reader appropriates the event. Further, the theme recedes in her later poems, suggesting she has moved to a new focus on the Christ story. Two poems will serve here as representative of the poet's meditations: "Christmas Approaches, Highway 401" (*AN* 2.97) and "Waking and Sleeping: Christmas" (*AN* 2.101–02), in their different approaches will reveal a thematic coherence of the beginning of a story ending in resurrection and glory.

"Christmas Approaches, Highway 401" (*AN* 2.97) is the first of the group of Christmas poems in the volume *sunblue*.[46] Typical of Avison's oblique style in her incarnational creation poems, there is little in the poem to suggest an Advent theme and initially it seems out of place in this discussion of poems on biblical texts. Instead, there is a rendering of snow and light, curiously working together to signal an important event. Here the snow of a winter night witnesses to the light. In the structure of the poem three lines stand out flush with the margins as a poem in miniature.

> Seed of snow
> [. . .]
> is particle
> [. . .]
> is sown tonight with the beauty

are the framing lines which determine the central meaning of the arrival of the Light of the world. Dense and indented lines, crowded by details of a busy winter Toronto highway, give no hint of the approach of Christmas,

44. Ibid., 57.

45. The organizational pattern of *sunblue* has a seasonal sense to it with the poems of Christmas all placed together near the end of the volume.

46. See Appendix for complete text.

and in fact, can distract from the central image. The location suggests the speaker is probably in a vehicle speeding across that highway, observing the snow and its surroundings, both what it affects, and what repels its effects.

The fast-paced blocks of text interspersed between the haunting and delicate lines are a patchwork of human creation—for good and ill—and natural landscape. The mere "seed of snow," so small and graceful, [falls—or is fallen]

> on cement, ditch-rut, rink-steel, salted where
>
> grass straws thinly scrape against lowering
>
> daydark [. . .]

The mix of highway salt and snow suggest the brevity of the beauty. The words rush by as the vehicle blurs the details. The speaker continues, "[the seed of snow] is particle"

> unto earth's thirsting,
>
> spring rain,
>
> well-spring

[but also]

> Roadwork, earth work, pits in hillsides
>
> [. . .]
>
> unkilned pottery broken and strawed about,
>
> minibrick people-palaces

The speaker reverses the usual order of seeing:

> by day all lump and ache
>
> is sown tonight with the beauty
>
> of light and moving lights, light traveling, light
>
> shining from beyond farthestness.

Here she uses the night's limitations, fears, and distortions of reality to see differently with the lights from the moving cars on the busy highway, shining on the seed of snow. The imagination awakens the awareness of the "light / shining from beyond farthestness." The title of the poem directs a transformation of the various combinations of light into the light that guided the Wise Men so many years ago. Even that suggestion is insufficient; the "light / shining from beyond farthestness" must be the source of light—Light himself. "Light has come into the world," the Gospel writer announces (John 3:19). On the 401 Highway, an unexpected place, Christmas approaches.

Christmas in all its mystery is not for the dull, the faint-hearted, the unreflecting. "Waking and Sleeping: Christmas" (*AN* 2.101–2) sets up a series of dramatic oppositions as the title indicates. There are both "childbirth and a dying bed"; Abraham's sacrifice of Isaac and "the branched ram";

> We carol as our earth
> swings some to outer nightward
> and sunfloods the Antipodes.

Intensity in the oppositions increases when "the newborn in his mortal fairness" produced "helpless, awestruck jubilance," but "hard on the manger vigil came Herod's massacre" "and Rachel's / heart then broke." The frontier woman and doctor who have not been shielded from the stark realities of both birth and death are the ones who are already familiar with the experience of awe and "tremblings that reach your heart." In light of these contrasts, Christmas for the welcoming and aware world is a

> welling
> from past the horizoning why
> a new light flows, is filling:
>
> coming far down, away
> from the enduring Father.

It is pure inexplicable light, "pure gift," "waking" for the world. For the "newborn in his mortal fairness" Christmas means something else: "the Child, alone, sets out upon His way / to the cursed tree, His altar" and no branched ram waits to take his place. The closing stanza is unclear:

> People tremble and yearn;
> our dark hearts thud
> in case that light will burn
> and wake the dead.

The trembling and yearning seem to come from an awareness of the implications of the incarnation—salvation and suffering in strange combination. These deep emotions may also suggest the opposite. There is no response in those who are spiritually in the dark. The Christmas light may be finally about waking the dead.

The dramatic oppositions of "Waking and Sleeping: Christmas" point to the darker theme of judgment that Avison does not evade in her witness to the Christ. In fact, a series of poems in her *Winter Sun* pre-conversion collection suggests a preoccupation with judgment, doom, and alienation in her thinking. She speaks of "slow sure estrangement from the sun" in "The Fallen, Fallen World." (*AN* 1.75–76).[47] She mourns, "Myrrh, bitter myrrh, diagonal, / Divides my gardenless gardens" in "Not the Sweet Cicely of Gerardes Herball" (*AN* 1.64–65). "Watershed" (*AN* 1.101) begins with open cynicism:

> The world doesn't crumble apart.
> The general, and rewarding, illusion
> Prevents it.

In the last stanza the speaker notes "a change in the air": 'Yes, and you know / In your heart what chill winds blow." "Apocalyptic?" (*AN* 1.104) is equally pessimistic:

> "We must accept the baptism of the gutter"
> (Yeats). "We must love one another or die"
> (some other poet). "We must eat and marry
> And give our children college educations [. . . .]
> Accept, yes. Choose what we accept. *And* die.

The poem's ending suggests no resolution:

> The old man reels.
> Love in absurdity rocks even just men down
> And doom is luminous today.

So concludes a litany of despair.

Judgment is still present in later volumes but the tone has changed as Avison interacts with the biblical story of Jesus. In *The Dumbfounding's* "Controversy" (*AN* 1.163) she outlines the self-imposed struggle against goodness:

> They licked the salt at their lip-edge
> and fixed how to feed, sleeping on it
> and sweating, and went blind
> into the flesh. And some god
> you say is God says, "that lot's lost"
> and rolls them loose
> like water on silky dust

47. See chapter 4 for a fuller discussion of "The Fallen, Fallen World."

> rolling away (and if some sparrows
>> dropt by and pecked at water globules –
>> your god keeps accounts of
>> them and their drinks there?)
> . . . centuries gone . . . neither here nor there . . .
> done for . . . ("Shove off then").
>
> Judgement? Not His. It's gaming
> with loaded dice, and a god made like men
> or men with power behind their couldn't-care-less,
> and *not* the Truth with the
> bite of final cold, and marveling in it
> of bleeding, and waiting, and joy.

The speaker's misconception of God is made obvious with his declaration of an indifferent or vindictive god. A new image of sparrows "dropt by and peck[ing] at water globules" intrudes and counters the argument. Words more famous than the speaker's overlay and transform his own angry denial as Jesus's declaration from the Sermon on the Mount is invoked: "Yet not one of [the sparrows] will fall to the ground apart from your Father" (Matt 10:29). Therefore, the poem's conclusion is not totally unexpected. The last lines signify a familiar Avisonian turn, reflecting her experience with the biblical counterpart of judgment—mercy. Cross, grave, and empty tomb settle the controversy.

Two important poems in *Concrete and Wild Carrot* suggest her sense of urgency regarding impending judgment. In "Other Oceans" (*AN* 3.146–54) she laments those who do not embrace rescue: "Behold the immured, the lost champion, / the dangerously young," and

> us who merely persevere
> along the borders of
> the always unthinkable!

In particular her last section "AFTER" (*AN* 3.153–54) speaks of the

> Post-modern:
>
> i.e. those who (he said)
> in honesty of heart
> deny any eternal verities;

The lines go on to describe them as searchers too:

being
searchers for plausible
truth, they humbly
substitute for the old symbols,
what they affirm as
'the logocentric.'

She commends them for their thoughtfulness and sense of responsibility and "shoulder[ing]" "their part of the / burden of living," but finally offers her judgment, echoing the Scriptures:

How different it would be, today, to
'take up your cross and follow Me,' to
'take My yoke upon you, learn . . .'
Take both?

She is confident of the legitimacy of her witness of words:

It makes no sense today
to talk this way, nor did
in A.D, thereabouts.
No, but once heard it condenses
somehow. Cautions. Compels – can
flood a person, earth and sea and sky – all that
originated in a like
mystery (all who will die from
this reasonable lifetime we have known) –
with one
overwhelming focus.

The process of "condensing," "cautioning," "compelling," and "flooding a person" is reminiscent of her own conversion and subsequent cost of following Christ.

In "Alternative to Riots But All Citizens Must Play" (*AN* 3.179–82), the poet speaks in more dramatic language.

To myself everywhere:
Cry out, 'Break!' Break
all our securities, and break out!

she cries. This poem can be read as a critique of a bankrupt society that needs unspecified revitalizing at its very core; but one can also read it as a biblically prophetic warning of spiritual disaster:

> Disrupt these
> almond-eyed visions, spongy with
> yearnings, for prophesied
> pre-dawn light, this very day.
>
> Nightfall is near.
>
> Break in! Break up
> all our so solid structures for the
> glory of
> nothing to hold on to
> but untried air currents,
> the crack and ricochet
> of impact. Risk
> survival!

Jesus's death, burial, and resurrection have changed everything, as she delineates with particular poignancy in her poem "Uncircular" from *Concrete and Wild Carrot* (*AN* 3.167–69), so it makes sense to "risk survival."[48] In the opening two stanzas of "Uncircular," she announces the profundity of both the death and resurrection of the Son of God, but she frames the two stanzas and the closing stanza of the poem with the word "entombment":

> The entombment of all that wrath
> bespeaks the stench of a
> fragmenting into
> finality.
> To me, this matters.
> I anchor there as to a lifeline,
>
>   ***
>
> there where
> what other self-bound persons
> had wrapped and lovingly
> laid, a total

---

48. See Appendix for complete text.

loss for all, for all
was found in purity, among his friends
changed, but the same time opening
everything on earth to the
power that lifted him.

No wonder Paul cried out,
'I count all loss . . .' – above all, loss.

The poem concludes with an awkward and terse announcement that connects with the opening lines but strangely inhibits closure of its large theme:

Entombment, however, is
new in all history.
What it is for.

Before those enigmatic closing lines Avison offers five detailed scenes from what she calls "the intractability of history"—that narrative of Yahweh's stubborn and hard-to-cure people. Scene 1 is from the Davidic Kingdom but the description is one of weakness:

His are the evenings of a
king in a cave kept wakeful by
deftly deciphering the poems
he found written in his heart.

In scene 2 "He" (Yahweh?—the antecedent is ambiguous) watches his people "brokenheartedly" trying to

rouse them to the dread, in time,
that dragged them down
into sensibility.

Scene 3 is "the besieged city" of a doomed people "among the panic-crazed" and scene 4 is the later exiled "strangers far from home" who "knew the wreckage to be / faced." These vignettes out of Israel's history show both the breaking of the covenant and the prophesied consequences. Scenes 4 and 5 blend together those exiles and the Jewish people of Palestine in Jesus's day, and twice the poet explains Jesus's activity, described as a kind of poem-making—a calling to account:

Among us, Jesus found
encrusted words and structures;

> he washed and brushed them clean
> and out of [that] intractability
> of history.

Again, there is resistance,

> when some who so cherished
> the traditional that they urged
> stains, gritty particles, dust
> must be left, too, untouched.

Nevertheless,

> His words flowed from a
> clear wellspring always till now
> a little tainted by the
> hand that cupped to drink, or the
> crafted ladle.

For his efforts Jesus was "dragged off and left abandoned to / indifferent cruelty once." The poem then circles back to its strange and puzzling conclusion. Death has been inevitable since Eden's loss, so entombment is not new. The closing line is a sentence fragment evoking the opening lines of the poem and clarifying its newness: "What it is for." Mercy and grace are realized fully in "the entombment of all that wrath" and the "fragmenting into / finality" of all humanity's "intractability." Both St. Paul who "cried out, / 'I count all loss . . .'" and the poet who "anchor[s] there as to a lifeline" are buoyed up by this recognition.

When Avison speaks in her poems of Jesus's resurrection, the core event of the Christian faith, she engages in the Christ story with increased intensity. The young woman in "A Story" reluctantly admits that "[p]erhaps a few / who beached the boat and / stayed, would know" where the "gardener-storyteller" is (AN 1.164–67).[49] In her resurrection poems there are listeners who stayed close to Jesus and have news to tell.[50] The witnesses in

49. See earlier section of this chapter.

50. "Continued Story" (AN 1.48–49), "To Emmaus" (AN 2.59), "The Unshackling" (AN 2.208), "Thoughts on a Maundy Thursday" (AN 2.213), "Our Only Hour" (AN 2.228–30), "That Friday Good?" (AN 3.84), "Interim" (AN 3.85), "Third Hand, First Hand" (AN 3.141), "The Whole Story" (AN 3.155), "Uncircular" (AN 3.167–69), "On a Maundy Thursday Walk" (AN 3.174–75), and "'Early Easter Sunday Morning Radio" (AN 3.195) are all devoted to retelling and musing on the climax of the biblical story—the empty tomb. Furthermore, these are not Avison's only references to the resurrection of Jesus Christ. Several other poems make mention or imply the theme: For example,

these poems who confront the mystery of the risen Christ are pulled directly into the story. "Come and see" becomes "come and be transformed and participate in the cosmic event."

Avison's poems about Christ's resurrection are not the intense puzzles of some of her other theological lyrics. She does not explain or defend the historicity of the empty tomb. She merely embraces the mystery of the risen Christ and by extension invites her readers to do the same. As she recounts the grand conclusion to the fate of the "Christmas Light" in "From Christmas through This Today" (*AN* 2.248), she emphasizes the implication of resurrection for anyone who accepts or rejects the witness role:

> Then from the tomb the terrible light
> outburst
> emptying all we'd gained and He
> had lost.
>
> The light that seeks us out
> is as at first
> but darkness now is different, only ours by choice.

She parallels David Jasper's observation of the privacy of the actual moment of resurrection in his comments about George Herbert's seventeenth-century poem "Easter":

> The tomb, then, would be found empty at the break of day, so that, as in the Gospels themselves, the central event, the resurrection itself is missed and not described. Here scripture, poetry, and history are all silent. . . . At this central moment of the story, language dissolves, and history moves into eternity.[51]

Instead, the event of resurrection must be accessed through its eyewitnesses. She, in turn, presents the resurrection refracted through their experience. She takes the simple vignettes of these biblical witnesses, each struggling with their incredulity with first devastation and then eucatastrophe before their eyes, and imaginatively embraces the words of the Word.[52]

"Person?" (*AN* 1.191); "The Dumbfounding" (*AN* 1.197–98); "The Christian's Year in Miniature" (*AN* 1.206); "The Circuit" (*AN* 2.61); and "The Bible to Be Believed" (*AN* 2.62–63) all have recognizable Easter lines.

51. Jasper, *The Study of Literature and Religion*, 40.

52. A word coined by J. R. R. Tolkien to signal "the sudden happy turn in a story . . . ." He goes on to explain, "And I was there led to the view that it produces its peculiar effect because it is a sudden glimpse of Truth, your whole nature chained in material cause and effect, the chain of death, feels a sudden relief as if a major limb out of joint

In her identification with the early followers of Christ, the poet amplifies their struggle to come to terms with their new reality. In "To Emmaus" (*AN* 2.59) she notes one experience of doubt turned to belief, as Luke has noted (Luke 24:13–35):

> The Risen One wandered their road with them.
>
> Their beclouding had not cleared
>
> and did not lift even from
>
> His word
>
> He simply came when asked at evening
>
> and broke bread there, a third, with them.
>
> And abruptly they were assured,
>
> beyond all that seeing had suffered
>
> joyful.

She makes the event all about the witnesses' transformation—their new capacity to "see." His presence became visible, she suggests, when they asked. Their response was spontaneous. "They hurried / to those who had not heard" (*AN* 2.59). She describes doubt, disbelief, and guilt in "The Unshackling" (*AN* 2.208), intimating unstated emotions in the Johannine record of Jesus's post-resurrection appearance to the disciples (John 20:19–23):

> Locked in   in fear
>
> that evening   where
>
> ten were huddled   came
>
> the eternal Lamb.

At the same time the poet is reminding her readers of the connection with John the Baptist's earlier announcement, "Here is the Lamb of God who takes away the sin of the world." She condenses the Gospel writer's promise of peace, His presence, the Holy Spirit, and ministry of forgiveness in spare stanzas. The simple language addresses their prison of fear without naming it:

> 'You, vulnerable (too),
>
> with truth I breathe,
>
> with My love, you can go
>
> out (too). See, you are with

---

had suddenly snapped back[;] . . . the Resurrection was the greatest 'eucatastrophe' possible and produces that essential emotion: Christian joy which produces tears because it is qualitatively so like sorrow, because it comes from those places where Joy and Sorrow are at one, reconciled, as selfishness and altruism are lost in Love." See Letter 89 to Christopher Tolkien.

Me still.
Just as We will:
you will forgive,
receive.'

Avison does not explain the disciples' response, "'Then it's not *that* we feared,'" except to deepen their awareness of grateful responsibility: "With their gladness and grief, / waiting, now, interfered." "Third Hand, First Hand" (*AN* 3.141) discussed earlier in this chapter, singles out doubting Thomas with his defensive explanation for his need for proof: "heartsick, tormented, not / open to silly words," "[A]lind in his mirrory grief." The announcement of Christ's presence is understated:

And
they heard 'Stretch out your hand . . .'
Thomas abandoned proof.

The miracle of the event is filtered through his consciousness with a subtle model for belief for future witnesses.

"Continued Story" (*AN* 1.48) imagines the anguish of Mary Magdalene before the empty tomb in a daring comparison with a woman abandoned by her lover:

What woman would not know?
　　　He was gone.
What woman would not try
blindly every device – vigil
by the night window, perfumes –
before facing it? No
lover beloved. Nobody.

The title of the poem guides the movement of Mary's evolving anguish and bewilderment through the separate events of death and burial to empty tomb. The first stanza suggests she slowly faces the reality of death: "What woman would not know? / He was gone." "No lover beloved." The second stanza has abruptly moved past the recorded journey to the tomb with spices to prepare a dead body for burial.[53] The poem focuses on the solution—the stone is moved—which brings no comfort and raises a new dilemma:

53. In the biblical story the women wonder who will move the stone for them (Mark 15:47—16:3; Luke 23:53—24:2).

> Cut off by stone?
> worse, cut off by
> no visible barrier:
> then all the more, her hope
> lay dying in her.

Jesus is not only dead, but now even his body has disappeared. Mary's pain is raw and immediate, without reflection.

> What woman would not
> scald her eye-sockets with those
> painful slow tears, largely unshed?
> to have lost even
> loss in an
> empty new day?

Her visceral reaction is framed in dramatic irony: "Whoever did this thing / is enemy: to me, now –." The impulse to turn to this perceived enemy—the "authorities," she believes—is out of a lover's desperation. The delicate interaction between her and Jesus, "supposing him to be the gardener" recounted in John (John 20:11–18), is curtained off by an abrupt shift in the poem and draws on the Lukan account (Luke 24:6) as well: "(He had purposed no riddle– / 'Did I not tell you?')." The question of "enemy" has been laid aside. A marked new section of the poem reveals resurrection transformation in Mary's experience and optic heart: "I don't know. But I saw, / she cried. He told me to tell you . . ." Now the question of having her testimony believed emerges as the point of the story in the climactic last three lines of the poem:

> What woman, what man
> dared believe her
> here in enemy country?

The ambiguous and again, ironic, last line lingers in the air. "Enemy country," pointing to the resistance the good news encounters, is balanced by the assurance of presence and power of the "Enemy" who emptied the tomb.

In another poem with a parallel title, "The Whole Story" (*AN* 3.155), a similar transformation occurs. Avison presents a witness who has moved beyond that initial panic into the realization of essential meaning for her own person.

> Behind that stone before
> it was rolled away

a corpse lay.

There lay all I deplore:

fear, truculence – much more

that to any other I need not say.

But behind that stone I must be sure

of deadness.

"Continued Story" has been completed in the mind of the speaker in St. Paul's theological explanation of identity with Christ's death, burial, and resurrection. Echoes of St. Paul's declaration, "But if we have died with Christ, we believe that we will also live with him" (Rom 6:8), are obviously sounding in this particular rendition of the theme:

Once it is clear

it was a corpse that day,

then, then, we know the glory

of the clean place, the floor

of rock, those linens, know the hour

of His inexplicable 'Peace'; the pour

– after He went away –

of wonder, readiness, simplicity,

given.

The pain of death—of death to self—must be enacted before one can know "the glory of the clean place." Then follows "inexplicable 'Peace'" and "pour"—a peculiar noun echoing Joel's fulfilled prophecy, "I will pour out my Spirit upon all flesh," at Pentecost (Joel 2:28; Acts 2:17) and suggesting something similar to the English poet George Herbert's "glass of blessing" in "The Pulley."[54]

"Our Only Hour" from *No Time* (AN 2.228–30) imaginatively connects the biblical witness and its witnesses with the "blessed . . . who have not seen and yet have come to believe" via Avison's familiar juxtaposition of a wonder of the created world with the narrative of the Scriptures, in this case, a "sun-gilded" shrub by an apartment wall.[55] The poem's opening lines

54.
Let us' (said he) 'pour on him all we can'
[. . . .] So strength first made a way;
Then beauty flowed, then wisdom, honour, pleasure [. . . .]
Rest in the bottom lay.

55. See Appendix for complete text. The striking phrase "sun-gilded" is used again in "Window Conversation" in *Momentary Dark* (MD 57).

explode with the poet's dramatic vision, gaining in analogical significance as the poem progresses:

> In the sunslick a shrub, its buds sealed in,
>
> is skeleton'd in light. Sand clumps on
>
> > sand cast shadows.
>
> Out of strange oceans day has unscrolled,
>
> > (low shining) has smoothed
>
> a HERE from among
>
> farness and blueness and more, more, mounting and melting
>
> > to indigo, and the centripetal
>
> > fires of gold.

Beginning with her familiar sun metaphor she announces, "[D]ay has unscrolled" something to read: "a HERE from among / farness." The connection with the Easter story is abrupt and intense, moving from sunlight to lightning: "*His look was lightning.* / The extraordinary angel / stood [. . .] / the keepers were as dead men." In the unfolding of the poem's story that follows (and drawing from Matthew's singular account), the emphasis is first on the "extraordinary angel"—a lesser being than the risen Christ—one sent to announce the event, in short, a witness, and then the guard of soldiers at the tomb, reluctant and unhappy secondary witnesses.[56]

> The keepers till the day they died
>
> could not forget. Blindness still stabbing, from the
>
> > fierce glare of such a
>
> > countenance (in the undwindling moment
>
> when they blacked out).

> Not everybody sees
>
> something like that in his time.
>
> And then can never
>
> distance it by
>
> words ('I always remember
>
> > The morning . . .')
>
> Nobody could have heard.

The repeated and emphasized statement in the poem, "*His look was lightning*," points to the essential moment, "our only hour," for these keepers at

---

56. Matt 28:1–15.

the tomb. In another shorter lyric in the same collection "Bolt from the Blue" (*AN* 2.232), the poet dramatizes the profound experience of a god or God as lightning,

> [w]hen something . . . split? – bright
> terror, eardrum-crack,
> conveyed, not the daylight
> beyond sky's iodined mask
>
> but the mask's volt,
> discharge within the veil
> (Zeus with his bolt
> they used to envisage).

Here in "Our Only Hour" the experience is, in retrospect, memory that will not recede:

> It is a disappointment
>   to have seen
>   the singular brightness and be
>   only as dead men,
> and then exist, later that day and on and on:
>   the point of it
>   searching you, idly now, somehow, in
>   a gathering silence, a history
> compulsively reviewed.

Mid-point in the poem in a brief three-line stanza a subtle contrast is introduced. There is the keeper "waiting it out in the hours of his darkness" and the agony of a "gathering silence" of now not seeing or hearing. It is a far different moment for the women receiving the angel's message at the tomb. Three stark sentences sum up their joy and suggest the same for future witnesses:

> Three women were there.
>   God kept them from terror.
>   Truth shone, and shines.

The meaning of the story seems obvious at this point as the poem returns to interpreting the shrubbery transformed by the "keen north sun" and broadening out to "wide continents" and "our multifarious kind":

> we receive 'all' easily but
> glimpse something, once or twice,
> which in our only hour will be
> massively known.

It is vital, Avison seems to suggest, to join the women at the tomb, not the guards.

But there is a delicate surprise at the end of the poem that captures her own gentleness of witness, perhaps even offering hope to the keeper in the silence and darkness. The poem ends not with the angel with the look of lightning, but

> the man, torn, stained,
> left in mummy-wrappings,
> stone under stone.

Once again, there is the blending of sight and sound, of seeing and hearing that fits with hearing and receiving the Word:

> the man then seen
> alive, known
> powerful, heard
> in the heart's ear?

>   He does not so stagger belief
>   as overwhelm our grieving.

Furthermore, the poem highlights the inclusivity of the invitation—both the women and the keepers—with the embracing pronoun "our."

One of Avison's very late poems in "Too Toward Tomorrow: New Poems," "Early Easter Sunday Morning Radio" (*AN* 3.195), is a muted Easter reflection of a long perseverance of faith in what she calls

> the not yet except
> for a breath of, a
> far-off heralding of,
> sun.[57]

In this poem she embodies the mystery of receiving the word/Word with ultimate clarity. Earlier in "Interim" (*AN* 3.85), she has noted the difficult struggle to carry on when "He has come / to vanish—out of human reach"

---

57. See Appendix for complete poem.

and described the inevitable strain to see what is not yet to be seen.[58] "Our troubled faces clear to see him," she has explained. In the later poem, she listens on the radio to the youthful choir (reminiscent of shepherds on the hillside hearing the angel choir): "'Gloria!' they sing, / 'Gloria!'" The poet simply responds, "Why weep, old eyes, when / so suffused with joy?" Here is a moment of epiphany, when the veil is lifted temporarily.[59] Here is her unadorned testimony of settled hope. "Come and see."

58. See chapter 2 for additional discussion of this poem.

59. These poems about spiritual sight transcending physical sight echo Milton's apostrophe to "holy Light" in Book 3 of *Paradise Lost*, climaxing in his appeal:
So much the rather thou Celestial Light
Shine inward, and the mind through all her powers
Irradiate, there plant eyes, all mist from thence
Purge and disperse, that I may see and tell
Of things invisible to mortal sight (*PL* 3.51–55).

CHAPTER 6

"Go and Tell"
The Missionary Impulse in Avison's Poetry

Learning, I more and more
long for that simplicity,
clarity, that willingness
to speak (from anonymity . . .)
all those impenetrables.
("Concert" *AN* 3.65)

And yet I see you [. . .]
torn inside too
by your own torrent of words,
all through, you resolutely breathed in
sun and rain's sweetness
with simple joy.
("Seer, Seeing" *AN* 3.60–62)

What woman, what man
dared believe her
here in enemy country?
("Continued Story" *AN* 1.48–49)

In the same way Avison's poetry is a beckoning to "come and see," there is
a corresponding energy suggesting an active impulse to "go and tell." She

embraces the imperative to "go [to my brothers] and tell" that prompted Mary Magdalene to announce to the disciples, "I have seen the Lord" (John 20:18). In her writing merge the dual roles of witness and poet. When she speaks of the poet writing "as a mix of the resurrection life and marred everyday living," she provides an interpretive guide to the witness of her poetry as a persevering and unabashed telling, no matter how veiled the language.[1]

THE MISSIONARY IMPULSE

"The Apex Animal" (*AN* 1.53), the opening poem of the poet's first volume of poetry, *Winter Sun*, sets the tone and introduces the peculiar style of announcement characteristic of her witness. "A Horse, thin-coloured as oranges ripened in freight-cars," or "rather, the narrow Head of the Horse," begins a storyteller who assumes a reader's assent to an imaginative and mysterious reality:

> It is the One, in a patch of altitude
> troubled only by clarity of weather,
> Who sees, the ultimate Recipient
> of what happens, the One who is aware
> when, in the administrative wing
> a clerk returns from noon-day, though
> the ointment of mortality
> for one strange hour, in all his lusterless life,
> has touched his face.

Here is a mixture of fancy ("and from experience / commend the fancy to your inner eye") and concrete reality of an office worker whose inner life has been changed by some mysterious event but whose exterior conceals the transformation. No explanation or defense is offered for the strange details of the story. But the atmosphere of essential imaginative hiddenness has been established for the many poems to follow, confirming Daniel Doerksen's early assessment that the first two volumes, *Winter Sun* and *The Dumbfounding*, represent two different faces of religious orientation—the earlier one "searching" and the later "discovery."[2]

Again, in this first "searching" volume of poetry, and before she has formally declared her conversion to Christianity, Avison dramatizes the

1. Avison, Letter to Tim Bowling, October 5, 2001.
2. Doerksen, "Search and Discovery," 7–20.

activity and attitudes of a reporting witness in a particularly joyful poem, "Birth Day" (*AN* 1.127–28), arguably the happiest in this austere and complex collection of poems. While the poem is highly allusive and dense, so characteristic of her earlier style, its narrative frame is straightforward and clear, embodying the essential elements of Christian witness. The speaker of the poem seems to be a messenger bearing important news—good news, in fact—that generates an appropriate response of joy from receptive hearers. The messenger is totally absorbed not in self, but in his message—that is, pointing to another. The compelling force of the poem is the actual news the messenger announces; his significance as a witness is dependent on the story he has to tell. The news, veiled and somewhat hidden, has an inherent darkness in its own obscurities and complexities. The poem's narrative is as follows:

> Saturday I ran to Mytilene.
> Bushes and grass along the glass-still way
> Were all dabbled with rain
> And the road reeled with shattered skies.
>
> Towards noon an inky, petulant wind
> Ravelled the pools, and rinsed the black grass round them.
>
> Gulls were up in the late afternoon
> And the air gleamed and billowed
> And broadcast flung astringent spray
>   All swordy-silver.
> I saw the hills lie brown and vast and passive.
>
> The men of Mytilene waited restive
> Until the yellow melt of sun.
> I shouted out my news as I sped towards them
> That all, rejoicing, could go down to dark.
>
> All nests, with all moist downy young
> Blinking and gulping daylight; and all lambs
> Four-braced in straw, shivering and mild;
> And the first blood-root up from the ravaged beaches
> Of the old equinox; and frangible robins' blue
> Teethed right around to sun:
> These first we loudly hymned;

And then
The hour of genesis
When first the moody firmament
Swam out of Arctic chaos,
Orbed solidly as the huge frame for this
Cramped little swaddled creature's coming forth
To slowly, foolishly, marvelously
Discover a unique estate, held wrapt
Away from all men else, which to embrace
Our world would have to stretch and swell with strangeness.

This made us smile, and laugh at last. There was
Rejoicing all night long in Mytilene.

The title "Birth Day" is unassuming, but it is not unambiguous, raising questions regarding its unnamed referent(s) and accompanying motivation for celebration for both messenger and waiting "men of Mytilene." The setting of the story generates curiosity by the specificity suggested in the poem's opening arresting sentence: "Saturday I ran to Mytilene."[3] Possibly Mytilene refers to one of those places the apostle Paul visited on his missionary journeys (Acts 20:14).[4] In one of its several variant spellings, Mytilene (or Mitilene) fits the coastal descriptions of the opening stanzas and a messenger on foot suggests a mode of travel of the early century of biblical times. The running messenger in the poem intuits an urgency to his task as, in contrast to the passive hills, "[t]he men of Mytilene waited restive / Until the yellow melt of sun." The allusive quality of the line suggests the prophet Isaiah's haunting poetic words: "People who walked in darkness have seen a great light" (Isa 9:2) and Zechariah's song: 'The dawn from on high will break upon us, to give light to those who sit in darkness' (Luke 1:73). Here the weather seems to be shifting from rain to "the yellow melt of sun," verifying the prophetic words.

3. In the original edition Avison spelled the place name "Mitilene." The Canadian poet Gwendolyn MacEwan writes of the emotional impact of that line when she first read it as a young poet: "That single stark naked line grabbed me in a stranglehold. . . . Can you plunk a line like that down at the very beginning of a poem and get away with it? How daring, and how glorious!" MacEwen, "Poetry and Honey Dew," 32. Her comment raises awareness of the role artistic appeal can play in witness. If creation can beckon one towards the Creator, the same appeal occurs with sub-creators.

4. On the other hand, Mytilene is also the place where the poet Lord Byron died. (Avison's MA thesis topic was "The style of Byron's *Don Juan* in Relation to the Newspapers of His Day.")

The messenger in the poem exclaims, "I shouted out my news as I sped towards them / That all, rejoicing, could go down to dark," an assertion responding to the restive men but also to the poet Wallace Stevens's dreaming "Sunday Morning" woman.[5] Repetitions in the poem link the "all" of the announcement with the next stanza: "All nests [. . .]," "all lambs [. . .]," "and the first blood-root," introducing a disorienting and ambiguous conflation of even bigger events in the central stanza. There "the hour of genesis" might speak of the world's original beginnings, "orbed solidly as the huge frame for this / Cramped little swaddled creature's coming forth." Key words—"firmament," "chaos," "swaddled creature"—signal allusions to distinctively recognizable stories of two birth days—the birth of the world in the book of Genesis and the birth of Christ in Luke's Gospel, evoking both Eden and Bethlehem in this twinned creation account. The syntax is ambiguous in the last four lines and allows for at least two possible readings. Avison's messenger perceives this "unique estate" as one "which to embrace / Our world would have to stretch and swell with strangeness." On the one hand, it could be the world that has to accommodate itself by some uncomfortable movement toward the unique estate of the Christ child. On the other, the peculiar phrase "to stretch and swell with strangeness" could intimate the suffering of the cross, suggesting it is the Christ child who is embracing the world. If so, there is an additional layer to the conflation of the major events, now including Christ's death.[6]

A third birth day is suggested in the potential birth of new Christians as the waiting men of Mytilene receive the message of hope. In Luke's Gospel "rejoicing" occurs when the shepherds respond to the announcing angels' proclamation, "Unto you is born this day, a Savior" (Luke 2:11), and they go to the manger to worship the Christ child. Rejoicing also occurs when the

---

5. "Sunday Morning's" bleak vision ends with lines that sound very similar.

6. It is not at all unexpected that other Christian poets' conceptions of the Christ story are evoked as Avison anchors herself in the full range of the tradition of English poetry. Her "'moody firmament / Swam out of Arctic chaos" sounds more Miltonic than biblical. The lines

Cramped little swaddled creature's coming forth
To slowly, foolishly, marvelously
Discover a unique estate

trigger several connections: Herbert's tenant in "Redemption" looking for a "new affordable lease" and finding the landlord has lately "gone / about some land which he had dearly bought" and T. S. Eliot's wise men in "Journey of the Magi" who look for the Christ child, finding instead the suggestion of three crosses. In these parallel moments there is a peculiar sympathy to see the full sweep of the redemption story. All four poets—Milton, Herbert, Eliot and Avison—play with time, making two events seem as one: the birth of Christ and the death of Christ meld into one salvation experience.

lost sheep, the lost coin and the lost son are found (Luke 15:1–32). In the context of the poems of *Winter Sun*, "Birth Day" stands out, anticipatory of the witness Avison's later poems bring. She moves beyond Stevens's picture of a tomb in "Sunday Morning," dispelling the gloom of his bird's downward flight, with a glimpse of Easter newness in the nests of "all moist downy young / blinking and gulping daylight" and "frangible robins' blue / Teethed right around to sun." Even the image of "the first blood-root up from the ravaged beaches / Of the old equinox" implies a miraculous transformation, with the toxic juice of its rootstalk producing a fragile wild white flower.

Here in this early poem of Christian witness is a glimpse perhaps, an imaginative experiment, of her "lighting up of the terrain" ("Voluptuaries and Others" *AN* 1.117). The allusive and elusive quality to "Birth Day" hints at the mystery and wonder involved in the sacred process of going and telling. Even the fact that this searching poem could be a pointer, a significant telling of the Christian story, suggests the delicate process. As one theologian has mused, "The witness is one who attempts the impossible: connecting the Unseen and the unseeing"; I would add, even when the witness herself is learning to see.[7]

In practice, the energy to go and tell is mostly hidden in the actual accounts of transformation and response to the risen Christ. Particularly in the poems of *The Dumbfounding* Avison says very little about the process of witness as telling. There are no stories of messengers hurrying to convey good news. Instead, the witness is already on the witness stand recounting in vivid and personal terms what could be her own experience in such lyrics as "Many as Two" and "Searching and Sounding."[8] "Many as Two" (*AN* 1.159) is conveyed as a dialogue reminiscent of Old Testament prophets arguing with Yahweh, sounding very much like an interrogation of a witness:

'Where there is the green thing
life springs clean.'
> *Yes. There is blessed life, in*
> *bywathers; and in pondslime*
> *but not for your drinking.*
'Where the heart's room
deepens, and the thrum
of the touched heartstrings reverberates – *Vroom* –
there I am home.'

7. Willmer, private conversation, June 5, 2007.

8. Other poems as well, such as "The Word" (*AN* 1.195–96), read like narrative testimony. See chapter 1 for commentary on the lyric.

Yes. And the flesh's doom
is – a finally welcome going out on a limb?
or a terror you who love dare not name?
(No thing abiding.)
No sign, no magic, no roadmap, no
pre-tested foothold. 'Only that you know
there is the way, plain,
and the home-going.'

Outside the heartbreak home I know, I can own
no other.
'The brokenness. I know.
Alone.'
(Go with us, then)?

From the outset the two speakers can be identified with the contrasting italicized and despairing lines of the witness and the ordinary typeset of the beckoning Christ. Additionally, and connecting with Yahweh, are the quotation marks. These are mediated words—interpretations of Scripture's declarations and intuitions of the faith required to embrace the Christian journey. In various statements throughout the Old and New Testaments, the prophets, poets, and apostles have elaborated on these themes. Now here Avison distills these faith statements into curious word pictures: "[W]here there is the green thing"—so startlingly vague for a precise poet— hints at the psalmist's images of tree and green pastures (Ps 1:3; 23:2); "where the thrum of the touched heartstrings reverberates" echoes the psalmists' songs emerging from pain (such as Ps 28:7; 30:11–12); "you know there is the way" evokes Jesus's words to the fearful disciples dreading his depar- ture (John 14:1–6). The two parenthetical phrases—"(No thing abiding.)" and "(Go with us, then?)"—extend the faith process as they are imagined, now condensed and reconfigured from the words of Scripture. *"No sign, no magic, no roadmap, no / pre-tested foothold"* exposes the witness's experi- ence of her deep fears. The response is only partially comforting: "'[T]here is the way, plain, / and the home-going.'" The poem's ending, *"Outside the heartbreak home I know"* matched by the "brokenness" and "aloneness" of the beckoning Lord and Savior, never named, reveals the speaker's intense vulnerability as reporting witness.

"Searching and Sounding" (*AN* 1.199–202), the most elaborate of explicit witness poems of *The Dumbfounding*, recounts the story of a rest- less searcher: "I look for you" [. . .], "find you here" [. . .], "run from you"

[. . .], "and as I run I cry."[9] In her search she sounds the depths of human experience:

> not in Gethsemane's grass, perfumed with prayer,
> but here,
> seeking to cool the grey-stubbled cheek
>   and the filth-choked throat
>   and the scalding self-loathing heart, and
> failing, for he is
> sick,
> for I [. . .]

It is in the difficult shared scenes of human pain, making her heart sore, and making her weep, that she unhappily intuits the requirements of finding the One whom she seeks. She identifies herself with those white dwarf stars that burn out:

> as though you can clear
> all tears from our eyes only
> if we sound the wells of weeping with
> another's heart, and hear
> another's music only [. . .]
>
> Dwarf that I am, and spent,
> touch my wet face with
> the little light I can bear now, to mirror [. . .]

The dream that follows takes her from recognizable desolation—"sandstone, baldness, the place / of jackals, the sparrow's skull" on further down "to the farthest reaches / where your Descent began, on the beach gravel" of the sea. "To what strange fruits in / the ocean's orchards?" she wonders. Once again, the focus of her reflections shifts to the great sacrifice of the Light's downward journey, making her own care of others seem not only possible, but essential:

> GATHER my fragments towards
> the radium, the
> all-swallowing moment
> once more.

9. This poem is introduced briefly in chapter 1.

This kind of telling, the poet suggests, originates in the mind and mystery of the invisible third person of the Trinity—"self-effacing" and "loving / with him [Jesus], yourself unseen" (". . . Person, *or* A Hymn on and to the Holy Ghost" *AN* 1.192). The pattern of narration is quietly transferred from the person's story to the larger Christ story. She condenses the mystery of the shared roles of human and divine witness as she elaborates the Spirit's miraculous freeing of one "from facelessness." There is the expectation of declaring that story; there is also the promise of on-going power and presence in the witness:

> Let the one you show me
> ask you, for me,
> you, all but lost in
> the one in three,
>
> to lead *my* self, effaced
> in the known Light,
> to be in him released
> from facelessness,
>
> so that where you
> (unseen, unguessed, liable
> to grievous hurt) would go
> I may show him visible.

What is suggested for the life of a witness—"so that where you" [. . .] "would go / I may show him visible"—applies to the poems as well.

St. Paul, as missionary and evangelist, embodies the passion and pattern of witness for her. Twice in "Branches" (*AN* 1.185–86) she refers to that powerful event that kindled the missionary impulse in the apostle. Early in the lyric she speaks of the "Light that blinded Saul / blacked out Damascus noon." Further down she compares the extremity of that Light, with its capital letter pointing to its metaphorical significance, with her specific locale, "Toronto's whistling sunset [. . .] / a pale, disheartened shine," bringing the two together. In her wordplay she establishes the power and appeal of that Light:

> Stray selves crowding for light
> make light of the heart's gall
> and, fly-by-night, would light on
> the Light that blinded Saul.

Later, the poet simplifies the witness motif and intensifies Paul's single-minded vision in *sunblue*'s "As a Comment on Romans 1:10" (*AN* 2.60). In three short stanzas she summarizes the dramatic story of Paul's missionary journeys, originating in his Damascus encounter:

> Paul petitioned to go
> to Rome 'by any means'
> and was led by the centurion
> to the Emperor's death-row.
>
> Yet he urged it. He was
> glad these new Romans existed.
> His wisdom was enlisted as
> their ally, to find them his.
>
> It did not save his neck
> or probably theirs:
> he knew beforehand that when light appears
> it must night split   and earth quake.

His Damascus "seeing" (Acts 9:1–19), emphasized here by spacing in the line and splitting apart the final word (changing noun to verb), sets off a chain reaction of shared divine and human activity, illustrated by his journey to Philippi and his announcement of salvation to the jailor in the earthquake (Acts 16:16–34). The silent implication of the narrative is a possibility of another chapter about witness in its repeated action—"when light appears" to other witnesses.

A third poem about St. Paul in the later collection *Not Yet But Still*, "A Basis" (*AN* 3.40–41), complicates the witness and suggests a different perspective on going and telling. "Most threads are twisted. / They tend to knot," she explains, by analogy,

> I.e. the best
> must be, on earth,
> only the worst in course of
> being transfigured.

She imagines the pressure exerted on both Paul and those around him in their collective enterprise, suggesting that "[t]he missionary 'call' / is part expulsiveness." The word choice is distinctive in its particularity. "Expulsive" can mean "driven out," and "repellant," allowing for accompanying ambivalent connotations.[10] There is a quality about going and telling that disrupts and disturbs those around the witness, the official "senders":

> In all, in Antioch,
>
> stresses through Paul, the saint
>
> (despite that gentle 'encourager' on his team)
>
> may have begun to fray a seam or two.

She wonders about this great missionary: "Was he / a venturesome unsettler?" There is the larger picture of the apostle's great accomplishments:

> Where he went,
>
> restlessly, on and on,
>
> his stays established outposts of the
>
> heavenly imperium which must
>
> in turn disrupt all empires.

But back at home ("in Antioch") the process of sending Paul out has been similarly disruptive for the "saints" who

> experienced then the senders'
>
> stresses, unsettlings, frayed seams;
>
> but also they experienced
>
> the saint's propulsive
>
> fire in the bones.

Therefore, the energy and restlessness of the missionary impulse in the great apostle suggest for the poet an uncomfortable uneasiness about the motivation for mission: "So an expulsive Paul / was after all the heartbeat of heaven's purposes?" she muses.

Avison explores the same lingering questions about the human element of witnessing in some of her prose reflections. She is direct and candid in a letter to her friend Anne Corkett about the twisted threads of being sent ones—now in the smaller arena of current relationships—when she writes,

> Your friend's being drawn by Holy Ghost power through your own drawn-ness is also lovely in excelsis. . . . More & more I'm trying to ted [sic] out what is evangelical sub-culture (conformity, slavery to others' ideals and notions of what is Right) and what is of the family of faith (slavery to Christ Jesus our Lord because in Him we are all children of one Father & stuck with

---

10. Admittedly, "driven out" is rare and "repellant" is obsolete (OED); nevertheless, Avison would mine all meanings in her word choice.

each other for all the natural puzzlement & even distaste that may cause any one of us—and stuck with obedience absolute). . . . Is 'witnessing' a 'gift of the Spirit?'—is it ever a flow, joyfully, for any but the most mature Christian? . . . if I go I have to go as I am, not according to anybody's idea of how-to or ought-to-be, but on those terms going is scarey [sic] but like you with your friend really?"[11]

One can hear in the letter a kind of anxiety regarding her own idiosyncratic approach to "witnessing." Does she need the Christian community's validation or is she confident to "go as [she is]"? Avison's poem "A Basis" takes the same questions about any injunction to "go and tell" and proposes that the process and outcome are not straightforward—even for the greatest of evangelists! Three options might account for the witness of St. Paul: "Expelled? Sent? Summoned?" The poet links herself to the apostle in her frank head note to the poem:

Preface. This is about
many of us. You deride
the stereotype of my peculiar
subculture? That would be good-
bye to something you might want understood.

In her quasi-defense of her "peculiar subculture" she does not identify the stereotype or its corrective; rather, she leaves the poem to speak for itself and also for her connection to St. Paul.

Surrendered to
impulse some venturers may go
alien ways – were these galling at home?
    Expelled? Sent? Summoned?

The outcome is the same,
there and even here.

She hints at her own *modus operandi* with her sometimes disturbing lyrics and a possible personal restlessness carried over into the poems.

11. Avison, Letter to Anne Corkett, December 17, 1981.

WITNESS FAITHFUL TO AVISON'S OWN PERSON

In identifying with the apostle Paul's "propulsive / fire in the bones," Avison reveals a complexity to her poetry's witness. What does the resurrection life look like for the poet? How does it "mix with marred everyday living?" How does she live? How does she speak? How does she write? She readily acknowledges limitations: "No fool-proof formula exists for using a poetic impulse to God's glory," she writes in "Muse of Danger." "The child of God claims the victory of Christ, and yet lives embattled from moment to moment, falling often and constantly knowing no power except through forgiveness."[12] Human fallibility and limitation are recognized from another angle. Years later in her Pascal lectures the poet remarks, "The truth given in the Holy Word is a disciplined, but not a manageable enterprise. . . . Truth is final, but our mortal grasp of it never can be final." In fact, the tables are turned, she goes on to suggest: "The word of truth is living and probes us continually as we live our days and nights."[13] These observations are enacted over and over in individual lyrics, as she works out her own salvation and in turn formulates her witness.

Witness in poetry with her particular stamp and coloring has distinctive characteristics. I suggest three to consider: (1) She reveals an independence of spirit. She sees and experiences life in complexity, contradiction, and hiddenness; consequently, her gospel-telling reflects that same trio of characteristics. (2) Her social consciousness in her concern for the environment and love for the city's most vulnerable inhabitants is an essential part of her telling-witness. (3) Words for the poet are pointers, not weapons.

AVISON'S INDEPENDENCE OF SPIRIT

The first volume of poetry after her conversion, *The Dumbfounding*, establishes her compulsion to tell. Obviously, she takes on St. Paul's passion as her own. When he exclaims, "For I am not ashamed of the gospel; it is the power of God for salvation to everyone who has faith" (Rom 1:16), she gives assent in these intense explorations of her new life in Christ. Almost half of the lyrics in that volume carry an explicit witness, most notably in the cluster of poems, including the already noted "The Word," "The Dumbfounding," and "Searching and Sounding." However, it is *sunblue*, twelve years later in 1978, that seals her reputation, and to some degree, determines a divided audience. David Kent has noted, "*sunblue* reveals Avison fully emerged as a

12. Avison, "Muse of Danger," 33.

13. Avison, *A Kind of Perseverance*, 70–71.

devotional poet in the English tradition and has confirmed her position as a major religious poet."[14] Her Oxford University Press edition *Selected Poems* in 1991 is even more unequivocal: "Her recent work records her conversion to Christianity, which now informs all of her poetry."[15] Clearly, her Christian witness is not a secret. At the same time, it is not a direct telling, even in the pages of *sunblue*, which has generated the most discussion regarding her Christian orientation. She embraces the burden of telling but shapes it in her own distinctive style. She can be bold but correspondingly subtle and obscure. She is often candid but also coy. She can be playful and serious, hidden and open. Her "whole tendency," described early on, is "to inquire, to probe, to try out, and to test possibilities. She is a poet who does what she must—what the passion to discover truth drives her to do."[16] Therefore, the exploring is integral to and shapes the telling. What she discovers and reports can be jarring sometimes, and even contradictory to the joy of the Christian message.

The significant religious and biblical content in the volumes of her poetry is the primary indication of boldness. In her eclectic and varied range of material, both direct and indirect religious lyrics dominate the landscape of her poetry. Twenty-two of the fifty-two poems in *The Dumbfounding* are focused on a Christian topic; thirty-two of eighty-two poems in *sunblue* are clearly religious; *No Time* has forty-five of its 115, *Not Yet But Still* has twenty out of its sixty-three, *Concrete and Wild Carrot* has twelve of its thirty-five and *Momentary Dark* has fifteen of its fifty poems speaking to the Christian faith. The essentials of the Christian life comprise a worthy poetic subject for Avison. Often titles of poems are strikingly bold and idiosyncratic.

". . . Person *or* A Hymn on and to the Holy Ghost" (*AN* 1.192) in *The Dumbfounding* openly invokes the Trinity. The volume *sunblue* begins with eighteen poems, including a series of sketches that record observations of everyday living and subtle hints of incarnational life.[17] "Water and Worship: An Open-air Service / On the Gatineau River" (*AN* 2.33), the next poem, is jarring in its introduction to a ritual, "an open-air service" of what she later calls her "peculiar subculture" (*AN* 3.40–41) and leaves no doubt of her missionary impulse. "The Bible to Be Believed" (*AN* 2.62–63); "The Cursed Fig-Tree: The form not the purpose of the parable" (*AN* 2.243–44); "Notes from Dr. Carson's Exposition of 1 John 5" (*AN* 3.142); and "On a Maundy Thursday Walk" (*AN* 3.174–75) all compel awareness of her interest in the

---

14. Kent, *Margaret Avison and Her Works*, 4.

15. Avison, *Selected Poems*, back cover.

16. Avison, *The Dumbfounding*, back cover.

17. See Chapter 3 for an earlier and fuller discussion of this theme.

Bible and Christian holy days. In effect, the poet is announcing the effect of the Christ story on her person—her activities, her reading, her thoughts.

At the same time and equally significant to her bold witness, religious and biblical content, while dominant, is not the sum total of her reflections. In fact, more of Avison's published poems are not about Christian subjects at all. The poet is not always writing about Jesus. In *Momentary Dark*, for example, Jesus is not even named until "Prayer of Anticipation" (*MD* 58), more than half way through the slender volume, and then only once more in "Two to One" (*MD* 64–65). Any book of her poetry will yield a broad range of themes, embedded in the natural everyday events of an ordinary Christian living out her life. Her experiences parallel the lives of other ordinary people. She is awakened in the middle of the night when

> Around 4 a.m.
> the hermits come
> and gun a jalopy
> apiece down the empty
> unseen car-track

in "Contemplatives *or* Internal Combustion" (*AN* 2.42). "Lament for Byways" (*AN* 3.161–62) evokes familiar nostalgia for a city that has changed:

> Through spy-
> holed fences, we inspect
> the backs of streets we knew
> before.

She calls women working in offices "Lemmings" (*MD* 14):

> In cruel office shoes
> Five o'clock ladies pound
> past, toward their release.

She reflects on the necessity of two-income families in "A Women's Poem: Now" (*AN* 3.55):

> Women are breadwinners perforce
> when their pay is their sole resource.
> Or when couples aspire to arrive
> at a house – not a cell in a hive.

She knows how to articulate the empty home in "Loss" (*AN* 2.262):

> Trees are long gone,
> and the clutter of children gone
> and the sun washes in to the bone.
> Here pain hit home.

Parallel experience in "Meeknesses" (*AN* 2.166)—

> an examination room, to the examiner,
> whether medical or academic,
> whether with stretcher and gowned patient or
> young scholars flushed intent submissive –

the poet suggests, "presents pathos." In "Technology Is Spreading" (*AN* 2.43),

> Two men hatless plodding
> behind, in the rain
> one to the other confiding

catch her attention with their familiar "stratagem":

> 'When using a
> computer it is always desirable
> to stick to one language.'

Avison can see and then articulate the unusual in the ordinary experience, giving heightened significance to what often goes unnoticed and unnoted. These lyrics with their common, but uncommonly noted, events, ideas, and emotions produce a striking foil for the Christian poems that accompany them. The resonance in the one poem verifies the integrity of the religious experience in the other.

While she is, indeed, capable of bluntly speaking (and often does) about the joys and obligations of Christian witness, her poetic method is often more subtle and indirect. Frequently, she enacts Jesus's parable about the kingdom of God as she beckons and then sends her readers looking for the treasure she found hidden in a field and then hides it herself.[18] The opening poems of *sunblue* again provide an example. They establish a reverent atmosphere of delicate detail, and even a sense of the holy, a quality in George MacDonald's writing that attracted C. S. Lewis.[19] She sets up memorable

---

18. "The kingdom of heaven is like treasure hidden in a field, which someone found and hid; then in his joy he goes and sells all the he has and buys that field" (Matt 13:44).

19. See Lewis, *Surprised By Joy*.

contrasts between "the yellow-helmeted men," "a work gang on Sherbourne and Queen," and "the hostel's winter flies" of destitute men across the street (*AN* 2.18); or again, the "cold layered beauty / flowing out there" and "such creatureliness" "indoors promises" in "End of a Day *or* I as a Blurry" (*AN* 2.23). She notes the "miles of beeswax mist" from one train window (*AN* 2.21) and "grasses bronze and tassel-tawny" (*AN* 2.20) from yet another; she observes "necklacing ant-feet; robins' toe-pronging and beak-thrust" at "grass-roots level" (*AN* 2.25).

> Behind the rainmurk
> is, I persuade myself,
> a mountain shouldering
> near enough [. . .],

she thinks in "Let Be" (*AN* 2.32). In each of these opening lyrics there is a kind of privacy and intimation of the holy Other rather than an obvious heralding of Christian good news.

One of these subtle early poems in *sunblue*, "Stone's Secret" (*AN* 2.26–27), attempts and achieves more in its strange revelations.[20]

> Otter-smooth boulder
> lies under rolling
> black river-water
> stilled among frozen
> hills

sets off an imaginative tour of outer space. The impenetrable stone under water here on earth is nothing compared to the secretive stones in space:

> Out there – past trace
> of eyes, past these
> and those memorial skies
> dotting back signals from
> men's made mathematics [. . .]

> out there, inaccessible
> to grammar's language the
> stones curve vastnesses,
> cold or candescent [. . .]

---

20. See Appendix for complete text.

Their privacy and mystery are sustained which neither mathematics nor language can access "out there." The poem takes another turn, however, intimating a secret that supersedes any mystery nature affords. In its closing stanza creation has pointed to the Creator and announces a dramatic movement in time and space:

> Word has arrived that
> peace will brim up, will come
> 'like a river and the
> glory . . . like a flowing stream.'
> So.
> Some of all people will wondering wait
> until this very stone
> utters.

The words of both Second Isaiah and Luke are evoked, uniting the anticipated peace of Jerusalem with Jesus's triumphal entry into Jerusalem: "I tell you, if these were silent, the stones would shout out" (Luke 19:40).[21] The allusions establish the poem as a vehicle for announcing the good news of the gospel. Movement expands beyond the stones of earth and space. Now it is a matter of witnesses releasing the secret of the King's arrival.

The delicate and subtle can soften and even transform the obvious. While the direct title "Water and Worship: An Open-air Service / On the Gatineau River" (*AN* 2.33) places her probably at the scene of a baptismal service, the poet's attention, however, is drawn to the image of the sun on moving water:

> currents within us course
> as from released snow, rock-
> sluiced, slow welling from
>   unexpected hidden springs,
> waters still acid,
> metallic with old wrecks –
>   but Love draws near,
>   cut-glass glory, shattering everything
>   else in
>   the one hope known.

---

21. "For thus says the Lord: 'I will extend prosperity to her like a river, and the wealth of the nations like an overflowing stream'" (Isa 66:12).

Her musings on the "waters still acid, / metallic with old wrecks" touched by the "cut-glass glory" of Love (the sun/Son) become an epiphany and an unexpected metaphor of the painful process of a person's transformation only partially realized, but nevertheless secure in its hope. The analogy provides the assurance.

But her subtlety does not preclude candor. In a number of poems the poet assumes the role of prophet, pointing a finger at human fallibility, sinfulness, and evasion. "Almost All Bogged Down" (AN 1.45–46) presents a picture of sinners who do not understand their desperate predicament. Four stanzas categorize different kinds of sinners by their self-presentations. Stanza 1 speaks of the most obvious but least harmful: "Some scamps are visibly so; their smell / repels their fellows." Stanza 2 raises the ante:

> Some rogues are adequately clean
> in clothes and under them, but have their tongues
> cankered.

Stanza 3 contains the defensive "victims" who are not as innocent as they assume:

> A handful shuffle haplessly, prefer
> to make the victimizers make their part
> plain, for the gain of foreheads clear
> and eyes that say, It's not my fault I'm hurt.

Her fourth group of modern counterparts of Pharisees is readily familiar to any audience:

> The rest? rascals as well, immersed in place
> of power or public service; oh, acquainted
> with others' taint. Their own they can suppress
> secure in the nice role of the anointed.

She does not allow sin any dignity or grandeur with her pointed titles "scamps," "rogues," and "rascals," implicating one and all. The gospel story is all the more startling in this context, introducing "once always one not one of us / choosing to be of us" with an offer of transformation that only "some few may following find":

> Vagrant, in ambush, challenger, masked
> or barefaced, everyone at risk
> gambles his own way. And the one
> of us not one of us is gone

a way some few may following find,

just, one by one.

The preacher in the poet has offered both a caution and challenge reminis-
cent of Jesus's Sermon on the Mount: "For the gate is narrow and the road is
hard that leads to life, and there are few who find it" (Matt 7:14).[22]

Avison employs Amos's memorable phrase "cows of Bashan" twice,
connecting the Old Testament prophet's blistering critique of exploitation
to her fear of the same. Amos "fulminates," the poet observes. "Hear this
word, you cows of Bashan . . . who oppress the poor, who crush the needy,
who say to their husbands, 'Bring something to drink!'" (Amos 4:1).[23] She
uses the image first in "Incentive" (AN 2.261) to identify the unrecognized
need of her generation:

(cows of Bashan

slaking our thirst, calling for more,

squashing poor people and not even noticing

and on the right days all in good order

sailing down aisles, heaping up

flowers on the altar etc.)[24]

In turn, she trembles at the possibility of judgment:

we look to him for

?no bread

no rain

leaf-shrivel and pests and

fevers and sores and

violence?

These calamities, she hopes, will be enough incentive to incite repentance—
"would but these bring us back to / [. . .] the waiting, the hope." The second
time she evokes the phrase is in the opening lines of "Seer, Seeing" (AN

22. Or "If any want to become my followers, let them deny themselves and take up
their cross daily and follow me" (Luke 9:23).

23. The prophet's words of judgment that follow are relevant to Avison's borrowing
of the phrase: "The time is surely coming upon you, when they shall take you away
with hooks, even the last of you with fishhooks. Through breaches in the wall you shall
leave, each one straight ahead; and you shall be flung out into Harmon, says the Lord"
(Amos 4:2–3).

24. See Appendix for complete text.

3.60–62), an intense dialogue with Amos where she agonizes over her iden-
tification with her culture:

> I am no cow of Bashan, Amos.
> No. I'm not poor, for all I've tried to end up
> understanding that, by being it.
> It didn't work. I work.
> My meals are
> ordinary, and by no means
> easily shared in
> fact—though gestures can
> make maybe some
> trifling difference somewhere.

Even as she herself tries to resist oppressing the poor and crushing the
needy, she recognizes her unwitting complicity with her society. Neverthe-
less, she voices her critique, casting judgment on deficiencies and error, her
own included. As a result, she may elicit agreement on her diagnosis of the
human condition, bringing her readers to a point of crisis in choosing her
source of remedy. Indirection frequently softens the appeal as she stops
short of demanding assent. The closing lines of "Almost All Bogged Down,"
discussed above,

> And the one
> of us not one of us is gone
> a way some few may following find,
> just, one by one,

articulate the instinctive pattern.

In suggesting this link between candor and witness, I am not implying
a didacticism or agenda in her poetry. The witness is faithfully reporting
what she has seen, heard, and experienced. The poems do their own work.
One enthusiastic critic, David Mazoff, suggests this pattern of witness is
deliberate and intentional in 'her use of rhetoric, those skills and strategies
that she uses both to destabilize the text and to defamiliarize the reader.'[25]
In an exchange of correspondence between author and critic, Avison speaks
of "a few quibbles" she has with Mazoff's observations:

> I write by ear rather than from rhetorical "strategy" (perhaps
> the ear can apply tactics unbeknownst?), and some things you
> credit me with as strategies or "techniques" are just ear, sense,

25. Mazoff, *Waiting for the Son*, 19.

and insight "clicking"—it feels good after it happens but I can
never plan to bring it off.[26]

At the same time, she exerts a clever coyness in some of her poems that
resists closure. Her first volume of poems *Winter Sun* is filled with vivid
and memorable lines that cannot be pinned down. What is "the ointment
of mortality" which "has touched [the] face" of the clerk in "The Apex Ani-
mal" (*AN* 1.53)? What is "the sweet surrender" in "Dispersed Titles" (*AN*
1.55–59) when she writes,

> Something wrought by itself out of itself
> must bear its own
> ultimates of heat and cold
> nakedly, refusing
> the sweet surrender?

What does she mean when she suggests, "Things of the heart occur here. /
Some wilt before sea-level" in "Rich Boy's Birthday through a Window" (*AN*
1.109)? It is her signature style to hint and hover around an idea and elude
tidy conclusions.

Agnes Cleves, in the dramatic monologue concluding *Winter Sun*
(*AN* 1.132–43), speaks for a poet capable of holding a person at bay if she
chooses:

> What story do you want?
> Tales of young love, or of that horse with wings
> The pink-striped circus lady rode, standing?
> Why should I tell such things
> Except to force myself, your peer.
> In the strange perfumed anterooms
> Of the fastidious voluptuaries.
> Have you remarked
> How few persist in penetrating farther
> And all of the rumour that subsides after them [. . .]

---

26. Avison, Letter to Mazoff, January 4, 1990. Her response sounds very much like
C. S. Lewis's correction of his assumed motivation for the Chronicles of Narnia: "Some
people seem to think that I began by asking myself how I could say something about
Christianity to children; then fixed on the fairy tale as an instrument. . . . Everything
began with images. . . . At first there wasn't even anything Christian about them; that
element pushed itself in of its own accord." (Lewis, "Sometimes Fairy stories may Say
Best What's to be Said, 36).

Go home, my dear. It is too late
And you are all abrim and pent
And the dark streets are tilted to a vacuum
Where things may happen [. . .]

One evening, just a year or two ago,
The simple penetrating force of love
Redeemed me, for the last perhaps. I've seldom dared, since
To approach that [. . .]
The need to tell you is exciting
And very bleak [. . .]

How is it that by now
The shaft of vision falling on obscurity
Illumines nothing, yet discovers
The way of the obscure? [. . .].

So it is not surprising that the poet will adopt a persona who can withhold a direct answer to a religious question, all the while revealing just enough to disturb the reader-listener. "Strong Yellow, for Reading Aloud" (*AN* 2.44–46), the poet explains, is "written for and read to English 389's class when asked to comment on my poem "'The Apex Animal,' etc.," and calls attention to her evasiveness and inventiveness. She creates a new horse for this new poem. This time it is a

[a] painted horse,
a horse-sized clay horse, really,
like blue riverclay, painted
with real mural eyes [. . .]
on the rainy Sunday diningroom wall.

Contrasting details between the painted blue horse "with / white hairs, the eyes / whited too" and the original "strong yellow" one of "The Apex Animal" (*AN* 1.53) dominate the poem and control the conversation, all the while she is aware of the essential question:

Q: 'The Head of the Horse
        "sees" you say in that poem.
Was that your vision of
God, at that period
in your development?"

The poet assesses the person asking the question.

> But I think, reading the lines,
> the person looking *up* like that
> was squeezed solid, only a crowd-pressed
> mass of herself at shoulder
> level, as it were [. . .]

The person in the crowd seems incapable of empathy and understanding of the poet's experience in creating the original picture of the Apex animal:

> no heart, no surprises, no
> people-scope, no utterances,
> no strangeness, no nougat of delight
> to touch, and worse,
> no secret cherished in the
> midriff then.
> Whom you look up from that to
> is Possibility not
> God.
> I'd think . . .

Therefore, the poet withdraws and steers the discussion to talking about the color of the horse and the playful role of the artist in her verbal creation of the two contrasting horses. The poem resists closure even as the speaker in the poem sidesteps the question. In its elusiveness the poem echoes Jesus's parabolic method: "To you has been given the secret of the kingdom of God, but for those outside, everything comes in parables; in order that they may indeed look, but not perceive, and may indeed listen, but not understand" (Luke 4:11–12).

"A Work-Up" (*AN* 2.41), a poem in close proximity to "Strong Yellow," is a whimsical and strange sort of parable that achieves something similar—a testing of spiritual acuity. Here Avison uses odd-angled humor to defamiliarize a common but serious condition. It is appropriately titled "A Work-Up," suggesting "a diagnostic examination of a patient" (OED). The poem is set up as a simple but surreal three-act play with an angel "examining" the unresponsive patient:

THE ANGEL OBSERVES

> lips, as if stone-carved
> cold, the grit lying unfanned and

> sand-dry – an engine-hood of a
> cathedral, cabaret spotlights –
> moving to speak. . . .

THE ANGEL ENTERS.

> (Mildly):
>> 'What *are* you about?
>> You're itting yourself.'

> (The wind suspires.)

>> The astonied eyelids
>> fail even to blink.

THE ANGEL BEGINS TO LEAVE:

>> 'Wind and light want to be bare
>> to your unringing ear,
>> beloved. Oh, beware!'

As the angel "(mildly)" assesses the "lips" "moving to speak," he sees a kind of refusal of something—an unresponsiveness: "You're itting yourself"; the patient is self-destructing. When "the wind suspires"—set off in parentheses, as if a stage direction—the patient still does not respond.[27] The angel might as well leave. The closing lines of the drama change the mood as they clarify the urgency. Heaven's messenger is going to withdraw: "Wind and light," powerful symbols of the Trinity, "want to be bare / to your unringing ear, / beloved. Oh, beware." The serious implication, however missed by the patient, is clear to observers who themselves now need to respond.

A later poem, "Instrumentalists Rehearse" (*AN* 3.100), demonstrates a softer playfulness, perhaps in its witness of the natural world.

> Fishes off on cruises
> dream, staring up to sky.
>
> Maple keys let themselves be
> sodden and mashed down
> into the earth. Their biddable eyes
> still towards the trusted
> nurturer's, without

27. Suspires means "longs for, yearns after" (OED).

any idea what

'fruitful' may turn out to mean

(one papery inch from lofted leafiness!)

– or 'multiply.'

While the brief lyric is part of a group of poems "For the Fun of It" in *Not Yet But Still*, its closing stanza suggests a gentle humor informed by religious persuasion. Her allusion the "planets and constellations / danc[ing] to like music" calls attention to medieval cosmology with its music of the spheres. Here in this whimsical poem she seems to be imaginatively connecting with the pre-Copernican model of the cosmos, suggesting the fish and the maple keys are "instrumentalists rehears[ing]." But the larger performance is in the heavens:

Planets and constellations

dance to like music

not needing to know that

their lost millennia will

shine in a fledgling owl's

eyes in the dark forest deep

deep in the heart of

their fathomless night.[28]

Yet the poem's conclusion is fully rooted in earth and the eyes of the fledgling owl. William Butt draws the connection between planets, constellations, and owls in terms of Avison's comment in *A Kind of Perseverance* that "[w]e still speak of the *uni*verse, the whole, without losing in that wholeness one particle of life's marvelous array of particulars."[29] He suggests these last lines of the poem reveal Avison's understanding of "resonant plenitude": "[L]ike Blake's burning tiger in the night, a baby owl grows radiant with its context—with all the distant implications of the universe. In its eyes shines

28. C. S. Lewis explains this activity in *The Discarded Image*: "We are watching the activity of creatures whose experience we can only lamely compare to that of one in the act of drinking, his thirst delighted yet not quenched. For in them the highest of faculties is always exercised without impediment on the noblest object; without satiety, since they can never completely make His perfection their own, yet never frustrated, since at every moment they approximate to Him in the fullest measure of which their nature is capable. . . . Run your mind up heaven by heaven to Him who is really the centre, to your senses the circumference, of all; the quarry whom all these untiring huntsman pursue, the candle to whom all these moths move yet are not burned," 119.

29. Avison, *A Kind of Perseverance*, 64.

light that eons ago left stars.[30] Obviously the humor and playfulness do not leave aside depth of insight.

At the opposite end of Avison's range of emotions is a profound seriousness that sounds the depths of human suffering. The resonance of harmony and light in the natural world in its "array of particulars" has its counterpart in distance, darkness, and polarization in turning away from the light. The poet explains her terrifying subject in the head note of "The Familiar Friend, But by the Ottawa River" (*AN* 3.66–67): "The person addressed is Judas Iscariot. The words centuries later reflect a possible train of thought in the human mind of his human-divine friend whom he would betray. And die of it." Several things complicate a familiar theme. Her note is typically ambiguous. To whom is she referring with the sentence fragment "And die of it"? The poem's title also blurs time and place. The setting by the river is established in the first stanza—in twentieth-century Canada:

> River, enriched in the last light:
> [. . .] the
> stillness brimming, like those
> muscular waters in the lingering light.

But she goes on to suggest this is "a possible train of thought" from scenes centuries earlier.

The second longer stanza has the "human-divine friend" revisiting the three years

> when we were
> at peace breathing companionability
> together

and reinterpreting "fleeting expressions, wordless mealtimes"—in short, engaging memory to explain a possible motive for such a terrible deed.

> I knew I am the one
> you one day, towards
> evening, would
> leave. You had prepared for
> what had to happen.

> When it did it burned
> deeper than your mind.
> Nothing will medicine the sore [. . .]

---

30. Butt, "Word and Action in Margaret Avison's *Not Yet But Still*," 845.

If the poem ends mid-stanza, it is understandable, for reliving betrayal has that particular inconsolable ache about it. But the poem has a startling Avisonian turn in the last two lines of the stanza: "[B]ut an abiding with the wordless glory – / mirroring waters flowing." The poem returns the focus to "by the Ottawa River" to the person speaking the thoughts of the one who was betrayed. This is another version of her '*uni*verse, the whole, without losing in that wholeness" a sense of the particular. Judas Iscariot's betrayal is the speaker's betrayal as well. The only comfort for the speaker is "an abiding with the wordless glory" (in contrast or in keeping with the earlier "wordless mealtimes"). There is "medicine" to be appropriated, the poem suggests, not something Judas seemed to act upon in the biblical account (Matt 27:3–8). The poem ends in its closing two-line stanza with a sobering realism not diminishing the horror of betrayal: "If only memory were not / one function of mind."

Similar to the other pairings reflected in Avison's distinctive style—bold and obscure, candid and coy, playful and serious—the poet moves between hidden and open in her witness of telling. There is a degree of hiddenness in most of the poet's lyrics, accounting for some of the difficulty in interpretation and immediate appreciation. Many of the poems already discussed have contained layers of hiddenness, often locked in a single word or phrase. One very short poem with its very long title "Miniature Biography of One of My Father's Friends Who Died a Generation Ago" (*AN* 1.187) illustrates the withholding of interpretive keys:

> You, sovereign, Lord, have let this be,
> Love's gesture here on earth to me.
>
> Your touch would prove all.
> Shall I fear it, who want your approval?
>
> My friend's sorrow
> I cannot endure. Our
> shrinking is your pain.
>
> Let Love's word speak plain.

To begin, it is not clear who is addressing "You, sovereign, Lord." Is it the father? Is it the father's friend? Is it the daughter writing the poem? Then there is no antecedent for "this" in the first line—presumably the key unnamed event that is central to the father's friend. The best that can be reconstructed from these non-details is that some sorrowful event has happened either to the friend or to the father. Some thing—probably this experience—is interpreted as a hidden indication of "Love's" care, distilled in the phrase "Love's gesture." But something is needed to verify this "gesture." "Your touch would prove all," addressed to the sovereign Lord, seems essential to the speaker, but there is a holding back, which is recognized as causing the Addressee pain as well. The last line offers some resolution, summing up the person's life: "Let Love's word speak plain."

Part of the hiddenness of the poem is the sense that this story has been told before. The distinctive use of "Love" hearkens back to George Herbert's famous "Love (III)," with its eloquent dialogue between the unworthy guest and "Love" who offers his costly hospitality.[31] Here in Avison's poem there are the same emphases—the gesture, the need for approval, the shrinking back, the final plain words of command, and response of obedience. She builds on Herbert's dialogue with the curious subject of her title, "Miniature Biography." In its repeated pronouns of "you" and "your" the poem seems to be as much prayer as it is biography. Here might be the point: The story of "One of My Father's Friends" is a record of a lifetime of prayer and obedient submission to the One who is called Love. Now the title of the poem is brought into question. Perhaps "My Father" is not the poet's earthly parent, but one whose son taught his own friends to pray (Luke 11:1–4).

This reticent and private poet can surprise readers with her sometimes transparency about facets of gospel living, effectually disarming those who may be open but reluctant to embrace the Christian faith. In "Beginnings" (*AN* 2.224) she states the common position of believers—whether seasoned or neophyte.

---

31. Love bade me welcome: yet my soul drew back,
　　Guilty of dust and sin.
　　But quick-eyed Love, [. . .]
　　Drew nearer to me, sweetly questioning,
　　If I lacked any thing.

　　'A guest,' I answered, 'worthy to be here':
　　Love said, 'You shall be he' [. . .]

　　'You must sit down,' says Love, 'and taste my meat':
　　So I did sit and eat.

George Herbert, one of Avison's favorite poets, has already been introduced in chapter 4 in an earlier poem of hers, "Intra-Political: an Exercise in Political Astronomy." In this poem she refers to Herbert's poem directly:

(George Herbert – and he makes it plain –
Guest at this same transfiguring board
Did sit and eat) (*AN* 1.97–100).

Each of us has

some sense of God

and we're all coping

with realities in our

life.

I have trouble getting the

two together.

You do too.

Everybody does.

Paul does.

In a sense he starts there.

In "Oh, None of That! – A Prayer" (*AN* 2.251), she draws attention to the dangers of sentimentality in one's religious experience in using her own variation of a peculiar term "namby pamby."[32] She personalizes the tendency by naming it in a prayer with the first person pronoun—"the cloaking faith I wear."

From the namby-pams

of the cloaking faith I wear

deliver me [. . .]

oh, from the namby-pams that evade

the absolute scrutiny

and evade healing, oh, deliver me.

Whatever I read or hear or see

only declares what is in me,

an ominous freight

hidden – and worse let out.

Neither does she avoid talking about the painful, dark experiences of life when God seems absent. She expresses fear and anguish and disappointment, particularly over the death of friends, most notably in the Jo Poems cycle (*AN* 2.115–37):

32. Namby-pam means "weakly sentimental, insipidly pretty, affectedly or childishly simple" (OED). The word's etymology is particularly interesting, as the OED explains. It is "a disparaging alteration . . . in imitation of childish speech) of the name of an author of sentimental poems (especially concerning children)" (OED) Major eighteenth-century writers, the dictionary reports, ridiculed Ambrose Philips in print. It is likely that Avison might have first read the word in Pope's *Dunciad* (3.322): "'Beneath his reign, shall . . . Namby Pamby be prefer'd for Wit!' (OED)." A poet of Avison's bent undoubtedly winces at this particular weakness.

My Lord, in horrible need I
turn to the Book, and see
sin and death, life in thee
only, and can not see,
O living Word, I cannot see to see.

I love this friend we've lost.
And the two-dimensional good
that was all I knew
       apart so long from you,
I cannot now dishonour, or belie.

But the truth brooks no denying.
There is a word, are words,
   that do not lie.

My friend is dead.

At the beginning of her prose poem "Job: Word and Action" (*AN* 3.102–15), framed as "A Book Review," she begins with a kind of apology: "Nothing will do / but to read the book." She recognizes her own limitations in comparison with the book itself: "For one thing, it is immeasurably better, / and clearer, and probably more accessible." But she admits a writer's desire with a touching openness:

Why write about it then?
Because I want to,
to cope with it
in human company.

While Avison's poetry causes dismay and dismissal at times for its obscurity and difficulty, those very qualities are also sources of power in the witness of her verse. As she probes ideas to discover truth, she draws her readers into exploration as well. Readers are her "human company," not her adversaries to be felled or conquered by persuasion.

Her perception and experience of life's complexity, contradictions, and hiddenness affect how the Christ story is passed along. Even while there is evidence of divine presence and activity, she dares to voice what may be lurking underneath an event or experience—unfairness, aloneness, or pain. One such example is the opening poem of her late collection *Momentary Dark* with its strange title, "Milton's Daughters: The Prototypes" (*MD* 1–2).

The ambitious goal of the great seventeenth-century poet is silently pres-
ent in Avison's twentieth-century address to his daughters. In *Paradise Lost,*
Milton asserts,

> What in me is dark
> Illumine, what is low raise and support;
> That to the highth of this great Argument
> I may assert Eternal Providence,
> And justify the ways of God to men. (1.23–26)

Now the poet is wondering how Milton's ambitions were realized. She re-
flects on the high cost for everyone involved.

> Imagine, in the deeps of night,
> the blind man, haplessly resounding with a surge of
> line upon line till he could
> bear no burdening more.

The creative effort is demanding for the blind poet with such high expecta-
tions of himself. But a more painful reality falls to daughters—these "proto-
types"—in a patriarchal environment, who were sometimes expected to be
Milton's amanuenses.

> You heard, and wrote: a process
> bypassing mind, or heart,
> I'd guess,

this twentieth-century poet sympathetically observes. She addresses Mil-
ton's daughters at the beginning of the poem as "[C]hildren of celebrated /
fathers." At mid-point, their title has shifted:

> Children of dust, summons can come at
> difficult hours, disrupting
> the sleep of nature.
> The voice must be heeded, the incomprehensible
> words forming at best
> a promise that,
> somehow, someday, everything will
> come into clarity.

Besides the obvious comment on mortality in "children of dust," the poet
must be implying some critique of the famous father who biographers

suggested denied his daughters the education to appreciate what they were recording.[33] The closing lines are haunting in their ambivalence:

> Daughters, sleep well
> while time runs on.
> Rise, docile, dim
> of spirit. Someday someone
> will bless you for it.

The poem ends with unanswered questions. Of what are Milton's daughters the prototypes? What does Avison mean when she addresses them in the end, "Rise, docile, dim / of spirit"? Is it a lyric celebrating or critiquing "eternal providence" and "the ways of God"—to "men"; that is, might she be ironic, implying God's ways have not been justified to women as well? Or is the poem meant to encourage women writers not to be "dim of spirit"? The poem's placement at the beginning of a collection entitled *Momentary Dark* suggests a witness that is oblique and questioning.

A second poem in *Momentary Dark* is also about a woman, this time an unnamed witness from John's Gospel, the Samaritan woman at the well (John 4:28–29). In the Johannine account there is a triumphant conclusion to her encounter with Jesus, but no record of the woman's experience afterwards: "Many Samaritans from that city believed in him because of the woman's testimony" (John 4:39). The poem "Hot Noon" (*MD* 46–48) imaginatively picks up where the biblical text ends, probing the woman's particular circumstance. The poem opens with a puzzling aphorism:

---

33. An earlier draft has the poet chiding Milton for his parental neglect: ("John, did you hear your / demands as they would sound / to bored, biddable children?"). The final poem maintains the consistent address to the daughters:

> Warm-hearted Samuel
> Johnson must have been
> exasperated
> on your behalf, saying that you
> had been schooled only
> in alphabets and sounds
> of Greek, Arabic, Hebrew,
> not in the words.

The poem with its multiple drafts and revisions in the Margaret Avison fonds was initially in two parts: "'Milton's Daughters: I (Context)" and "Milton's Daughters: II (The Prototypes)" and dated "February 26, 2003." The early version included details revealing a sensitivity, and even anger, partially concealed in the final poem. She muses,

> Was it a meek sacrifice?
> a Puritan, meticulous obeying of
> the 5th commandment? (unpublished draft)

The labourer

in a constructed wilderness

is sometimes desiccated,

possibly connected to Jesus's discussion with his disciples while the woman is in the city telling of her conversation with Jesus: "I sent you to reap that for which you did not labor. Others have labored, and you have entered into their labor," Jesus says (John 4:38). "Wilderness" and "hot noon," of course, carry metaphorical meaning particularly for this Samaritan woman with her sultry history. Avison's summary captures the woman's "constructed wilderness" and "desiccated" outcome:

'I'm weightless, rootless. There's not a breath

stirring, to move me. If

only I could have one last

sip of life! Then

let it be night. For good.'

She was

human.

The theological discussion she has had with Jesus, not the focal point of the poet's attention, is assumed but not re-constructed in the poem. The woman's subsequent testimony, however, is charged with energy in its compression:

And then

she ran off.

(Who'd listen

to her?) But her shouts

caught many. Some

had heard about him and ran

with the others, reckless in that

punishing sun.

The woman's formal witness, her going and telling, is complete, but her life still goes on. Avison's familiar "eye is astray."[34] The poet is concerned with the aftermath of the woman's "labour" and witness and what has happened in her complicated life. In contrast to the "hot noon" of the title, the event is over and now

34. See Avison's definition of "poetry" in "Poetry Is" (*MD* 27–28).

> [i]n the cool of the evening, in twos and threes
> they left, he with his friends.
> She watched them fade from view,
> sighed, headed her own
> way, all but alone. Tomorrow,
> or ever, would this day
> have to be
> *remembered?* As are
> those surprises that
> linger, faintly strange and
> bright like yesterday's stars
> and planets? (*MD* 46–48)

The poem continues to focus on the woman's awareness both of the unique connection with Jesus and her usual aloneness. She wonders how or if her struggle with relationship (her "constructed wilderness"?) will change after her conversation with Jesus. "What makes a human being co- / alesce with the other"? The poet speaks for the woman. The poem's closing stanza anchors the conversion of the woman in terms of everyday living. The transformation is a work of art not without struggle:

> How does the sequel go
> after the story we've heard? Fidelity
> tomorrow? or a naturally
> unsupported, solitary,
> gradually less and less
> defensive life? with
> reverence now for
> anyone human,
> even herself.

Visually, the decreasing lines places the emphasis on the gradual healing of the woman's own psyche. This re-telling of the story is the poet faithful to who she is and how she sees. Here again Avison expresses her own longing for authentic utterance.

SOCIAL CONSCIOUSNESS INTEGRAL TO WITNESS

Strong indicators of witness faithful to Avison's own passions and com-
mitments are poems that draw on a highly developed and sensitive social
conscience. One of the many contradictions that characterize the poet is
her seemingly elitist poetry in its difficulty and inaccessibility embracing
the world of the city's poor and disenfranchised. This disparity is shown in
an early poem "Far Off from University" (*AN* 1.130), in both the title which
announces the polarization between the world of the educated and elite and
the poor and the homeless, and in the colorful and eloquent language de-
scribing the "smouldering derelict caboose":

> the counter-confessional priest
> at daybreak through limp whites
> showed the sharp scapulae
> turned from his greased grill to take cash
> and at the doorway, with his spatula
> pointed, past sheds and fluted morning pigeons,
> across the shining steel of crisscross tracks, to
> the villainous hovel still sodden in night,
> in spite of wire-thrum and the sky's empty clamshell.[35]

There are startling religious overtones in the scene (and hence, its original
title) that connect the poor with the one who was born among them and
shows favor to them (Luke 1.52–53):

> After the sour
> senility of night, suddenly,
> a more than animal joy, a sanity
> of holy appetite awoke:
> breast bared for its blind suckling
> a more than mother leaned, drew breath, tendering.
> cement and weeds, sky, all-night diner, flesh,
> gathered as being; fumbling, fed.

The tenderness in this strange lyric reveals a sensibility of one attuned to the
city's hidden poor, an awareness which emerged early in Avison's life. In her
anonymous article, "I Couldn't Have My Cake and Eat It," she reflects on the

---

35. The poem was originally titled "June at Christmas." The new title obviously
nuances a different contrast.

profound effect of two experiences of her adolescence, The Depression and illness (anorexia), when she explains how

> I first knew people who knew real hunger, real want. Then I began to walk, for hours: city walks that bared the truly grim time this was for many. I saw solitary frayed bony men staring in bakeshop windows, standing out in the dirty snow. Everything was dirty snow at that time for me. I thought the answer was easy: give all we had away at once, and it would be all daffodils tomorrow . . .
>
> I stopped eating; I stopped enjoying. I wanted to be lost with the stunted frail creature with wrists like sticks out of raveled sweater-cuffs whom I walked and walked among on the dirty streets around the idle and empty mills and railroad tracks.[36]

The poet's awareness of the poor took on practical significance in the various stages of her nomadic career. Particularly in the decades following the publication of *Winter Sun* in 1960 and her conversion to Christianity in 1963 she engaged in employment that registered her solidarity with the underprivileged.[37] She spent a year writing abstracts for *The Research Compendium* of the University's School of Social Work, published in 1964. She first volunteered at Evangel Hall, an inner city mission run by Knox Presbyterian church on Spadina in Toronto, as a "women's worker," and then worked full time there from 1968 to 1972. From 1978 to her retirement in 1986 she worked as a secretary to another outreach organization, Mustard Seed Mission. One co-worker at Evangel Hall writes about the poet:

> Margaret loved and understood the characters at the Mission. She identified with their poverty, mental illness and aloneness. For one of the Mission's windows, Margaret wanted to write, "You don't have to go it alone." . . . Margaret Avison's life has been like a [sic] effulgent rainbow arching over brilliant and il-literate minds and the poorest of the poor.[38]

---

36. Avison, [Martin, pseudo], "I Couldn't Have My Cake and Eat It," 90. Avison sounds strikingly similar to Simone Weil. "At the age of five, she refused to eat sugar as long as the soldiers at the front were not able to get it. The war had brought the sense of human misery into her protected milieu for the first time, and her typical" writes Leslie Fiedler, in his Introduction to *Waiting for God*, 14.

37. David Kent reminded me that this was not a new emphasis for her. "[S]ome of her earlier empathy took the form of political activism (with the CCF, for example.) The *Research Compendium* project was published in 1964, but the offer was made to her in June 1962 and a year later the work was 'nearly done,' according to letters I've seen." Private conversation, October 25, 2009.

38. McIlveen, "Rainbows and Worn Out Shoes."

In Avison's article ". . . at least we are together . . . ," she outlines the complexity of issues confronting the city's poor. To begin, she asserts, "To have choices is the luxury out of reach of 'the poor,' isn't it?" and then proceeds to identify the maze of difficulties the "poor" must navigate in their subsistence living.[39] She muses on the difficult relationship between the "helpers" and the ones who need "help." Her lyric "Needy" (*AN* 2.83) articulates one of these painful specifics:

> 'The poor are always being
> inspected: by the
>> Fire Department, for litter, oily rags, those
>> lamp-cords from the washing-machine to
>> the hall ceiling socket, etc.;
>> by the
>> "worker" with new forms
>> to be written on;
>> by the
>> mission visitor "to invite
>> you to the children's pageant";
> somebody even inspects
> to check on whether it's true you keep chickens and goats!'

The irony of the poem is contained in the social worker's freedom "to need yet never be / needy." Yet, the inequalities do not excuse non-involvement. She continues in ". . . at least we are together . . .":

> our corporate sin is very great, as we demonstrate in society by inhibiting some people's social choices. This is the why of corporate social action by the church. Contrition is only the first step. The evils of oppression go on. And we must go on "working out our salvation," i.e. experimenting and exploring to find the Way here too to go and sin no more.[40]

Her lyrics recognizing and giving dignity to the poor and honoring those who are of like mind are not many in her total collection, but they stand out in their openness and passion. When she grieves for her dead friend in the elegiac "Jo Poems" (*AN* 2.115–37), she eulogizes one who did "much good" in

39. Avison, ". . . at least we are together . . .," 15.
40. Ibid.

    tough-minded steps towards
    protection for the most exposed,
    e.g. the night-shift dishwashers etc.
      who come and go within a week
      too ill   too far forgotten
      to care that 'no work' is
      also 'the worst,' or maybe
      simply not able to recall
      which all night spot it was
      they should be turning up tonight.

The vivid picture of the exploited night worker is given a place of honor in her commemoration of her friend. In the sketch "A Work Gang on Sherbourne and Queen, Across from a Free Hostel for Men" (*AN* 2.18), the poet offers a sympathetic picture of the destitute men reminiscent of Gloucester's despairing comment in *King Lear*: "as flies to wanton boys are we to th' gods; / they kill us for their sport" (*Lear* 4.1.37–38). Avison sees similarly:

    The hostel's winter flies
    where morning spills them out
    fumble, undisturbed
    by street or curb.

She is dignifying Mr. Jollyben's courageous suffering in "Diminuendo" (*AN* 1.36–37), living in the highrise where

    (there are no
    windows in that seven-storey wall, none
    at all),

and where he is unable

        to tilt
    a human face
    as the earth's face is tilted early, early,
    into the pineboard light.

"Simon: finis" (*AN* 1.220), "[B]one rick man on an iron cot [. . .] / laid out now in his tatters" at last receives acknowledgement in his final "gradual smile." Perhaps the most memorable portrait of the urban poor is her "July

Man" '[o]ld, rain-wrinkled, time-soiled, city-wise, morning man" (*AN* 1.160).[41]

While needs are pressing, she does not sentimentalize the disenfranchised. For example, she acknowledges in her role as a social worker that sinners and rascals hide among the poor. Her lyric "For a Con Artist, Who Had Given / the Worker a False Address" (*AN* 2.161–62) speaks of limited expectations as the poem's speaker makes a home visit:

> and there
> was nobody that name there
> since, or before of course,

and the writer

> contemplates the absurd [. . .]
> and her not on this street but somewhere,
> indulged, a little, at least
> for now.

Furthermore, needs overlap and city issues are muddled. In "Exchanges and Changes" (*MD* 77–78) there are many "sufferer[s] of cities."

> [H]ear me for
> green pastures are
> everywhere despoiled.

While she is lamenting deep environmental concerns, the poor intrude:

> 'Change,
> please,' chants the street-corner fellow.
> Doesn't he know the
> verb is transitive? 'Change
> my lot with a quarter
> of your huge holdings! Change
> my role, make me a
> giver who keeps back
> only the minimal means for a
> simple life. I'd like
> to look employable again, in time to
> work again.'
> And then change everything

41. See chapter 4 for an extended discussion of "July Man," "a stillness, a pivot."

with not a single despoiler's energies
agglomerating, ever
again.

While the expression of her empathy with the poor is compelling, as noted above, it is not her last word on the subject. Avison's poems about the poor extend beyond human empathy and sympathy. Her Christian witness is more complex, as she suggests in the narrative of her own journey:

> I wish I had known that Jesus really did become one with them, with me too. And that nobody else needs to do it, nobody can do it any more than we can be good. We can be with Him, beyond His Cross because we come to Him there to accept the exchanged lots, our death, His life. And then there is a way of getting to be where His suffering goes—but this I only begin to glimpse . . .[42]

In spite of her deep commitment to serving the "needy" and vulnerable poor, she recognizes the fundamental limitation of the will "to be good" or the will to serve. Only the Savior of the world can truly save.[43] She suggests in "Psalm 80:1—'Thou that dwellest between the cherubim, shine forth!'" (*AN* 2.85) who takes responsibility for the poor—whether literal or figurative:

> You know, Lord, You know us
> out in the dark and cold –
> and never planned to leave us out
> although shut out of old.
>
> [. . .]
>
> We didn't know You, Jesus.
> You came out in the night
> and poked around the side streets
> to bring us to Your light.
>
> We waited where the wind blew
> and knifed You in the rain.
> Yet You still know who's scared and cold
> and doesn't dare complain [. . .].[44]

42. Avison [Martin, pseudo], "I Couldn't Have My Cake and Eat It," 90.

43. As George MacDonald tells his charge in Lewis's *The Great Divorce*, "Only the greatest of all can make Himself small enough to enter Hell," 139.

44. See Appendix for the complete poem.

The same theme of divine partnership is delicately introduced mid-point in part six of the "Jo Poems." She begins the section with another short eulogy mixed with critique of government and society who has failed the poor:

> Daily and lifelong, Josephine,
> you gave voice to the mute
> hoping the deaf would hear, who all
> too easily, in affluent times,
> relegated the poor to a category
> (the 'residual poverty' of efficient,
> ah, and political, theory).

With only a simple typographical marker to indicate a new theme, the poet seemingly changes the subject:

> *Having*
>
> Sir, you have nothing
> the woman said
> Nothing to dip into water
> or carry water in [. . . .]

As the next stanza talks about the cooperation of sky and earth in the changes of the seasons, the familiar story of the woman at the well of John 4 is evoked, allusively suggesting the One who gave the Samaritan woman's life meaning and allowed her to serve him.

> The heart listens.
>
> 'You have a cup
> when I have nothing.
> Both must be
> for still refreshing overflowing new-day
>   joy to be.'

"Giving voice to the mute," in spite of obstacles, is a witness with its clear reward of companionship in shared purpose. The refrain ending the lyric, "Psalm 80:1—'Thou that dwellest between the cherubim, shine forth!'" carries a confidence in the sense of solidarity both with the poor and with the "Lord of Heaven" who watches over the lowly.

Some You have given food and warmth
now can go back out to
be with You in the darkness,
vagrants, focused on You –

[. . .]

Bless us, Lord of Heaven,
Bless us, Mary's child,
and keep our courage high with You
through steep and storm and wild.

The poet sees that sharing in Christ's suffering is an ongoing experience, a journey into and "in the darkness," and it is somehow connected with His concern for those "out in the dark and cold."

"Cross Cultural *or* Towards Burnout" (*AN* 3.48–49), a later poem, evokes a different situation altogether, raising a troubling specter for Avison, friend of the poor.[45] Instead of the knowledge of "at least we are together," she is drawn into the critical divide between cultures—once a far off reality, now plainly visible in a city in multi-cultural flux. The dominant word in the poem is rage:

Your rage is bearable
[. . .] yet your rage hurts / [. . .]
We are outraged at your
raw grief
[. . .] Therefore your rage is the long held under
knowledge [. . .]

She is facing her unwitting involvement with social injustice:

A post-colonial white woman, I am
therefore a thing-hog,
easy taker-for-granted, helpless
to unmake the bed
others made for me, even before
grandpa (and even he was
simply another fellow working long hours,
kindly respectful, whether paid or not).
And I lie, tossing, in that
incontestably comfortable bed.

45. See Appendix for complete text.

The witness in the poem is suggested in her confrontation with the biblical text, first through the prophet's announcement of judgment of one culture by another—a judgment ordained by a God who understands the slave's suffering and calls the exploiter(s) to account: "Through Jeremiah I had / faced up to God's fierce anger." Then the poet curiously submits herself to the other woman's rage—perhaps because she has already experienced the judgment of God in her knowledge of Christ.

> Therefore your rage is the
> long held under
> knowledge of the holy child's
> knowledge of
> the spittle, the
> flogged back, the suave
> manipulator's deathly mockery,
> present, every wracked
> generation, as if helplessly.

In the meantime, two separate single-line stanzas frame the vision of a future judgment on her own culture ("Ours," she emphasizes), which has exploited another. Her admission, "Your work is dark and bitter," is countered ambiguously with "Our God endures." The poem is a somber one as its title suggests—". . . Towards Burnout," and as its closing lines reinforce, with only one word "restoration" hinting at some possible hope:

> The sentinel trees
> on a far hilly ridge
> remind us of perennial
> destruction, restoration, on
> wave lengths much too vast to ease
> you and the child today
> or us into tomorrow.

As usual, she speaks with frankness and troubled honesty, admitting no ready solution—only recognition of the divide between her and the one she wishes could be in solidarity with her.

It is a short distance in Avison's poetic vision between concerns for the marginalized and the poor and the world's careless treatment of the earth. In "Transients" (*AN* 2.88), she dryly observes that

> The affluent city shaves the turfs
> (laid one sun-streamy March morning)
> by tractor-mower, tenders them chlorinated
> and fluoridated rain from
> sunken spigots,

only to be later undone by "a high-rise / enterprising developer" who

> uproots
> the lawnstuff, uncouples the subsurface
> aqueduction system.

The city does its part as it

> lays and trims and turfs up and
> replenishes and hardens in vacant lots and
> parking lots.

The comment carries with it an undertone of critique: "We are forever / doing, done-to." In "Exchanges and Changes" (*MD* 77–78) years later, there is less patience with the obsessive activity:

> Cement and paving
> seal off the hope of
> loam for more than our
> sons' and daughters' lifetimes.

She holds out hope in "We Are Not Desecrators" (*AN* 3.36), observing that "[m]y kind out there sullies / it all, as I do being here"; yet, "[a]fter a noisy night of rain / sun comes flooding." This promise of sun suggests

> Yet we, providing an unlikely
> context for miracle, maybe, alone
> are inwardly kindled.

Or again, in "The Implicit City" (*MD* 39–40), by its comparison to the future city of God:

> Yet O my city, rich as
> fistfuls of raisins, down here
> already, are you not,
> in spite of the
> rancid smell, the milling of

every sprig that has

found its foothold through a

broken sidewalk,

are you not, in

some breathtakingly

scary or brilliant moment

momentarily touched by,

bathed in,

a far-breathed holiness?

Nevertheless, she accepts a prophet's responsibility to speak out and call for change. This speaking out is part of her role as witness. "Ecologist's Song" (*AN* 2.266) is perhaps her most overt announcement of and call for concern and acknowledgement of its witness. Her opening lines of the poem have a sense of nostalgia: "Sometimes, where the sky bent brown / above a creased doeskin of new earth" brings to mind Hopkins's reverence of an ever-revitalizing nature:

Oh, morning, at the brown brink eastward springs –

Because the Holy Ghost over the bent

World broods with warm breast and with ah! bright wings.[46]

But here there is not that hope as "pillars plunge upwards, and through the thinning air / the pelting hail sweeps down." In the initial indications of trouble, the tension between the beauty of creation and its damage is almost indecipherable in the eloquent language describing the "[a]bsorbing, glittering" "beach at noon / welter[ing] with silence." Earth receives its wounds without complaint like the poor who have no voice. Someone has to speak for it:

There a separate pool

has formed, plum-coloured, richer than water, cool,

shadowed by stillness in the naked sun.

A sudden gust whisks a gold shower

of stinging sand on the dark sheen.

Who brings the petals, cupped and shyly white?

Why are they bruised?

Who glassblows dew shaking the droplets out

46. Hopkins, "God's Grandeur."

> to burn in icy leaf-tip and grass-blade
>
> clear of the clustering wood?

Avison warns of the interconnectedness of pollution in one part of the "lovely planet" affecting the rest:

> Everywhere's ocean of sun, late-flowing, knows
>
> the dark tides too, the netted shores
>
> of land and air wrapping the lovely planet
>
> round, and one knot of the net
>
> loosed, one strand plucked in the net,
>
> wake resonances through the hemispheres.

Therefore, she announces emphatically, "Attend. Attend": "[H]ere is / significant witness of an event." The damaged earth shows its wounds and she speaks for it.

In "Seer, Seeing" (*AN* 3.60–62), the poet continues to wrestle with the fact of collective guilt—of unintentional responsibility, but this time she invokes biblical authority.

> Institutions have all the words, but
>
> there's not an institution speaks for
>
> you, or for me hearkening for you,

she tells the prophet Amos,

> any more than for

> > her, left alive, with listening eyes
> >
> > sitting amid a strew of
> >
> > bodies where a passing gust
> >
> > ruffles, idly.

She works her way through Amos's "tides of holy anger" as he sees ancient Israel's complacency and self-indulgence. She distills the prophet's words of judgment, "I will tear down the winter house as well as the summer house; and the houses of ivory shall perish, and the great houses shall come to an end, says the Lord" (Amos 3:15), to the terse announcement: "Tear down / Tear down." She applies his vision to her twentieth-century world:

> Din into my ears
>
> your dirge, Amos. Set my last
>
> gaze on
>
> a whole people convulsed [. . . .]

She is disgusted by an abused environment and damaged people, and she cannot contain herself:

> I cannot yet
> see, my vision blurred by vapour trails,
> riot-torn cities' smoke,
> hot breathings from cored mountains,
> oh, by the too-late industries
>> puncturing pre-sunset smog
>> seeking too late to trans-
>> mogrify tropical and
>> other swarming nowheres to
>> spitefully replicate club men
>> and women and their
>> clubs and memories.

Amos, she recognizes, is a model in his role as prophet: He is a modest spokesperson seeking nothing for himself: "I am no prophet . . . I am a herdsman, . . . and the Lord said to me, 'Go, prophesy to my people Israel'" (Amos 7:14).[47] His range of language, both harsh and beautiful, establishes a pattern of witness to emulate in her own generation and place. But it is the mixture of pain and hope in the Old Testament prophet that speaks most to her and finally through her:

> And yet I see you
>> banking on seed and
> embers and all through
>> the world of bombast and
>> frozen-eyed bewilderment,
>> and torn inside too
>> by your own torrent of words,
>> all through, you resolutely breathed in

47. He speaks confidently of the one he represents—"the one who forms the mountains, creates the wind, reveals his thoughts to mortals" (Amos 4:13). The prophet employs dramatic and powerful language in his passion for justice. He condemns "the cows of Bashan" who "oppress the poor'" (Amos 4:1). He speaks God's words, "I hate, I despise your festivals. . . . Take away from me the noise of your songs . . . But let justice roll down like waters, and righteousness like an everflowing stream" (Amos 6:21, 23, 24). His words of hope speak of restoration for the land: "The mountains shall drip sweet wine, and all the hills shall flow with it . . . they shall rebuild the ruined cities and inhabit them; they shall plant vineyards . . . they shall make gardens and eat their fruit" (Amos 9:13, 14).

sun and rain's sweetness

with simple joy [. . .]

This strange combination of "torn inside" and "resolutely breathed in" "with simple joy" points to the familiar paradoxical way of thinking and experiencing life that so characterizes the colorful prophet.

WORDS AS POINTERS RATHER THAN WEAPONS

As important as her independence of spirit and social conscience are in understanding Avison's witness, it is in her view of language, "Adam's lexicon" and her "working tools," that her witness is most distinctive and individual.[48] When an interviewer questions her about the "deeply provocative statement" from "A Kept Secret" (AN 3.96)—

Darkness is changed

once it is comprehended; it becomes

knowledge, beyond our reach –

she dodges the religious subtext in the question. She describes the process of arriving at that observation: "I vividly remember the superb moment which occasioned that poem: a large bird flew up into a tree, and the combined play of tree-shadow and sun, darkness and light, were part of the exhilaration of the event." She goes on to explain,

Poetry can use concepts without taking them too seriously, as in this poem. I was writing poetically, not philosophically, even though "comprehended" might seem to refer to Isaiah's statement [Isa 9:2 perhaps]?[49] The poem merely tries to express the wonder of creation as seen in a flash.[50]

While the poem obviously explores different kinds of metaphorical darknesses—

The dark was not

Thomas Hardy's not

the West's gaunt watershed:

bedaubed everyman, ducking

from any horizon –

48. Avison and Martin, "A Conversation with Margaret Avison," 74.

49. "The people who walked in darkness have seen a great light; those who lived in a land of deep darkness—on them light has shined" (Isa 9:2).

50. Avison and Martin, "A Conversation with Margaret Avison," 74.

she insists the poem's fundamental focus is not philosophical (or theological or apologetic) analysis. The arena of persuasion, argument and apologetics is not the domain of her lyrics. "Writing poetically" is some other process. "It is a truism," William Butt notes, "that poetry does not urge or require belief; that is the task of rhetoric."[51] Even if her poetry finally convinces a reader to take the claims of Christianity seriously and to respond to Jesus's invitation, "Follow me," the primary impulse of her lyrics cannot be said to be specifically rhetorical or persuasive. She writes as a poet and she is a witness as a poet. Consequently, in her witness, her words are not weapons, but rather pointers.[52] In fact, she is unhappy when she sees poetry put to other uses. In her poem "Songs" (*MD* 32–33), she is troubled by poetry celebrating the triumph of warfare. As she wonders how the connection comes about, her attitude of mourning and disapproval over both the exploitation of language and the triumph of one people over another is unmistakable:

> The source of song – by the brook Kishon, by
> the waters of Megiddo – ancient records
> gloat over, appropriating all
> the conquered's inclement cruelties.
> [. . .]
>
> why is a peaceable company nourished on the
> songs of railroad strikers, of
> shipwrecks, disastrous cyclones, fires
> engulfing whole communities [. . .]
>
> Is the clemency
> all in the singing narrative?
> [. . .]
>
>   Too many long
> (foolishly) for the
> right-angled, upright, sovereign voice, the
> singing celebrant, one foot up on
> the prone subjected first.

In contrast to "Songs," in her earlier poem from *The Dumbfounding*, "Words" (*AN* 1.161), she demonstrates a happy coincidence of "heart-warmed lungs"

51. Butt, "Word and Action in Margaret Avison's *Not Yet But Still*," 839.

52. See The Introduction for my first reference to this phrase essential to the thesis of this book.

and "de-ciphering heart." While the opposite seems to be suggested in the poem's opening stanza with its metaphor of heraldry and its peculiar language of warfare, old and new, the first line hints at a different direction in its "breath-clouded brass":

> Heraldry is breath-clouded brass,
> blood-rusted silks, gold-pricked even threadbare
> memorials of honour
> worn
> a shield when napalm and germ-caps and fission are
> eyeless towards colour, bars, quarterings.

The second stanza, in its change of the form of the word—"heraldry" to "herald"—totally alters the connotations accompanying it, as nature's creatures and creation take on the role of voicing (and "revoicing" in the later poem "Knowing the New" *AN* 3.28) "daybreaking glory":

> A herald blares in a daybreaking
> glory, or foolishly carols –
> robin under a green sky – or, a
> green earth-breaking tip, is still
> but with bodily stillness, not the
> enemy's voicelessness.

"The enemy's voicelessness" has been neutralized by speech, but with a sense of life-giving joy rather than triumphant defeat. This combination of "still / but with bodily stillness" of "green earth-breaking tip" with the "herald blaring" of the "robin under a green sky" is repeated over and over in Avison's celebratory poems of trees and birds. But it is in the human expression of words that "[t]he ancient, the new, / confused in speech, breathe on" most vividly, even intimating perhaps the connection between the "ancient scriptures" and the new and modern witness:

> involving
> heart-warmed lungs, the reflexes
> of uvula, shaping tongue, teeth, lips,
> ink, eyes, and de-
> ciphering heart.

At the same time, this distinction of poetic witness merely pointing toward Christ is not diminishing poetry's impact of witness. In her important observation about her craft—"When he is writing poetry, a person is at his most intense, his most clear-sighted"—Avison, speaking as both a poet and critic, insists on a distinct validity, even superiority, of poetry's "pressure-point of crystallization."[53] Writing poetically may mean paradoxically both more and less than she suggests. It may "merely try to express" one thing, as she qualifies her intention in "A Kept Secret" for the interviewer quoted above; but it may do far more in the process.

Her major prose statements about her view of language—all statements well-mined by her critics and admirers—may clarify how her witness unfolds in her poetry. Both sound and sense are essential considerations and she speaks of both. Responding to Sally Ito, the poet explains:

> Sounds in poetry are musical, words are primarily tactile: to paraphrase some French writer, a writer's words are primarily not the ones in the dictionary, but the ones he knows from the reverse side where he can feel their surfaces, texture, knobbiness, curves. . . . Playing with sound and texture becomes instinctive.[54]

The poet Carmine Starnino, sensitive to Avison's aesthetic considerations, recognizes her "unremitting inventiveness" and "encoding her devotion in distinctive and compelling language," insisting that "Avison is a poet who, first and foremost, lets herself be led by sounds, so that her assertions, however theological, are always authenticated by her ear." In his admiration of her accomplishment, he suggests, "No Canadian poet has pushed to such an extreme the relationship of form to content . . . reading her poems always leaves our relationship with language somewhat re-angled." It is obvious Starnino's interest is in what her faith experiences do to her unusual poetry as he uses speaks of poetry revolutionized by her witness. He challenges the fundamental thematic emphasis in what he notes is in the "ear of such a style."

> [T]he "Christianity" of Avison's poems isn't seen to rest in any self-evidently formal trait. The poems are instead read backwards from her faith. That is, they are read thematically . . . as quirky memorable, fiercely individualistic networks of image and syntax. Christianity, however, did more than just flavour Avison's poetry with unfashionable surmises; it revolutionized it.

If the music of her poetry is one outcome of her Christian faith experience, as Starnino seems to suggest, it is a possible corollary that her "poetry's

---

53. See Chapter 1 for an initial reference to this quotation.
54. Ibid.

sharp, uncommon notes" and "acoustic value" contribute in some intangible way towards her witness. The poet's love of language in its varied sounds may be a means of drawing readers to its intrinsically linked sense of "Avison's veer towards God."[55]

When Avison herself speaks of "writing with my ear in our good language," she is calling attention to her lifelong affection for words. One of her earlier prose statements announces her understanding of what a poet does: "Any Canadian writer, for example, is aware of a scuffle to find his own words, his own idiom. . . . In trying to find his language-level, then, a Canadian poet is trying to assert both an identity and an aesthetic."[56] Years later, speaking to a university audience in the Pascal lectures, she comments on her sensitivity to words: "In everyday, received languages, as one linguist put it, 'all grammars leak'; they lack ultimate precision, much of the vocabulary being poetry, i.e. metaphor, stained with history and faraway cultures."[57] Later in the lectures, she reiterates the observation: "What an awesome phenomenon language is, an echo chamber of ancestral insights and of our human psyches."[58] In the interview with Sally Ito, Avison speaks of "'lyric flow" as part of [her] poetry in youth," eventually followed by "a more deliberate style" when "word, music, word sounds, images no longer simply cluster." "[L]ife experience and aging led to delight in words' derivations and histories."[59] In each of these observations, and in either phase of her writing—"lyric" or "deliberate"—the poet is not interested in using words as weapons.

Rather, she invests her energy, delighting in and scuffling with words, as Jon Kertzer writes, to identify "how she regards words: how they assert, convey, conduct, contain, create, direct, or reveal meaning." In his essay "Margaret Avison and the Place of Meaning," he demonstrates the shift he sees in her view of language that occurred with her Christian conversion:

> Before, she looks inward for the place of meaning as well as outward at the world, coordinating the two by means of the "inrushing floodlight of imagination" [quoting from a letter to Cid Corman]. After, she continues to rely on the imagination,

55. Starnino, "He From Elsewhere Speaks," 140–43.

56. Avison, "Poets in Canada," 182.

57. Avison, A Kind of Perseverance, 37.

58. Avison sounds very similar to Owen Barfield in his colorful image of "metaphor bending over the cradle of meaning." Poetic Diction, 88. Kertzer interprets Barfield as offering a theory of language where "words contain their past. They have a 'soul' which is dormant, but which the poet can revive" ("Margaret Avison and the Place of Meaning," 11–12). Avison, A Kind of Perseverance, 73.

59. Avison and Ito, "The Quiet Centre Inside," 160, 168–69.

but directs it upward, subordinating it to the revelation of "the
flower-light of Beyond" ["Midsummer Christmas" *AN* 2.100].[60]

Perhaps Kertzer has stopped too soon in tracing her "place of meaning."
"Upward" replaced "inward" in her imaginative focus; in her experience
of life in Christ, "downward"—to the city in which she lives—has followed
"upward." As the poet seeks to "go and tell," passing on that discovery of
meaning, she maintains a respectful and unmeasured openness to further
discovery, dialogue, and understanding.

Avison's appreciation for language is an open window, allowing breez-
es to blow in, softening the human impulse to dogmatism and that "right-
angled, upright, sovereign voice" she deplores in "Songs." Several of her later
poems, some whimsical, speak of this consummate commitment to respect
for the "other." She introduces the "artless art" (*AN* 3.46) of children who

> contrive
> a secret language? – nobody 'else' to know
> the key, for ever.

In "Relating" (*AN* 3.135–36) she observes an ant, reflecting on the
limitation in communicating between two parties. Even more important,
she recognizes she has only a partial understanding of the significance of
living side by side in "unsegmented, unsmall / shared reality":

> Many speak languages
> I've never learned.
> Is your being one
> pictograph, seed of a
> word, the gateway to
> a language nobody speaks?
> So none can read this
> unsegmented, unsmall
> shared reality.
>
> The radii of power
> are focused down and in
> on you and me over our
> warped little shadows; they
> adjust, this midday instant, to
> us, moving [. . . .]

60. Kertzer, "Margaret Avison and the Place of Meaning," 10.

She introduces her portrait-poem "To Wilfred Cantwell Smith," with an epigraph she says "records one comment he made in passing":

> When asked, What is an intellectual? he said: "An intellectual is
> a participant in his own society, listening to people. That kind
> of truth cannot be put anywhere by us, not in words, never put
> in its place. The human mind can apprehend, not comprehend"
> (*AN* 3.171–72).[61]

The mixture of humility and intellect he embodies attracts the poet's attention and clarifies afresh her self-understanding as a witness. Again, the three very different poems—"Artless Art," "Relating," and "To Wilfred Cantwell Smith"—affirm her attitude of openness and respectful dialogue. The language of both speaker and listener shapes the witnessing act. The telling presupposes first a listening, which is an apprehension, not a comprehension. What is contrived in fun for the child—the secret language—is a limiting reality for the adult musing on "the warped little shadows" of both person and ant who can only imaginatively communicate. Language both isolates and unites, hides and reveals, confuses and explains. "We say we 'see,' at moments of understanding. But we do not see with the multi-faceted eyes an insect brings to the act," Avison tells her university audience in the Pascal lectures. "Our limitations, once we acknowledge them, liberate us to steady plodding, and occasional awe."[62] Now in her portrait of one with his knowledge of multiple languages in "To Wilfred Cantwell Smith," she can both identify those limitations and speak of one who has the "de-ciphering heart" to transcend them:

> Our native language shapes us, does it not
> even as it shapes itself upon the page?
> The languages you've learned, in life and college,
> carve and emboss characters in your thought?
>
> > Hebrew's ornate iron, its quirks around the line
> > (vocal or consonant) in you have wrought
> > the odd intransigent openness—and untaught
> > much we grew up to mimic—or disdain.

---

61. Author of such books as *Patterns of Faith Around the World* and *On Understanding Islam*, Professor of Comparative Religion, and new friend in her seniors residence.

62. Avison, *A Kind of Perseverance*, 68.

Myopic, skeptical, sometimes distraught,
slowly your readers see ourselves as foreign,
trotting for safety through our little warren
of walled ways. Now, perilously, we're out

in a big world of foreigners, finding that they are not!
Ink on white paper keeps informing those
who learn, to listen long, until there glows
within the friendly signs of being understood [. . . .]

Avison's celebration of this irenic and gentle scholar provides a description of characteristics and attitudes that make witnessing even possible: an "odd intransigent openness," a re-learning (a process described as "untaught") of much that reflects "myopic, skeptical, sometimes distraught" behavior, a reinterpretation of what is foreign, an absorption of learning and listening, "until there glows / within the friendly signs of being understood" or "what's been sought / within shines there."

This sensitivity towards language enables the witness to know when to withhold words and be silent.

Come, quietness, to the man
love-wrung and turbulent
and alone.
Come, largeness [. . . .]

she intones in "In Truth" (*AN* 1.188–89). "Words are too many. In this place / loss is torn." Again, in "There Are No Words For" (*AN* 3.25), she pictures a scene of pain where "[t]wo together / each quite alone" "now frozen out by / that odd proscenium, privacy, respected." The poem concludes,

Having no words is not
safe. It is
then the only good.

"When Their Little Girl Had Just Died" (*AN* 3.26) suggests a similar call for silence:

Does pain prise people apart?
It can.
[. . .]
None can give counsel re the split
to two, lopped so [. . .].

There is unspoken but acceptable irony in these calls for no words in delicately crafted word-filled lyrics, articulating obvious empathy by one who understands language—here, a peculiar language of silence.

One of her most provocative prose observations is tucked into an early review of another poet. "[E]verybody's speech is defective," she points out; and poets need to "discipline speech into clarity."[63] There is irony again, of course, in Avison's perception of clarity, for her disciplined speech is filled with ambiguity and often indeterminate meaning, or at best, nuanced in puzzling ways that belie what is usually meant by "clarity." A stanza, a phrase, a line, even a word of her verse can evade confident interpretation. She comments on the writer's intentions of "precision" as she compares sonnets to butterfly specimens in jars in "Butterfly Bones: Sonnet against Sonnets" (AN 1.71):

> The sweep-net skill,
>
> the patience, learning, leave all living stranger.
>
> Insect – or poem – wait for the fix, the frill
>
> precision can effect, brilliant with danger.

Ambiguity rings in the multiple metaphors and uncertain syntax of "leave all living stranger"; "brilliant with danger" is equally puzzling in the odd connection of adjective and noun. The metaphor in the title of her essay "Muse of Danger" inviting connection between poem and witness is the same sort of clarifying puzzle. David Kent suggests a motive in his 1989 overview of her published works:

> Her own work only occasionally fulfils her Eliotesque definition of poetry given in 1948: "to discipline speech into clarity" . . . that is because of her effort to make reading an act of imaginative and moral discrimination prompted by a poetry as fraught with ambiguity, multivalency, and motion as experience itself.[64]

This explanation can speak to Avison's religious experience as well. Clarity for her is the articulation of the radiating mystery of the God who can only be partially known and understood and expressed. "How can we catch the illimitable in our little bottles?" she queries.[65] Clarity is an opening out, an enlarging of vision even as she seeks "precision with particulars'" and "spa-

---

63. The context of the statement is Avison's review of *The Rocking Chair and Other Poems* by A. M. Klein. "Like Demosthenes, Mr. Klein knows that everybody's speech is defective, and he has in his humility accepted Demosthenes' corrective pebbles . . . that their whole purpose is to discipline speech into clarity," 191.

64. Kent, *Margaret Avison and Her Works*, 20.

65. Avison, *A Kind of Perseverance*, 64–65.

cious thinking across centuries."[66] Starnino admires her "determination to compress the language into fierce oddities" in her "tireless search for the form most fit to recall the passion of Christ."[67] In a similar vein, Avison speaks of her motivation to write her "Job: Word and Action" poem where the search is for the subject to match her experience: "For this poem, my search was for God, THE Friend. Underlying it was a recurring incredulity about the Father's love for me, I think."[68]

Another more elusive quest is implied in the lyric "Concert" (*AN* 3.65), summing up her desire for clarity and simplicity all the while engaging the reader in her perpetual maze of wondering and wandering enquiry:

> Learning, I more and more
> long for that simplicity,
> clarity, that willingness
> to speak (from anonymity . . .)
> [. . .]
>
> You fret because the underbrush
> is dense, the way uncleared it seems
> where you now find yourself?[69]

In her longing, the poet-witness now raises as many questions as she answers. To whom is she speaking—the "you" "fret[ting] because the underbrush is dense" in the second stanza? What is she learning in that opening line? Why does she call attention to the desire for anonymity in her parentheses? What are "all those impenetrables"? The simile

> when words
> are more like bluebell petals under
> an absorbed heaven

is puzzling in spite of its elegance. The poet may be thinking of a present experience of delicate, but ineffective words, separated from heaven's intentions and attention. Or alternatively, the words may be part of "all those impenetrables" in a future fulfillment, effectively blending with and being absorbed into heaven's will. Either way, they compel a meditative response.

---

66. Ibid., 65.

67. Starnino, "He From Elsewhere Speaks," 143.

68. "Nobody has yet accepted my 'Job' as a poem, so maybe it isn't," she wryly observes. Nevertheless, the point still stands that this kind of search with its attendant result is what she may mean by "clarity." Avison and Ito, "The Quiet Centre Inside," 169.

69. See Appendix for an uninterrupted version of the poem.

The lack of simplicity and clarity in this paradoxically precise but ambiguous image is illustrative of her great longing.

The third stanza, in contrast, is definitive and even majestic in its particulars. Here the speaker has provided creation's words—simple, clear, perfectly placed and completely productive.

> Words have been given. Once.
> Words that are storm and sun and rain.
> Listening earth, where they have fallen,
> finds seed casings begin
> to split,
> roots throb. As though
> some unimaginable response is
> implicit in that speaking.

The word merely has to be spoken and "seed casings begin / to split, / roots throb." The poet has depicted the "implicit," "unimaginable response" in the arrangement of those lines, vividly isolating "to split." The closing two-line stanza is her hopeful conclusion pointing to success.

> Fulfilment is in promise
> and still more resonant longing.

She is in "concert" with that other Speaker in her "resonant longing" and fulfilled promise. Consequently, her "language, as she stretches words to their very limits," as her friend and publisher William Pope suggests in a letter to the poet, takes on a life and power "go[ing] beyond challenge to transformation." He continues, "I have read 'Concert' many times, but it will take me a lifetime and more to fully experience the blessings and glories of which it eloquently speaks."[70] The poem seems to resist closure, not unlike many of Jesus's parables. Nevertheless it speaks of—it announces, it witnesses to—the mystery of a God who communicates with His creation. It awakens a sense of wonder about the divine energy in language that produces "some unimaginable response": "Words have been given. Once." The poet's longing produces "still more resonant longing" in the poem's reader. The exquisite subtlety of the poem does not negate clarity; it redefines it in terms of mystery.

Back in 1957 Northrop Frye singled out Avison's bleak picture "Neverness Or, The One Ship Beached On One Far Distant Shore" (*AN* 1.24–26)

---

70. Pope, Letter to Avison, 1977.

as at the center of "a certain structure of imagery" for the then young poet.[71] Her vision alters and softens over the years, albeit still rich in ambiguity and complexity. "Concert" may be the new center climaxing her missionary impulse. "Resonant longing" has replaced the nostalgia and despair of earlier days. The "unfixed vision" of "Neverness" has been superseded with "some unimaginable response" to the "words that have been given." Eager witness has replaced weary critic as the poet presses on in her commitment to "go and tell."

71. See chapter 4 for a discussion of this poem. Frye, "Preface to an Uncollected Anthology," 35.

Conclusion

A Persevering Witness

WHEN AVISON SPEAKS OF her conversion experience as "the Jesus of resurrection power" making himself known to her, she echoes the disclosure of the risen Christ to Mary Magdalene in John's Gospel with its injunction to "go and tell." In language of the numinous she describes "the overwhelming presence of Jesus Christ in the room" initiating immediate transformation.[1] At the same time, in her Pascal lectures, she implies an ongoing perseverance from that encounter: "The priority, Christ's pervasive Presence, was primary and clear."[2] Witness to the resurrection is both an instantaneous event and a continuous experience.

In *A Kind of Perseverance* she draws on the poem of the Irish poet W. R. Rodgers, "that traces a twelve-month journey of the Magi—a course through promise and bewilderment to the darkest hour," to reminisce on her "watershed year" when "the "all's' of the Gospels were hitting [her]." One journey follows another: "Next came the painful part: that was the beginning of the *really* long journey!"[3] She understands well the spirit of the author of *Pilgrim's Progress* as she honors him in "For Tinkers Who Travel on Foot" (*AN* 1.174):

> What if it *was* a
> verse in the
> Epistle to the Hebrews that
> kept Bunyan
> at concert pitch through
> deaf and dumb months?

---

1. See chapter 1. Avison and Simone, "A Religious Experience," 6.
2. Avison, *A Kind of Perseverance*, 25.
3. Ibid., 72, 21, 72.

He found

resonance.

He stuck it out till then, too:

not for one instant sure it

would come to anything, in all his

mute madness, nor ever

diverted for one instant.

Again Avison evokes the famous story of Bunyan's Christian when she writes in "We Are Not Poor, Not Rich" (*AN* 2.87):

And I can barely snatch

my foot free when the soppy sand

goes slack

and fills in my old track.

Yet looking up from this Despond, I note

a pilgrim firm of foot

and think he's on a better road

– and think then wrong.

When the poet speaks of "a person's climate . . . with emotional seasons and variations within seasons," she calls to mind both the literal and the metaphorical in "In Sultry Weather" (*AN* 2.189):

It is the going on (not

storm and relief, or an escape

to a wind-clean shore, or a warm sweetgrass knoll)

that surprises, daylong.[4]

Her poem "Interim" (*AN* 3.85), mentioned earlier, speaks of this '*really* long journey' after Easter when "[o]ur troubled faces clear to see Him."[5] Again, in language of weather, she describes her kind of perseverance:

but doggedly set out, against a sting

of rain, moved by His plan,

through night and shale-blue dawn, remembering

at least to follow on.

The many poems across decades of writing I have explored in this study have provided a picture of this "going on" or "following on"—the poet's

4. Ibid., 39.

5. See chapter 2.

persevering witness. In her two lectures given in 1993, "Misunderstanding Is Damaging" and "Understanding is Costly," Avison candidly gives her perspective on the life of the Christian in a specific intellectual context, validating Christianity for those who are already believers and challenging those who are skeptical. In the process, she indirectly offers an interpretation of the witness of her own poetry.

She begins her first lecture with a series of six propositions developing along the following line of thought:

> No mortal person has perfect understanding.

> A growing person keeps facing misunderstanding, and keeps breaking through. The old is damaged, but ahead is new understanding—of self or of another . . .

> . . . the growing process is dangerous, and essential.[6]

Speaking as one who has been on the road for a long time, she calls attention to the recognition of the life principle embedded in her propositions that apply to "Christian" and "counter-Christian" alike.[7] Painful breakthroughs in understanding are necessary for any growing person.

In the longest poem in *The Dumbfounding*, "The Earth That Falls Away"(*AN* 1.175–84), Avison presents a complex interweaving of vignettes of people who experience blindness and various degrees of seeing. Their varied reactions register painful breakthroughs of growing persons and the damage they endure in facing misunderstanding.[8] One of the poem's several contrasts involves children who are merely enacting the experience of unseeing. "There is screaming in blind man's buff," the speaker notes apprehensively. The blind man's own child

>   tried
> for real, being blind.
> About two minutes. It bled
> black like, all *at* me.
> I couldn't bear it
> even two minutes.

6. Avison, *A Kind of* Perseverance, 20.

7. Avison opens her second lecture with the observation: "Everyone has a counter-Christian bias or a Christian bias, at any given stage of life, in any given circumstance." Ibid., 47.

8. I run the risk of oversimplifying this rich and allusive poem in isolating this one dimension. See Ernest Redekop, *Margaret Avison*, 130–140, for example, for a more elaborate reading of the poem.

Even imaginatively facing misunderstanding—role playing blindness—is dangerous.

In contrast, one of the central figures in the poem, a blinded soldier is puzzlingly uneasy about a possibility of recovery.

> 'It's winter where I live.
> I've had a northern summer, that
> is more than some, let's leave it
> at that' – I said.

When the operation is successful, he is dismayed. His new experience of seeing involves discomfort and disorientation and the old way of interpreting life is damaged:

> Please. Leave me alone.
> Bandage my eyes again.
> The dream of seeing
> I want, as it has been, open
> daybreak blue, with the sting
> of the far-off; not this urging
> of person, colour, thing.
> Unclutter me. Relieve
> me of this visible. Give
> back my sealed-off dayshine . . .

The Scriptures and epigraph from Beddoes's "Death's Jest Book" framing the poem point to its religious and metaphorical significance.[9] The closing lines are simultaneously fearful and glorious in their obvious reference to the God of Scripture:

> Your beauty and holiness,
> Your fair-seeing, scald.
>
> In the intolerable hour
> our fingers and fists
> blunder for blindfolds
> to have You in our power!
>
> 'He does not resist you,'
> said James

9 Ps 27:9; Neh 1:6; Jas 3:6, and "Can a man die? Ay, as the sun doth set: / It is the earth that falls away from light."

looking to

Him who, in his hour,

comes.

As Redekop notes, "Man, like the blind soldier accustomed to a Nomans-land of 'illusory gleam-and-gone,' cannot endure without great pain the face of God, the beholding eyes of the Lord, despite his hope for sight and his desire for light."[10] Yet there is also hope for the ones who "look to / Him who, in his hour, / comes." The prose propositions of *A Kind of Perseverance* imply the same dilemma and its resolution.

Within the framework of the lectures, Avison announces a life of courageous confronting of mortal limitations in understanding, beginning with facing up to misunderstanding. The Christian witness is one who faithfully points to Another, but through partial understanding. This "dangerous" and essential pattern of growth affects all parties—both the one who faces the witness and hears the witness's report, but also the witness herself. In her poem "Dead Ends" (*AN* 3.159) she suggests: "There's no finality out here: a sphere / too vast, too growthful, too / mischievous":

There's too much

of us for us to know.

But closing heart, and ear

is a terminus I

fear, too.

             We slam

into it, often, though knowing is a peril

almost as terrible as

never being sure

where

the dead end will

appear.

The speaker in her dramatic monologue "To a Seeking Stranger" (*AN* 2.234–35) declares "to a man who wants life to the full, / wants absolutely. Wants. For God's sake yes," that it is a lifetime of adjustments, "turmoil" and "battle" engaging combatants of unequal strength. The speaker revives the familiar phrase "For God's sake yes" with a new inflection, implying that the person is missing the meaning of his own exclamation. At some point, however—"in time"—clarity will come:

10. Redekop, *Margaret Avison*, 139.

> In time, farnesses
>
> open. The bright large place
>
> we must all need who would
>
> be, begins to be.

In the meantime, the last stanza speaks of that inevitable taking up of one's cross daily: "[t]he terrible, blood-guttering wood / can be everyday, too. / Yes."

Refusal to move out from places of misunderstanding is also dangerous, she suggests at the end of her first lecture with her ironic twist of phrase announcing its opposite: "The greatest danger is to stop evading [Jesus Christ]. Unless you consider it damaging not to grow." At the same time, understanding is costly:

> Pain, loss, is defined as a beginning-point in the Gospels. You must spend all, i.e. lose all, to gain more than all, qualitatively speaking. Love defined himself ("God is love") by total loss . . . he wants us to share this loss, for love's sake.[11]

Much of this cost has been articulated in the poems already discussed earlier. For example, "'*Forsaking all*'—You mean / head over heels, for good" ("The Word" *AN* 1.195); or "There is a sword / enters with hearing" ("Listening" *AN* 2.64); or "Keep our courage high with You / through steep and storm and wild" ("Psalm 80:1— 'Thou that dwellest between the cherubim, shine forth!'" *AN* 2.85).

The propositions propelling her second lecture specifically challenge the eager witness:

> Objective: understanding without compromise.

> Alien doctrine, i.e. someone else's doctrine, grew in a different soil; something can be learned from anything or anybody who is alive and growing.

> Conviction does not preclude listening.

> Contention tends to defensiveness.

She brings the propositions to a head with her mind-bending aphorism:

> The true believer's problem: how to say 'I am here,' and not be saying 'I am not not-there.[12]

11. Avison, *A Kind of Perseverance*, 44, 55.

12. Ibid., 48.

Here she calls all her hearers to practice receptiveness. Avison explains, "A Christian's obligation to absorb the other is both bane and blessing, all entangled as it is with both compromise and compassion."[13] The implication, as her propositions outline, is one of difficulty, restraint, and compassion learned through a lifetime of careful awareness. In the lowly identification with fellow subway travelers, for example, she can speak of "Learning Love a Little" (*AN* 2.267):

> . . . therefore in the clattering
> tunnel, in the subway car
> hustled, borne, we are
> strangers averted, and together.
> Respect seeds the unbreathable air with
>   a certain dotted-Swiss, a
>   scent, and one dumbly welcomes
>   this, and them.

Many of her poems draw on a similar implied companionship of circumstance which calls for this unusual articulation of respect "seed[ing] the unbreathable air" creating "a scent" and sense of welcome. It can be an intentional gift to another; it can also come unbidden, as one of her most poignant poems, "Balancing Out" (*AN* 3.130), suggests. The poet voices the painful thoughts of a widow who recognizes her husband's coat on a "ruined fellow" who had received it from a mission. Tangled emotions surge in the woman:

> The giver of his topcoat eerily
> watched, her widow's desolation clearly
> inconsolable now
> (a pang – like joy!),
> to see what she had seen
> on a fine and steady man
> made come full circle on this ruined fellow.
>
> Still, he had his coat,
> and she, the echoing years.

---

13. She invokes Shakespeare's vivid phrase from Sonnet 110, "my nature is subdued to what it works in, like the dyer's hand" (and already appropriated by W. H. Auden, applied to literary criticism), to apply it yet another way. In the lecture she suggests that "the supposedly bigoted Christian" may be ahead of his or her "counter-Christian majority" just by virtue of necessity, 65–66.

The poet's picture of both widow and indigent man in their unplanned connection in the concluding stanza embodies the costly understanding of "a Christian's obligation to absorb the other" of which she speaks in *A Kind of Perseverance*.[14]

This costly understanding of which the poet speaks prevents both defensiveness and aggression, and points to a humility learned from "heartfelt sympathy." She pointedly observes, "One of our craftiest evasions is trying to manage [the truth given in the Holy Word]. . . . Truth is final, but our mortal grasp of it never can be final." Therefore, there is no place for arrogance or triumph over another; and there is no need for defensiveness. Rather, the life and words of the witness will reflect their source and the one to whom they point. Her concluding words in *A Kind of Perseverance* characteristically deflect her own efforts: "It will never be *our* understanding or intelligence that will rescue us. Oddly, that is the shining hope."[15]

What she articulates in her prose Avison works out in her poetry. A prayer-poem in her collection *The Dumbfounding*, when she is new on the journey, articulates her early intuition of the mystery of resurrection life and its attendant witness for the Christian believer. She begins "A Prayer Answered by Prayer" (*AN* 1.203) boldly declaring her position on the witness stand as she reworks a common saying, "My heart was on my sleeve, / I knew it, barely warm." Words of testimony become a prayer: "'This was what I believe, / How can I hold firm?'" even while she senses the tenuous hold of her new found faith expressed in familiar optical disorientation:

> On a flat earth, solid
> I stand 'upright' and stare
> at sunset's moon-globe pallid
> in a skied nowhere.

Jesus's words to Thomas, "Blessed are those who have not seen and yet have come to believe" (John 20:29), take on new meaning with the poet's assertion:

> What only Christ makes real
> rests in astonishment
> in one Uncommonweal.
> Love is heart-rent.

14. Ibid., 66.

15. Ibid., 49, 70–71, 74.

Perseverance in faith and witness is a mysterious gift—"What only Christ makes real"—and a costly one for both the Giver and the witness. She now offers a completely different kind of prayer from a new vantage point.

> 'All creating Son
> whose badge I thought to wear,
> where you have found me, burn
> me, your beacon fire.'

This new prayer, with its expression of both costly submission and comfortable recognition of the prime witness with his "beacon fire," characterizes the witness of her poetry published in ensuing decades. She continues to convey a sense of the triune God cloaked in mystery.

> In the cold February sun
> I sit, silent, with a presence
> not known within. Yet, known?

begins a much later poem from *Momentary Dark* ("Prayer" *MD* 15). "Let the unknowing structure what is known," she prays with familiar ambiguity. A peculiar receptivity follows from her awareness of the "human hearer who / proved He could be trusted / in death, in life, always":

> Let inner hearing
> create listening, so that
> the presence not here
> (not yet?)
> may speak.

She does not clarify the audience of the speaking "presence," but presumably it involves the poet herself as the receiving witness. At the same time, this audience is also the poet as sending witness, obeying the injunction to "go and tell" in each lyric she crafts out of what she has heard.

The reflections from *A Kind of Perseverance* contain the essence of Avison's understanding of and approach to Christian witness articulated in this book. Her first cluster of teasing propositions regarding the dangerous and essential growing process prods her audience to take seriously the person of Jesus "who is everywhere concerned, everywhere Sovereign."[16] Her second cluster of propositions draws the focus to what she calls "the true believer's problem" and the role of the poet-witness. In her posthumous autobiography, the poet explains the origin of her enigmatic axiom. When she served

---

16. Ibid., 21.

on a panel at the Vancouver Poetry Conference in 1963, she and her fellow poets were asked, "What makes a poet's language distinctive?" "We all fell silent, trying to pin it down, then attempted answers," she writes:

> *Not* just affection for words, which is common to all good writers; *not* necessarily a matter of cadence, formal structures, rhythm. The answer that came to me, forced out of minutes of dismissing options, was new to me too: "It is saying 'I am here and not not-there.'"[17]

It is an answer, she notes, that resonated with other poets. In her Pascal lectures, years later, she continues to brood on that formulation, then connecting it to witness. In this enigmatic way of talking about poetry and witness and their possible connection—"a modifying one learns from the experience of heartfelt sympathy"—the poet has clarified (and declarified!) her twin passions.[18]

In light of this persevering and faithful witness, there is one issue yet to address: an audience for the witness. "I write to be read. . . . My readers are the completers of what the text began. I address them as co-creators, unknown but for sure out there, and exacting," Avison tells her interviewer Sally Ito.[19] The poet describes her "scuffle to find [her] own words, [her] own idiom" through the years "to assert both an identity and an aesthetic," but as I have emphasized throughout this study, her "completers of what [her] poems] began" and "co-creators" share in another "scuffle," one of potentially more difficulty.[20] How might they—how do they—receive her witness and even contribute to it? Further, her particular poetry poses a difficulty in two directions. Because Avison has positioned herself in mainstream literature, the overt (and covert) Christian themes of her lyrics disturb those who prefer religion to remain in the private domain. At the same time, the complexity and obscurity of her poetry limit her readership, and hence, access to her witness, in a culture already disinclined to the literary form. Admittedly, reading her complex and concentrated lyrics with sensitivity and understanding requires intense intellectual and spiritual effort.

A. J. M. Smith, her early critical champion, prefaces his selections of her poetry in his 1943 anthology with the succinct description: "Her poetry

---

17. Participants included such American poets as Charles Olson, Robert Creeley, Allen Ginsberg, Robert Duncan and Denise Levertov. Avison was the sole Canadian poet in the group. Avison, *I Am Here and Not Not-There*, 145.

18. Avison, *A Kind of Perseverance*, 49.

19. Avison and Ito, The Quiet Centre Inside," 162.

20. Avison, "Poets in Canada," 182.

is metaphysical poetry—passionate, intellectual, and essentially religious."[21] In his "Poetry" entry for the *Literary History of Canada*, Laurie Ricou categorizes her among the select few Canadian "metaphysical poets" in style and sympathies for her poems' "sense of closure" and "variations on the conceit." He goes on to note, "Compounding and alliteration remind us first of Hopkins, an appropriate analogy given Avison's eloquent Christian commitment to 'the achieve of, the mastery of' God's world."[22] David Kent emphasizes the poet's location in the English literary tradition as a "devotional poet," "anticipated by her debts to George Herbert and Gerard Manley Hopkins."[23]

While she shares such stylistic similarities to these earlier poets with her love of wit and paradox and her concision and conceits, she may share more of a kinship with what Louis Martz, in his classic study of *The Poetry of Meditation,* describes as the "mastery of the art of [religious] meditation." Better still, content and form are inextricably mixed in these "devotional poems." The introduction to Martz's book sounds like a gloss on Avison's method of seeing, particularly her method of studying the Bible. He writes:

> Such meditation is the subject of this study: intense, imaginative meditation that brings together the senses, the emotions, and the intellectual faculties of man; brings them together in a moment of dramatic, creative experience. One period when such meditation flourished coincides exactly with the flourishing of English religious poetry in the seventeenth century.[24]

Martz clarifies the religious significance intended by spiritual writers of the seventeenth century drawing on such writers as St. François de Sales. In his *Treatise on the Love of God*, the spiritual writer interprets meditative practice as "an attentive thought iterated, or voluntarily intertained in the mynd, to excitate the will to holy affections and resolutions." Again, de Sales in his *Introduction to the Devout Life* explains: "Brieflie, devotion, is nothing els but a spirituall swiftnesse and nimbleness of love . . . ."[25] Clearly, while Avison's primary source of light comes from Scripture, her poetry resonates with the spirit of these earlier spiritual writers, both directly and indirectly. In fact, some poems allude to these writers. For instance, the poem "Prayer" (*MD* 15), quoted above, takes as its theme the apophatic tradition or *via negativa* explained by the anonymous fourteenth-century author of *The Cloud of Unknowing* in tandem with Scripture. In the second

21. A. Smith, *The Book of Canadian Poetry*, 441.

22. Ricou, "Poetry," 20, 24.

23. Kent, *Margaret Avison and Her Works*, 7.

24. Martz, *The Poetry of Meditation*, 2, 1.

25. Quoted in ibid., 15.

stanza of "Prayer" (*MD* 15), the obvious word play on the title of the classic emphasizes her connection:

> For the cloud, of unknowing
> (not of night or day
> or time or place)
> I yearn as David did for
> springs in a dry land.

Margaret Avison, however, is not a devotional writer with a seventeenth-century audience. She is writing in the twentieth and early twenty-first century, with literary fashion and interests less inclined to the devotional poetry of which Martz speaks. As has been shown here, her poetry is neither sensational nor easily accessible, garnering a large reading public. Poetry as an art form in general has a smaller coterie of followers in a world dominated by other print forms and media. The Canadian scene is relatively small to attract interest in a poet not aggressively marketing her work.[26] Further, the initial excitement and admiration for her sophisticated poetry lessened after Christian content seemed more pronounced with the publication of *sunblue* in 1978.

In spite of continued recognition in terms of awards and honorary doctorates in the later years, the 1970s is the decade that produced the major surge of criticism and interest in her poems in academic circles. Since that time, appreciative articles have been more occasional, until her receiving the Griffin Prize in 2003 and then her death in 2007. In his critical overview in 1989, Kent comments on "the bifurcation of Avison's audience," particularly noting the critics Willmot, Scobie and Djwa for their critical stance.[27] Rod Willmot, showing a familiarity with evangelical language, has particularly harsh words in one of his reviews of *sunblue*: "The wages of faith, one might say, are intellectual and linguistic diminution." Later in the review, while he acknowledges a "formally and rhetorically perfect" poem, he laments, "It is through cracks in the evangelical plaster that poetry pokes out again and flourishes."[28]

---

26. David Kent mentions in his tribute after her death: "In 1988 Northrop Frye told me that around 1950 he and A. J. M. Smith believed that Margaret Avison would some day have the kind of profile that Margaret Atwood has since come to enjoy. That did not happen. Frye noted: Atwood 'knows what the public wants, whereas Margaret Avison says to hell with them.'" "Margaret Avison, Poet," 59.

27. Kent, *Margaret Avison and Her Works*, 12. See chapter 2 for a discussion of Scobie courting Avison's endorsement for his work.

28. Willmot, "Winning Spirit," 115, 116.

On the other hand and more hopeful, Avison's connections within the poetic tradition draw attention to her lyrics. Her poems still regularly appear in anthologies with sections of twentieth-century poetry.[29] She is innovative enough to catch the attention of a discriminating critic. As a result, appreciation of her art can raise attention to the witness inherent in the poems. Furthermore, in recent years, an increased interest in spirituality, Christian or otherwise, harkens back to the meditative tradition that has shaped religious poetry for centuries, creating appeal in a twentieth and turn-of-the century poet who has followed in the footsteps of Herbert, Hopkins, and T. S. Eliot with her meticulous and incisive verse.

How effective, then, can Avison's poetry be as witness to the secular world? I take encouragement from Simone Weil in her account of the influence of a poem and poet on her Christian conversion, in her "Spiritual Autobiography" (Letter IV to Father Perrin) in *Waiting for God*:

> In 1938 I spent ten days at Solesmes, from Palm Sunday to Easter Tuesday, following all the liturgical services. I was suffering from splitting headaches. . . . There was a young English Catholic there . . . [who] told me of the existence of those English poets of the seventeenth century who are named metaphysical. In reading them later on, I discovered the poem of which I read you what is unfortunately a very inadequate translation. It is called "Love." I learned it by heart. Often, at the culminating point of a violent headache, I make myself say it over, concentrating all my attention upon it and clinging with all my soul to the tenderness it enshrines. I used to think I was merely reciting it as a beautiful poem, but without my knowing it the recitation had the virtue of a prayer. It was during one of these recitations that, as I told you, Christ himself came down and took possession of me.[30]

Weil is a powerful and unusual model of a person responding to the witness of a poem, compelling in her account of transformation. Moreover, the very nature of her out-of-the-ordinary experience calls attention to the poem's witness. Weil is illustrative of Avison's observation of Christ and his potential followers in "All Bogged Down" (*AN* 1.45–46):

---

29. See, for example, Lecker and David, *The New Canadian Anthology* (1988); Bennett and Brown, *A New Anthology of Canadian Literature in English* (2002); Scholes et al., *Elements of Literature, Poetry/Fiction/Drama* (2004); Stamp, *Writing the Terrain* (2004); Prufer, *Dark Horses* (2005); Rosengarten and Godrick-Hones, *The Broadview Anthology of Poetry*, 2nd ed. (2005); and Geddes, *20th-Century Poetry and Poetics*, 5th ed. (2006).

30. Weil, *Waiting for God*, 68–69.

                              the one

          of us not one of us is gone

          a way some few may following find,

          just, one by one.

The audience may be a select few, but any reader can be one who is the key
in influencing many more. In her own brief essay "Who Listens and How
Come?" she clarifies the responsibility of the witness and neutralizes the
concern regarding a limited audience:

> True enough, Jesus forbade us to cast our pearls before swine
> lest they trample them and rend us—but He let us rend Him,
> and bade us preach the Gospel to every creature. Every way is,
> ultimately, a way to Him, when the Holy Spirit will. It's a wide
> open subject, and I expect it will take a moment more than a
> lifetime for me to know who listens and how come.[31]

Furthermore, the co-creation of readers, "unknown but for sure out
there, and exacting" of which she speaks, can aid her witness by calling at-
tention to her excellent poems.[32] There have been a small but faithful and
articulate group of critics who have done what critics should do, in Harold
Bloom's words, "practice their art in order to make what is implicit in a
book finely explicit."[33] In this case they have played a dual role. Their occa-
sional essays have both reminded the literary public of Avison's poetry and
helped elucidate her difficult work. These include Kent, Mathews, Kertzer,
Redekop, Merrett, Quinsey, and others, contributing to the miracle of which
Avison delineates in "Discovery on Reading a Poem" (AN 2.206):

> One sail
>
> opens the wideness to me of the waters,
>
> the largeness of the sky.

Because she is more than an inspirational and skilled poet, these critics are
potentially reenacting the same miracle in the same elusive ambiguity of
witness with which I began this book reviewing "Rising Dust" (AN 1.45–46):

> But never any of us
>
> physiologist or fisherman
>
> or I
>
> quite makes sense of it. We

31. Avison, "Who Listens and How Come?" 5.

32. Avison and Ito, "The Quiet Centre Inside," 162.

33. Bloom, How to Read and Why, 19.

find our own level

as prairie, auburn or
snow-streaming, sounds forever
the almost limitless.

As poets and critics share in this witness, they are achieving what Etty Hillesum longed to do in her "witness" in a Nazi prison camp: "It is not enough simply to proclaim You, God, to commend You to the hearts of others. One must also clear the path toward You in them, God."[34] Part of that clearing of the path involves Avison's "open[ing] the wideness . . . of the waters" and "the largeness of the sky." The metaphors are naturally unexplained, only suggesting the direction upward and outward to the One who is larger and higher.

The difficulty lies in the mystery of humankind's connection with the ineffable Creator-Redeemer who is still just out of reach, still eluding "the fix, the frill / precision can effect, brilliant with danger" (*AN* 1.71). The poet and her critics can only "tell it slant." The witness of poetry is, in Farrer's words, "projected in images which cannot be decoded, but must be allowed to signify what they signify of the reality beyond them."[35] The readers who seem to best understand Avison's necessary ambiguity and complexity recognize the distinctive mystery that poetic witness is. Jacques Ellul reminds readers that "in a trial, the witness furnishes the key fact that *changes* the certitudes or view of the reality held before his appearance." He goes on to explain that

> the witness to the Word of God produces the greatest change, innovation, and rupture that can be imagined. He testifies to the Wholly Other, the Invisible, the imperceptible dimension we call Eternity, Absolute, Ultimate, or some other name. . . . The witness introduces this Wholly Other into our visible, concrete, measurable, and analyzable reality.[36]

He is speaking of truth which cannot be managed by the witness, a reality Avison intuits and articulates in her poetry. Ellul suggests, "The Wholly Other takes this reality upon himself, limits it, measures it, and gives it another dimension."[37] Avison explains in her inimitable way,

---

34. Hillesum, *Etty: The Letters and Diaries of Etty Hillesum, 1941–43*, 518.

35. Farrer, "Poetic Truth," 148.

36. Ellul, *The Humiliation of the Word*, 110.

37. Ibid.

> But when someone tells it, something,
> a Presence, may briefly shine
> showing heaven again,
> and open (*AN* 2.168).

Here too is an interpretation of her waters, sky and prairie, "'sound[ing] forever / the almost limitless" (*AN* 3.163–164), images which cannot quite be explained—only experienced.

Avison has, or should have, a second significant audience—another community of reception. I am speaking of the church, in its sometimes zealous witness—or sometimes lack thereof. The same factors that hinder a large secular reading public equally affect this second audience: her poetry is neither sensational nor easily accessible; poetry as an art form, in general, attracts a smaller number of readers; the Canadian scene is relatively small. Even, strangely, her religious emphasis with its counter-cultural vision can deter a Christian public from reading and appreciating her lyrics. Her prophetic voice speaks out against packaged, agenda-driven, and unreflective presentations of the gospel. Christian ministries and activities that are imitations of the larger context in which they are placed often have workers impatient with the seemingly unproductive exercise of meditation that the poet espouses and embodies. As a result, there is a hidden danger for this more specific reading community who claim to have the truth but are inadvertently missing the Truth. There is more urgency that her gift of poetry to the church be recognized and received.

C. S. Lewis, in his imaginative story *The Great Divorce*, offers salutary caution, reflecting on why souls from hell, given the opportunity to remain in heaven, choose not to stay. His guide on the journey has sobering words for the apologist Lewis:

> There have been men before now who go so interested in proving the existence of God that they came to care nothing for God Himself . . . as if the good Lord had nothing to do but *exist*! There have been some who were so occupied in spreading Christianity that they never gave a thought to Christ. Man! Ye see it in smaller matters. Did ye never know a lover of books that with all his first editions and signed copies had lost the power to read them? Or an organiser of charities that had lost all love for the poor? It is the subtlest of all the snares.[38]

Avison's lyrics resonate with her recognition of this snare, but it is articulated less in caution than in invitation. Her "come and see" and "go and

38. Lewis, *The Great Divorce*, 73–74.

tell" approach to witness is a call for people to move away from the surface of an unreflective faith at its core, to go deeper in and with Christ. She sees things "slant" and she beckons her readers to join her. In its puzzling riddles, her poetry prevents a too obvious or too literal articulation of gospel truth. She points to the crucified and risen Christ through her varied and unusual lyrics, but the complexity and paradox pervading the poems cause readers to brood on the inherent mystery in Christ's saving work. Looking translates into experience as her poetry invites solidarity with the one whose way is the cross. From beginning to end of her poetry, she "tells it slant," but also sure. Her poetry is a model to the missionary church in its invitational presentation—without weapons—of the good news of Christ. At the same time, it is a training ground. The struggle to truly access her work produces a deep sense of humility before a wise intellect.

There are signs of hope that her poetry can and will affect the Christian public. Besides her continued exposure in university settings and peer-reviewed publications, there are a number of thoughtful Christians across Canada who respond to her poetry as evidenced in writing workshops and seminars. There are clergy and writers who have discovered her poetry and refer to them in public presentation. Individual faculty members of seminaries and Christian colleges in Canada—among them, Regent College, Trinity Western University, Redeemer University, and Tyndale University College and Seminary—have promoted her poetry among friends and students. Both Professors Maxine Hancock, formerly of Regent College in Vancouver, and Deborah Bowen of Redeemer University encouraged me in this project, hoping that Avison would receive a wider readership. Finally, the encouragement I take from Simone Weil in responding to George Herbert I also apply to a potential Christian audience for Margaret Avison. There is someone who might read a poem by her, and as a result, "step out of the [Christian] world's parade," absorbing her lyrics in a transforming way.[39] That experience, in turn, might change the way the church thinks about and fulfils its mission.

Avison's long persevering witness is brought to a fitting close with two subtle markers of her dual vocations. Near the end of her life she invokes the names of two very early English poets, the Pearl Poet and Caedmon, suggesting some sort of affinity with both poets—in their craft and in their similar aspirations of witness. Her last collection before she died, *Momentary Dark*, contains a dedication "for the Pearl Poet," drawing attention, in itself, since it had not been her custom until her last publications to dedicate her books to anyone.[40] The connection with the poet of many centuries earlier

39. Tozer, *The Pursuit of God*, 102.

40. The volumes of The Collected Poems: *Always Now* are dedicated to her close friend Joan Eichner, variously identified as "sensitive editor" (*AN* 1:254) and "primary

is another of her teasing riddles inviting speculation. The Pearl (or Gawain) Poet was anonymous and unknown for a long time. The fourteenth-century poet was one whose poetry gained the world's attention years after its writing. The Pearl Poet apparently placed deeply religious poetry and secular verse together for "publication."[41] In his or her anonymity the poet achieved recognition as innovative and highly sophisticated. All these characteristics might resonate with the Canadian poet at the late date of publication of *Momentary Dark*. An excerpt from her commemorative poem, "Thinking Back," published in 1978 in *Acta Victoriana*, suggests further significance:

> We learned how far it can be to horizons
> and how to mourn by the Pearl Poet's brook
> in wind-wracked January.
> We all remember: voices, faces,
> moments, across the years;
> truths, and a glimmer that is light.
>
> Light broken has its beauty.[42]

Acquaintance with the medieval poem and its story directs the oblique references to Avison's subtle witness in *Momentary Dark*. While she makes less direct mention of Christ in this late collection, there is a peculiar veiled intensity about her drawing to a close both her witness and the writing of her poems. There is a kind of melancholy about "Finished When Unfinished" (*MD* 23), when she remarks,

> No one
> is left, writer or some
> incurious wanderer now
> long gone

---

sensitive reader" (*MD*:91) and the one who has prepared typescripts in the latter years of her "cryptic handwriting" (*MD*:91).

41. In the British library a single anonymous and untitled manuscript MS Cotton Nero A.x of four early Middle English alliterative poems (with names given to them by modern editors)—"Pearl," "Purity" or "Cleanness," "Patience," and the better known "Sir Gawain and the Green Knight"—are understood to be the work of one poet. A. Edwards reports that the history of the manuscript was unknown before the early seventeenth century ("The Manuscript: British Library MS Cotton Nero A.x," 198); Borroff remarks that it is the one manuscript that "testifies to [the poems'] existence" (*Sir Gawain and the Green Knight, Patience, and Pearl*, xi). Scholars acknowledge that "[n]othing is known about the author except what can be inferred from the works" (Abrams et al., *Norton Anthology of English Literature*, 119). These general facts create interest in themselves.

42 In the Margaret Avison Fonds.

with the image

> On a flat stone, in the
> plain light, lies a
> torn paper with something written
> on it. All the wide shore, the
> calm lake, the reeds
> listen in the sun, in
> silence, as do other flat stones.

In contrast, there is acceptance and responsiveness to "the presence not here / (not yet?) in the yearning "Prayer" (*MD* 15):

> Let the unknowing
> structure what
> is known.

There is quiet expectation expressed in the Christological poem "Diadem" (*MD* 41):

> To the
> awakened eye, although
> sea-wrack green and bronze are un-
> promising, fresh growth peers visible forth.

The dedication to the Pearl poet provides an interpretive key of hope to her "momentary dark" in its varied forms. She does not minimize the darkness and pain of inevitable diminishments, similar to that great twentieth-century witness Flannery O'Connor.[43] But the Pearl poet calls to Avison's mind that "[l]ight broken has its beauty," as the narrator in the old poem tries to reach his lost "Pearl" across the brook in the dream-garden, and accepts the instructions of the young maiden who assures him of some day being united with her again.

A friend who attended her private funeral expressed his disappointment to me that none of her poems was read at the service.[44] Instead, the order of service she planned opens with a poem and tribute to the other much older poet, Caedmon, with her opening comment, "I was impressed by the humility of this seventh-century Anglo-Saxon poet and by his

---

43. O'Connor, in turn, borrows from Teilhard de Chardin from *The Divine Milieu* the phrase "passive diminishments." *The Habit of Being,* 509.

44. Private conversation with Don MacLeod, August 2007. Avison's poem "Godspeed" (*AN* 2.215) is dedicated to Judy and Don MacLeod.

obedient response."[45] She quotes an excerpt from a biography of his humble and retiring life that emphasizes his poetic output as a reluctant response to a divine call, inviting comparison to her own aspirations:

> "Caedmon, sing me something." But he answered, "I cannot sing and for that cause I left the banquet and returned hither, because I could not sing." "Nevertheless, thou must sing to me." "What must I sing?" he asked. "Sing the beginning of Creation," said the other. Having received this answer, he straightway began to sing verses to the praise of God the Creator . . . .[46]

From there the order of service directs her friends to multiple passages from Old and New Testaments and some familiar hymns of "joyfulness," "time-lessness," and "holiness," all pointing to some facet of the Eternal Father and Son. One brief prayer—in prose—is her only sustained composition, and with no mention of her poetic achievements or love of the same:

> Prayer (In my words, at age 86, for me in old age:) O Lord my God, Your love has been like a salve preparing my skin for the stretches of bitter cold. . . .
>
>   How did you draw me and at last visit me? You were longsuf-fering through all my resisting and stalling. Such love hurts while it heals. Now I am launched, not into darkness, but into awe-some Love that, step by step, You have proved is trustworthy.[47]

She makes a final cryptic statement of witness in her gesture of silence. There are no more poems to be written. Nothing more needs to be said. Instead, she frames her closing comments on her life and poetry by first turning witness-like to the poet who early on established the model for poetry—"to the praise of God." Then she concludes with her final pointing to the One to whom she belongs and declares in her chosen scriptural benediction, Jude 24–25:

> Now to Him who is able to keep you from stumbling,
>
> And to present you faultless
>
> Before the presence of His glory with exceeding joy,
>
> To God our Savior,
>
> Who alone is wise,

45. Avison, "Funeral Program." Perhaps the poem "Caedmon" by her friend Denise Levertov was also called to mind in her selection. (See Kent, *"Lighting Up the Terrain,* 1–2).

46. Ibid. The excerpt, she writes, is taken "from *The Caedmon Poems,* tr. into Eng-lish by Charles W. Kennedy."

47. Ibid.

> Be glory and majesty,
>
> Dominion and power,
>
> Both now and forever.
>
> Amen (Jude 24–25).

Margaret Avison's last words of testimony are not her own but from the Book she called her own, pointing as always to the "Amen, the faithful and true Witness" (Rev 3:14).[48]

---

48. Avison, *A Kind of Perseverance*, 44.

Appendix

The Appendix is my concession to the difficulty of discussing poems that are new and unfamiliar and requiring a sense of the whole to understand isolated parts. It would be unwieldy and inappropriate to provide the text for all of Avison's poems I have quoted, but I have made a selection of lyrics that may help readers to follow my argument more clearly. They are arranged according to the section in which they are considered in some detail and are varied enough to present a good sampling of what I consider the poet's witness through her writing. They do not necessarily represent her "best" poems or my favorite ones.

CHAPTER 1

The Word

"*Forsaking all*" – You mean
head over heels, for good,
for ever, call of the depths
of the All – the heart of one
who creates all, at every
moment, newly – for
you do so – and
to me, far fallen in the
ashheaps of my
false-making, burnt-out self and in the
hosed-down rubble of what my furors
gutted, or sooted all
around me – you implore

me to so fall
in Love, and fall anew in
ever-new depths of skyward Love till every
capillary of your universe
throbs with your rivering fire?

"*Forsaking all*" – Your voice
never falters, and yet,
unsealing day out of a
darkness none ever knew
in full but you,
you spoke that word, closing on it forever:
"Why hast Thou forsaken. . . ?"

This measure of your being all-out, and
meaning it, made you
put it all on the line
we, humanly, wanted to draw – at
having you teacher only, or
popular spokesman only, or
doctor or simply a source of sanity
for us, distracted, or only
the one who could wholeheartedly
rejoice with us, and know
our tears, our flickering time, and
stand with us.

But to make it head over heels
yielding, all the way,
you had to die for us.
The line we drew, you crossed,
and cross out, wholly forget,
at the faintest stirring of what
you know is love, is One
whose name has been, and is
and will be, the
I AM.
        The Dumbfounding (AN 1.195–96)

CHAPTER 2

Poetry Is

Poetry is always in
unfamiliar territory.

At a ballgame when
the hit most matters
and the crowd is half-standing
already hoarse, then poetry's
eye is astray to a
quiet area to find out
who picks up the bat the runner
flung out of his runway.

Little stuff like that
poetry tucks away in
the little basket of other
scraps. There's the

cradling undergrowth in
the scrub beside a
wild raspberry bush where
a bear lay feet up feeding
but still three rubied berries
glow in the green.
He had had enough.

Then there's the way
a child's watering can
forgotten in the garden
no faucet, but the far
sky has filled. When sun
shines again it has
become a dragonfly's pretend
skating rink.

Scraps. Who carries the basket?
What will the scraps be used for?

Poetry does not care
what things are for but is
willing to listen to
any, if not everyone's
questions.
It can happen that poetry
basket and all *is*
the unfamiliar territory
that poetry is in.
    Momentary Dark (MD 27–28)

"Tell them everything that I command you; do not omit a word" (Jer. 26.2b)

Night? barely past noon?
an eerie quiet, then
the crack and rustle of fear.

But in that hour
just before the storm/doom
crashed down,

with force and immediacy, heard
by every child, woman and man,
came the word, spoken
through Jeremiah who
moved past darkness.

Yes, they had heard
his long-range forecasts.
But now, they knew, believing now
had them closed in with seeing.
    Not Yet But Still (AN 3.35)

Proving

"... do not omit a word" (Jer. 26.2b)

Truth speaks
all things into being.
No word more, but
not one left unspoken.
Truth carves, incises,
to the bone,
and between bone and marrow.
No wonder
we want none of him.
The wonder is
truth loves;
died of it, once.

Truth lives.
Acting on what is spoken,
not a syllable extra,
nothing omitted,
brings into being
just what is prophesied.
That is the test –
not of what has been spoken
but for the hearer,
his act.

Not Yet But Still (*AN* 3.79)

.

CHAPTER 3

A Nameless One

Hot in June a narrow winged
long-elbowed-thread-legged
living insect lived
and died within
the lodgers' second-floor bathroom here.

At six a.m.
wafting ceilingward,
no breeze but what it living made there;

at noon standing
still as a constellation of spruce needles
before the moment of
making it, whirling;

at four a
wilted flotsam, cornsilk, on the linoleum:

now that it is
over, I
look with new eyes
upon this room
adequate for one to
be, in.

Its insect-day
has threaded a needle
for me for my eyes dimming
over rips and tears and
thin places.

      The Dumbfounding (AN 1.225)

What John Saw (Revelation 4)

The black holes out there, of pure (physical) force
in the heavens,
those in-and-out plosions, focused,
remote, in a rhythm of
incomprehensible infrequency
but nonetheless in time,
speak the extremes absolute of a rhythm
we mortals know.
They are like us contained in
creation's "Let it be so."

Who can comprehend, with a heart hungry
for meaning?
who does not feel the uprooting
tremor of one event –
one person's or, in the stupefying
astronomers' book of hours, one
pulse of the megalorhythm?

Yes yes I know
this bronzing beech tree, the
blackening myrtle at its foot
(event in all my seasons,
seasoned for this long before I was
born) exists in a mere
twitch, is rushing towards the node
millennia away, and that just one
of many, just one episode.
Time curls on itself.

Least moments given, though,
can open onto
John's comprehender: here,
there, then always
now, because unchanging, who
made light and ponderous rhythms, time, and all
pulsing particulars.
John saw him rainbowed in glory –
compact of all our music, hearing the farthest
compositions, and the most intricately
present. Magnet. Intensifier. Agonizingly
rediscovering, in shards, the shapes
design is satisfied to see.
One. White. Whole.

Secret within
all that John saw
is the bronzing beech tree

of this October twilight
though I do not yet see,
even in mind, being not yet out of time.
    Not Yet But Still (AN 3.74–75)

CHAPTER 4

'On' from Other Oceans

When the convulsive earth
arched under the sea
its craggy ribs were
blurted out where reefs had been
into the golden warmth for a
fraction of a second of the one
day that's a thousand years.
In the same breath, on what was risen up
swarms of wee morsels mightier than
seafoam, rockface, under weather
brought what had emerged to be
grasses of the field
breathing that sun-washed sky.
On the face of the earth
trees and tiny Arctic flowers
face upwards; animals
with velvet paws, or hoofs,
all seem to look away towards the
falling-away edge of the earth.
My face, among these others,
ours, are not as though
among these others.
    Concrete and Wild Carrot (AN 3.146)

Neverness, or, The One Ship Beached On One Far Distant Shore

Old Adam, with his fistful of plump earth,
His sunbright gaze on his eternal hill
Is not historical:
His tale is never done
For us who know a world no longer bathed
In the harsh splendour of economy.
We millions hold old Adam in our thoughts
A pivot for the future-past, a core
Of the one dream that never goads to action
But stains our entrails with nostalgia
And wrings the sweat of death in ancient eyes.

The one-celled plant is not historical.
Leeuwenhoek peered through his magic window
and in a puddle glimpsed the tiny grain
Of firmament that was before the Adam.

I'd like to pull that squinting Dutchman's sleeve
And ask what were his thoughts, lying at night,
And smelling the sad spring, and thinking out
Across the fullness of night air, smelling
The dark canal, and dusty oat-bag, cheese,
And wet straw-splintered wood, and rust-seamed leather
And pearly grass and silent deeps of sky
Honey-combed with its million years of light
And prune-sweet earth
Honey-combed with the silent worms of dark.
Old Leeuwenhoek must have had ribby thoughts
To hoop the hollow pounding of his heart
Those nights of spring in 1600-odd.
It would be done if he could tell it us.

The tissue of our metaphysic cells
No magic window yet has dared reveal.
Our bleared world welters on
Far past the one-cell instant. Points are spread

And privacy is unadmitted prison.
Why, now I know the lust of omnipresence!

You thousands merging lost,
      I call to you
Down the stone corridors that wall me in.

I am inside these days, snug in a job
In one of many varnished offices
Bleak with the wash of daylight
And us, the human pencils wearing blunt.
Soon I'll be out with you,
Another in the lonely unshut world
Where sun blinks hard on yellow brick and glazed,
On ads in sticky posterpaint
      And fuzzy
         At midday intersections.
The milk is washed down corded throats at noon
Along a thousand counters, and the hands
That count the nickel from a greasy palm
Have never felt an udder.
      The windy dark
That thrums high among towers and nightspun branches
whirs through our temples with a dry confusion.
We sprawl abandoned into disbelief
And feel the pivot-picture of old Adam
On the first hill that ever was, alone,
And see the hard earth seeded with sharp snow
And dream that history is done.

          ****

And if that be the dream that whortles out
Into unending night
Then must the pivot Adam be denied
And the whole cycle ravelled and flung loose.
Is this the epoch when the age-old Serpent
Must writhe and loosen, slacking out

To a new pool of time's eternal sun?
Old Adam, will your single outline blur
At this long last when slow mist wells
Fuming from all the valleys of the earth?
Or will our unfixed vision rather blind
Through agony to the last gelid stare
And none be left to witness the blank mist?

From Elsewhere (AN 1.24–26)

July Man

Old, rain-wrinkled, time-soiled, city-wise, morning man
whose weeping is for the dust of the elm-flowers
and the hurting motes of time,
rotted with rotting grape,
sweet with the fumes,
puzzled for good by fermented potato-
peel out of the vat of the times,
turned out and left
in this grass-patch, this city-gardener's place
under the buzzing populace's
square shadows, and the green shadows
of elm and ginkgo and lime
(planted for Sunday strollers and summer evening
families, and for those
bird-cranks with bread-crumbs
and crumpled umbrellas who come
while the dew is wet on the park, and beauty
is fan-tailed, grey and dove grey, aslant, folding in
from the white fury of day).

In the sound of the fountain
you rest, at the cinder-rim, on your bench.

The rushing river of cars
makes you a stillness, a pivot, a heart-stopping
blurt, in the sorrow

of the last rubbydub swig, the searing, and
stone-jar solitude lost, and yet,
and still – wonder (for good now) and
trembling:

> The too much none of us knows
> is weight, sudden sunlight, falling
> on your hands and arms, in your lap,
> all, all, in time.
> *The Dumbfounding* (*AN* 1.160)

CHAPTER 5

Meditation on the Opening of the Fourth Gospel

Un-tense-able Being: spoken
for our understanding,
speaking forth the 'natural world' –
'that,' we (who are part of it)
say, 'we can know.'

Even in this baffling darkness
Light has kept shining?
(where? where? then are we blind?).
But Truth is radiantly here,
Being, giving us to Become;
            a new unfathomable genesis.

Come? in flesh and blood?
seen? as another part
of the 'natural world' his word
flung open, for the maybe imperiller,
in what to us was the
Beginning?

The unknown, the unrecognized, the
invisibly glorious
hid in our reality

till the truly real
lays all bare.
The unresisting,
then, most, speaks
love. We fear
that most.
    No Time (*AN* 2.148)

The Bible to Be Believed

The word read by the living Word
sculptured its shaper's form.
What happens, means. The means are not blurred
by Flood – or fiery atom.

    He reads: a Jewish-Egyptian
    firstborn, not three years old;
    a coal-seared poet-statesman;
    an anointed twelve-year-old.

The Word dwells on this word
honing His heart's sword,
ready at knife-edge to declare
holiness, and come clear.

    Ancient names, eon-brittled eyes,
    within the word, open on mysteries:
    the estranged murderer, exiled, hears at last
    his kinsman's voice;
    the child, confidingly question, so close
    to the awful ritual knife,
    is stilled by another, looking to His Father –
        the saving one, not safe.

The Word alive cherishes all:
doves, lambs – or whale –
beyond old rites or emblem burial.
Grapes, bread, and fragrant oil:

all that means, is real
now, only as One wills.

Yes, he was tempted to wash out
in covenanting song
the brand on the dry bone;
he heard the tempter quote
the texts he meant and went embodying.

The Word was moved
too vitally to be entombed
in time. He has hewn out
of it one crevice-gate.

His final silencing endured
has sealed the living word:
now therefore He is voiceful, to be heard,
free, and of all opening-out the Lord.
        sunblue (AN 2.62–63)

For the Murderous: The Beginning of Time

Cain brought grain on his forearm
            and a branch with grapes
        to the plain earth
        under the wide sky:
vaguely he offered to the far-borne light
what the slow days had sweetened.

Abel killed, from his flock.
On the fire he made sacrifice.
Fat-brisk rose smoke and sparks,
and blood darkened the stone place.

            That this was 'better' than that
            kindled in Cain a murderer's heart –
            he was watched over, after; but he kept apart.

In time the paschal lamb
before the slaying did
what has made new the wine
and broken bread.
> *sunblue* (*AN* 2.54)

Aftermath of Rebellion

When runners came with news

after the Battle in the Forest
the King's hopes stirred – here was
no rout, no loyal remnant
straggling home to defend
an indefensible throne.

Yes, the first praised the Lord his God
(the King's), obviously glad in
the monarch and his kingdom
made secure. Yet
(and hope flickered):
'What of Absalom?'

The second, the official slower
runner, with a word
stifled the air and
hope went out.

'Would God that I had died for *him*.'

The father's lament
has lingered on the ancient air of grief
at least till now.

a vain, muscular, risk-defying,
fine-looking heir to
prospects that one day would
amaze the Queen of Sheba,
a rebel, a contemptuous

underminer, had flung off

– forever now –
in his young man's euphoria,
his father's hand.

For such a delinquent
even, a sovereign, sick at heart,
learned what it is when
a father loves.
        Not Yet But Still (*AN* 3.57–58)

All Out or Oblation

(as defined in 2 Sam. 23:13–17 and 1 Chron. 11:17–19)

Where sandstorms blow
and sun blackens and withers, licks up
into empty bright glare
any straggler
            who is exposed
                        being still alive,
there:
        clean   cold   water
            throat-laving
            living
                water.

    Look! – a little group of men:
    sun flashes
    on the water poured from leather pouch
    into a bowl, shining,
        now uplifted.
God.
God.
            Saltwater has etched
            their cheeks, their mouthcorners.

WHAT ARE THEY DOING?

They are crazy. They are
                    pouring it
                            out.
Sand coats the precious drops and darkens with the life-stain.
                                                Earth's
            slow and unspasmodic swallowing is slowly, slowly
                                    accomplished.

No. I do not understand.

yet with the centuries still gaze at them
        to learn to expect to
        pour it out

        into desert – to find out what it is.
        sunblue (AN 2.55–56)

A Story

        Where *were* you then?
                    At the beach.
        With your crowd again.
        Trailing around, open
        to whatever's going. Which one's
        calling for you tonight?
                    Nobody.
        I'm sorry I talk so. Young
        is young. I ought to remember
        and let you go and be glad.
                    No. It's all right.
                    I'd just sooner stay home.
        You're not sick? did you
        get too much sun? a crowd,
        I never have liked it, safety in numbers
        indeed!
                    He was alone.

Who was alone?
>The one
>out on the water, telling
>something. He sat in the boat that
>they shoved out for him, and told
>us things. We all just stood there
>about an hour. Nobody
>shoving. I couldn't see
>very clearly, but I listened
>the same as the rest.

What was it about?
>About a giant, sort of.
>No. No baby-book giant.
>But about a man. I think –

You *are* all right?
>Of course.

Then tell me
so I can follow. You all
standing there, getting up
out of the beach-towels and gathering
out of the cars, and the ones
half-dressed, not even caring –
>*Yes.* Because the ones
>who started to crowd around were
>so still. You couldn't
>help wondering. And it spread.
>And then when I would have felt out of it
>he got the boat, and I could
>see the white, a little, and
>hear him, word by word.

What did he tell the lot of you
to make you stand? Politics?
Preaching? You can't believe everything
they tell you, remember –
>No. More, well a
>fable. Honestly, I –

I won't keep interrupting.

I'd really like you to tell.

Tell me. I won't say anything.

     It is a story. But

     only one man comes.

     Tall, sunburnt, coming

     not hurried, but as though

     there was so much power in reserve

     that walking all day and night

     would be lovelier than sleeping if

     sleeping meant missing it, easy

     and alive, and out there.

Where was it?

     On a kind of clamshell back.

     I mean country, like round about here,

     but his tallness, as he walked there

     made green and rock-grey and brown

     his floorway. And sky a brightness.

What was he doing? Just walking?

     No. Now it sounds strange

     but it wasn't to hear.

     He was casting seed,

     only everywhere.

     On the roadway out

     on the baldest stone,

     on the tussocky waste

     and in pockets of loam.

Seed? A farmer?

     A gardener rather

     but there was nothing

     like garden, mother.

     Only the queer

     dark way he went

     and the star-shine of

     the seed he spent.

(Seed you could see that way –)

     In showers. His fingers

     shed, like the gold

                of blowing autumnal
                woods in the wild.
                He carried no wallet
                or pouch or sack,
                but clouds of birds followed
                to buffet and peck
                on the road. And the rock
                sprouted new blades
                and thistle and stalk
                matted in, and the birds
                ran threading the tall grasses
                lush and fine
                in the pockets of deep earth –
You mean, in time
he left, and you saw
this happen?
                The hollow
                air scalded with sun.
                The first blades went sallow
                and dried and the one
                who had walked, had only
                the choked-weed patches
                and a few thin files
                of windily, sunnily
                searching thirsty ones
                for his garden
                in all that place.
                But they flowered, and shed
                their strange heart's force
                in that wondering wilderness –
Where is he now?
                The gardener?
No. The storyteller
out on the water?
                He is alone.

                Perhaps a few

who beached the boat and
stayed, would know.
The Dumbfounding (AN 1.164–67)

Christmas Approaches, Highway 401

Seed of snow
on cement, ditch-rut, rink-steel, salted where
grass straws thinly scrape against lowering
daydark in the rise of the earth-crust there
(and beyond, the scavenging birds
flitter and skim)
is particle
unto earth's thirsting,
spring rain,
wellspring.
roadwork, earthwork, pits in hillsides,
desolation, abandoned roadside shacks
and dwelt in,
unkilned pottery broken and strawed about,
minibrick people-palaces,
coming and going always
by day all lump and ache
is sown tonight with the beauty
of light and moving lights, light traveling, light
shining from beyond farthestness.
sunblue (AN 2.97)

Uncircular

The entombment of all that wrath
bespeaks the stench of a
fragmenting into
finality.
To me, this matters.
I anchor there as to a lifeline,

***

there where
what other self-bound persons
had wrapped and lovingly
laid, a total
loss for all, for all
was found in purity, among his friends
changed, but the same time opening
everything on earth to the
power that lifted him.

No wonder Paul cried out,
'I count all loss . . .' – above all, loss.

***

Among us, Jesus found
encrusted words and structures;
he washed and brushed them clean
and out of the intractability
of history learned by rote
stepped, in simplicity the exemplar,

into the prairies of
dutiful days, each with the taste
of moving slowly towards . . . without
the horizon coming any closer.

His are the evenings of a
king in a cave kept wakeful by
deftly deciphering the poems
he found written in his heart.

When most of his people trailed
about in moulting plumage –
aping, through fear and envy,
those not themselves –
he brokenheartedly
tried to put heart in them

again, or rouse them to the dread, in time,
that dragged them down
into sensibility.

In the besieged city
he moved among the panic-crazed;
and where skin-and-bone
cannibals crept or
by the walls, rocked against the rock
like a cribbed infant.
Once for a time
all of them were
strangers far from home.
They knew the wreckage to be
faced and put together somehow
on their return some day.

Once again there, Jesus too found
words twisted, rubble about and
again he swept and tended them
gently, almost smiling
when some who so cherished
the traditional that they urged
stains, gritty particles, dust
must be left, too, untouched.
His words flowed from a
clear wellspring always till now
a little tainted by the
hand that cupped to drink, or the
crafted ladle.

Why was this one then
dragged off and left abandoned to
indifferent cruelty once, with no
home left, anywhere?

       ***

Entombment, however, is
new in all history.
What it is for.
    Concrete and Wild Carrot (*AN* 3.167–69)

Our Only Hour

In the sunslick a shrub, its buds sealed in,
is skeleton'd in light. Sand clumps on
        sand cast shadows.
Out of strange oceans day has unscrolled,
        (low shining) has smoothed
      a HERE from among
farness and blueness and more, more, mounting and melting
        to indigo, and the centripetal
          fires of gold.

His look was lightning.
The extraordinary angel
stood, where history cleft
BC – AD:
the keepers were as dead men.

    The keepers till the day they died
      could not forget. Blindness still stabbing, from the
          fierce glare of such a
           countenance (in the undwindling moment
              when they blacked out).

Not everybody sees
something like that in his time.
And then can never
distance it by
words ('I always remember
    the morning . . .')
Nobody could have heard.

Often in the night
the old keeper would
butt again at the wall
Of fact: the stone,
    the hurried debriefing to
        hide what was done
        and keep them each alone
        and dumb.

His look was lightning.

It is a disappointment
        to have seen
        the singular brightness and be
        only as dead men,
and then exist, later that day and on and on:
        the point of it
        searching you, idly now, somehow, in
        a gathering silence, a history
compulsively reviewed.

Could those keepers have actually
stifled the world?
One of them wondered,
waiting it out in the hours of his darkness.

        Three women were there.
          God kept them from terror.
          Truth shone, and shines.

The shrubbery by an apartment wall is
wire-bright in the keen north sun
        (sky jet-stream-sundered)
          and I think
          how it is the angel
          staggers belief.

Wide continents, telescope-swathed marine sky, our
    multifarious kind, spilling out, over, around:
    we receive 'all' easily but

glimpse something, once or twice,
which in our only hour will be
massively known.

The angel, we
hardly expect,
can hardly credit.

But the man, torn, stained,
left in mummy-wrappings,
stone under stone?

the man then seen
alive, known
powerful, heard
in the heart's ear?

He does not so stagger belief
as overwhelm our grieving.
No Time (AN 2.228–30)

Early Easter Sunday Morning Radio

The young voices,
the students' choirs
stir wonder. It's

the sting of new day
clear chill delicately
touched on the damp
grey-cloth east by a
thin brush, watery colours
faint in: tints run
sidewise and dis-
solve upward in the not yet except
for a breath of, a

far-off heralding of,
sun.

   'Gloria!' they sing,
   'Gloria!'

Why weep, old eyes, when
so suffused with joy?
   Too Towards Tomorrow: New Poems (AN 3.195)

CHAPTER 6

Stone's Secret

Otter-smooth boulder
lies under rolling
black river-water
stilled among frozen
hills and the still unbreathed
blizzards aloft;
silently, icily, is probed
stone's secret.

Out there – past trace
of eyes, past these
and those memorial skies
dotting black signals from
men's made mathematics (we
delineators of curves and time who are
           subject to these) –
out there, inaccessible
to grammar's language the
stones curve vastnesses,
cold or candescent
in the perceived
processional of space.

        The stones out there in the
        violet-black are part of a

slow-motion fountain? or of a
fireworks pin-wheel?
i.e. breathed in and out
as in cosmic lungs? or
one-way as an eye looking?
what mathematicians must,
also the pert,
they will
as the dark river runs.

Word has arrived that
peace will brim up, will come
'like a river and the
glory . . . like a flowing stream.'
So.
some of all people will
wondering wait
until this very stone utters.
  sunblue (AN 2.26–27)

Incentive

One walked the roads, slept
on a boat-cushion, waited alone
in enemy country at blazing noon for
water even,
paced it out to the end
in such clear strength

that (cows of Bashan
      slaking our thirst, calling for more,
      squashing poor people and not even noticing
      and on the right days all in good order
      sailing down aisles, heaping up
      flowers on the altar etc.)
we look to him for

?no bread

no rain
leaf-shrivel and pests and
fevers and sores and
violence?

would but these bring us back to
the footpaths and open
skies among night-breathing olive trees,
back to the waiting,
the hope.
    No Time (AN 2.261)

Psalm 80:1 – "Thou that dwellest between the cherubim, shine forth!"

In autumn dark comes early,
the wind goes to the bone,
the crowds are very busy
and a person feels alone.

You know, Lord, You know us
out in the dark and cold –
and never planned to leave us out
although shut out of old.

The windows of the glory
were open, and You knew
Your power was for outpouring
in time to make this new.

We didn't know You, Jesus.
You came out in the night
and poked around the side streets
to bring us to Your light.

We waited where the wind blew
and knifed You in the rain.
Yet You still know who's scared and cold
and doesn't dare complain.

Some You have given food and warmth
now can go back out to
be with You in the darkness,
vagrants, focused on You –

until all the windows
of the Kingdom shine
and we can all be very sure
You wanted every one.

> Bless us, Lord of Heaven,
> Bless us, Mary's child,
> and keep our courage high with You
> through steep and storm and wild.
>   *sunblue* (AN 2.85–86)

Cross-Cultural or Towards Burnout

Your rage is bearable as your
swallowed insults and the limp
collusion with us were not
to you, were to us echoes only of
our inauthentic guilt.

Yet your rage hurts.
A post-colonial white woman, I am
therefore a thing-hog,
easy taker-for-granted, helpless
to unmake the bed
others made for me, even before
grandpa (and even he was
simply another fellow working long hours,
kindly respectful, whether paid or not).
And I lie, tossing, in that
incontestably comfortable bed.

What has been crafted in behind
green hedges of 'our heritage'

took centuries, took lives.
It formalized, in time, our
savage sorrow into this
chamber music. We need
a life half-lived-out, maybe more
to be constrained to music in
quiet fullness of sorrow.

We are outraged at your
raw grief, at
the bony barricades of
borne indignity:
your five-year-old coming in
defeated, facing still
another day of what
our five-year-old will say and do.

Through Jeremiah I had
faced up to God's fierce anger.

Therefore your rage is the
long held under
knowledge of the holy child's
knowledge of
the spittle, the
flogged back, the suave
manipulator's deathly mockery,
present, every wracked
generation, as if helplessly.

Your work is dark and bitter.

Ours, rounded up at last from the
once fortress city, picking our way
out through its rubble, bound
for forced labour in remote Asian
cities, or
slavery in
others' mansions and palaces.

Our God endures.

The sentinel trees
on a far hilly ridge
remind us of perennial
destruction, restoration, on
wave lengths much too vast to ease
you and the child today
or us into tomorrow
Not Yet But Still (*AN* 3.48–49).

Concert

Learning, I more and more
long for that simplicity,
clarity, that willingness
to speak (from anonymity . . .)
all those impenetrables, when words
are more like bluebell petals under
an absorbed heaven.

You fret because the underbrush
is dense, the way uncleared it seems
where you now find yourself?

Words have been given. Once.
Words that are storm and sun and rain.
Listening earth, where they have fallen,
finds seed casings begin
to split,
roots throb. As though
some unimaginable response is
implicit in that speaking.

Fulfilment is in promise
and still more resonant longing.
Not Yet But Still (*AN* 3.65)

Bibliography

Abrams, M. H. *A Glossary of Literary Terms*. 7th ed. Fort Worth, TX: Harcourt Brace, 1999.

———. *The Mirror and the Lamp: Romantic Theory and the Critical Tradition*. New York: Norton, 1958.

Abrams, M. H., and Stephen Greenblatt, eds. *The Norton Anthology of English Literature: The Major Authors*. 7th ed. New York: Norton, 2001.

Aide, William. *Starting from Porcupine*. Ottawa, ON: Oberon, 1996.

Alighieri, Dante. *The Divine Comedy*. Translated by C. H. Sisson. Oxford: Oxford University Press, 1993.

Anderson, A. A. *Second Samuel*. Dallas: Word, 1989.

Anderson, Mia. "'Conversation with the Star Messenger': An Enquiry into Margaret Avison's Winter Sun." *Studies in Canadian Literature* 6.1 (1981) 82–132.

Aristotle. "The Poetics." In *Criticism: Major Statements*, 4th ed., edited by C. Kaplan and W. Anderson. Translated by S. Butcher, 18–46. Boston: Bedford/St. Martins, 2000.

Armstrong, Isobel. *Victorian Poetry*. London: Routledge, 1993.

Atwood, Margaret. *Survival: A Thematic Guide to Canadian Literature*. Toronto: House of Anansi, 1972.

Auden, W. H. *The Dyer's Hand and Other Essays*. New York: Random House, 1968.

Augustine. *Confessions*. Translated by H. Chadwick. Oxford: Oxford University Press, 1991.

Avison, Margaret. *Always Now: The Collected Poems,* 3 vols. Erin, ON: Porcupine's Quill, 2003–5.

———. ". . . at least we are together . . ." *Crux* 8.2 (1970–71) 15–19.

———. *Concrete and Wild Carrot*. London, ON: Brick, 2002.

———. *The Dumbfounding*. New York: Norton, 1966.

———. *History of Ontario*. Toronto: Gage, 1951.

———. *I Am Here and Not Not-There: An Autobiography*. Erin, ON: The Porcupine's Quill, 2009.

———. [Angela Martin, pseudonym]. "I Couldn't Have My Cake and Eat It." In *I Wish I Had Known . . .* , edited by M. H., 86–89. London: Scripture Union, 1968.

———. *A Kind of Perseverance*. Hantsport, NS: Lancelot, 1994.

———. Letter to Tim Bowling. October 5, 2001. The University of Manitoba: Margaret Avison Fonds.

———. Letter to Anne Corkett. December 17, 1981. The University of Manitoba: Margaret Avison Fonds.

———. Letter to Cid Corman. March 9, 1961. In *Origin* 2.4 (1962) 10–11.

———. Letter to Michael Higgins. April 4, 2000. The University of Manitoba: Margaret Avison Fonds.

———. Letter to Denise Levertov. 1995. The University of Manitoba: Margaret Avison Fonds.

———. Letter to David Mazoff. January 4, 1990. The University of Manitoba: Margaret Avison Fonds.

———. Letter to Stephen Scobie. December 30, 1993. The University of Manitoba: Margaret Avison Fonds.

———. Letter to Stephen Scobie. March 15, 1994. The University of Manitoba: Margaret Avison Fonds.

———. *Listening: Last Poems.* Toronto: McClelland & Stewart, 2009.

———. "Muse of Danger." *His*, March 1968, 33–35.

———. News clippings, correspondence from Margaret Avison. York University, Scott Library Archives: Margaret Clarkson Fonds, 1963–70.

———. *No Time.* Hantsport, NS: Lancelot, 1989.

———. *Not Yet But Still.* Hantsport, NS: Lancelot, 1997.

———. "Poets in Canada." *Poetry* [Chicago] 94 (1959) 182–85.

———. "Reading Morley Callaghan's 'Such Is My Beloved.'" *Canadian Literature* 133 (1992) 204–7.

———. "Readings." Audio Recording at Regent College, 1972. Vancouver, BC.

———. *The Research Compendium: Reviews and Abstracts of Graduate Research, 1942–1962.* Toronto: University of Toronto Press, 1964.

———. Review of *The Canticle of the Rose: Selected Poems 1920–1947*, by Edith Sitwell. *The Canadian Forum*, February 1950, 262–63.

———. Review of *Collected Poems*, by W. B. Yeats. *The Canadian Forum*, February 1951, 261.

———. Review of *Day and Night*, by Dorothy Livesay. *The Canadian Forum*, June 1944, 67.

———. Review of *Here and Now*, by Irving Layton. *The Canadian Forum*, May 1945, 47–48.

———. Review of *New Poems*, by Dylan Thomas. *The Canadian Forum*, September 1943, 143.

———. Review of *The Rocking Chair and Other Poems*, by A. M. Klein. *The Canadian Forum*, November 1948, 191.

———. Review of *Selected Poems*, by Kenneth Patchen; and *Residence on Earth and Other Poems*, by Pablo Neruda. *The Canadian Forum*, April 1947, 21–22.

———. Review of *The Soldier, a Poem*, by Conrad Aiken. *The Canadian Forum*, January 1945, 241.

———. *Selected Poems.* Toronto: Oxford University Press, 1991.

———. "The Style of Byron's *Don Juan* in Relation to the Newspapers of His Day." M.A. thesis, University of Toronto, 1964.

———. *sunblue.* Hantsport, NS: Lancelot, 1978.

———. Telephone Interview with Elizabeth Davey, April 6, 2004.

——— "Undated and Untitled Poem." The University of Manitoba: Margaret Avison Fonds, n.d.

———. Unpublished letters, poems. The University of Manitoba: Margaret Avison Fonds, 1929–.

————. Unpublished letters, poems. York University, Scott Library Archives: Margaret Avison Fonds, 1959–83.

————. "Who Listens and How Come?" *Crux* 6.2 (1969) 4–5.

————. *Winter Sun.* Toronto: University of Toronto Press, 1960.

————. *Winter Sun/The Dumbfounding: Poems 1940–66.* Toronto: McClelland and Stewart, 1982.

Avison, Margaret, and Sally Ito. "'The Quiet Centre Inside: Margaret Avison interviewed by Sally Ito.' In *Where the Words Come From: Canadian Poets in Conversation,* edited by Tim Bowling, 159–73. Roberts Creek, BC: Nightwood Editions, 2002.

Avison, Margaret, and D. S. Martin. "A Conversation with Margaret Avison." *Image: Art, Faith, Mystery* 45 (Spring 2005) 65–76.

Avison, Margaret, and Rose Simone. "A Religious Experience." *The Second Mile,* February 1994, 48.

Babstock, Ken. Review of *Concrete and Wild Carrot* by Margaret Avison. *Globe and Mail,* June 21, 2003, D13.

Baldick, Chris. *The Modern Movement: 1910–1940,* Vol. 10. The Oxford English Literary History. Oxford: Oxford University Press, 2004.

Barfield, Owen. *Poetic Diction: A Study in Meaning.* 3rd ed. Middletown, CT: Wesleyan University Press, 1973.

Barratt, David et al., eds. *The Discerning Reader: Christian Perspectives on Literature and Theory.* Grand Rapids: Baker, 1995.

Barrett, C. K. *The Gospel according to St. John: An Introduction with Commentary and Notes on the Greek Text.* 2nd ed. London: SPCK, 1978.

Barth, Karl. *Church Dogmatics.* Vols. 1/4. 2nd ed. Edited by G. Bromiley, and T. F. Torrance. Edinburgh: T. & T. Clark, 1975.

————. *Evangelical Theology: An Introduction.* Translated by Grover Foley. Grand Rapids: Eerdmans, 1963.

Bartholomew, Craig, and Michael Goheen. *The Drama of Scripture: Finding Our Place in the Biblical Story* Grand Rapids: Baker Academic, 2004.

Baym, Nina, et al., eds. *The Norton Anthology of American Literature,* Vol. 1. 5th ed. New York: Norton, 1998.

Bennett, Donna, and Russell Brown, eds. *A New Anthology of Canadian Literature in English.* Don Mills, ON: Oxford University Press, 2002.

Bloom, Harold. *How to Read and Why.* New York: Simon & Schuster, 2001.

Boice, James Montgomery. *The Gospel of John.* Grand Rapids: Zondervan, 1979.

Booth, Wayne. *A Rhetoric of Irony.* Chicago: University of Chicago Press, 1975.

Borroff, Marie. *Sir Gawain and the Green Knight, Patience, and Pearl: Verse Translations.* New York: Norton, 2001.

Bowen, Deborah. "Phoenix from the Ashes: Lorna Crozier and Margaret Avison in Contemporary Mourning." *Canadian Poetry* 40 (Spring/Summer 1997) 46–57.

Bowering, George. "Avison's Imitation of Christ the Artist." *Canadian Literature* 54 (Autumn 1973) 56–69.

————. "Her Moment, Ours." *Canadian Poetry* 59 (Fall/Winter 2006) 14–15.

Brown, David, and Ann Loades, eds. *The Sacramental Word.* London: SPCK, 1996.

Brown, Frank. "Transfiguration: Poetic Metaphor and Theological Reflection." *The Journal of Religion* 62 (1982) 39–56.

Brown, Raymond E. *The Gospel according to John.* 2 vols. Garden City, NY: Doubleday, 1966.

———. *The Gospel and Epistles of John: A Concise Commentary.* Collegeville, MN: Liturgical, 1988.

Browning, Robert. *Robert Browning's Selected Poems.* New York: Crowell, 1896.

Brueggemann, Walter. *Cadences of Home: Preaching among Exiles.* Louisville: Westminster John Knox, 1997.

———. *Isaiah 40–66.* Louisville: Westminster John Knox, 1998.

Brunner, Emil. *The Christian Doctrine of Creation and Redemption, Dogmatics,* Vol. 2. Translated by Olive Wyon. Philadelphia: Westminster, 1952.

Bultmann, Rudolf, et al. *The Gospel of John: A Commentary.* Oxford: Blackwell, 1971.

Busch, Eberhard. *The Great Passion: An Introduction to Karl Barth's Theology.* Edited by Darrell Guder and Judith Guder. Translated by Geoffrey Bromiley. Grand Rapids: Eerdmans, 2004.

Butt, William. "Word and Action in Margaret Avison's 'Not Yet But Still.'" *University of Toronto Quarterly* 70.4 (2001) 839–56.

Cairns, David. *The Image of God in Man.* London: Fontana Library Theology & Philosophy, 1973.

Calverley, Margaret. "The Avison Collection at the University of Manitoba: Poems 1929–89." *Canadian Poetry* 28 (Spring/Summer 1991) 54–84.

———. "A Reconsideration of Margaret Avison's 'Dispersed Titles.'" *Essays on Canadian Writing* 47 (1992) 163–80.

———. "'Service is Joy': Margaret Avison's Sonnet Sequence in Winter Sun." *Essays on Canadian Writing* 50 (1993) 210–23.

Calvin, John. *The Epistle of Paul the Apostle to the Hebrews and the First and Second Epistles of St Peter.* Translated by W. Johnston. Grand Rapids: Eerdmans, 1963.

———. *The Gospel according to St. John 1–10.* Translated by T. H. L. Parker. Grand Rapids: Eerdmans, 1961.

———. *Institutes of the Christian Religion,* Vols. 1–2. Edited by John T. McNeill; translated by Ford Lewis Battles. Philadelphia: Westminster, 1960.

Chronology. Margaret Avison Fonds. The University of Manitoba.

The Cloud of Unknowing and Other Works. Translated by Clifton Walters. Harmondsworth, UK: Penguin, 1978.

Coenen, L. "Witness, Testimony." In *NIDNTT* 3: 1038–51.

Cohn-Sfetcu, Ofelia. "To Live in Abundance of Life: Time in Canadian Literature." *Canadian Literature* 76 (1978) 25–36.

Coleridge, Samuel T. "From *Biographia Literaria.*" In *English Romantic Writers,* edited by David Perkins, 448–91. New York: Harcourt, Brace & World, 1967.

Craddock, Fred B. *Luke.* Louisville: John Knox, 1990.

Culler, Jonathan. *Literary Theory: A Very Short Introduction.* Oxford: Oxford University Press, 1997.

Culpepper, R. Alan. *Anatomy of the Fourth Gospel: A Study in Literary Design.* Philadelphia: Fortress, 1983.

———. *The Gospel and Letters of John.* Nashville: Abingdon, 1998.

de Dietrich, Susanne. "You Are My Witnesses." *Interpretation* 8.3 (1954) 273–79.

Dickinson, Emily. "Poems." In *The Norton Anthology of American Literature,* Vol. 1, 5th ed., edited by Nina Baym et al., 2488–531. New York: Norton, 1998.

Dijwa, Sandra. "Letters in Canada: 1979. Poetry." *University of Toronto Quarterly* 49 (1980) 348–49.

Dillard, Annie. *Pilgrim at Tinker Creek.* New York: Harper & Row, 1974.

Doerksen, Daniel. "Search and Discovery: Margaret Avison's Poetry." *Canadian Literature* 60 (1974) 7–20.

Donne, John. *Poetry and Prose*. Edited by Frank J. Warnke. New York: Random House, 1967.

Dostoyevsky, Fyodor. *The Brothers Karamazov: A Novel in Four Parts with Epilogue*. Translated by David McDuff. New York: Penguin, 2003.

Douglas, J. D., and Earle E. Cairns, eds. *The New International Dictionary of the Christian Church*. Grand Rapids, Zondervan, 1978.

Edwards, A. S. G. "The Manuscript: British Library MS Cotton Nero A.x." In *A Companion to the Gawain-Poet*, edited by Derek Brewer and Jonathan Gibson, 197–220. Woodbridge, UK: Boydell & Brewer, 1997.

Edwards, Jonathan. "Personal Narrative." In *The Norton Anthology of American Literature*, Vol. 1, 5th ed., edited by Nina Baym et al., 441–52. New York: Norton, 1998.

Edwards, Michael. *Towards a Christian Poetics*. Grand Rapids: Eerdmans, 1984.

———. "Wordsworth and the 'Mystery of Words.'" In *The Interpretation of Belief: Coleridge, Schleiermacher and Romanticism*, edited by David Jasper, 143–57. New York: St. Martin's, 1986.

Edwards, Ruth. *Discovering John*. London: SPCK, 2003.

Eliot, T. S. *Collected Poems 1909–1962*. London: Faber & Faber, 1963.

Ellul, Jacques. *The Humiliation of the Word*. Grand Rapids: Eerdmans, 1985.

Empson, William. *Seven Types of Ambiguity*. 3rd ed. London: Pimlico, 2004.

Erickson, Millard. *Christian Theology*. 2nd ed. Grand Rapids: Baker, 1998.

Facts about Niagara Falls. No pages. Online: www.niagarafallslive.com/Facts_about_Niagara_Falls.htm.

Fagles, Robert, trans. *The Iliad of Homer*. New York: Viking, 1990.

Farrer, Austin. "Poetic Truth." In *Reflective Faith: Essays in Philosophical Theology*, 24–38. Grand Rapids: Eerdmans, 1974.

Fiedler, Leslie. Introduction to *Waiting for God*, by Simone Weil. New York: Harper & Row, 1973.

Fitch, William. *Knox Church Toronto: Avant-garde, Evangelical, Advancing*. Toronto: Deyell, 1971.

Fitzgerald, Robert, trans. *The Odyssey of Homer*. New York: Farrar, Straus, and Giroux, 1998.

Fox, Gail. "Dancing in the Dark." In *"Lighting up the terrain": The Poetry of Margaret Avison*, edited by David Kent, 55–57. Toronto: ECW, 1987.

Frye, Northrup. *The Educated Imagination*. Toronto: House of Anansi, 1963.

———. "Preface to an Uncollected Anthology." *Studia Varia: Royal Society of Canada, Literary and Scientific Papers*, edited by G. D. Murray, 35. Toronto: University of Toronto Press, 1957.

Gaventa, Beverly. *Acts*. Nashville: Abingdon Press, 2003.

Geddes, Gary, ed. *20th-Century Poetry & Poetics*. 5th ed. Don Mills, ON: Oxford University Press, 2006.

Hair, Donald. "Avison at Western: Writing at the Limits of Vision." *Canadian Poetry* 59 (Fall/Winter 2006) 53–61.

Hanson, Paul. *Isaiah 40–66*. Louisville: John Knox, 1995.

Hardy, Daniel, and David Ford. *Jubilate: Theology in Praise*. London: Darton Longman & Todd, 1984.

Harvey, A. E. *Jesus on Trial: A Study in the Fourth Gospel.* Atlanta: John Knox, 1976.

Hatch, Ronald. "Poetry." *University of Toronto Quarterly* 60.1 (1990) 24–42.

Hauerwas, Stanley. *With the Grain of the Universe.* London: SCM, 2002.

Hay, Elizabeth. Endorsement. In *Always Now: The Collected Poems*, Vol. 3 by Margaret Avison, back cover. Erin, ON: The Porcupine's Quill, 2005.

Hays, Richard B. "Reading the Bible with Eyes of Faith: The Practice of Theological Exegesis." *Journal of Theological Interpretation* 1.1 (2007) 5–21.

Heft, Harold. "In Griffin's Grip: The Canadian Shortlist." *Books in Canada* 32.5 (2003) 41.

Herbert, George. "From *The Temple.*" In *Seventeenth Century Prose and Poetry*, 2nd ed., edited by Alexander Witherspoon and Frank Warnke, 842–59. New York: Harcourt, Brace & World, 1963.

Hillesum, Etty. *Etty: The Letters and Diaries of Etty Hillesum, 1941–1943.* Edited by Klaus A. D. Smelik and Arnold Pomerans. Grand Rapids: Eerdmans, 2002.

The Holy Bible. The New Scofield Reference Bible, Authorized King James Version. New York: Oxford University Press, 1967.

The Holy Bible. New Revised Standard Version, Anglicized Text. Oxford: Oxford University Press, 2003.

Honan, Park. *Browning's Characters: A Study in Poetic Technique.* New Haven: Yale University Press, 1961.

Hopkins, Gerard. In *The Norton Anthology of English Literature: The Major Authors*, 7th ed., edited by M. H. Abrams and Stephen Greenblatt, 2155–65. New York: Norton, 2001.

Hutcheon, Linda. *A Poetics of Postmodernism: History, Theory, Fiction.* New York: Routledge, 1988.

———. "'Snow Storm of Paper': The Act of Reading in Self-Reflexive Canadian Verse." *Dalhousie Review* 59 (1979) 118–27.

Iser, Wolfgang. *The Act of Reading: A Theory of Aesthetic Response.* Baltimore: Johns Hopkins University Press, 1978.

James, William. *The Varieties of Religious Experience: A Study in Human Nature.* London: Longmans, Green & Co., 1902.

Jasper, David., ed. *The Interpretation of Belief: Coleridge, Schleiermacher and Romanticism.* New York: St. Martin's, 1986.

———. *The New Testament and the Literary Imagination.* Atlantic Highlands, NJ: Humanities Press International, 1987.

———. *The Study of Literature and Religion: An Introduction.* Minneapolis: Fortress, 1989.

Jefferson, Ann, and David Robey. *Modern Literary Theory: A Comparative Introduction.* 2nd ed. Totowa, NJ: Barnes & Noble, 1986.

Jeffrey, David Lyle. *Houses of the Interpreter: Reading Scripture, Reading Culture.* Waco, TX: Baylor University Press, 2033.

———. "Light, Stillness, and the Shaping Word: Conversion and the Poetic of Margaret Avison." In *"Lighting up the terrain": The Poetry of Margaret Avison*, edited by David Kent, 58–77. Toronto: ECW, 1987.

———. "Margaret Avison: Sonnets and Sunlight." *Calvinist Contact,* 19 October 1979, 3–4.

———. *People of the Book: Christian Identity and Literary Culture.* Grand Rapids: Eerdmans, 1996.

Jeffrey, David Lyle, and Gregory Maillet. *Christianity and Literature: Philosophical Foundations and Critical Practice.* Downers Grove, IL: IVP Academic, 2011.

Jennings, Elizabeth. *Every Changing Shape: Mystical Experience and the Making of Poems.* Manchester: Carcanet, 1996.

Johnston, Gordon. "Ongoingness and Nearer Farnesses: The Place of 'Too Towards Tomorrow: New Poems' in *Always Now: The Collected Poems.*" *Canadian Poetry* 59 (Fall/Winter 2006) 82–94.

Jones, D. G. "Cold Eye and Optic Heart: Marshall McLuhan and Some Canadian Poets." *Modern Poetry Studies* 5.2 (1974) 170–87.

Judges' Citation. On line: http://www.griffinpoetryprize.com/shortlist_2003.

Karr, Mary. Introduction to *The Waste Land and Other Writings*, by T. S. Eliot. New York: The Modern Library, 2002.

Kent, David. "Composing a Book: Denise Levertov, Margaret Avison and The Dumbfounding." *Canadian Poetry* 59 (Fall/Winter 2006) 40–52.

———. ed. *"Lighting up the terrain": The Poetry of Margaret Avison.* Toronto: ECW, 1987.

———. "Margaret Avison and Her Works." In *Canadian Writers and Their Works*, Poetry Series, Vol. 6, edited by Robert Lecker et al. Toronto: ECW, 1989.

———. *Margaret Avison and Her Works.* Toronto: ECW, 1989.

———. "Margaret Avison, Poet." *Canadian Notes & Queries* 73 (2008) 51–59.

———. "Wholehearted Poetry; Halfhearted Criticism." *Essays on Canadian Writing* 44 (1991) 67–78.

Kent, David, and Katherine Quinsey. "Introduction, Margaret Avison." *Canadian Poetry* 59 (Fall/Winter 2006) 5–13.

Kertzer, Jon. "Margaret Avison and the Place of Meaning." In *"Lighting up the terrain": The Poetry of Margaret Avison*, edited by David Kent, 7–26. Toronto: ECW, 1987.

———. "Margaret Avison's Portrait of a Lady: 'The Agnes Cleves Papers.'" *Concerning Poetry* 12 (Fall 1979) 17–24.

———. "Margaret Avison: Power, Knowledge and the Language of Poetry." *Canadian Poetry* 4 (Spring-Summer 1979) 29–44.

———. "Margaret Avison" In *Profiles in Canadian Literature* Vol. 2, edited by Jeffrey M. Heath, 33–40. Toronto: Dundurn, 1980.

———. "Passion of Age (Review)." *Canadian Literature* 129 (1991) 195–96.

Koester, Craig. *Symbolism in the Fourth Gospel: Meaning, Mystery, Community.* 2nd ed. Minneapolis, MN: Fortress, 2003.

Korg, Jacob. "Imagism." In *A Companion to Twentieth Century Poetry*, edited by Neil Roberts, 127–37. Oxford: Blackwell, 2003.

Krieger, Murray. *A Window to Criticism: Shakespeare's Sonnets and Modern Poetics.* Princeton: Princeton University Press, 1964.

Kubacki, Maria "Canadian Poet Occupied Upper Echelons of Craft." Obituary, *National Post,* August 14, 2007.

Lakoff, George, and Mark Johnson. *Metaphors We Live By.* Chicago: University of Chicago Press, 1980.

Lane, Tony. "Karl Barth." In *A Concise History of Christian Thought.* Rev. ed. London: T. & T. Clark, 2006.

Lane, William L. *Hebrews 9–13* Word Biblical Commentary. Dallas: Word, 1991.

Lawall, Sarah, et al., eds. *The Norton Anthology of Western Literature*, Vol. 1. 8th ed. New York: Norton, 2006.

Lecker, Robert. "Exegetical Blizzard." *Studies in Canadian Literature* 4.1 (1979) 180–84.

Lee, John B. "Groundhog Day." *Canadian Poetry* 59 (Fall/Winter 2006) 59–61.

Lennard, John. *The Poetry Handbook*. Oxford: Oxford University Press, 1996.

Levinson, Michael, ed. *The Cambridge Companion to Modernism*. Cambridge: Cambridge University Press, 1999.

Lewis, C. S. *An Experiment in Criticism*. Cambridge: Cambridge University Press, 1961.

———. *The Four Loves*. Glasgow: Collins, 1960.

———. *God in the Dock: Essays on Theology and Ethics*. Edited by Walter Hooper. Grand Rapids: Eerdmans, 1970.

———. *The Great Divorce* San Francisco: Harper Collins, 2001.

———. *The Magician's Nephew*. New York: HarperCollins, 1994.

———. *Mere Christianity* London: HarperCollins, 1997.

———. "On Three Ways of Writing for Children." In *Of Other Worlds*, edited by Walter Hooper, 22–38. New York: Harcourt Brace Jovanovich, 1975.

———. *Studies in Words*. 2nd ed. Cambridge: Cambridge University Press, 1967.

———. *Surprised By Joy: The Shape of My Early Life*. New York: Harcourt Brace & Co., 1956.

———. *Till We Have Faces: A Myth Retold*. London: Bles, 1966.

———. "The Weight of Glory." In *The Weight of Glory and Other Addresses*. New York: Simon & Schuster, 1975.

Lincoln, Andrew T. "The Beloved Disciple as Eyewitness and the Fourth Gospel as Witness." *Journal for the Study of the New Testament* 85 (2002) 3–26.

Loomis, Jeffrey B. *Dayspring in Darkness: Sacrament in Hopkins*. Cranbury, NJ: Associated University Presses, 1988.

Lundin, Roger, ed. *Disciplining Hermeneutics: Interpretation in Christian Perspective*. Grand Rapids: Eerdmans, 1997.

———. "Hermeneutics." In *Contemporary Literary Theory: A Christian Appraisal*, edited by Clarence Walhout and Leland Ryken, 149–71. Grand Rapids: Eerdmans, 1991.

MacEwen, Gwendolyn. "Poetry and Honey Dew: My First Meetings with Margaret Avison." In *"Lighting up the terrain": The Poetry of Margaret Avison*, edited by David Kent, 32. Toronto: ECW, 1987.

Malthus, Thomas. *An Essay on the Principle of Population*. 1798. Reprint. Oxford World's Classics, n.d.

McDowell, Josh. *Evidence Demands a Verdict: Historical Evidences for the Christian Faith*. San Bernardino, CA: Here's Life Publishers, 1979.

McFague, Sallie. *Metaphorical Theology: Models of God in Religious Language*. Philadelphia, PA: Fortress, 1982.

———. *Speaking in Parables: A Study in Metaphor and Theology*. London: SCM, 1975.

McIlveen, Esther. "Rainbows and Worn Out Shoes." No pages. Online: http://www.renewal-fellowship.ca/47.

Marshall, I. Howard. *The Acts of the Apostles*. Sheffield, UK: Sheffield Academic Press, 1990.

———. *The Gospel of Luke*. Grand Rapids: Eerdmans, 1978.

Martz, Louis L. *The Poetry of Meditation*. New Haven: Yale University Press, 1962.

Mather, P. Boyd. "Paul in Acts as 'Servant' and 'Witness.'" *Biblical Research* 30 (1985) 23–44.

Matterson, Stephen, and Darryl Jones. *Studying Poetry*. London: Arnold, 2000.

Mathews, Lawrence. "Stevens, Wordsworth, Jesus: Avison and the Romantic Imagination." In *"Lighting up the terrain": The Poetry of Margaret Avison*, edited by David Kent, 36–54. Toronto: ECW, 1987.

Mazoff, C. D. "Through the Son: An Explication of Margaret Avison's 'Person.'" *Canadian Poetry* 22 (Spring/Summer 1988) 40–48.

———. *Waiting for the Son: Poetics/Theology/Rhetoric in Margaret Avison's "sunblue."* Dunvegan, ON: Cormorant, 1989.

Merrett, Robert J. "Faithful Unpredictability: Syntax and Theology in Margaret Avison's Poetry." In *"Lighting up the terrain": The Poetry of Margaret Avison*, edited by David Kent, 82–110. Toronto: ECW, 1987.

———. "Margaret Avison on Natural History: Ecological and Biblical Meditations." *Canadian Poetry* 59 (Fall/Winter 2006) 95–110.

———. "'The Ominous Centre': The Theological Impulse in Margaret Avison's Poetry." *White Pelican* 5.2 (1976) 12–24.

Messenger, Cynthia. "Canadian Poetry." In *A Companion to Twentieth-Century Poetry*, edited by Neil Roberts, 304–17. Oxford: Blackwell, 2003.

Middleton, J. Richard, and Brian Walsh. *Truth Is Stranger Than It Used to Be: Biblical Faith in a Postmodern Age*. Downers Grove, IL: Intervarsity, 1995.

Milton, John. *Paradise Lost*. Edited by Merritt Y. Hughes. New York: Macmillan, 1986.

Molesworth, Charles. "The Centers of the Modern." In *The Heath Anthology of American Literature*, Vol. 1, 3rd ed., edited by Paul Lauter et al., 884–916. Boston: Houghton Mifflin, 1998.

Moltmann, Jürgen. *God in Creation: A New Theology of Creation and the Spirit of God*. Minneapolis: Fortress, 1993.

Moss Laura, and Cynthia Sugars, eds. *Canadian Literature in English: Texts and Contexts*, Vol. 2. Toronto: Pearson Canada, 2009.

Moss, Robert V., Jr. "The Witnessing Church in the New Testament." *Biblical Theology* 3 (1960) 262–68.

Mudge, Lewis S. "Paul Ricoeur on Biblical Interpretation." In *Essays on Biblical Interpretation*, edited by Lewis S. Midge, 1–40. Philadelphia: Fortress, 1980.

Muers, Rachel. *Keeping God's Silence: Towards a Theological Ethics of Communication*. Oxford: Blackwell, 2004.

Murfin, Ross, and Supryia M. Ray. *The Bedford Glossary of Critical and Literary Terms*, 2nd ed. Boston: Bedford/St. Martin's, 1998.

NASA Goddard Space Flight Center. "White Dwarf Stars." No pages. Online: http://imagine.gsfc.nasa.gov/docs/science/know_l2/dwarfs.html.

Nederlanden, Harry der. "Margaret Avison: The Dumbfoundling [sic]." *Calvinist Contact* 19, October 1979, 1, 3–4.

Neufeld, James. "Some Pivot for Significance in the Poetry of Margaret Avison." *Journal of Canadian Studies* II.2 (1976) 35–42.

New, William H., ed. *Inside the Poem: Essays and Poems in Honor of Donald Stephens*. Toronto: Oxford University Press, 1992.

———. "The Mind's Eyes (I's), (Ice): the Poetry of Margaret Avison." *Twentieth Century Literature* 16 (1970) 185–202.

Newbigin, Lesslie. *Foolishness to the Greeks: The Gospel and Western Culture*. Grand Rapids: Eerdmans, 1986.

———. *The Gospel in a Pluralist Society* London: SPCK, 1989.

Newman, Robert C. "Natural Theology." In *NIDCC* 695.

Nicholls, Peter. *Modernisms: A Literary Guide.* Basingstoke, UK: Palgrave Macmillan, 1995.

North, John. Introduction to *A Kind of Perseverance,* by Margaret Avison, 7–17. Hantsport, NS: Lancelot, 1994.

Obituary notice *Globe and Mail,* August 10, 2007.

O'Connor, Flannery. *The Habit of Being: Letters of Flannery O'Connor.* Edited by Sally Fitzgerald. New York: Farrar, Straus & Giroux, 1988.

Olscamp, Paul J. "How Some Metaphors May Be True or False." *Journal of Aesthetics and Art Criticism* 29.1 (1970) 77–86.

Osborne, John. "Black Mountain and Projective Verse." In *A Companion to Twentieth Century Poetry,* edited by Neil Roberts, 168–92. Oxford: Blackwell, 2003.

Oxford English Dictionary Online. Oxford: Oxford University Press, 2008.

Pearce, Joseph. *Literary Converts: Spiritual Imagination in an Age of Unbelief.* San Francisco: Ignatius, 2000.

Perkins, David, ed. *English Romantic Writers.* New York: Harcourt, Brace & World, 1967.

Perloff, Marjorie. "Postmodernism/Fin de Siècle: Defining 'Difference' in Late Twentieth-Century Poetics." In *Poetry On and Off the Page: Essays for Emergent Occasions,* 3–33. Evanston, IL: Northwestern University Press, 1998.

Peterson, Eugene. *Christ Plays in Ten Thousand Places: A Conversation in Spiritual Theology.* Grand Rapids: Eerdmans, 2005.

Pope, William. Unpublished letter to Avison, 1977. University of Manitoba: Margaret Avison Fonds.

Pollock, Zailig. "A Response to Michael Taylor's 'Snow Blindness.'" *Studies in Canadian Literature* 4.1 (1979) 177–79.

Pound, Ezra. "A Few Don'ts." In *20th-Century Poetry & Poetics,* 5th ed., edited by Gary Geddes, 1042. Don Mills, ON: Oxford University Press, 2006.

Prickett, Stephen. "On Reading Nature as a Romantic." In *The Interpretation of Belief: Coleridge, Schleiermacher and Romanticism,* edited by David Jasper, 126–41. New York: St. Martin's, 1986.

———. *Words and The Word: Language, Poetics and Biblical Interpretation.* Cambridge: Cambridge University Press, 1986.

Punter, David. *Metaphor.* London: Routledge, 2007.

Purdy, Al. "On First Looking into Avison's 'Neverness.'" In *"Lighting up the terrain": The Poetry of Margaret Avison,* edited by David Kent, 30–31. Toronto: ECW, 1987.

Quinsey, Katherine. "The Dissolving Jail-Break in Avison." *Canadian Poetry* 25 (Fall/ Winter 1989) 21–37.

———. "'Our own little rollicking orb': Divinity, Ecology, and Otherness in Avison." *Canadian Poetry* 59 (Fall/Winter 2006) 111–38.

Redekop, Ernest H. *Margaret Avison.* Toronto: Copp Clark, 1970.

———. "sun/Son light/Light: Avison's elemental sunblue." *Canadian Poetry* 7 (Fall/ Winter) 21–37.

———. "The Word/word in Avison's Poetry" In *"Lighting up the terrain": The Poetry of Margaret Avison,* edited by David Kent, 115–43. Toronto: ECW, 1987.

Ricoeur, Paul. *Essays on Biblical Interpretation.* Philadelphia: Fortress, 1980.

Ricou, Laurie. "Poetry." In *Literary History of Canada: Canadian Literature in English* Vol. 3, 2nd ed., edited by Carl F. Klinck, 3–45. Toronto: University of Toronto Press, 1976.

Roberts, Neil, ed. *A Companion to Twentieth Century Poetry.* Oxford: Blackwell, 2003.

Ryken, Leland. "Formalist and Archetypal Criticism." In *Contemporary Literary Theory: A Christian Appraisal*, edited by Clarence Walhout and Leland Ryken, 1–23. Grand Rapids: Eerdmans, 1991.

———. *The Literature of the Bible.* Grand Rapids: Zondervan, 1974.

———. *Windows to the World: Literature in Christian Perspective.* Grand Rapids: Zondervan/Probe, 1985.

———. *Words of Delight: A Literary Introduction to the Bible.* 2nd ed. Grand Rapids: Baker, 1992.

Ryne, Linn. "Leif Ericson." No pages. Online: www.mnc.net/norway/ericson.htm.

Schneiders, Sandra. *Written That You May Believe: Encountering Jesus in the Fourth Gospel.* Rev. ed. New York: Crossroad, 2003.

Scobie, Stephen. Letter to Margaret Avison. February 17, 1993[sic]. The University of Manitoba: Margaret Avison Fonds.

———. Letter to Margaret Avison. November 10, 1993. The University of Manitoba: Margaret Avison Fonds.

———. "Poetry and Fiction." *Queen's Quarterly* 87 (1980) 158–60.

Seitz, Christopher R. *Figured Out: Typology and Providence in Christian Scripture.* Louisville: Westminster John Knox, 2001.

Shastri, Sudha. *Intertextuality and Victorian Studies.* Hyderabad: Orient Blackswan, 2001.

Shepherd, Victor. "A Summary of Calvin's Doctrine of Scripture." Unpublished and undated lecture notes.

Simone, Rose. "A Religious Experience." *The Second Mile,* February 1994, 6.

Smedes, Lewis. "Theology and the Playful Life." In *God and the Good*, edited by Clifton Orlebeke and Lewis Smedes, 46–62. Grand Rapids: Eerdmans, 1975.

Smith, A. J. M. *The Book of Canadian Poetry: A Critical and Historical Anthology.* Chicago: University of Chicago Press, 1943.

———. "The Confessions of a Compulsive Anthologist." In *On Poetry and Poets*, 106–22. Toronto: McClelland & Stewart, 1977.

———. "Critical Improvisations on Margaret Avison's Winter Sun." *The Tamarack Review* 18 (Winter 1961) 81–86.

———. *On Poetry and Poets.* Toronto: McClelland & Stewart, 1977.

Smith, Mark K. "Michael Polanyi and Tacit Knowledge." The Encyclopedia of Informal Education, 2003. No pages. Online: http://www.infed.org/thinkers/polanyi. htm.

Soards, Marion L. *The Speeches in Acts: Their Content, Context, and Concerns* Louisville: Westminster/John Knox, 1994.

Somerville, Christine. "The Shadow of Death: Margaret Avison's 'Just Left or The Night Margaret Laurence Died.'" In *Inside the Poem: Essays and Poems in Honor of Donald Stephens*, edited by William H. New, 55–59. Toronto: Oxford University Press, 1992.

Sonderegger, Katherine. "El Resurrexit Tertia Die: Jenson and Barth on Christ's Resurrection." In *Conversing with Barth*, edited by J. McDowell and M. Higton, 191–213. Farnham, UK: Ashgate, 2004.

Soskice, Janet Martin. *Metaphor and Religious Language.* Oxford: Oxford University Press, 1985.

Starnino, Carmine. "Are You There, God? It's Me, Margaret." Review of *Always Now: The Collected Poems*, Vol. 2. *The Globe and Mail*, February 19, 2005, D5.

———. "He From Elsewhere Speaks: Avison's Spiritualized Syntax." *Canadian Poetry* 59 (Fall–Winter, 2006) 139–49.

Stevens, Wallace. *The Collected Poems of Wallace Stevens*. New York: Knopf, 1971.

Stibbe, Mark. *John's Gospel: New Testament Readings*. New York: Routledge, 1994.

Strathman, Hermann. "Witness." In *TDNT* 474–514.

Swiss, Margot, ed. *Poetry as Liturgy: An Anthology by Canadian Poets*. Toronto: St. Thomas Poetry Series, 2007.

Taylor, Michael. "Snow Blindness." *Studies in Canadian Literature* 3 (1978) 288–90.

Teleky, Richard. "The Poet as Translator: Margaret Avison's 'Hungarian Snap.'" *Canadian Literature* 135 (1992) 112–22.

Temple, William. *Readings in St. John's Gospel*. London: Macmillan, 1968.

Thesen, Sharon, ed. *The Griffin Poetry Prize Anthology 2003*. Toronto: House of Anansi, 2003.

Tinsley, John. *Tell It Slant: The Christian Gospel and Its Communication*. Bristol: Wyndham Hall, 1990.

Tolkien, J. R. R. Letter 89 to Christopher Tolkien, November 7–8, 1944. In *The Letters of J. R. R. Tolkien,* edited by Humphrey Carpenter, 115–17. London: George Allen & Unwin, 1981.

———."On Fairy-Stories." In *Essays Presented to Charles Williams*, 38–39. Grand Rapids: Eerdmans, 1966.

Tozer, A. W. *The Pursuit of God*. Harrisburg, PA: Christian Publications, 1958.

Trites, Allison. *The New Testament Concept of Witness*. Cambridge: Cambridge University Press, 1977.

Vander Weele, Michael. "Reader-Response Theories." In *Contemporary Literary Theory: A Christian Appraisal*, edited by Clarence Walhout and Leland Ryken, 125–48. Grand Rapids: Eerdmans, 1991.

Van Helden, A. "The Galileo Project." No pages. Online: http://galileo.rice.edu/sci/brahe.html /.

Van Rys, J. "'A Tangle of Vegetation': Suffering in Margaret Avison's 'Jo Poems.'" *Canadian Poetry* 59 (Fall/Winter, 2006) 62–81.

Vendler, Helen. "Author's Notes for Teaching Poems, Poets, Poetry." In *Poems, Poets, Poetry: An Introduction and Anthology*. 3rd ed. Boston: Bedford/St. Martin's, 2010.

———. *Coming of Age as a Poet: Milton, Keats, Eliot, Plath*. Cambridge: Harvard University Press, 2003.

———. *Poems, Poets, Poetry: An Introduction and Anthology*. 3rd ed. Boston: Bedford/St.Martin's, 2010.

———. *Poets Thinking: Pope, Whitman, Dickinson, Yeats*. Cambridge: Harvard University Press, 2004.

Waggoner, B. "Antony van Leeuwenhoek (1632–1723)." No pages. Online: http://www.ucmp.berkeley.edu/history/leeuwenhoek.html /.

Walhout, Clarence, and Leland Ryken, eds. *Contemporary Literary Theory: A Christian Appraisal*. Grand Rapids: Eerdmans, 1991.

Walton, Martin. *Witness in Biblical Scholarship: A Survey of Recent Studies 1956–1980*. Leiden: Interuniversitair Instituut Voor Missiologie, 1986.

Warnke, Frank, ed. *John Donne: Poetry and Prose*. New York: Modern Library, 1967.

Watts, John D. W. *Isaiah 1–33*. Word Biblical Commentary. Dallas: Word, 1987.

———. *Isaiah 34–66*. Word Biblical Commentary. Dallas: Word, 1987.

Weil, Simone. *Waiting for God*. New York: HarperCollins, 1973.

White, R. E. O. *Luke's Case for Christianity*. Harrisburg, PA: Morehouse, 1987.

Wien, J. "Avison and the Postmodern 1960s." *Canadian Poetry* 59 (Fall/Winter, 2006) 27–39.

Wilder, Amos. *Early Christian Rhetoric: The Language of the Gospel*. Cambridge: Harvard University Press, 1971.

Willimon, William H. *Acts*. Atlanta,: John Knox, 1988.

Williams, Rowan. *On Christian Theology*. Oxford: Blackwell, 2000.

———. *Tokens of Trust: An Introduction to Christian Belief*. London: Canterbury, 2007.

Willmer, Haddon. Personal correspondence by conversation and email, 2004–10.

Willmot, Rod. "Winning Spirit." *Canadian Literature* 87 (Winter 1980) 115–16.

Wimsatt, Jr., William. *The Verbal Icon: Studies in the Meaning of Poetry*. Lexington, KY: University of Kentucky Press, 1954.

Witeymeyer, Hugh. "Modernism and the Transatlantic Connection." In *A Companion to Twentieth Century Poetry*, edited by Neil Roberts, 7–20. Oxford: Blackwell, 2003.

Wood, Brent. "Irony in Avison's Winter Sun." *Canadian Poetry* 59 (Fall/Winter, 2006) 16–26.

Wordsworth, William. "Lines, composed a few miles above Tintern Abbey . . . July 13, 1798." In *English Romantic* Writers, edited by David Perkins, 209–11. New York: Harcourt, Brace & World, 1967.

———. "Preface to Second Edition of the Lyrical Ballads." In *English Romantic* Writers, edited by David Perkins, 320–33. New York: Harcourt, Brace & World, 1967.

World Transformation "R. Buckminster Fuller." http://www.worldtrans.org/whole/bucky.html /

Wright, T. R. *Theology and Literature*. Oxford: Blackwell, 1988.

Zezulka, J. M. "Refusing the Sweet Surrender: Margaret Avison's 'Dispersed Titles.'" *Canadian Poetry* 1 (1977) 44–53.

Zichy, Francis. "'Each in His Prison / Thinking of the Key': Images of Confinement and Liberation in Margaret Avison." *Studies in Canadian Literature* 3 (1978) 232–43.

———. "A Response to Robert Lecker's 'Exegetical Blizzard' and Michael Taylor's 'Snow Blindness.'" *Studies in Canadian Literature* 4.2 (1979) 147–54.

Index of Works by Margaret Avison